THE CARIBBEAN AND THE MEDICAL IMAGINATION, 1764–1834

During the eighteenth and nineteenth centuries, the Caribbean was known as the 'grave of Europeans'. At the apex of British colonialism in the region between 1764 and 1834, the rapid spread of disease amongst colonist, enslaved and indigenous populations made the Caribbean notorious as one of the deadliest places on earth. Drawing on historical accounts from physicians, surgeons and travellers alongside literary works, Emily Senior traces the cultural impact of such widespread disease and death during the Romantic age of exploration and medical and scientific discovery. Focusing on new fields of knowledge such as dermatology, medical geography and anatomy, Senior shows how literature was crucial to the development and circulation of new medical ideas, and that the Caribbean as the hub of empire played a significant role in the changing disciplines and literary forms associated with the transition to modernity.

EMILY SENIOR is Lecturer in Eighteenth-Century and Romantic Literature at Birkbeck College, University of London. She has had articles published in the *Journal for Eighteenth-Century Studies*, *Eighteenth-Century Studies* and *Atlantic Studies*.

This series aims to foster the best new work in one of the most challenging fields within English literary studies. From the early 1780s to the early 1830s, a formidable array of talented men and women took to literary composition, not just in poetry, which some of them famously transformed, but in many modes of writing. The expansion of publishing created new opportunities for writers, and the political stakes of what they wrote were raised again by what Wordsworth called those "great national events" that were "almost daily taking place": the French Revolution, the Napoleonic and American wars, urbanization, industrialization, religious revival, an expanded empire abroad and the reform movement at home. This was an enormous ambition, even when it pretended otherwise. The relations between science, philosophy, religion, and literature were reworked in texts such as *Frankenstein* and *Biographia Literaria*; gender relations in *A Vindication of the Rights of Woman* and *Don Juan*; journalism by Cobbett and Hazlitt; poetic form, content and style by the Lake School and the Cockney School. Outside Shakespeare studies, probably no body of writing has produced such a wealth of comment or done so much to shape the responses of modern criticism. This indeed is the period that saw the emergence of those notions of "literature" and of literary history, especially national literary history, on which modern scholarship in English has been founded.

The categories produced by Romanticism have also been challenged by recent historicist arguments. The task of the series is to engage both with a challenging corpus of Romantic writings and with the changing field of criticism they have helped to shape. As with other literary series published by Cambridge University Press, this one will represent the work of both younger and more established scholars, on either side of the Atlantic and elsewhere.

See the end of the book for a complete list of published titles.

THE CARIBBEAN AND THE MEDICAL IMAGINATION, 1764–1834

Slavery, Disease and Colonial Modernity

EMILY SENIOR

Birkbeck College, University of London

CAMBRIDGE
UNIVERSITY PRESS

CAMBRIDGE
UNIVERSITY PRESS

University Printing House, Cambridge CB2 8BS, United Kingdom

One Liberty Plaza, 20th Floor, New York, NY 10006, USA

477 Williamstown Road, Port Melbourne, VIC 3207, Australia

314-321, 3rd Floor, Plot 3, Splendor Forum, Jasola District Centre, New Delhi - 110025, India

79 Anson Road, #06-04/06, Singapore 079906

Cambridge University Press is part of the University of Cambridge.

It furthers the University's mission by disseminating knowledge in the pursuit of education, learning and research at the highest international levels of excellence.

www.cambridge.org
Information on this title: www.cambridge.org/9781108404198
DOI: 10.1017/9781108241977

© Emily Senior 2018

First published 2018
First paperback edition 2020

A catalogue record for this publication is available from the British Library

Library of Congress Cataloging in Publication data
Names: Senior, Emily, 1978– author.
Title: The Caribbean and the medical imagination, 1764–1834:
slavery, disease and colonial modernity / Emily Senior.
Description: Cambridge, United Kingdom; New York, NY: Cambridge
University Press, 2018. | Series: Cambridge studies in romanticism; 119 |
Includes bibliographical references and index.
Identifiers: LCCN 2017059327 | ISBN 9781108416818 (hardback)
Subjects: LCSH: Medicine – Caribbean Area – History – 19th century. |
Medicine – Caribbean Area – History – 20th century. | Communicable diseases –
Caribbean Area – History – 19th century. | Communicable diseases – Caribbean
Area – History – 20th century. | Medical literature – History. | BISAC: LITERARY
CRITICISM / European / English, Irish, Scottish, Welsh.
Classification: LCC RA482.C27 P67 2018 | DDC 614.4/2729–dc23
LC record available at https://lccn.loc.gov/2017059327

ISBN 978-1-108-41681-8 Hardback
ISBN 978-1-108-40419-8 Paperback

To Ian, Avery and the next chapter

New-come buckra,
He get sick,
He tak fever,
He be die;
He be die.

Slave song reported by
Robert Renny, *An History of Jamaica* (1807)

Everyone who is born holds dual citizenship, in the kingdom of
the well and in the kingdom of the sick. Although we all prefer to
use only the good passport, sooner or later each of us is obliged, at
least for a spell, to identify ourselves as citizens of that other place.

Susan Sontag, *Illness as Metaphor* (1978)

how astonishing, when the lights of health go down, the undiscov-
ered countries that are then disclosed, what wastes and deserts of
the soul a slight attack of influenza brings to view, what precipices
and lawns sprinkled with bright flowers a little rise of temperature
reveals, what ancient and obdurate oaks are uprooted in us by the
act of sickness, how we go down into the pit of death and feel the
waters of annihilation close above our heads and wake thinking to
find ourselves in the presence of angels and the harpers.

Virginia Woolf, 'On Being Ill' (1926)

Contents

Illustrations

Acknowledgements

This book began as a doctoral thesis under the supervision of Karen O'Brien, whose energy and historical precision remain a source of inspiration. Many thanks are also due to Lynn Festa for her assiduous, interested and invaluable criticism, to John Gilmore for sharing his encyclopaedic knowledge of Caribbean writing and to Markman Ellis for his attentive reading, which helped propel the project to the next stage.

I am grateful to the Arts and Humanities Research Council for funding my doctoral studies. I also benefited from a Research Exchange Fellowship at the University of Wisconsin, Madison, funded by the University of Warwick and the University of Wisconsin. Thanks to the organizers and members of the Harvard International Seminar on the History of the Atlantic World 2009 for a wonderful summer of conversation about Atlantic histories of science and medicine. Thanks also to staff at the Beinecke Library, the Lewis Walpole Library, the Huntington Library, the William Blake Archive, the Ebling Library at the University of Wisconsin and the James Ford Bell Library at the University of Minnesota.

My colleagues at Birkbeck have been a great source of support. I am particularly grateful to Luisa Calè for her boundless energy and curatorial vision, to Louise Owen for her incisive reading of Chapter 5, to Isabel Davis, Richard Hamblyn and Sue Wiseman for sharing ideas, and to Gill Woods for unfailing support and scholarly generosity. Colleagues in the Eighteenth-Century Research Group and the Centre for Nineteenth-Century Studies have made Birkbeck a wonderful place to bring this project to fruition.

During the course of writing this book I collaborated on projects with Sarah Easterby-Smith and Sarah Thomas, and I am grateful to them for discussions which bolstered its progress. I am also indebted to Judith Thompson for her generosity in sharing her expansive knowledge of Thelwall's life and works. In the latter stages of the project, two anonymous readers gave the manuscript careful consideration on behalf of Cambridge University Press and I thank them for their detailed and valuable guidance.

My parents, Daphne Muir and Bruce Senior, and my brother Patrick have put up with this project with humour and kindness, and for longer than they should have had to. My grandparents present and departed, Tom and Marjorie Senior and Mary and Andrew Mango, and the rest of the Mango clan, gave steady encouragement. Thanks to Abbie Hastings, Eve Leegwater, Laura Montag, Annie Stancheris for much-needed distraction. I owe a great and cherished debt to Ian and Avery, for more than words can express. This book is dedicated to them, with love.

An earlier version of Chapter 2 appeared in Emily Senior and Sarah Easterby-Smith (eds.), 'The Cultural Production of Natural Knowledge', a special issue of the *Journal for Eighteenth-Century Studies* (2013). A previous version of Chapter 3 was published in *Eighteenth-Century Studies* (2010).

Communicating Disease
Literature and Medicine in the Atlantic World

In the modern-day vernacular, the flu can be 'caught', one might 'give' another person a stomach virus, and medical science is said to be in a state of perpetual 'war' in the effort to 'kill' cancer: the imaginative lives of illness pose questions about individual agency, social interaction and the violent colonization of bodies. Figures of disease are harnessed to an array of ideological ends, and the association between colonialism and disease gives metaphorical form to the rampant sickness and staggering death rates which mark the history of the British Empire. Disease often had the final word in defining imperial boundaries, determining the outcome of power struggles and the contours of colonial dominions. At the apex of British colonialism in the Americas between the conclusion of the Seven Years' War in 1763 and the abolition of slavery in 1834, the rapid spread of disease amongst colonist, enslaved and indigenous populations made the Caribbean notorious for being one of the deadliest places on earth, winning it the epithet 'the grave of Europeans'. Understanding medical knowledge and anxieties about illness as shaping colonial existence, this book is a study of colonial disease as it was imagined by the literary and medical texts of the Caribbean. *The Caribbean and the Medical Imagination* considers how literary and medical discourses were related at this point, how they expressed anxieties about illness and how they organized colonial environments and bodies (healthy and sick, literal and figurative) and articulated models of humanity and identity through figures of disease. Working at the interface between literary criticism and the cultural history of colonial medicine, this book reveals the conceptual and linguistic frameworks – aesthetic, philosophical, poetic, political, psychological, racial, religious and scientific – of literary and medical encounters with colonial disease.

As well as new territories in West Africa, the Seven Years' War brought the conquest of Canada, Florida, Dominica, Grenada, Havana, Saint Lucia and Saint Vincent, making Britain the dominant power in the

Atlantic world. It was, as Linda Colley has written, 'the most dramatically successful war the British ever fought.'[1] Colley has shown that the British reaction to the enormous pressures of such a massive increase in global power and territory, as well as the problems of staggering debt, helped to force a 'major reassessment of the meanings of Britishness and of the implications of empire.'[2] A key element in the reconfiguring of identity, knowledge and power that took place at this peak moment of British imperial control, however, and to a far greater extent than has been recognized until recent historical accounts, was disease.[3] The Seven Years' War itself had seen ground lost or gained because of disease.[4] More broadly, as Europeans distributed themselves across the globe, and forcibly distributed others, the colonial encounter between nations merged previously separate pathogenic environments. The British slave ships which, between 1740 and 1807, carried 2.2 million African people from their homes, had an enormous part to play in the transport of pathogens to the Caribbean, and were notorious as breeding grounds for disease.[5] Recent estimates put the death toll for those shipped across the Atlantic (and imprisoned in West African barracoons) at somewhere between 10 and 50 per cent.[6] The grim environment of the slave ship was one of brutal, cramped and unsanitary conditions which meant that contagious fevers, fluxes (dysentery and bowel complaints), measles, smallpox, influenza and parasites could spread above and below deck with exceptional speed.[7] The disease environments Europeans encountered in Africa played a major role in the expansion of the Caribbean sugar plantations, but because the process of shipping African slaves to the Caribbean meant African diseases came too, European health did not fare much better on the other side of the Atlantic. In the Caribbean, the meeting between diverse populations allowed the different diseases found amongst African, European and indigenous populations to prey on the weaknesses of each group. Biological protections and susceptibilities that people had accumulated from generations of prior exposure to, or isolation from, particular pathogens left them vulnerable to the new diseases they were now encountering. As Richard Harrison Shryock puts it, 'Europeans, Africans, and Indians engaged in a free exchange of their respective infections' and the Caribbean functioned as a 'melting pot for diseases'.[8]

In Kingston, the ratio of funerals to baptisms was 7:1.[9] For Europeans, life expectancy in Kingston was not much better than it was in West Africa, where more than 60 per cent of Europeans died within a year and only 10 per cent lived for more than three years.[10] This extraordinarily high death rate was inflicted not by the Maroon Wars and slave rebellions which disrupted the authority of the Jamaican plantocracy, but by rampant and uncontrollable disease. Death rates across the Caribbean were usually higher than birth rates and, for the most part, neither black nor white populations sustained themselves by natural increase.[11] The exceptions were the Bahamas and Barbados, which saw a natural increase in their slave populations during the early nineteenth century – their much flatter landscapes made them reputedly healthier than other islands.[12] It soon became clear to planters that it was cheaper to buy slaves and work them to death than to raise them from birth – despite the fact that African slaves often arrived in the West Indies in a very poor state of ill health and suffering from diseases contracted on the cramped and filthy slave ships.[13] While Europeans suffered most from fevers (malaria and yellow fever in particular), Africans tended to suffer from different diseases: yaws (frambœsia – a highly infectious disease endemic to Africa and resulting in deforming and painful lesions of the bones and skin), leprosy, elephantiasis, Guinea worms, geophagy (dirt eating), as well as dropsies (oedema), fluxes, tetanus and ulcers.[14] But it was the New World indigenous communities who were most fatally devastated by the combined influx of African and European diseases: smallpox, measles, diphtheria, whooping cough, bubonic plague, malaria, typhoid fever, yellow fever, dengue fever, scarlet fever, influenza, Guinea worm, yaws, leprosy and hookworm. The previously isolated indigenous Caribbean people were the group worst affected by the Atlantic pathogenic exchange – partly because the South American mainland was exposed to fewer outsiders and diseases, and partly because some Caribbean landscapes and the nature of the plantation system harboured greater numbers of deadly mosquitoes.[15] On the plantations, the particularly high concentration of people, plants and animals in the lowland tropical areas used for growing sugar – which took up increasing quantities of land – released the contents of what Richard Sheridan has called a 'Pandora's box of debilitating and lethal pathogens'.[16]

Disease was widely understood to originate from climatic conditions. From the middle of the eighteenth century, a reinvigorated Hippocratic model of environment and health emerged as the dominant medical framework, and became allied to the empirical observation of new geographical territories. Earlier versions of Hippocratic epidemiology and meteorology, which focused on a causal relationship between geographic space and health, were expanded, and centred on a hypothesis of aerial contagion according to which dirt and stagnation spread disease via miasmatic particles.[17] Through this theory of inanimate infection, and following Thomas Sydenham's influential work on the significance of seasonal weather changes, disease came to be associated with bad air – *mal aria*, or what the colonial surgeon Robert Jackson called 'the exhaling surface of the earth'.[18] The geographical focus ushered in an age of regionalized medicine which sought to map localities, climates and environments according to which diseases were found to be present. Within this model of disease, tropical climates were perceived as particularly deadly. Military physician George Pinckard emphasized the expedited progress of disease in the West Indies and colonial medicine's struggle to stem the tide of death:

> In all climates, a sound judgement, and an acuteness of discrimination, together with a correct knowledge of the human frame, are necessary to the successful treatment of diseases: but in the West Indies, where the attack is frequently sudden, and the progress destructively rapid, if the malady be neglected or badly treated, in its incipient stage, medicine becomes inefficient, and, too often, the disease cannot be subdued by all the art of the wisest Physician.[19]

Despite the insufficiency of European medicine's powers in tropical climates, the medicalization of the climate and atmosphere created a new role for physicians in relation to the social and environmental management of disease. Both the need to control disease and the new supervisory role of medical professionals were particularly apparent in plantation societies, and large numbers of doctors and surgeons took upon themselves the project of medically analyzing tropical environments.[20]

Ideas about human difference were also structured by this climatic model of health. From very early in the era of Caribbean plantation slavery, Europeans believed that Africans were particularly immune to the effects of tropical climates, while perceiving themselves as uniquely susceptible to climate-related illnesses. The indigenous peoples of the West Indies were seen as especially vulnerable to other types of diseases, which explained the rapidity of their decline in numbers after European colonization. Fascinated by the fact that Africans, Creoles, Europeans and Indigenes often suffered from different forms of illness, colonial medical practitioners invested in cataloguing and describing these differences. The idea of national character also emerged in relation to the climatic theory of human difference. John Huxham, who had written an influential book on fevers, drew on Hippocratic ideas to claim that 'the Heat of the Torrid Zone exhausts the liquids of the inhabitants', and that the effects altered the 'Temperaments and very manners of men'.[21] Physician William Falconer described the different characters shaped by climatic differences: while individuals from temperate climates were gentle and mild-mannered, those hailing from tropical locations were hot-tempered, violent and vengeful.[22] The understanding of the relationship between climatic and social differences varied. David Hume's 'Of National Characters' (1748) argued for the distinction of 'moral causes' from 'physical causes' such as climate. For Hume, European national character could be largely explained through moral causes such as rules and manners, which 'run, as it were, like a contagion' – but this did not hold for black people, whose differences indicated that there was an 'original distinction' between the races.[23] Unsurprisingly, then, an important preoccupation for Europeans came to be the question of whether or not the arts and sciences could offset the effects of climate.[24]

Medicine and natural philosophy were undergoing a period of considerable change, and classical theories co-existed with newer ideas and treatments.[25] Key developments in anatomy, pathology, neurology and cardiovascular understanding shifted some of the underlying principles of medicine and natural philosophy, leading to the call for systematic diagnoses of individual diseases as a way to find more effective cures. There was interest in new medical procedures such as smallpox inoculation, and many celebrated William Harvey's work on the circulation of the blood as having 'dispelled the darkness' enshrouding the understanding of the human body.[26] Yet despite major changes in the understanding of the body and the challenges to humoralism presented by new discoveries, treatments for disease remained remarkably unaltered. Physicians still studied the medical doctrines of Hippocrates and Galen, and used the medical treatments introduced by the ancient Greek humoralists, retaining the emphasis on the careful maintenance of the body's natural balance. While defensive regulation of this balance could be ensured through an appropriate regime of diet and exercise, the founding principle of therapeutic treatment was the expulsion of toxic substances from unhealthy bodies. When the body's mechanical processes faltered or were offset, this was usually considered the result of a corruption of the fluids. Many diseases were the result of 'plethora', an excess of matter in the bodily system. Any excess or corrupted matter had to be removed, and it was the physician's role to evacuate contaminating fluids from the body. Phlebotomy, although experiencing something of a decline in popularity, was advocated by the eighteenth-century Dutch founder of clinical education, Herman Boerhaave, and was still practised regularly in Britain and its colonies – along with other heroic medical procedures such as sweating, vomiting, purging and blistering. Such treatments seldom did anything to cure patients of their ills and frequently resulted in harm. Medicaments and palliative treatments – which could include anything from herbal remedies to chemical, mineral and metallic preparations laced with poisonous ingredients such as mercury or antimony – were not much more successful in their attempts to alleviate pain or treat infection. The majority of surgical operations resulted in septic or gangrenous body parts and frequently caused painful or fatal complications. Overall, in Roy Porter's words, 'medicine's powers to save lives had barely advanced since antiquity.'[27]

Earlier generations of colonists had high hopes for the health and success of European inhabitation of the West Indies. In his *True and Exact History of the Island of Barbados* (1657), planter Richard Ligon appealed for more doctors to treat the island's growing population, which was then establishing the sugar monoculture which would dominate the region for the next two centuries:

> But when able and skilfull Physicians shall come, whose knowledge can make the right experiment and use of the vertues of those simples that grow there, they will no doubt finde them more efficacious, and prevalent to their healths, than those they bring from forraine parts. For certainly every Climate produces Simples more proper to the cure the diseases that are bred there, than those that are transported from any other part of the world: such care the great Physician to mankind takes for our convenience.[28]

While Ligon expressed the hope that Barbados would offer up the natural means of treating its own endemic diseases, Captain Edmund Hickeringill, then secretary to the Governor of Jamaica, dismissed claims that Jamaica was an inherently unhealthy country in *Jamaica Viewed* (1661):

> That the island of Jamaica was rather the grave than the granary to the first *English* Colony ... cannot modestly be denied ... But that such a Mortality should proceed, either from the *Clime*, being situate in the *Torrid Zone*, (a Heresie unpardonable in the Ancients;) or from any accidental *Malignity* in any of the Elements, peculiarly *entail'd* upon it, whereby it should be less habitable than any other most auspicious Settlement remains here to be controverted.[29]

Hickeringill particularly emphasized the 'suitableness' of the Jamaican climate to 'English Complexions'. But from this early optimism that the Torrid Zone was not inherently or irretrievably diseased, medical opinion shifted so that by the early nineteenth century hopes for the possibility of European acclimatization to the West Indies had faded.[30] In his *Tour through the Island of Jamaica* (1823), Cynric R. Williams remarks satirically that the island 'is a superb country for physicians'.[31] While the West Indies was a place to be approached with both ambition and trepidation, the ravages of yellow fever and malaria were the risk many Europeans were willing to take as the promise of land, status and wealth drew flocks of hopefuls to

Caribbean shores. The eighteenth century had, as Ligon had earlier hoped, swelled the ranks of qualified physicians and trained surgeons, and many of these set forth for the Caribbean colonies with hopes of social advancement and financial gain. But with Africans and Europeans dying in their droves, a wealth of new diseases to treat and callous, parsimonious slave-owners, plantation health care was generally of very poor quality.[32] Until Britain abolished its Atlantic slave trade in 1807, planters attributed the high rates of disease to the spread from imported sick Africans, when in reality brutal work demands, unsanitary conditions and dietary deficiencies accelerated the onset and severity of illness amongst slaves. After 1807, acquiring new slaves was less straightforward, and some planters took steps to improve medical care. Some colonial medics drew attention to the ways in which enslaved people's health was affected by malnutrition, fatigue, poor sanitation and lack of proper clothing and shelter. They urged slave-owners and those involved in transporting people on ships from Africa to improve living conditions and to provide hospitals for sick slaves, as well as pregnant women and mothers. Many chose to ignore this advice, and despite small attempts at improvement medical practice on the plantation failed to do much to treat the overwhelming numbers of diseased and dying enslaved people. Often, slaves preferred to be treated by black doctors and medical attendants, who gained power and influence in some colonies partly because their herbal remedies contained effective drugs. Even when they did not succeed as cures, these treatments seldom harmed the patient, unlike many Western medical treatments. 'In truth', as Kenneth Kiple puts it, 'the slaves would probably have been better off with their own practitioners, for white medicine in the West Indies was, to put it charitably, of low quality.'[33]

The fatal prospects of new diseases loomed large in the intrepid traveller's imagination, as slave-owner and politician John Stewart wrote in 1823:

> Previous to his crossing the Atlantic, [the European traveller] is terrified and alarmed by exaggerated accounts of the intolerable heat of the climate, the unwholesomeness of the atmosphere, the fatal ravages of the yellow fever, the savage and treacherous disposition of the negroes, and the *huge serpents and other venomous reptiles* with which the country is infested. But he is at the same time instigated and encouraged by happier representations – He is told of the riches with which it abounds, the facility with which these may be acquired – in short, the prospect of realizing in a few years, in this land of promise, the fortune of a nabob.[34]

The Caribbean represented both the zenith and the disaster of European imperial endeavour: there were bountiful opportunities to make a fortune, but one had to survive long enough to spend it, and many did not. The rapid spread of illness and the inability of the medical community to cope with sick populations prompted the rearticulation of national, racial and social identities in terms of the rhetoric of disease and cure as bodies, landscapes and people came to be categorized in terms of health, illness, disease susceptibilities, physical strengths and weaknesses and ideas about contagion and contamination. Many colonist and Creole authors depicted the West Indies as a land of fertile and luxurious abundance – one which would repay its visitors with health and wealth – while others used the medicalization of the Caribbean to legitimize imperial conquest and chattel slavery. Colonial disease invoked questions about social encounter, movement and otherness. Jamaica-based planter Edward Long and other pro-slavery writers drew on ideas about health and illness to situate slave bodies in a medicalizing discourse which explicitly figured blackness as malignant and polluted. The idea of the Caribbean as an inherently diseased set of spaces also provided a convenient justification for colonial intervention and the introduction of European agricultural, medical and social practices.

The threat of colonial illness emerged in literary texts in various ways, but not least in terms of a thematic and figurative focus on the idea of contagion, and abolitionists leant on acute anxieties about the spread of colonial disease. Hannah More's *Slavery: A Poem* (1788) figures abolitionist sentiment in terms of the infectiousness of fellow feeling: 'From soul to soul the spreading influence steals, / Till every breast the soft contagion feels'.[35] Others warned of the medical dangers of slavery to the metropole. William Hutchinson's anti-slavery play *The Princess of Zanfara* (1789) describes the horrific consequences of the crowded, putrid conditions aboard the slave ships that sailed the Middle Passage, picturing them spreading illness as they sailed into English docks:

> New cargoes crowd our shores, and on the beach
> The squalid multitudes are pouring forth,
> From over-loaded ships, which, like the curse
> Of vile Pandora's box, bring forth disease,
> With misery, and pallid want,
> Crippled and maim'd, whose ulcerating sores
> Cling to the canker'd chains, that rankle deep,
> And seek the bone.[36]

Abolitionist writings also imagined in medical terms the moral threat posed to British society by its participation in slavery. The Caribbean, as Kathleen Wilson writes, 'seemed to promise obliteration for the enslaved, the penurious and the prosperous alike. As economic boon and cultural miasma, they hinted at the strangeness and hybridity of colonial power and the danger it posed to the honour of the English nation and the virtue and integrity of its imperial project.'[37] Anna Letitia Barbauld's poetical *Epistle to William Wilberforce* (1791) conceives of the British national body as infected by the moral 'contagion' of slavery: 'The spreading leprosy taints ev'ry part, / Infects each limb, and sickens at the heart.'[38] The all-consuming greed of colonialism, Barbauld predicts, will degrade society: 'By foreign wealth are British morals chang'd, / And Afric's sons, and India's, smile aveng'd'.[39] Scottish hymn writer and poet James Montgomery, meanwhile, constructs the avarice of profit-hungry sugar planters as a kind of sickness, spread by the slaver's 'fungus form' which 'taints the air', leaving clouds of miasmatic and moral contagion in his wake.[40] For Montgomery, as for Barbauld, the spread of disease (especially the notorious yellow fever, which focused its attentions on susceptible European populations) is the righteous punishment for participation in the slave system.

But this book does not focus on the metaphorical lives of colonial disease in the metropolitan abolitionist imagination. The colonial Caribbean is often taught and written about through an abolitionist lens that risks being employed anachronistically to suggest a beguiling proximity between historical and current anti-slavery perspectives that erases the specificity and nuance of both. Indeed, the particularities of the Caribbean as a set of localized material places with unique literary and cultural histories risks being subsumed within (nonetheless crucial) accounts of Romantic articulations of human violence, suffering and sympathy. Besides this point, a great deal of excellent and important scholarly work already exists which focuses on the history of abolitionist lives and literatures.[41] Instead, this book focuses largely on the limited, erratic, biased and unreliable body of works marked by centuries of violence, erasure and loss that is the colonial archive. Putting colonial spaces, settings, texts and authors in the foreground, *The Caribbean and the Medical Imagination* deals primarily with works by planters, slave-owners, Creoles, travellers, soldiers, physicians and surgeons. Disease defined colonial existence, and this study endeavours to grapple with the daily, constant, gruelling and terrible fact of colonial illness by examining it in its local contexts.

Despite the material and metaphorical relationships between colonialism and disease, as well as the wealth of evidence that has emerged from the burgeoning field of medical humanities that Romantic literature was often grounded in emerging scientific ideas, there has not been a great deal of scholarly attention to the medical concerns of literature written in and about the colonies. Tim Fulford, Debbie Lee and Peter Kitson have shown that the joint public articulation of colonialism in literature and science 'gave Britons the confidence to imagine and execute further exploration for the benefit of empire.'[42] Jonathan Lamb's *Preserving the Self in the South Seas* and *Scurvy: The Disease of Discovery* have revealed the significance of diseases of travel and colonization to the narrative production of colonial selves. Alan Bewell's meticulous, wide-ranging *Romanticism and Colonial Disease* brought the global significance of colonial disease to the attention of scholars working on the literatures of the period. Bewell uses the history of British anxiety about the spread of illness from the tropical colonies to British shores to contextualize and inform readings of national identities in British Romanticism from William Wordsworth to Mary Shelley. In the context of concerns about 'foreign' diseases, Bewell shows how those in the metropole 'attempted to understand their own biomedical identities in relation to these new, more dangerous disease environments that colonial contact had brought into being.'[43] Here, though, colonial spaces, settings, texts and authors inform metropolitan ones, rather than taking centre stage. Indeed, Bewell notes that his project began with a more colonial focus; the fact that his study redirected to British shores reflects the existence of colonial literatures on the margins of the Romantic canon, despite the interconnections between Romanticism and colonialism – which are so deep – Mary Louise Pratt writes, that 'one might be tempted to argue that Romanticism originated in the contact zones of America, North Africa, and the South Seas.'[44]

This book's focus on a body of texts that emerge from a closer relationship to Caribbean peoples, spaces, settings and social realities enables it to emphasize the great significance of African-Caribbean medical knowledge both on the plantation and in the wider Atlantic world. While the medical practices that Europeans brought with them to the Caribbean were often ineffective or even deadly, the Caribbean became a major entrepôt for botanical, medical and natural philosophical exchange, as new networks of transnational knowledge production emerged at the meeting points between different peoples, species and knowledge forms. Elizabeth Bohls describes the captive spaces of the colonial Caribbean as a 'laboratory for modernity'.[45] As well as the demographic and ecological changes after 1492 that Bohls describes, the Caribbean was, more literally, the site of important knowledge production and cultures of experiment. Work to understand new floras, faunas and geologies prompted the collection of botanical specimens on a massive scale, with both commercial and medical aims.[46] Empire, as Richard Drayton has shown, 'transformed the scope and character of European knowledge, as it brought apothecaries and philosophers into contact with both strange plants and with the science and pharmacy of non-European peoples.'[47] As Bewell notes, colonial natural history was much more than merely a taxonomic activity serving to classify knowledge imported from new worlds. Rather, it was a 'translational world-making activity, which mediated colonial natures through their portable forms'.[48] In this translational practice, local natures – and indeed local knowledge forms – were subject to profound material and cultural transformations.

But the role of African and indigenous American sources in this new botanical knowledge remains underexplored. Western medical science had much to learn from indigenous populations' knowledge of plants and minerals, as well as from African medical treatments, both of which were often better suited to the diseases found in tropical regions.[49] While most European medical practitioners derided treatments of African and Caribbean origin, some prominent individuals observed slaves' medical treatments in order to advance their own knowledge. William Hillary, an influential English physician who practised medicine on sugar plantations in Barbados, acknowledged that African-Caribbeans had discovered an herbal cure for yaws, a debilitating and pernicious disease which was widespread among slaves and which European doctors were at a loss to treat.[50] Other European travellers reported learning about herbal treatments for ophthalmia, dysentery and fevers; techniques for extracting the notoriously troublesome Guinea worm as well as surgical practices and bonesetting.[51] Often associated with rebellion and revolution, practices such as obeah – a syncretic range of African-Caribbean magical, medical and spiritual practices – were largely prohibited and forced into fugitive practice. Nonetheless, it had a powerful impact on British ideas about health and illness as well as literary representations of the slave plantation.

Scratching at the surface of British and white Creole accounts, it is possible to catch glimpses of enslaved people's botanical, medical and natural knowledge and practices. This study reads British and white West Indian medical treatises and articulations of African-Caribbean medical practices through what Vincent Brown calls the 'acts of triangulation' which shape the practice of reading the history of enslaved peoples.[52] Examining slaveholder documents and British medical texts against what is known about African-Caribbean history and the illicit practices of subordinate communities, engaging with enslaved people's medical knowledge and their relationship to the history of resistance is a partial, provisional work that depends upon uneven source materials and the deeply problematic attempt to reconstruct enslaved subjectivities. But, as Paul Youngquist and Frances Botkin write in their proposal for a 'Black Romanticism', scholarship on the period must, urgently, attend to the literary and historical multiplicity that is still too often marginalized.[53] By participating in what Srinivas Aravamudan calls postcolonial 'tropicalization', Peter Hulme calls practices of 'reading athwart the articulating acts of colonial power' and Edward Said terms 'contrapuntal reading', I gesture toward ways of reading the illicit medical practices of enslaved populations in order to re-evaluate their cultural importance on the plantation and beyond.[54]

The scientific turn in the humanities has brought a number of initiatives across various disciplines that address the central role of the Caribbean, its natural history and its plantation economy in empire building, capitalist economies, intellectual sensibilities, scientific ideas and literary and artistic production. Engaging with recent scholarship in the study of empire, and in British and Caribbean literary and cultural histories, this study goes beyond the comparison of the British and Caribbean contexts in order to develop an approach that is not nominally transatlantic or comparative. Rather, it considers the communication between various geographical locales and the Atlantic networks which shaped the literary production of medical knowledge. Keeping materials drawn from different areas of the globe in sustained conversation, it is possible to move away from the easy binaries – of colonizer and colonized, self and other – that both imperialist discourse and the rhetoric of disease simultaneously suggest and undermine. Indeed, the attempt to articulate or recover African-Caribbean knowledge and practices of resistance displaces the nation as the defining category of knowledge. Paul Gilroy's momentous *Black Atlantic: Modernity and Double Consciousness* emphasizes the mobile, de-centred production of Atlantic cultures, while Joseph Roach's *Cities of the Dead* models a 'circum-Atlantic' model of history, memory and performance cultures, and David Lambert describes the 'decentring ebbs, flows, currents, eddies and tides of Atlantic approaches' as a vital means for exploring competing articulations of colonial identities.[55] There is also a wealth of scholarship on the history of Atlantic science: James Delbourgo and Nicholas Dew's *Science and Empire in the Atlantic World,* Neil Safier's *Measuring the New World* and Londa Schiebinger's *Plants and Empire,* to take just a few examples. Ideas from this body of work about intercultural and transnational formations and the re-evaluation of the Latourian centre-periphery model of scientific production in 'centres of calculation' inform this book as it addresses the complicated relationships between African-Caribbean, European and Creole ideas about health and illness, colonial bodies and the webs of knowledge networks developed during this era in which scientific development was so fundamentally allied to colonial movement and power.[56] The acts of partial recovery involved in examining enslaved, indigenous and Creole knowledge cultures are important. The dawning of the Enlightenment and the 'cultural vanguard of the Romantic era', as Youngquist and Botkin put it, 'look different from the perspective of the living death sentence of slavery.'[57]

But the aims of this book are not structured by the history of medicine: it is not a survey of colonial medical methods that uses literature to answer questions about plantation health or medical practice or to diagnose particular illnesses with the benefit of retrospective vision. Rather, this is a fundamentally literary and cultural project which seeks to illuminate the discourses of health and illness which defined colonial life. The word 'imagination' in the title signals the book's central questions: what are the imaginative forms and functions of ideas about health, illness and cure? What was the cultural and literary impact of such widespread illness and death? How did medical concerns become embedded in the literature of the Caribbean? How were literary texts and modes of expression implicated in the articulation of new epidemiological concerns and physiological models?[58] This perspective does, however, mark a deliberate attempt to refocus some of the discussions that have surrounded work in the medical and scientific humanities. It is widely understood that the experience, articulation and understanding of disease, treatment and cure are shaped by and within language.[59] Yet George Rousseau's call in 1981 for a dialogue in social history that would take account of the influence of literature on medicine has yet to be heeded. As Rousseau wrote then, the interdisciplinary field of literature and medicine 'cannot advance very far until the medical world is persuaded that the territoriality of language extends far beyond the borders imagined by most medical practitioners and researchers.'[60] Scholarship in the medical humanities has examined a literary paradigm engaged with medical knowledge, and explored the idea of illness as an experience which is shaped as much by language and culture as by biology and environment. But the questions of how medical discourse emerges in literary forms and, perhaps more pressingly, how literary forms structure the textual production of medical knowledge, still linger. Research modelling a multidisciplinary approach to the period can be seen in the body of work that has established the huge impact of medical and scientific knowledge on Romantic literary themes and cultural concerns.[61] These works have expanded our understanding of eighteenth- and nineteenth-century medical and scientific contexts and their influence on literary texts. Yet a model of literature as a reactive form, with literary themes understood to emerge from scientific models of disease, contagion and cure, still dominates. Histories of medicine have operated to contextualize and inform the study of literature, yet have not attended to the influence of literary form and theme on medical discourse. Some discussions have begun to rework this approach. David Shuttleton structures his literary and cultural history of smallpox in terms of the important role of literature in the 'cultural framing' of the disease.[62] Candace Ward takes up the eighteenth-century fascination with fever as a lens through which to examine the social construction of class, gender and race, and argues that physicians and sentimental readers were united by the practice of 'reading' the fevered female body.[63]

Understanding medical and natural philosophical texts as cultural documents, this book argues that they require critical interpretation and attention to their stylistic form as well as to their subject matter. It focuses not only on the literary expression of medical knowledge, but also on the generic characteristics of medical discourse, and on the impact of literary forms on medical ideas and scientific ways of knowing. Rather than singling out theme or content at the expense of form, this project synthesizes a range of different fields in order to consider how overlap between different epistemologies demands innovations in narrative form. The 'medical imagination', here, refers not only to the medical sensibility that weighed so heavily on the literature and culture of the Caribbean, but also to the ways in which medicine drew on literary strategies. The intention is to examine the processes of medicine's textual production, as well as the various imaginative forms employed to make sense of health and illness in New World environments. Addressing not only the issues of why the vocabulary of medicine featured so prominently in colonial literary texts and how this medical impetus took shape, but also the effects of literary form on medical writing, makes it possible to establish the imaginative contours of illness in the colonies and yields different approaches to the study of historical interactions between the arts and the sciences.

The Caribbean and the Medical Imagination seeks to blur the late modern disciplinary divisions which have limited our understanding of the nature of the literary production of medical ideas, and to query the anachronistic separation of the 'arts' and the 'sciences' in what was a predisciplinary period. Luisa Calè and Adriana Craciun, Noah Heringman, Jon Klancher and Simon Schaffer have in various ways tackled the problem of addressing earlier historical moments from a post-disciplinary perspective, and their work has prepared the ground for future reassessments of the relationship between 'imaginative' literature and other textual forms.[64] This book allies itself with such efforts to historicize and demystify post-Enlightenment cultural formations of disciplinarity, institutionalization and professionalization that shaped the discourses of the human sciences in the nineteenth century and continue to dominate Western formulations in the twenty-first century, in order to reveal how modern scientific disciplines were born of conceptual and methodological interactions with literary work. By reaching beyond the attempt to tackle the use of figurative language as a form of colonial mystification, it is possible to interrogate the productive aspects of literary figures and narrative forms – the ways in which they construct the medicalized identities and social categories central to the exercise of imperial power, and the challenges made to it. Exploring the relationship between imaginative and medical discourses of disease, this study pays attention to the distinctive social motivations and linguistic modes of expression of different kinds of writing.

This book works toward three primary, joint objectives. Firstly, it argues that literature written in and about the Caribbean became a central cultural arena for the circulation of British and colonial medical and epistemological models. Medical and natural philosophical discourses played a key role in the thematic and stylistic development of empire writing, from the imperial georgic poetry at the peak of British Atlantic expansion in the mid-eighteenth century, through the colonial picturesque and sentimental modes of the revolutionary period to the gothic fiction, pantomime and melodrama of the post-abolitionist era. Secondly, the book recasts the history of literature written in and about the Caribbean in terms of its significant participation in and influence on medical discourses. Focusing on the relationship between literary form and medical ideas, it reveals how the medical knowledge that underpinned discourses of race, nation, climate and landscape was informed, articulated, produced and circulated by colonial literary texts. Incorporating the study of literary form into the history of medicine and natural knowledge expands historical understanding of interactions between colonial literature and medical science and develops our knowledge of the aesthetic, cultural, epistemological and textual models which shaped colonial cultures. Thirdly, by modelling a variety of approaches to its broad primary text base, *The Caribbean and the Medical Imagination* develops critical frameworks for addressing the historical relationship between literature and medicine. The key contribution is to literary and cultural studies of the Romantic period, but, in its expansion of the range of arenas in which medical science was created and communicated, the book has broader interdisciplinary implications.

This multidisciplinarity contributes to the understanding of historical interactions between different forms of knowledge: between literature and medical science, and between African-Caribbean and European
models of health, illness and cure. Suggesting a paradigm of knowledge
produced through intercultural encounter and global mobility, the book
situates ideas about disease in relation to postcolonial models of social
encounter. The Caribbean was a focal point in the American, English
and Scottish Atlantic worlds, and a web of cultural influences centred
on the sugar islands. This study reveals the forms of medical and natural
knowledge that emerged at particular moments of syncretic social change,
examines the contested development of specifically African-Caribbean
and British Creole medical ideas which existed in competition with those
of European physicians and addresses the role that literature played in
producing and articulating these new ideas about health, illness and colonial bodies. Concentrating on new fields such as dermatology, medical
topography and medical theories of creolization – work which emerged
from specifically colonial agendas but had global implications – the book
examines the points of intersection between literary and medical narratives
of health and humanity, and shows that moments of crossing between
cultural, disciplinary and professional boundaries were uniquely productive of different kinds of medical ideas and textual forms. Ultimately, this
is a story about colonial modernity. I use this term not to suggest a distinction from metropolitan modernity but rather, as Elizabeth Maddock
Dillon does, to suggest a modernity that is 'constitutively entwined with
colonialism'.[65] The Caribbean was, during this period, the 'principal ful-
crum' of the emerging social and economic system of capitalism which
transformed the global movement of capital as well as people, plants,
animals, goods, ideas and pathogens.[66] The changing attitudes, disciplines,
epistemologies, landscapes, practices, relationships and material and discursive forms associated with modernization emerged in the context and
conditions of the Caribbean as the hub of empire.[67] Yet, as Christopher
Iannini argues, 'the importance of the Caribbean to the culture of modernity was obscured by a long history of conscious negation'.[68] Revealing the
plantation as a unique site of experimental and hybrid forms of medical
discourse, and emphasizing the multivalent forms of Romantic period
knowledge, I work towards a view of the Caribbean colonies as places at
the centre of the types of conflict, exchange and hybridity which characterize the emergence of the 'modern'.

Tracing a rich literary history of the colonial medical imagination,
this study draws on a wide variety of both well-known and understudied

drama, fiction, poetry and travel narratives, as well as medical treatises, letters, diaries and colonial and parliamentary reports. Taking its cue from its pre-disciplinary context, my approach to colonial and medical writings is purposefully eclectic. Medical practice was professionalized, to be sure, but medical texts and ideas nonetheless drew on, articulated and responded to other discourses in ways very different to today. Attending to the contingencies of Romantic-period textual forms enables a nuanced exploration of the relationship between medical knowledge, literary figures and themes and textual form, and of the ways in which medical meanings proliferate and migrate in different historical moments and narrative forms. In five case studies focusing on different elements of health and medicine, I examine texts written in and about the Caribbean by William Beckford, William Earle, Maria Edgeworth, Bryan Edwards, John Fawcett, James Grainger, George Heriot, Matthew Lewis, John Marjoribanks, James Montgomery, William Murray, John Gabriel Stedman, John Thelwall and Helena Wells, alongside the medical writings of James Lind, William Hillary, Benjamin Moseley, George Pinckard, Robert Whytt and others. By combining archival research and neglected writings with some better-known works, I bring to the fore a wealth of colonial and metropolitan writing that uncovers the powerful effect of illness on the Atlantic cultural imagination, producing a literary genealogy of colonial medical knowledge from the georgic to the gothic.

Chapters 1 and 2 focus on the conjuncture of aesthetics, geography and health. Addressing the poetry of landscape and the fusion of literary and medical languages, they explore key points of thematic and stylistic intersection in writing about health and tropical space, and show how the georgic and picturesque forms which dominated the representation of colonial environments in the mid- and late eighteenth century played a significant role in articulating and shaping new medical ideas. Chapter 1 addresses James Grainger's efforts to endow disease with poetic form in his 'West-India georgic' *The Sugar-Cane* (1764). The colonial rhetoric of tropical disease and European cure relocated the literature of the period within a framework of medical anxiety that processed disease through a series of figurative and symbolic bodies: animals, landscapes, plants, race and weather all became implicated and mobilized in efforts to understand and describe illness. Grainger's poetics of disease are voiced in terms of an emerging environmentalism and georgic organicism which reconfigure the natural and social hierarchies of colonial nation building. His hybrid georgic form and use of African-Caribbean medical sources reveal colonial literature and medicine as deeply intertwined. Examining the connection between poetic and scientific innovation, I argue that Grainger's interest in non-European medical treatments from slaves and local sources not only gave metropolitan audiences a flavour of the Caribbean, but also shaped *The Sugar-Cane* as a unique example of the Atlantic production of medical knowledge in literary form.

In *Disease and Representation*, Sander Gilman points to the aesthetic structures of comprehension in scientific knowledge: 'science often understands and articulates its goals on the basis of literary or aesthetic models, measuring its reality against the form and reality that art provides'.[69] The imagery of disease, Gilman argues, encompasses both medical and aesthetic understanding. Chapter 2 addresses the formal relationship between literature and medicine in relation to the new sciences of medical geography and topography which developed at the end of the eighteenth century and coincided with the literary and artistic fashion for the picturesque representation of landscape. Colonial land was conceived within a medical imaginary that drew together ideas of space, health and aesthetics, grounded in the Hippocratic theory which emphasized the causal relationship between environment and health. Chapter 2 describes the points of thematic and formal intersection between medicine and the picturesque in terms of the contemporary cultural prioritization of visual experience. It examines the well-documented crisis of diseased colonial nature imagined in travel writing and poetry of the 1780s and 1790s, presenting a new perspective on the medical context of this writing by demonstrating the powerful influence of aesthetic ideals on medical knowledge, and arguing that the meeting between medical topography and picturesque aesthetic ideals provoked changes in both literary and scientific narrative forms.

Charting the rise of new physiological models which told the story of human difference in medical terms, Chapters 3 and 4 focus on the cultural and textual politics of colonial bodies and the specific ways in which they were subject to medicalization in the turbulent era leading up to 1807. Most widely associated with the striking engravings by William Blake that embellished its publication in 1796, John Gabriel Stedman's *Narrative of a Five Years Expedition against the Revolted Negroes of Surinam* has much to offer scholars of colonial history and literature beyond this connection. Chapter 3 reads Stedman's account of military life in the troubled Dutch colony of Suriname in terms of his fascination with the effects of the violent colonial environment on skin. Having newly displaced dress and religion as the primary markers of human difference, skin was the point of convergence for social narratives of the body in terms of beauty, feeling, health and race. Skin's vulnerability and its semiotic ambiguity as a marker of human identity and difference make it the motif through which Stedman tries to make sense of the disease, death and disorder that surround him. Drawing on treatises from the emerging discipline of dermatology, this chapter examines cultural concepts of complexion in the context of empire and intercultural encounter and skin's increasingly important role at the centre of ideas about sympathetic response and sentimental feeling. Situating these ideas in conversation with recent scholarly work on sentimental forms of narrative, this chapter argues that the reciprocal significance of medical and racial theories of skin's sensitivity and literary models of sentiment can offer new ways of understanding the historical relationship between race and feeling.

Chapter 4 introduces the figure of the medical Creole. Renowned for being avaricious, extravagant, oversexed and slothful, white West Indian planters were vilified as cartoonish slobs in the anti-slavery press. While the British-Caribbean use of the term 'Creole' both during the Romantic period and in postcolonial studies today usually denotes a non-indigenous individual born in the Caribbean, the 'Creole' within colonial medical discourse referred to another type of body: an individual who had become 'creolized' through the medical process of 'seasoning' or acclimatization to the tropics. Recovering the medical etymology of the term 'Creole' enables a reconfigured postcolonial model of the Creole as hybrid through the lens of colonial medical discourse. Situating this unique category of colonial identity within a tripartite Atlantic network of American, British and Caribbean scientific knowledge, this chapter also maps the contours of a specifically Creole medical empiricism which emerges from the white West Indian's liminal social position between European and Other, colonizer and colonized. The texts examined in this chapter – George Pinckard's medical epistolary collection *Notes on the West Indies* (1806) and John Thelwall's Haitian Revolution novel *The Daughter of Adoption* (1801) – also reveal the West Indian as not just a figure of fun, but of reform. Pinckard's and Thelwall's Creoles, through their claims to alternative modes of knowledge, are affiliated with a colonial modernity which overhauls metropolitan tradition.

Chapter 5 is set during the years leading up to the abolition of slavery, as plantation societies experienced a period of renewed resistance and revolution but also the deterioration which followed declining numbers and fading hopes for the health of European colonies. The chapter examines the relationship between obeah, African-Caribbean medical knowledge and slave revolution. Revealing the impact of alternative approaches to health and the natural world on the plantation and beyond, this chapter argues that obeah implicates African-Caribbean medical and spiritual practices in syncretic cultural processes and revolutionary strategies in a way that redefines Eurocentric models of the history of science and the colonial-periphery dynamic in which scientific knowledge has been located. Obeah was framed by a theatricalizing discourse: colonial medicine rejected 'superstition' and equated obeah with theatrically produced delusion. But colonial authorities also used spectacle to compel belief in the power of the colonial project, to strategically deploy the Christian faith and to break the spell cast by the powerful performances of obeah doctors. Through readings of the anonymous novel *Hamel, the Obeah Man* (1827), as well as fiction, pantomime and melodrama by Maria Edgeworth, William Earle, John Fawcett and William Murray, Chapter 5 shows how theatrical structures shaped the understanding of obeah and the changing politics of knowledge. It offers a model of obeah as a form of slave resistance which depends not only on its ability to inspire slaves in joint acts of rebellion, but also upon its conceptual capacity to unsettle British colonial representations of African-Atlantic medical and spiritual practices. Indeed, obeah presented an alternative narrative of health, life and the afterlife that challenged European medical and ontological narratives, and this chapter identifies the obeah practitioner as a figure of colonial modernity at the centre of crucial moments of intercultural encounter that brought exchange, instability and revolution.

PART I

Health, Geography and Aesthetics

CHAPTER I

'What New Forms of Death'
The Poetics of Disease and Cure

> The poets did well to conjoin music and medicine in Apollo, because
> the office of medicine is but to tune the curious harp of man's body
> and to reduce it to harmony.
>
> Francis Bacon, *The Advancement of Learning* (1605)

With the Baconian concept of the duality of music and medicine in mind, this chapter turns to the work of the colonial physician and poet James Grainger, who practised on St. Christopher (now known as St. Kitts) in the 1760s. In his 'West-India georgic', *The Sugar-Cane* (1764), Grainger set himself the task of writing a poetic advice manual for cane planters.[1] His four-book Virgilian work celebrates the industry of the sugar planta- tion, incorporating agricultural, botanical and medical information and instruction, as well as advice on organizing communities of African slave labourers. The poem was read widely at the time of its publication, though it was praised, imitated and satirized to varying degrees: its bathetic alter- nation between neoclassical European imagery and tropical cockroaches, worms and skin diseases won it a mixed reception. It is now best known by James Boswell's notorious anecdotal account of a draft reading of the poem before an audience of 'assembled wits' including Joshua Reynolds: the verse 'Now Muse let's sing of rats' prompted the group to 'burst into a laugh', and explains why the author poetically refurbished his rats as the 'whisker'd vermine-race'.[2] Grainger's work has overthrown its humble beginnings, however, and come to exemplify not only the graceless attempt to repre- sent colonial agriculture in verse and the decline of the georgic form, but also the first origins of a specifically West Indian body of literature.[3] Such weighty literary baggage belies the humble request Grainger makes in the poem's preface that he be 'understood as a physician, and not as a poet.'[4] Yet Grainger certainly did have literary aspirations, as evidenced both by his neoclassical choice of form and by the fact that on returning to London from his home in St. Kitts he obtained corrections and advice on the poem from his intellectual circle – an illustrious group which included Robert Dodsley, Samuel Johnson, William Shenstone and Thomas Percy (who included Grainger's West Indian ballad 'Bryan and Pereene' in the *Reliques of Ancient English Poetry* [1765]). Indeed, Grainger claimed that the 'importance and novelty' of his tropical context and agricultural subject matter 'could not fail to enrich poetry with many new and picturesque images'.[5]

Grainger's poem did not only render colonial agriculture and disease in poetic form. The 'new and picturesque images' of the verse have their parallel in his interest in colonial medical and botanical discovery, and the 'arduous undertaking' of his georgic labour reaps its rewards in the aesthetic, agricultural, economic and medical 'enrichment' offered by the Caribbean islands.[6] Imagining Columbus's transatlantic voyage, Grainger ponders 'What storms, what monsters, what new forms of death, / In a vast ocean, never cut by keel' might have been encountered by the 'boast of science' and his crew.[7] Just as Columbus met with new diseases and 'new forms of death' on his arrival in the Americas (though not with the same devastatingly fatal effects as those suffered by indigenous North Americans as a consequence of European infectious diseases), so Grainger's planter and colonial physician meet with a host of unknown diseases in the West Indies. Disease and cure dominate the poem's fourth book, which addresses the particular illnesses to which African slaves were susceptible, but disease is also significant to the poem's focus on the agricultural health of the plantation. Taking care of the health of slaves and of the precious cane plant was a relentless task:

> When may the planter idly fold his arms,
> And say, 'My soul take rest?' Superior ills,
> Ills which no care nor wisdom can avert,
> In black succession rise.[8]

The 'superior ills' encountered on the plantation demand even more superior agricultural practices and medical treatments to stem the constant tide of disease, pests and weeds, and Grainger's efforts to meet this challenge find him seeking sources of local cure. Tropical botanical specimens, indigenous remedies and African expertise provide the materials for hope that treatments for the many and varied diseases to which Africans and Europeans were subject in the West Indies might yet be found. Positioning himself as participating in the transatlantic quest for new medical knowledge, Grainger emphasizes the pharmacological fecundity of the West Indies: 'medicines of such amazing efficacy, as I have had occasion to make trials of in these islands, deserve to be universally known.'⁹ While Grainger's neoclassical form and invocation of 'all Apollo's arts' signify his appeal to classical authority and European literary associations, his medical sources deploy African and Indian knowledge alongside that acquired during his Edinburgh medical training.¹⁰ The poem not only represents the attempt to generate a literary encounter between Europe and the Caribbean but also brings together European medicine with other forms of knowledge, with Grainger's medical 'trials' suggesting a model of colonial experiment that is attentive to the usefulness of West Indian, indigenous and African treatments and practices.¹¹ *The Sugar-Cane*'s literary and medical encounters and experiments are the subjects of this chapter. Examining the connection between poetic and scientific innovation, I argue that the poem's 'new and picturesque images' endow colonial disease with poetic form and create a joint literary and medical response to the 'new forms of death' Grainger finds in existence on St. Kitts. Grainger's significant interest in non-European medical treatments from slaves and local sources not only gave metropolitan audiences a flavour of the Caribbean, but also shaped *The Sugar-Cane* as a unique example of the Atlantic production of medical knowledge in literary form.¹² Often read in terms of its neoclassical Europeanization of the Caribbean landscape, *The Sugar-Cane* is not in fact a standard example of mid-century georgic verse. Highlighting the tensions between classical authority and medical modernity, Grainger's poetics of disease and cure represents his engagement with formal innovations in the georgic mode, as well as the endeavour to combine the medical practices of different cultures and articulate them poetically. Far from the regulated, neat extension of metropolitan agricultural landscape represented by other neo-georgics, the unruly parasites, pests and weeds of Grainger's tropical landscape reimagine the colonial order in terms of organic intimacy between human and non-human beings, and construct the plantation as a privileged site of new and experimental natural knowledge. Indeed, it is through the many disruptions of the georgic structure – the poem's prioritization of medical instruction over agricultural aesthetics, expansive medical and botanical footnotes and displacement of British farmhands and swains by enslaved Africans – that Grainger's plantation is revealed as participating in a discourse of colonial modernity which foregrounds experimental literary, medical and natural philosophical knowledge.

'West-India Georgic'

Grainger was born in Berwickshire in the 1720s. Having studied medicine at Edinburgh, he served as surgeon to Lieutenant-General Pulteney's infantry regiment during the Jacobite rebellion of 1745, and in the Netherlands in 1746–8. He settled in London in 1753, built a medical practice and established himself in literary circles. In 1759 Grainger journeyed to St. Kitts on a four-year tour as travelling companion to John Bourryau, an heir to property on the island, but stayed when he met Daniel Burt, the daughter of Nevis planter and former St. Kitts Governor, William Burt. Unable to afford a full-size plantation himself, Grainger invested his modest funds in the purchase of slaves, managed estates belonging to his wife's uncle and practised medicine. He followed up his poem with his *Essay on the more common West-India diseases* (1764), which is in many ways a prose extension of the poem, and particularly of Book IV, which focuses on the medical treatment of slaves. The *Essay* was the first medical manual published on the health and medical treatment of slaves in the British West Indies, was read widely in medical circles and was praised by William Wright, a well-regarded physician and a Fellow of the Royal Society, when he added notes and a Linnæan index to a second edition of the *Essay* in 1802.[13]

Grainger was one of many Scottish medical practitioners who travelled to the colonies in the hope of becoming wealthier and more successful than was possible in their native land.[14] Recent significant changes to Scottish medicine had seen its transformation from a unique national system to a transnational institution, and Scotland's place on the imperial periphery was going through radical changes during the eighteenth century partly due to the fact that it was now renowned as a centre for European medical education. Despite the exclusions imposed by the Royal College of Physicians on those without Oxbridge degrees, Scottish institutions began to dominate the Atlantic medical world.[15] The vast majority of medics entering naval service were trained, as Grainger was, at Edinburgh, and many Scots travelled to the colonies, and the Caribbean in particular, either as army medics or to fulfil the medical requirements of slave plantations. 'For medical education', Douglas Hamilton writes, 'Scotland, and especially Edinburgh, was the hub of the empire.'[16] Scottish medical involvement in the Caribbean colonies bound England and Scotland together in a joint Atlantic enterprise and played a key role in the emergence of the British nation and the formation of the eighteenth-century Atlantic world. Investment in empire, as Linda Colley has shown, presented Scots with an opportunity to redress, to some extent, the inequality in wealth and power between themselves and the English.[17] Grainger marks Scotland's relative poverty in the Scots miners whose hellish labours compare unfavourably with those of enslaved Africans:

> Nor, Negroe, at thy destiny repine,
> Tho' doomed to toil from dawn to setting sun.
> How far more pleasant is thy rural task,
> Than theirs who sweat, sequester'd from the day,
> In dark tartarean caves[18]

But Grainger also identifies Scotland with both good health and medical knowledge in relation to his Scottish Muse, a 'poor exile' originating from 'Annan's pastoral hills' and longing to revisit her homeland to 'tread, flush'd with health, the Grampian hills again!'[19]

The Sugar-Cane reflects Grainger's dual interests in plantation management and the medical care of slaves, taking the form of a didactic instruction to the planter – with a brief direct address to the 'Genius of Africk'.[20] The poem gives directives on all aspects of plantation management, including technical advice on cultivation and vermin control as well as directions for the medical care of slaves. Representing the great cultural and economic significance of medicine to the British Empire, Grainger's plantation physician takes on a crucial role in relation to both medical treatment and the other sciences of plantation management: agriculture, botany and chemistry. In the context of extremely high morbidity and mortality rates among African slaves, the poem advises its planter readers to take better care of their slaves' health and explicitly casts medicine in a supporting role to slavery as a commercial enterprise.[21] Instructing the planter to 'let humanity prevail' and treat his slaves with care and kindness, Grainger emphasizes the importance of healthy slaves to the plantation's productivity: 'would'st thou see thy negroe-train encrease, / Free from disorders; and thine acres clad / With groves of sugar'.[22] Epidemiological discourse was central to the justification of slavery's ongoing necessity: rather than abandoning slaves to fend for themselves, Grainger counsels that 'the good man feeds his blind, his aged steed'.[23] Without the authoritative plantation physician – whose humane wisdom is evoked by the use of various classical accolades, from 'Machaon' to 'Pæan' – it is assumed that Africans would be helpless to treat themselves.[24] The idealized 'Celsus', in whose presence 'pining Illness, flew', is the ameliorative balm on the harsh realities of the slave plantation:

> His gate stood wide to all; but chief the poor,
> The unfriended stranger, and the sickly, shar'd
> His prompt munificence: No surly dog,
> Not surlier Ethiop, their approach debarr'd.[25]

Medicine was the convenient location of the ameliorative middle ground, and Grainger drives home the significance of the professional medic's role on the plantation in the *Essay on the more common West-India diseases*: 'planters should remember the sixth commandment. Those who presume to prescribe to the sick, and are not qualified by study and experience, must be murderers.'[26] This stern advice was aimed not only at penurious planters who refused to pay for proper medical care for their slaves, but at the host of unqualified medics practising in Britain and the colonies who presented obstacles to medicine's professionalization.[27]

Grainger's medical georgic articulates the many challenges awaiting medical practitioners in the West Indies, and strives to articulate disease and cure in poetic form. 'Say, shall the muse the various ills recount', Grainger asks, 'which Negroe-nations feel?'[28] Describing the highly contagious yaws, Grainger recommends that patients suffering from it should be housed separately from other sick slaves:

> Or, shall she sing, and not debase her lay,
> The pest peculiar to the Æthiop-kind,
> The yaw's infectious bane?—The infected far
> In huts, to leeward, lodge.[29]

The conversational style in these lines structures Grainger's didactic aims. Rather than arrange his poetry so that the question mark appears at the end of a line, however, Grainger uses the cæsuric dash to separate the question from its response. In the context of a virulent infection transmitted via bodily contact, this dash signifies the physical distance which the planter must place between slaves with yaws and the rest of the population. A similar punctuative gesture poeticizes the description of the several stages of yaws as it progresses through the body. The first phase, after initial infection, brings a painless, wart-like nodule called the 'mother yaw' or the 'master yaw'. In some cases a cluster of 'daughter yaws' appear simultaneously around the infected area. The second stage occurs months or even several years later, with an eruption of many more ulcerated lesions and loss of skin. These ulcerations can heal after six months, but the final stage of the disease is characterized by the spread of the infection to the bones and joints, and is both extremely painful and disfiguring.[30] Warning the planter to be wary of the possibility that the symptoms might reappear, bringing 'successive crops / Of defœdations' which 'will spot the skin', Grainger outlines the progression of the disease:

> A virulent contagion! — When no more
> Round knobby spots deform, but the disease
> Seems at a pause: then let the learned leach
> Give, in due dose, live-silver from the mine.[31]

Here, disease itself is punctuated by the long dash, which marks the movement from one stage of the disease to the next. In this instance, the dash marks a temporal, rather than a spatial, division. A subsequent colon then makes aural and visual sense of the 'pause' in the disease which allows the revered physician or 'learned leach' to administer his treatment. This second cæsura punctuates not only the pause in disease itself but also the anxious interlude between disease and cure.

For Grainger, poetry functions to dress up agricultural labour and medical treatment to 'best adorn / What Wisdom chuses, in poetic garb!'[32] But he also suggests that poetry itself has preventative and curative functions: 'my soft pipe, and my dittied song', Grainger proclaims, 'Should hush the hurricanes tremendous roar, / And from each evil guard the ripening Cane!'[33] There are many obstacles which threaten the success of the plantation and 'check the progress of the imperial cane' – the destructive hurricane; the racialized, parasitic 'monkey-nation'; the myriad insects; troublesome weeds, or the many diseases attacking either the cane plant or the slaves who cultivate it.[34] The poetic labour of formulating these 'evils' in aesthetic form enacts a kind of protection over the planter's possessions, as Grainger asks after the infinite scope of poetry's curative powers: 'What cannot musick?'[35] The idea of poetry as having a dual role in aesthetic expression and medical treatment mirrors Grainger's own twin endeavours in literature and medicine. Emphasizing the factual basis for his verse – 'the precepts contained in this Poem' are the 'children of Truth, not of Genius; the result of Experience, not the productions of Fancy' – Grainger suggests that aesthetic and natural knowledge enhance and inform one another.[36] Just as 'art transforms the savage face of things' in that the georgic form provides the tropical Caribbean wilderness with European agricultural and poetic structure, so poetry can soothe the planter's troubles – the foremost of these being disease.[37] Grainger's poetic labour not only functions to create the Caribbean landscape within a European conceptual and textual framework, and to describe diseases and their symptoms in literary form: it also imaginatively cures the plantation's ills. Language is endowed with significant powers of healing as the figures of physician and poet become entwined and the Muse offers a soothing Grampian balm to the planter's diseased African slaves – 'What cannot song? all nature feels its power'.[38]

Published at the end of the Seven Years' War, *The Sugar-Cane* came at a pivotal moment in the history of the British Empire, and Grainger's agricultural interests arise in a period during which Britain's dominions were seen by those in the metropole as a tropical wilderness to be brought under imperial control. Imperial fantasies of wild and exotic landscapes abounded, and the Caribbean islands were pictured as rural havens. 'Empire', as Simon Pugh describes it, 'was the countryside writ large: an idyllic retreat, an escape, and an opportunity to make a fortune.'[39] Grainger's part in what Anthony Low has called a 'georgic revolution' responded to the contemporary taste for neoclassical verse, and brought a civilizing sense of metropolitan order to the colonial plantation.[40] Like other new georgics such as James Thomson's *The Seasons* (1730), John Dyer's *The Fleece* (1757), Christopher Smart's *The Hop-Garden* (1752) and Richard Jago's *Edge-Hill* (1767), *The Sugar-Cane* emphasizes the beauty and dignity in what Dyer calls the 'arts of trade' and the 'wide felicities of labour'.[41] 'An empire', as Low writes, 'cannot be built without sweat and toil.'[42] Georgics were employed with the imaginative work of nation building, poetically cultivating Britain's countryside or the wilderness of the tropics, to produce an agricultural and economic harvest, subsuming rural and colonial spaces within the imperial domain by identifying them as the extension of the metropolitan centre. Shaun Irlam suggests that Grainger's use of the georgic was a means to import metropolitan literary and social practices to the colonies as well as to 'exhibit that cultural artefact called the British West Indies for metropolitan and colonial audiences, and also to assert – given its composition during the Seven Years War with France (1756–63) – the pre-eminence of Britain as a nation and as a rising imperial power.'[43] Like Grainger, Thomson's *The Seasons* modelled the British Empire as built upon the foundations of the patriotic rural labourer. Thomson had also voiced the dangers of tropical disease. The revised version of 1744 registers the cultural significance of the massive losses of British troops to illness in the failed Cartagena campaign of 1742 (the notoriously calamitous attempt to seize the Spanish stronghold of Cartagena on the Caribbean coast of modern Colombia lasted only two months and saw English forces lose between two-thirds and three-quarters of their twelve thousand troops to disease). The 'dire Power of pestilent disease', as Thomson writes, 'quenched the British fire.'[44] Thomson records the association between the Torrid Zone and disease in his images of corrupted natural surroundings: the swamps 'where putrefaction into life ferments' and woods which harbour 'sick Nature blasting' cast down 'the towering hopes and all the pride of Man'.[45]

Grainger also followed Nathaniel Weekes, who had glorified the cane plant and other West Indian harvests in *Barbados: A Poem* (1754).[46] Weekes set a precedent for Grainger – not only in his use of descriptive poetry to aestheticize Caribbean agriculture, but in his emphasis on the use of locally sourced cures and the bathetic language used to describe them. On the pomegranate, Weekes writes: 'What nobler Drug can chemic Power prescribe, / To stop a Diarrhea's sanguine Course, Than your Balsamic Fruit's astringent Rind?'[47] Like Weekes and the authors of the metropolitan georgics, Grainger used descriptive poetry to construct a sense of agricultural and social order, celebrating the aesthetic and agricultural virtues of the cane plant through the precision of English landscaping and punctuative balance: 'the spectators charm / With beauteous prospects: let the frequent hedge / Thy green plantation, regular, divide.'[48] But while other poets made landscape and industry beautiful, singing the temperance of agrarian scenes for a metropolitan readership, Grainger's didactic purpose sets a different agenda that focuses on pests, disease and the racial and social order of the plantation:

> What soil the Cane affects; what care demands;
> Beneath what signs to plant; what ills await;
> How the hot nectar best to christallize;
> And Afric's sable progeny to treat
> A Muse, that long hath wander'd in the groves
> Of myrtle-indolence, attempts to sing.[49]

Breaking with Virgilian convention, Grainger replaces the georgic's final vision of a bountiful estate with a fourth book that offers advice on the medical care and social oversight of slaves. Grainger's medical georgic, like John Armstrong's four-book medical poem *The Art of Preserving Health* (1744) before it, puts disease and cure at the centre of the georgic form, as part of the struggle to maintain order amid the surrounding sickness and death.

As a 'West-India georgic', *The Sugar-Cane* blended classical and colonial forms of instruction. Climatic knowledge determined agricultural and medical practice, and observing the tropical environment for signs of meteorological change was a vital part of adapting European farming and health practices to the Caribbean environment. Grainger advises his planter to follow the Virgilian model of agricultural and meteorological prognostication based on the observation of natural signs – what Mary Favret calls 'georgic weather' – to manage a healthy and fruitful plantation:

> Let then Sagacity, with curious ken,
> Remark the various signs of future rain.
> The signs of rain, the Mantuan Bard hath sung
> In loftiest numbers; friendly to thy swains,
> Once fertile Italy: but other marks
> Portend the approaching shower, in these hot climes.[50]

The Caribbean weather brought new challenges, and Grainger's polarization of temperate and tropical climates emphasizes the different agricultural, botanical and medical knowledge required in the colonies. The conspicuous allusion to the Scots 'ken' of the planter adds another dimension.[51] While his 'ken' locates the colonial physician's new knowledge within a European frame of reference, the distance between the classical knowledge of the 'Mantuan Bard' and Grainger's modern Scottish medical understanding renders Grainger's 'ken' rather less metropolitan. In the tripartite relationship between the Caribbean, Italy and Scotland set up in this passage, scientific curiosity is codified as Scottish, and relates to both classical and modern knowledge. While in this era of British imperial dominance Scotland occupied a liminal space between colonizer and colonized, Grainger identifies it as having a crucial role to play in the production of colonial knowledge. The Scottish medic was situated within the doubled space of colonizer/colonized, and was both an agent of and subject to networks of imperial power. It is the sense of the Scottish colonial planter–physician as displaced outsider which affords him a unique medical and social perspective.

On this Scots-Caribbean plantation, miners and agricultural labourers are replaced by enslaved Africans, and Grainger's poetic labour strives to effect a seamless integration of slaves into the image of the regulated plantation:

> As art transforms the savage face of things,
> And order captivates the harmonious mind;
> Let not thy Blacks irregularly hoe
> But, aided by the lines, consult the site
> Of thy demesnes; and beautify the whole.[52]

But appropriating enslaved bodies into neoclassical poetry was difficult work. The language of lines, fences and rows – the physical and conceptual structures through which European landscaping was figured as enclosure – do not easily accommodate African slave labourers.[53] From Grainger's ameliorative perspective, the slaves are a blithe and carefree gang:

> Thy Negroe-train, (in linen lightly wrapt,)
> Who now that painted Iris girds the sky,
> (Aerial arch, which Fancy loves to stride!)
> Disperse, all-jocund, o'er the long-hoed land.[54]

The effort to describe enslaved workers as content and accepting of their lot falters in stumbling parentheses and clashing, multiple georgic lines (a train of slaves, a rainbow, a hoe line), making for an uncomfortable poetic integration of African bodies into British poetic and agricultural discourse. Beth Tobin argues that the inclusion of slave labour in georgic form presented Africans as 'agronomists', inadvertently portraying their 'agricultural knowledge, skill and virtue'.[55] Contemporary metropolitan readers found it difficult to digest. The anonymous author of *Jamaica: a Poem in Three Parts* (1777) responded directly to Grainger's work, rejecting slavery as a fitting poetic subject: 'Th'ingrateful task a British Muse disdains. / Lo! tortures, racks, whips famine, gibbets, chains, / Rise on my mind, appal my tear-stain'd eye'.[56] While Gilmore emphasizes that *The Sugar-Cane* later found success in new editions, reprints and anthologies and achieved 'canonical' status among early nineteenth-century readers, for Karen O'Brien the poem represents the beginning of the end for the georgic mode.[57] Grainger's colonial and agricultural focus, O'Brien argues, forced the uncomfortable issue of slavery, highlighting the troubling incorporation of slave labour, which simply 'could not be digested' by the British georgic.[58] While georgic was always, as David Fairer describes it, 'a genre located in the fallen world of decay, disease, war, and death, the changing seasons, the pressures of time, and the precariousness of human labour', slaves were at the limits of what the form could accommodate.[59]

In addition to the aesthetic and moral problem of appropriating slaves into neoclassical verse, the history of Grainger's poem has been marked by reactions to its colonial bathos. Boswell gives the following account of Johnson's view of the work and its author: 'Dr Grainger was an agreeable man; a man who would do any good that was in his power', but *The Sugar Cane* 'did not please him; for, he exclaimed, "What could he make of a sugar cane? One might as well write the 'Parsley Bed, a Poem;' or 'The Cabbage Garden, a Poem.'"'[60] In a seven-page piece in the *Critical Review*, however, Johnson praised the work, agreeing with Grainger's view of the distinctness of the subject and imagery and announcing that 'a new creation is offered, of which an European has scarce any conception ... we have been destitute till now of an American poet'.[61] But while Johnson's softer public words emphasized Grainger's close adherence to Virgilian principles despite an uphill struggle to 'reconcile the wild imagery of an Indian picture to the strict rules of critical exactness', he left little doubt that the language of colonial dirt, disease and cure sat uneasily in verse.[62] Grainger's medical interests and enslaved patients, as well as his tropical agriculture, made the work uncomfortable reading for a metropolitan audience. Grainger himself admits to the incongruity of his technical terminology: 'it must be confessed, that terms of art look awkward in poetry'.[63] Despite his best attempts to poeticize rats, flies and beetles, the alliterative efforts to describe in poetic terms the 'loathsome leprosy' and cholic's 'pungent pang' sit uneasily alongside the less apologetically bathetic 'dung-heaps', 'mould' and 'weeds' which he instructs his muse to 'descend to sing'.[64] Struggling under the weight of such cumbersome 'terms of art' and mundane agricultural and medical concerns, Grainger repeatedly questions whether his oft-invoked Muse should 'debase her lay' by addressing the unpoetical subjects of illness, insects and composts on the plantation, as well as the slave system itself.[65] The neoclassical language he uses to frame dirt and disease, and the hesitant, often graceless descriptions of tropical disease symptoms result in what Grainger apologetically describes as his 'imperfect strain'.[66] Recent critics have echoed Grainger's unappreciative first audience in their derision of his colonial agricultural bathos. 'Of greater interest to modern readers than Grainger's treatment of cockroaches, rats, dunghills, and the cultivation of sugar', writes Vincent Carretta, 'will be his ethnography of African slaves in the last section of his poem,'[67] But Grainger's pest-ridden plantation is more than an ugly scar on the expanding imperial horizon, and in a 'West-India georgic' the perpetual incursion of pests, moulds and weeds on the plantation, and how they relate to the representation of slave labour, require close attention.

Georgic Organicism

Grainger's plantation is one in which nature is imbued with agency, where moulds are 'impregnated' with 'every power of vegetation', soils have an emotional life and plants have a 'soul'.[68] Compared to that of 'old' Europe, this West Indian vegetable life is more abundant, and more active: 'a fertility, unknown of old, / To other climes denied, adorns thy hills; / Thy vales, thy dells adorns.'[69] O'Brien writes that Grainger's 'insistence upon the exotic superabundance of the land ruptures the sense of spatial continuity between colony and mother country'.[70] Tropical plant life works both within and against the georgic genre to claim the West Indian landscape as an extension of, but more vital than, that of the metropole. Viewed in its disordered and disordering glory, nature battles the planter's efforts at regulation, and poses new medical challenges to the physician. But, more than this, the St. Kitts plantations are alive with earthy fecundity:

> Shall the Muse celebrate the dark deep mould,
> With clay or gravel mix'd? —This soil the Cane
> With partial fondness loves; and oft surveys
> Its progeny with wonder.—Such rich veins
> Are plenteous scatter'd o'er the Sugar-isles.[71]

Grainger's luxuriant, mysterious and hybrid earth, the cane plant's sensitivity and self-will and the blood running through the veins of the planter's fields create a tropical environment defined by its fertility but also by its sense of agency. Other georgics also imagined farmlands with character: Smart poeticizes the responsive 'land that answers best the farmer's care', while Dyer's 'stubborn thorns' give some limited sense of vegetable resolve.[72] But Grainger goes beyond these figurative georgic staples, beyond the sighing forest and moaning mountain that might just as easily be found in British landscape poetry and beyond the field which is alive only insomuch as it responds to the farmer–planter's constant attention and assiduous care. Fairer describes the British georgic landscape in terms of the perpetual 'entropy' of nature, which 'threatens to frustrate human energy.'[73] For Grainger, though, the georgic order he strives to create in Book I – 'The beauty of holing regularly by a line' – later gives way to the sense of animate power that runs through the 'veins' of the 'imperial cane'.[74] More than agricultural fertility, the colonial environment offers the space to see and feel in tropical nature 'the organic spirit, principle of life!'[75]

Grainger's georgic organicism voices a sense of colonial environmental concern from a medical perspective, at a time when, according to Richard Grove, the beginnings of environmentalist colonial policies – starting with forest conservation and environmental legislation – were emerging in the British Eastern Caribbean.[76] *The Sugar-Cane*'s medical impetus stresses the need for preservationist work from the perspective of agricultural health. Echoing the sylvan imagery of *The Hop-Garden*, Grainger creates an image of the West Indian landscape as luscious, green and fertile, though threatened by the potentially devastating effects of incorrect agricultural and medical understanding:

> Yet some pretend, and not unspecious they,
> The wood-nymphs foster the contagious blast.
> Foes to the Dryads, they remorseless fell
> Each shrub of shade, each tree of spreading root,
> That woo the first glad fannings of the breeze.
> Far from the muse be such inhuman thoughts;
> Far better recks she of the woodland tribes,
> Earth's eldest birth, and earth's best ornament.[77]

As well as the deforestation described here, an abundance of destructive pests challenge Grainger's naturalist–planter and threaten the delicate balance of the plantation, as his earthy subject matter lends a sense of tight focus on the plantation's miniature colonists. While 'cockroaches crawl displeasingly abroad', noisy armies of plundering monkeys ('insidious

droles') attack at every opportunity, and 'bugs confederate, in destructive league, / The ants' republic joins; a villain crew'.[78] This is an imperial georgic, so it is framed in military terms: 'Gainst such ferocious, such
unnumber'd bands, / What arts, what arms shall sage experience use?'[79]
At the other end of this poetics of georgic scale, Grainger's model of an
organic tropical colony is imagined greatly expanded:

> Then earthquakes, nature's agonizing pangs,
> Oft shake the astonied isles: The solfaterre
> Or sends forth thick, blue, suffocating steams;
> Or shoots to temporary flame. A din,
> Wild, thro' the mountain's quivering rocky caves,
> Like the dread crash of tumbling planets, roars.
> When tremble thus the pillars of the globe.[80]

Against the kind of Eurocentric historical narrative described by Johann
Gottfried von Herder when he wrote that 'all peoples and parts of the world
are under our shade, so to speak, and when a storm shakes two twigs in
Europe, how the whole world quakes and bleeds', Grainger's plantocratic
ideal draws on a similar set of climatic terms to situate the West Indies at
the centre of a universal empire.[81]

   Within this global environmental vision, vegetation is imagined in the
context of the climatic model of life which defined eighteenth-century
models of health and illness. The movement of plant species across the
world was a crucial element of the imperial endeavour, and Grainger's
medical plantation is far-reaching in its pharmacological purview. The
vicissitudes of the tropics and the fiery south wind, though, prove fatal to
many foreign plants: 'when it breathes, / Europe and Asia's vegetable sons,
/ Touch'd by its tainting vapour, shrivel'd, die.'[82] Not all plant life suffers
from transplantation to the tropics – 'mint, thyme, balm, and Europe's
coyer herbs, / Shoot gladsome forth, nor reprobate the clime' – and, most
significantly, plants 'might be instructed to unlearn their clime, / And
by due discipline adopt the sun.'[83] Indeed, 'acclimatization gardens' for
plants imported to the tropics had an important part to play in the work of
empire.[84] Grainger's assertion that plant life is, with care, able to adapt to
new climates, situated in Book IV alongside his discussion of slave health,
is heavily invested in the colonial medical discourse of 'seasoning'. Just as
European plants might be transported and successfully cultivated in the
tropics, Grainger claims that 'salt-water' or newly imported Africans can
also be 'seasoned' to 'unlearn their clime' and adapt to new environments.[85]
In the context of overwhelming rates of death and disease, the poem
participates in the contemporary medical and scientific debate about the

effect of the Caribbean climate on minds, morals and constitutions, at a time when the possibility of seasoning was understood to be crucial to the success of the imperial endeavour.[86] Africans, Creoles and Europeans often had different disease susceptibilities, adding to the range of illnesses with which plantation medics were forced to grapple and for which they were untrained. While Europeans in the West Indies found themselves under attack from fevers such as malaria and yellow fever (Grainger also makes considerable mention of 'corrupted love', or venereal disease), slaves more frequently suffered from unfamiliar diseases such as yaws, leprosy, elephantiasis, Guinea worms, geophagy (dirt eating), as well as the more familiar dropsies (œdema), fluxes (bowel complaints), tetanus and ulcers.[87] Grainger's medical model draws on climatic theory to suggest that slaves' illnesses originate in their African constitutions, as well as adaptation to the Caribbean environment and life in slavery. Many of the diseases suffered by slaves, according to Grainger, had been brought with them from Africa, rather than contracted in the Caribbean. Diseases were often determined, in this understanding, by the specific region in West Africa from which individuals originated: 'Worms lurk in all', Grainger finds, but 'pronest they to worms, / Who from Mundingo sail'.[88] In Grainger's geographical medical model, it was a person's natural habitat which caused susceptibility to particular maladies, with climate and associated living conditions having significant effects. Tribes from the savannahs of the 'Golden Coast' (now Ghana), are the 'offspring of rude necessity' and their sturdy health befits them for the exhausting labour of the field.[89] By contrast, Africans from less barren climes such as the Congo, 'where lavish Nature sends indulgent forth / Fruits of high flavour', are used to living a gentler life.[90] These people 'ill bear / The toilsome field', being more suited to 'household offices'.[91] As well as predisposing people to a certain biological fate, home environments defined identity, and Grainger shared a widespread understanding of regional African 'character'. Scots traveller Janet Schaw commented in her journal account of the West Indies that 'it behoves the planter to consider the country from whence he purchases his slaves; as those from one coast are mere brutes and fit only for the labour of the field, while those from another are bad field Negroes, but faithful handy houseservants.'[92] For Grainger, while those who inhabit the region around the river Zaire (or the Congo) 'boast a docile mind, / And happiness of features', the 'Cormantees' are a 'breed too generous for the servile field' and are likely either to take their own lives or, 'fir'd with vengeance', seize the first opportunity to murder those who hold them captive.[93] Underlying these medical ethnological typologies in which slaves are predisposed to certain illnesses is an idea of the African body as the agent of its own disease.[94]

James Lind, one of the foremost authorities on colonial medicine in the West Indies, echoes Grainger's understanding of the parallel between human and vegetable acclimatization, writing that people who 'exchange their native soil for a distant climate may be considered as affected in a manner somewhat analogous to that of plants'.[95] In his *History of Jamaica* (1774), Edward Long explains 'seasoning' in humans as a process of adjustment to a new climate, new air and new diseases.[96] Indeed, even between Caribbean islands disease environments were understood to vary a great deal: Grainger writes that 'Creole Negroes, being transported from the place of their birth to another island, most commonly undergo a seasoning: nay, it has often been observed, that slaves carried from one plantation to another, though on the same island, are apt for some time to droop and be sickly'.[97] Like Long, Grainger notes that the seasoning process was complete after about twelve months. But Grainger's seasoning is one which emphasizes social, as well as physical, adaptation: 'When first your Blacks are novel to the hoe', he instructs, 'study their humours'.[98] While some Africans will need the planter's 'soft-soothing words' to placate them into submission, Grainger notes that others are easier to please: 'Some, presents; and some, menaces subdue.' Some, meanwhile, are so 'stubborn' that 'blows, alas! Could win alone to toil'.[99] It is only by investing in the welfare of his slaves that the planter will make them forget Africa, where they may have 'possesst large fertile plains, and slaves, and herds', and encourage them to become 'custom'd' to their new life of labour.[100] The processes of medical and social seasoning function to ameliorate the violence of plantation life as Grainger compels the planter to

> let gentle work,
> or rather playful exercise, amuse
> The novel gang: and far be angry words;
> Far ponderous chains; and far disheartening blows. —
> From fruits restrain their eagerness; yet if
> The acajou, haply, in thy garden bloom,
> With cherries, or of white or purple hue,
> Thrice wholesome fruit in this relaxing clime!
> Safely thou may'st their appetite indulge.
> Their arid skins will plump, their features shine:
> No rheums, no dysenteric ails torment.[101]

The language of merriment precedes and informs the description of the 'torment' of rheums and dysenteric ails, as well as the 'many Libyans' who 'pine in hourly agonies away' from want of the acajou (cashew) tree to prevent their ills.[102] Any sense of real suffering is effaced, whether by being located within the language of 'cheerful toil' that overwrites Virgil's more gruelling labour in order to accommodate an enslaved workforce, or hyperbolized in classical imagery or translated through the Muse, who, as well as embodying the idea of poetic inspiration, acts as a proxy who appropriates and dilutes the feelings of Africans as she 'sees, with grief' the enslaved 'in fetters bound'.[103] With appropriate care, Grainger instructs, enslaved Africans can be both medically 'seasoned' and persuaded to accept their lot. The project of Caribbean colonialism was entirely dependent on the successful transplantation of non-native species: sugar cane, breadfruit, people. Acclimatizing these human and vegetable bodies to their new environment was a monumental task, and *The Sugar-Cane* takes on the labour of aesthetically integrating the various bodies that were transported to the botanical, cultural and medical melting pot of the colonial plantation. Adjoining the medical language of 'seasoning' to contemporary discourses of botanical transplantation, as well as social processes of readjustment and hybridization, Grainger's imaginative appropriation of African bodies into the environmental system of the tropical plantation seeks to afford the planter the same ability to cultivate his slaves as the cane plant.[104]

The Sugar-Cane's agricultural and natural philosophical interests in the parallels between human and agricultural life in the tropics do not end there. Grainger's experimental agricultural practice identifies the islands as a space of human, animal and plant hybridity: 'In plants, in beasts, in man's imperial race, / An alien mixture meliorates the breed'.[105] Writing in the wake of 'Fairchild's mule', the first artificial plant hybrid created in 1717 by nurseryman Thomas Fairchild, Grainger's interest in the newer practice of experimenting with animal hybrids would have been more controversial, though the demand for farming development meant that Robert Bakewell and other agriculturalists were developing methods of animal cross-breeding.[106] Shaun Irlam reads the insertion of Africans into the georgic genre as an attempt 'to "landscape" slavery by zoologizing slave labour as some additional species of exotic fauna alongside the extensive botanical and zoological information he accumulates.'[107] When Grainger asks after the emotional life of the plantation – 'What must thy Cane-lands feel?' – he appropriates and displaces the feelings of African slave labourers. What is at stake in Grainger's interest in transplantation is revealed in the connection the poem draws between the cane plant, which 'surveys / Its progeny with wonder' and 'Afric's sable progeny', suggesting the twin significance to the success of Caribbean colonialism of sustaining these two types of foreign bodies.[108]

Grainger's hybrid bodies also work towards ideas about disease which emerge from encounters between human and non-human life forms. The georgic plantation's bugs and pests do more than threaten the precious cane plant: they also murder the planter's enslaved labour force. Of the human parasites, worms are by far the most troublesome and the most deadly, being fatal to 'more people in the West-Indies than all other diseases, the flux only excepted'.[109] The poem dedicates a long section to worms, to which it attributes a boundless array of painful and perplexing symptoms:

> Yet, of all the ills which torture Libya's sons,
> Worms tyrannize the worst. They, proteus-like,
> Each symptom of each malady assume;
> And, under every mask, the assassins kill.
> Now, in the guise of horrid spasms, they writhe
> The tortured body, and all sense o'er-power.
> Sometimes, like Mania, with her head downcast,
> They cause the wretch in solitude to pine;
> Or frantic, bursting from the strongest chains,
> To frown with look terrific, not his own.
> Sometimes like Ague, with a shivering mien,
> The teeth gnash fearful, and the blood runs chill:
> Anon the ferment maddens in the veins,
> And a false vigour animates the frame.
> Again, the dropsy's bloated mask they steal;
> Or, 'melt with minings of the hectic fire.'[110]

This image of the worm as a metamorphic infestation capable of putting on the 'mask' of any number of other illnesses is also described in the *Essay*, which notes that 'there is scarce one symptom which the animal œconomy may be affected, which Worms are not capable of exciting'.[111] While in the *Essay* Grainger notes that worms provoke or 'excite' various symptoms, *The Sugar-Cane* describes the parasite as able to 'assume' the symptoms of other diseases.[112] The sensibility of vegetation described in Book I here becomes a more active kind of agency. Disease is imitative and sinister, outsmarting the European physician, who, faced with such a mystifying array of symptoms, is left wondering what can be done by way of a cure: 'Say, to such various mimic forms of death; / What remedies shall puzzled art oppose?'[113] The description of the worm represents more than the attempt to rise above the bathos of tropical disease by endowing the humble parasite with a neoclassical poetic sensibility. The European physician's frustration in his endeavour to treat new diseases is only redoubled by the fact that he must also treat new kinds of patients, and the worm's defiance of medical expertise is echoed in the description of Africans suffering from the mystifying effects of 'imaginary woes' which the physician finds to be 'no less deadly' than 'real ills' and which 'baffle oft the wisest rules of art'.[114] Slaves afflicted by such false diseases exhibit a similarly various and changing set of symptoms to those suffering from a worm infestation:

> They mope, love silence, every friend avoid;
> They inly pine; all aliment reject;
> Or insufficient for nutrition take:
> Their features droop; a sickly yellowish hue
> Their skin deforms; their strength and beauty fly.
> Then comes the feverish fiend, with firy eyes,
> Whom drowth, convulsions, and whom death surround…[115]

The symptoms of the person suffering from an imagined illness, who first mopes and is then possessed by a violent fever, bear a striking similarity to the outward appearance of the individual infested with worms – by turns maniacal and pining. The 'luckless' planter who finds himself with a slave suffering from imaginary disease will find the only cure, Grainger advises, to be the powerful influence of the syncretic magical and medical practice of obeah (which may also have been the cause).[116] The colonial physician's frustration at having to deal with unknown illnesses understood as specifically African in origin is compounded by having to compete with 'subtle' African health practices: 'In magic spells, in Obia, all the sons / Of sable Affrick trust'.[117] Grainger's reliance on the magical healing touch of the obeah doctor highlights the dearth of medical tools at his own disposal. Like the worm's capacity for demonic mimicry, which mocks the efforts of medicine to discover it, the hypochondriac effects of imagined ailments frustrate the plantation medic, who is powerless to treat them. Disease, here, takes over body and mind as the victim of the worm loses all 'sense' as well as self. It is strangely unnatural, even artificial: just as the victim of obeah imagines he is sick, the person suffering from a worm infestation finds himself transformed into a 'frantic', 'frowning' puppet that displaces the agency of the sick person into the colonizing worm. Yet the connections Grainger draws between worms, mental disorder, and the magical and medical practices of obeah also point to the sense of agency which might be found in slaves' 'imaginary woes'. For Ramesh Mallipeddi, the medicalized discourse of colonial 'melancholy' or 'nostalgia', described by nautical medics as a psychosomatic phenomenon which was the cause of many ship-board suicides, 'functioned as a weapon of the oppressed, seized by the enslaved to influence the outcome of a social contest during the Middle Passage'.[118] The worm's protean agency originates in the particular space of the plantation, in which were formed a set of social structures that misappropriated the divide between human and non-human for imperial and commercial ends.[119] The worm further deranges this human and non-human binary and, like the multitude of other parasites described by the poem, signifies the tropical plantation as an organic system. The connection drawn between the worm, imaginary disease and the practice of obeah suggests the proximity of the human to non-human beings, bodies and forces, just as it recognizes the proximity of the medical to the magical and the resistant potential effected by the hybridizing forces at work on the tropical plantation.

The Sugar-Cane's organicism imagines an active, animate plantation in which the new proximity between different species, breeds and peoples and interactive relationships between human and non-human beings make the tropics a privileged site of experimentation and new natural knowledge. 'The eighteenth-century organic', as Fairer writes, 'celebrates mixture, not purity'.[120] The georgic processes of vegetable and human adaptation, hybridization and transformation align human and non-human bodies in a model that Monique Allewaert describes in terms of 'ecological personhood'. Grounded in the 'transformative power' of tropical vegetable life, Allewaert's tropical subjectivities arise from 'the entanglements that proliferated in the plantation zone' which 'disabled taxonomies distinguishing the human from the animal from the vegetable from the atmospheric, revealing an assemblage of interpenetrating forces'.[121] For Allewaert, the 'literal and figurative disaggregation of the human body in the American tropics' with their alternate ecologies, enslaved bodies and different models of personhood 'gave rise to an alternate materialism of the body' and constructed agency as an ecological phenomenon.[122] Indeed, Grainger's West India georgic, where moulds come to life and worms perform theatrical versions of other diseases, is a prime site of such colonial plantation ecology. As well as celebrating the West Indian plantation as a space in which the meeting of disparate species and life forms presents the opportunity for developing medical and natural knowledge, the poem hints at the blurry boundaries between life forms in an organic island space where, in Grainger's rearranged colonial order, insects are the colonizing forces to be defeated and plants and entomological life take on human agency.[123]

Empire of Experiment

Grainger's experimental georgic breaks important ground in its participation in the circum-Atlantic production of agricultural, botanical, medical and natural historical discourses. Rachel Crawford describes the idealized agrarian work of the georgic imagination as defined by the point of meeting 'between traditional husbandry and the new commercialism, between the poetry of the earth and the science of agriculture'.[124] *The Sugar-Cane* combines 'ancient' forms of labour with new technologies as part of the project of a colonial modernity invested in observation and experiment:

> Planter, improvement is the child of time;
> What your sires knew not, ye their offspring know:
> But hath your art receiv'd Perfection's stamp?
> Thou can'st not say. —Unprejudic'd, then learn
> Of ancient modes to doubt, and new to try:
> And if Philosophy, with Wisdom, deign
> Thee to enlighten with her useful lore;
> Fair Fame and riches will reward thy toil.[125]

Using the language of agricultural, chemical, medical and meteorological observation and trial and error, Grainger frames such new scientific and technical practices within an experimental sensibility. On the most successful techniques for processing sugar, for example, 'The skill'd in chemia, boast of modern arts / Know from experiment, the fire of truth'.[126] Agricultural practice, too, must be formed by experience – the best method, the poem advises, 'is undetermin'd: Trials must decide.'[127] This experimental method focuses on the rich potential of the West Indies. Just as the benefits of an 'alien mixture' in 'plants, in beasts, in man's imperial race' identify the Caribbean as the location of unique forms of human and non-human hybridity and the site of particular kinds of experimental potential, the poem also claims that the islands hold new specimens and new knowledge that might be of global use: 'doth the love of nature charm; / Its mighty love your chief attention claim? / Leave Europe'.[128] Grainger advises naturalists to travel to the West Indies, and,

> With candid search,
> Examine all the properties of things;
> Immense discoveries soon will crown your toil,
> Your time will soon repay.[129]

An experimental agricultural practice, as well as the proximity and parallels between human and non-human bodies in Grainger's organic plantation, are also evident in the planter's struggles against the 'base insects' and 'vile paricides' which attack the cane plant that supports them and spread disease:

> First pallid, sickly, dry, and withered show;
> Unseemly stains, succeed; which, nearer viewed
> By microscopic arts, small eggs appear,
> Dire fraught with reptile-life, alas, too soon
> They burst their filmy jail, and crawl abroad,
> Bugs of uncommon shape; thrice hideous show![130]

The 'microscopic arts' of the plantation's colonizing pests must be matched by the planter's microscopic attentions, who will find that the only treatment is to 'wipe every tainted blade, and liberal lave / With sacred Neptune's purifying stream.'[131] Grainger's micro-vision draws on European optical technology and new scientific practices of observation to create the all-seeing eye necessary to the planter's endeavour to maintain control over the plantation ecology.[132]

Elsewhere, though, Grainger's medical and natural philosophical practice is far less metropolitan. If the planter is able to control the pests and diseases which threaten his cane fields, he still has to contend with maintaining not only the wellbeing of his workforce but also his own health. For the British colonist 'who journeys then from home, / No shade to screen him' even 'all Apollo's arts' will not guarantee to 'bribe / The insidious tyrant death'.[133] Invoking Apollo's classical authority, the poem nonetheless identifies the limits of European medicine in relation to climatic disease, and the final lines of Book III set the stage for the medical investigations of Book IV with an exhortation to the planter to join the quest for new medical and natural knowledge.[134] In the context of uncertainty about how to treat the new diseases found in the West Indies, Grainger reaches beyond received authority and his Edinburgh medical training to incorporate a wealth of other medical and natural knowledge from across the globe. This knowledge materializes through *The Sugar-Cane*'s rich botanical footnotes, aimed at bringing into European view the 'wondrous' local plant life, 'Old as the deluge' but 'to botany unknown'.[135] The search for new drugs in the Americas was crucial to the colonial scientific and commercial enterprise.[136] Lamenting 'the short limits of a note', Grainger in fact uses extremely lengthy notes to append a wealth of information to his verse. David Shields writes that 'for a reader interested in the botany, material culture or history of the West Indies, these footnotes can be fascinating reading', while Jim Egan describes the notes as sometimes 'so copious they threaten to dwarf the poem.'[137] But to view the footnotes as simply supplementary reading, or as overwhelming poetic sensibility, is to lose sight of the significance of the footnote in historical context: eighteenth-century footnotes, as Anthony Grafton argues, signalled an epistemological shift from credulous scholasticism to analytical and historical methodologies.[138] While Gilmore's edition of *The Sugar-Cane* annexes the wealth of additional information as thirty-six pages of endnotes, the original 1764 publication was footnoted, giving a stronger sense on each page of the significance of the notes and an invitation to read simultaneously and interactively with the poem. In Egan's reading, Grainger suggests that the 'immense discoveries' of the Caribbean's natural potential have been left untouched and rendered 'useless' until the arrival of the British.[139] But the copious annotations point to the far broader geographical and cultural scope of colonial knowledge gathering. Including Creole, English, French, Indian, Spanish and Latinate names for indigenous plants, as well as their different uses in various medical cultures, Grainger's notes create the sense of multiple botanical languages and forms of medical and natural knowledge coexisting in the Caribbean, translated by the poem for a European reader: 'such words as are not common in Europe, I have briefly explained: because an obscure poem affords both less pleasure and profit to the reader'.[140] In a characteristically cosmopolitan footnote on tamarind, Grainger notes the Arabian introduction of the plant into medical practice, Creole practices for preserving its fruit, its botanical name and various other points of information on its medical qualities and practical uses. *The Sugar-Cane's* transnational notes construct botanical specimens and medical practices as examples of hybridized transnational knowledge.[141] The footnotes also become the repository for a disparate body of information: botany and medicine are included alongside histories of colonial conquest and literary reference, with Chaucer, Milton and Shakespeare conferring the authority needed to justify such sprawling notes, unfamiliar terms and foreign practices. The brutality of slavery is also relegated to the notes: the practice of grinding to death disobedient slaves is buried here, too bloody for the Muse's eyes.[142] But although they are relegated on the page, the footnotes nonetheless play a significant role in structuring the poem: like the corresponding poetic section on the picturesque 'tamarind-vista', Grainger's footnotes on tamarind are spread over two pages, marking their equal significance with his verse and prompting the reader to work back and forth between poetry and prose and between the pages of the text.

The footnotes, and the supporting *Essay*, include some key points of African and indigenous botanical, medical and natural knowledge. Grainger comments with reticence that, much like the plantation's composts, rats and weeds, endemic diseases and indigenous treatments are an inconvenient interruption into his more aesthetically pleasing poetical musings: 'in a West-India georgic, the mention of many indigenous remedies, as well as diseases, was unavoidable'.[143] He goes on to confess, however, that he 'rather courted opportunities of this nature, than avoided them', not least because the 'amazing' indigenous treatments he comes across are proven by his own 'trials' and 'deserve to be universally known.'[144] Such bold claims for the sources of treatment and cure he finds in the West Indies would have reassured his reader. As Grainger's dependence on 'soft-soothing words' and poetic strains to cure unwell slaves and sugar crops alike might suggest, finding effective medical treatments for slaves posed significant challenges for planters and physicians.[145] If Grainger's focus on Africa as the source of slave diseases sustains an image of a naturally healthy West Indies, it also suggests the problems of dependence on European methods to treat African slaves. Unlike Hans Sloane, who had earlier written that, but for one or two exceptions, he 'never saw a disease in Jamaica, which I had not met with in Europe', Grainger understands many diseases to be specific to the plantation or to African bodies and emphasizes the value of familiarity with local surroundings and patients in the development of medical knowledge fitted to the sugar plantation, urging the planter to let 'experience sanctify the fact'.[146]

On the basis of his own local observations, Grainger suggests that a method for preventing the painful and debilitating disease yaws might yet be found in the practice of inoculation:

> Say, as this malady but once infests
> The sons of Guinea, might not skill ingraft
> (Thus, the small-pox are happily convey'd;)
> This ailment early to thy Negroe-train?[147]

As Grainger points out, inoculation was already in use to provide immunity to smallpox. First practised in Africa, inoculation was introduced to Europe in the 1720s by Lady Mary Wortley Montagu, who had witnessed its use in Constantinople. Reverend Cotton Mather, the American Puritan and supporter of the Salem witch trials, also used inoculation for smallpox after learning of the method in 1706 from his slave

Onesimus, who had been inoculated as a child in Africa. Nevertheless, the practice remained a contentious one. Some devalued the efficacy of inoculation because of its African origins. Writing in 1722, the Scottish physician William Douglass had discredited smallpox inoculation on the grounds that accounts of its use had come from African slaves who were, quite simply, 'False Lyars'.[148] Vehement objections continued to be made for religious reasons after Grainger's time of writing. In his *Sermon against the Dangerous and Sinful Practice of Inoculation* (1772), the Reverend Edmund Massey denounced inoculation as a 'Diabolical Operation', prompting a debate over the ethics of physicians' intentionally infecting their patients.[149] Grainger counters such arguments by emphasizing the evidence for the success of inoculation. In the second edition of Grainger's *Essay* (1802), editor William Wright comments that 'Dr. [William] Cullen, and other nosologists, have classed the yaws among the *Cachexiæ*, whereas it aught to be amongst the *Exanthemata*, immediately after small-pox. Our author is the first who viewed it in its proper light.'[150] Scottish chemist and physician William Cullen was one of the most well-respected and widely read eighteenth-century nosologists and was at the forefront of the medical interest in the nervous system. Cullen classified yaws with other diseases such as scurvy which he argued were caused by a 'bad habit of body', but Grainger recognized that yaws was contagious and only infected an individual once, categorizing it alongside other skin diseases to which patients were immune after a single infection.[151] By 1799, the Jamaican Surgeon General Benjamin Moseley wrote that 'the cure of yaws is now understood by skilful practitioners. Inoculation is performed with success.'[152]

Grainger's inclusion of new methods and local cures emerges in the context of ongoing European discussions about the validity of non-European medical philosophies and the ways in which medical treatments might be comparatively evaluated.[153] In his natural history of Jamaica, Sloane writes that there are many '*Indian* and Black Doctors, who pretend, and are supposed to understand, and cure several Distempers'. Dismissing the expertise of Amerindian and slave healers, Sloane claims that 'they do not perform what they pretend' and describes African and indigenous natural knowledge as irrational, unreliable and even dangerous.[154] Yet it is because of what Sloane calls 'the great effects of the Jesuits Bark, found out by them' that he sets about investigating slave and indigenous medical practices.[155] The references in Sloane's *Voyage* to information 'a negro hunter told me' and a plant that was 'much esteem'd for its Vertues, by the Indian and Negro Doctors' attest to the significance and usefulness of such knowledge to Sloane's natural research, despite his protestations to the contrary.[156] Sloane was to find himself upstaged by one such medical practi-tioner when Sir Henry Morgan, lieutenant governor of Jamaica, expressed his dissatisfaction at Sloane's treatment by sending for a 'Black doctor'.[157] Other medics, though, were more open about their interest in seeking medical knowledge from non-European sources. The seventeenth-century physician Thomas Sydenham, whose work came to be so well respected in the medical world that he was later known as 'the English Hippocrates', wrote that the 'illiterate Indians' of the Americas had 'found out the best ways of cureing many diseases which exceeded the skill of the best read doctors that came out of Europe.'[158] Prominent Jamaican James Knight wrote in 1746 that he was 'of the Opinion, that many Secrets in the Art of Physick, may be obtained from the Negro Doctors, were proper Methods taken, which I think is not below our Physicians to Enquire into, as it may be of great Service to themselves, as well as mankind.'[159] The Leiden-educated William Hillary, who practised medicine in Barbados and wrote one of the most influential treatises on Caribbean diseases, also showed willingness to accept African herbal remedies. Hillary pointed out that it was local slaves, and not European-trained physicians, who had discovered a cure for yaws: 'the Negroes have by long observation and experience, found out a method of curing this disease with the caustic juices of certain escarotic plants'.[160]

Like Sloane's, Grainger's response to non-European medical practices is mixed. While he observes some treatments and methods to be useful, others are dismissed as 'pretend'.[161] The European physician has a role at the heart of empire, and the authority he invests in his colonial 'Pæan' suggests that, without European doctors, slaves would be unable to treat their own illnesses. Stephen Thomas writes that Grainger's plantation medicine was an important part of the ameliorative policy which promised to heal the sickness of empire by caring for slaves and improving tropical landscapes.[162] Besides the imperial gesture made by Grainger's elevation of the British physician, however, it is important to note that Grainger does learn from specific instances of effective medical treatments learned from Africans and black Creoles. Lamenting the lack of a known treatment for leprosy, which was widespread among slaves, Grainger is yet optimistic that the Caribbean will offer up a natural remedy, being 'still of opinion, that the Almighty has not left us without a cure for this disease; and per-suade myself it is to be found among the vegetables of the torrid zone.'[163] This hope, it seems, stems from Grainger's knowledge of a 'maroon negro' in Jamaica who had cured leprous blacks with a vegetable-based treatment, but who 'would not discover the secret of his art.'[164] As Schiebinger shows, the experience of being excluded from local botanical and medical secrets was a common one for Europeans, whose curiosity about African-Caribbean and Amerindian medicines was often frustrated by the unwillingness of slaves and Indigenes to divulge their knowledge.[165] Grainger succeeds in discovering other cures, however. In patients suffering from a swollen liver or spleen, which can cause 'an adhesion to the surrounding membrane', Grainger notes the method of successful treatment: 'the Negroes do certainly remove this adhesion, by frequent friction with their fingers, by laying the diseased across a hogshead; in short, by putting the body in such an attitude, as to enable them to insert their fingers below the small ribs.'[166] Significantly, though, this point is made in the notes, rather than the main text. This poetic erasure of African medical knowledge is also evident in the description of the chigoe flea, a parasite found in tropical climates:

> Fell, winged insects, which the visual ray
> Scarcely discerns, their sable feet and hands
> Oft penetrate; and, in the fleshy nest,
> Myriads of young produce; which soon destroy
> The parts they breed in; if assiduous care,
> With art, extract not the prolific foe.[167]

The poem emphasizes the chigoe as a parasite of the 'sable' body, commenting on the difficulty of removing the *'Chigoes* or *Chigres'*, which lay their eggs in a sack underneath the surface of the skin. The fact that Grainger has learnt this treatment from observing slaves is revealed only in the notes, where he describes having seen slaves successfully remove the sack 'without bursting, by means of a needle, and filling up the place with a little snuff; it soon heals, if the person has a good constitution'.[168] That the poetic version elides this point underlines the ambivalence of Grainger's attitude towards African-Caribbean medical knowledge and his tentative approach toward including it in his colonial georgic. Wanting to include African, indigenous and other forms of medical and natural knowledge, Grainger nonetheless avoids using African terms and treatments in the main body of *The Sugar-Cane*.

The Sugar-Cane was the first widely published and disseminated English-language text to detail some of the practices related to obeah – the 'dire spells' and 'poisonous drugs' brewed by 'cruel stepdames'.[169] It derides those who believe in its power, sympathizing with the 'Luckless' planter who owns 'The slave, who thinks himself bewitch'd; and whom, / In wrath, a conjurer's snake-mark'd staff hath struck!'[170] The notes, however, tell another story: 'as the negroe-magicians can do mischief, so they can also do good on a plantation, provided they are kept by the white people in proper subordination'.[171] Seeking antidotes for obeah's magical effects, Grainger turns to a plant native to the Americas: vervain, or wild liquorice, which the notes describe as a 'scandent plant, from which the Negroes gather what they call Jumbee Beeds.[172] These are about the size of pigeon-peas, almost round, of a red colour, with a black speck on one extremity. They act as an emetic, but, being violent in their operation, great caution should be observed in using them. The leaves make a good pectoral drink in disorders of the breast.'[173] Understating the significance of African knowledge, the verse gives the seeds their English name, with the African name reserved for the annotation. The 'Jumbie', or evil spirit, is erased from the poem in a manoeuvre that effaces the African medical and spiritual practices associated with the botanical specimen. Grainger implies, but does not say explicitly, that his knowledge of the plant's medicinal properties comes from his observation of the slaves who collect them. While his verse exoticizes and derides obeah poisons and spells, Grainger avoids attributing 'useful' knowledge to African sources beyond the footnotes. The use of local sources here also reveals that Grainger's medical and botanical poetics are shaped by the issues raised by this auxiliary knowledge: his uncertainty about how the plant might be articulated in poetic form – 'But, say what strains, what numbers can recite, / Thy praises, vervain; or wild liquorice, thine?' – is explained by its American origins and the fact that Grainger's understanding of its uses lies in African medical knowledge.[174] The *Essay*, like the poem, introduces its planter readership to several medical terms used by African-Caribbeans.[175] But most of Grainger's hybrid botanical and pharmacological knowledge emerges in the intersection between verse and footnote, as medical notes 'talk back' to neoclassical poetry and the reader works across and between poetry and prose to discover the full accounts of particular treatments and ideas. David Dabydeen emphasizes the poem's sense of aesthetic and cultural innovation: 'when we find [Grainger] introducing yams, okras and bonavist into his georgic, there is more than "novelty" to it; there is an artistic boldness which should not be underestimated. It is clear he had come to some understanding of the idea that a poem about the Caribbean could not be written in a manner that was entirely European.'[176] Where Grainger includes different kinds of plants, medicines and practices this 'artistic boldness' combines African and Caribbean medical and natural knowledge with European form, leaving neither untouched.

The references in the preface, notes and the *Essay* to various treatments shed light on Grainger's interest in African and Indian medical practices, as well as his focus on empirical evidence and regional bodies of botanical, medical and meteorological knowledge. While some colonial medical practitioners, notably Sloane, argued that diseases were the same in the Caribbean as they were in Europe, Grainger sees illnesses in the tropics as distinct and, therefore, looks to the Caribbean as a source of new cures for previously unencountered diseases. The emphasis on specific diseases found on the plantation meant understanding medical knowledge as local too – 'Each science useful to thy native isle!' – and prompted the search beyond his medical training to seek medicines and treatments on St. Kitts.[177] Grainger's methodological reasoning in the *Essay* suggests that a tropical cure best fits a tropical disease: 'both the old and new world boast of remedies to kill Worms; but as this fatal malady is more common in the torrid zone than in Europe, so the tropical remedies are more specifical in this complaint, than the European.'[178] This 'specifical' medicine is one that embraces not only local plant remedies but also other local forms of medical knowledge and practice – not in such a way as to displace the idea of European medical knowledge as primary or superior, but rather to challenge the idea that European medicine was a universal body of knowledge which might be simply exported to other parts of the globe without modification. Certainly, Grainger does not value African or Indian medical knowledge more highly than European, and he shares many of the same prejudices against obeah and other black doctors as his contemporaries. Creoles, likewise, 'are but too fond of quackery.'[179] Nevertheless, Grainger's incorporation of non-European medical practices into his work does make *The Sugar-Cane* truly a 'West-India georgic'. If *The Sugar Cane*'s neoclassical form represents an attempt to 'Europeanize' the West Indies, Grainger's transnational pharmacosm, experimental approach to medicine and agriculture, interest in the empirical observation of sick slaves and use of African-Caribbean medical treatments reveal another aspect to his work which stresses the importance of the West Indies to the rest of the world.[180]

Imitation and Innovation

Grainger's dialogue with African-Caribbean, indigenous and other international forms of natural knowledge and medical practice disturbs the hegemony of a European medical discourse which attempts to import itself wholesale into a colonial environment. Like the transplanted animals, plants and humans of colonial societies, medicine underwent processes of adaptation in colonial contexts, as local and transnational networks of medical knowledge coexisted, competed and interacted with each other. Grainger's cosmopolitan footnotes and experimental epistemology structure the plantation as a hybrid, shifting space in which new intimacies between temperate and tropical plants, insects, animals and humans created a hub for a multitude of diseases, while the condensed richness of the plantation environment also revealed new knowledge and sources of cure. The West India georgic, rippling with feeling plants and entomological agency, where footnotes bleed into verse and medical and natural knowledge is formed in transnational networks, structures a plantation ecology which the planter–physician must work to comprehend and control. The poetics of disease, pests and microscopic creatures expresses the difficulty of managing the many and varied life forms which make up the tropical plantation, as well as the reordering of natural and social hierarchies brought about by colonial nation building – an empire, in this georgic organic model, might be overthrown by the humble worm.

Grainger is notable among colonial medics and writers not only for incorporating African and indigenous treatments into his plantation practice but also in his endeavour to express illness and treatment in verse and his joint articulation of a localized and 'specifical' West Indian medical practice and poetic form. For Gilmore, the combination of European form and West Indian content is representative of Grainger's efforts to 'impose a European sense of order on the Caribbean landscape'.[181] Just as the colonial physician must 'rise superior to each menac'd ill' in the effort to contain disease, so Grainger's agricultural verse must 'transform the savage face of things', rendering the West Indian landscape audible and aesthetically pleasing to a European ear.[182] But *The Sugar-Cane* is not only characterized by its structuring of tropical spaces through neoclassical discourse and, as the Muse sings the praises of 'lofty Maro (whose immortal muse / Distant I follow, and, submiss, adore)', she identifies but from afar with the classical authority of 'Old Europe's letter'd climes'.[183] The footnotes have a key part to play here. Their cosmopolitan botanical, historical, literary and medical information and instruction confer authority and conceptual order. But the complex threads of the footnoted body of knowledge present the invitation to read in ways fundamentally atypical to the georgic form through cross-referencing and the movement between verse and note, creating a sense of disorder that runs counter to the standard georgic structure. Grainger's formal disorder is matched by the referential hybridity of the notes, which trace the transnational networks through which colonial knowledge was produced and highlight the production of different forms of knowledge that came with the movement of people, objects and ideas in ways peculiar to colonial societies. British imperial dominance in Grainger's era brought the deeper social penetration of knowledge-making networks and the global expansion of such networks through trade, migration and state-sponsored initiatives.[184] In contrast with the antique realms of 'Old Europe', Grainger emphasizes the novelty of Caribbean agricultural, botanical, medical and natural knowledge. It is the very newness of the climate and diseases Grainger encounters on St. Kitts which informs his poetry. Just as Hume wrote that 'the arts and sciences, like some plants, require a fresh soil', so too does Grainger's poem use an agricultural metaphor to describe the great potential for aesthetic and natural philosophical development presented by the Caribbean islands.[185] Their different climates, diseases and 'new forms of death' require new forms of poetry, and inspire the Muse's 'new and picturesque images'.[186] Grainger's climatically specific poetry is formed by his twin role as medical and poetical innovator and unique tropical poetics, and reaches toward an aesthetic and natural philosophical colonial modernity in which the planter–physician–poet's experimental knowledge takes up a central role in the conceptual, economic and scientific construction of empire.

The articulation of colonial disease in georgic form – through classical tropes as well as experimental knowledge – marks a key point in a medical trajectory which saw the aesthetic, cultural and medical issues explored in *The Sugar-Cane* being played out in various ways by different authors writing about the colonial Caribbean. The planter and politician Bryan Edwards echoed Grainger's reflections on the uniqueness of Caribbean landscapes: 'the beauty and novelty of the scene', notes Edwards, 'could not fail to supply an able artist with many new, striking and picturesque images'. Animated by this possibility, Edwards 'presumed to sketch out a West-Indian Georgick, in four books'. When the work was not yet halfway complete, however, Edwards felt that he 'had undertaken a task to which his abilities were not competent', and only the first book was included in his *Poems, Written chiefly in the West-Indies* (1792).[187] Modern critics have described Grainger's West India georgic as either an example of neoclassical imitation or a truly innovative Creole poetic development, and as embodying either the dying throes of the georgic mode or the moment modern Caribbean literature was born. O'Brien argues that the georgic's thematic plasticity did not prevent it from struggling to sustain certain aspects of colonial imagery – particularly images of enslaved Africans – and poets following Grainger began to avoid the georgic's 'tonal rupture'.[188] While Grainger's formal and thematic innovations did not rescue the georgic from its demise, his endeavour to bring the West Indies to a metropolitan literary audience was successful in many respects. *The Sugar-Cane* celebrates West Indian agriculture in a way that endeavoured to engage with local landscapes and to give a flavour of the plantation, and other colonial poets continued to exalt in the fertile abundance of the islands. This 'geo-poetical' literary strain is identified by Markman Ellis as constructing a set of 'island tropes' invested in establishing the 'benevolent dependency between island and metropolis' through descriptions of tropical nature and imperial agriculture.[189] John Singleton, for example, pays tribute to the 'tuneful Grainger, nurs'd in Fancy's arms' in his blank verse topographical and ethnographical poem *A General Description of the West-Indian Islands* (1767).[190] Like Grainger, Singleton's verdant, abundant tropical landscape features medicalized African bodies, though in a more vehemently racist and misogynist manner – Singleton warns, for example, against the white Creole practice of using black slave women as wet nurses: 'Infectious juice! for, with the milky draught, / The num'rous vices of the fost'ring slave / Deep they imbibe, and, with their life's support, / Draw in the latent principles of ill.'[191] The poetic union of medicine, landscape and climate appears again in George Heriot's *A Descriptive Poem, Written in the West Indies* (1781), which echoes Grainger's articulation of the problems faced by the colonial physician. While Heriot evolves the medical poetics that structured Grainger's work, his approach to landscape marks the move away from the georgic mode and the beginning of a trajectory towards the pastoral and picturesque models which would define writing about the colonies in the later years of the eighteenth century. In the 1780s and 1790s, the arduous labour of georgic geographies was largely replaced by the easier aesthetic views of pastoral and picturesque forms as the mode of articulation for colonial landscapes, with georgic lines, fences, furrows and routines replaced by the pleasingly irregular variety of scenic nature. It is to the colonial picturesque as the new vehicle for aesthetic and medical colonial description that Chapter 2 turns.

The Diagnostics of Description
Medical Topography and the Colonial Picturesque

In his colonial pastoral *A Descriptive Poem, Written in the West Indies* (1781), the Scots author and topographical artist George Heriot gives poetical voice to the widespread colonial anxiety that beneath the luxurious beauty of West Indian landscapes lay a hotbed of disease. 'All-bounteous Nature' and '*Vegetation's* ever active power' spread a 'verdant robe' over the 'sylvan shades' and 'fertile vales' of the tropical landscape and its natural riches. But the islands' exotic beauty is a façade that masks pollution and disease:

> while the virtues of the clime, my Muse
> In pleasing strains enum'rates, let her sing
> Its various corruptions; and th'effects
> From thence arising to the health of men
> And th'animal creation.[1]

Heriot's colonial Muse equivocates, celebrating the 'more various, more abundant' tropical landscape while lamenting the 'incessant' heat, which

> draws to the regions of the air, from swamps
> And waters stagnated, and noxious parts
> Of carcases to putrefaction turn'd
> And leaves and stems of trees, and plants decay'd,
> And from the open'd bowels of the ground,
> Sulphureous, septic particles; all these
> In th'atmosphere suspended, floating there,
> Involving men and animals around
> With a factitious and infecting air,
> Mix with the human breath, pass through the lungs,
> And stop the vital current of the blood.[2]

The rapid shifts between the framing concepts of health and appearance in Heriot's poem characterize colonial landscape description during this period, which is defined by a sense of discord as references to the horrific symptoms of deadly diseases sit uneasily amidst sweeping outlines of

vast mountains, lush valleys and green plantations. Heriot had travelled
to the West Indies in the late 1770s and published the poem on his return
to London. While enrolled at the Royal Military Academy, Woolwich,
Heriot was taught landscape painting by Paul Sandby, founder member
of the Royal Academy, before moving to Canada – some of his landscape
paintings of Montreal and Quebec are still in existence. His aesthetic sensibility is evident in the poem, but so too are his anxieties about colonial
health. Couching his language in the terminology of contemporary climatic medicine and animated by the fear of the 'factitious' and 'infecting'
miasmatic airs which caused the frequent 'putrid' and 'nervous' fevers
suffered by Europeans in the Caribbean, Heriot sums up the alarming
disjuncture between the lush beauty of the West Indian islands and their
deadly climates and geographies.[3]

Writing from Grenada, the Scots planter Colin Chisholm, then surgeon-
general to ordnance hospitals in the West Indies and one of the foremost
authorities on West Indian diseases, also articulates the association between
geography and disease in his *Essay on the malignant pestilential fever introduced into the West Indian Islands* (1795). Chisholm was an important figure
in the yellow fever debates of the 1790s which saw British, West Indian
and American medical practitioners locked in a heated controversy over
whether the disease was contagious or not, and the types of environments
to which it was endemic. In his account of the parts of Grenada where
endemic disease poses the greatest threat, Chisholm, like Heriot, describes
the 'singular scenery of this romantic country' in the same breath as he
warns of the dangers from the disease particles spread by miasmatic clouds:

> Rivers being here frequently shut up by mounds of loose sand thrown up in
> their mouths by the violence of the surf, much stagnant water and marshy
> tracts are found, at all times corrupting the air to leeward of them for sev-
> eral miles; these districts therefore, although incomparably the richest, and
> in many respects the most beautiful, are the most inimical to the health of
> any of the island.[4]

In their articulation of the common understanding that Caribbean
environments harboured a host of terrible diseases, Heriot and Chisholm
reveal that colonial land was conceived within a medical imaginary which
drew together ideas of geography, health and aesthetics. Chisholm goes
further than Heriot, however, in suggesting a positive correlation between
beauty and sickness. For Chisholm, the beauty of the lush Caribbean
landscape does not merely disguise disease – rather, it almost seems to
cause it.

As Chisholm and Heriot demonstrate, the late eighteenth century witnessed a conceptual alignment of disease and physical space. The geographical approach to disease was grounded in the new Hippocratism of two emerging scientific discourses which studied the causal relationship between climate and health: medical geography (the study of the distribution of disease) and medical topography (the detailed description of particular geographic locales with the aim of assessing the presence of disease). Health and illness were understood as geographical phenomena and the study of local environments became a central axiom of medical practice. As disease ravaged colonial populations and both Africans and Europeans in the Caribbean succumbed to illnesses outside their range of immunity, knowledge about which diseases were endemic to which regions came to be perceived as crucial to the success of the imperial endeavour. Colonial medical orthodoxy now emphasized the differences in the types and severity of diseases found in Europe and the Caribbean – though debate continued over whether certain climatic diseases such as yellow fever were in fact simply aggravated versions of domestic diseases found in England.[5] The epidemiological crisis prompted physicians to map disease onto the Caribbean islands themselves. It was largely through this identification of disease with space that the Caribbean became 'tropicalized': the notion of the Caribbean climate as tropical was conceptually structured by disease and by an understanding of 'the tropics' not simply as a climatic descriptive, but as harbouring distinct disease agents. The dismal mortality rate and the focus on pathogenic places structured the perception of colonial environments as sickly, and in need of a healing European hand. This medicalized formulation of space used descriptions of 'healthy' and 'unhealthy' environments to form the understanding of place, providing a justification for colonial intervention. Conversely, those invested in celebrating or promoting the Caribbean often invoked the same medicalized understanding of landscape but to different ends, emphasizing the fertility, health and superabundance of the islands.

Medical geographical knowledge had a cultural influence far beyond surgeons and physicians. Ludmilla Jordanova has shown that the synthesis of earth science and environmental medicine was 'embedded in all aspects of the life of the late Enlightenment'.[6] Alan Bewell has demonstrated the profound cultural significance of geographical medicine by highlighting its impact on the metropolitan imagination, showing that Romantic literature deployed disease geopolitically and drew on the widespread understanding of the colonies as fundamentally diseased in representations of domestic landscapes. But colonial medical geography did not simply provide Romantic writers with the vocabulary of disease to construct imaginative geographies. Heriot and Chisholm reveal the aesthetic and figurative dimensions of the geographical model of health that dominated medical discourse. The medical and environmental sciences emerged within literary texts and travel narratives written in and about the Caribbean, where authors employed a medicalized vision of landscape and climate to articulate and respond to colonial surroundings. Heriot and other colonial authors drew upon the language of medical geography and topography and signalled the beauty of colonial landscapes in relation to the discourse of health and illness, as well as positioning the Caribbean in comparison to European environments. But conversely, and with equal significance, medical authors drew on textual forms and aesthetic imagery from literary authors and travel writers in developing a body of knowledge which centred on establishing the visible environmental sources of disease – the stagnant waters, marshes and swamps, for example, identified by Chisholm and Heriot. Both medical and literary discourses appealed to a visual model which associated the appearance of a landscape with its perceived levels of disease, and the points of overlap between literary and medical approaches centre on textual practices of landscape description.

Addressing the relationship between medical and non-medical discourses in the imaginative construction of tropical environments, this chapter focuses on the points of intersection between the descriptive practices of medical topography and the literary aesthetics of Caribbean landscape. I argue that literature and medicine borrowed formal and thematic qualities from one another, and reveal the influence of aesthetic ideals on the production of medical knowledge. Considering the textual production of colonial medical knowledge in predisciplinary context, I present a consideration of textual contingencies, generic overlap and discursive reciprocity; in order to understand the structure of colonial medical knowledge, it is necessary to consider the stylistic characteristics of medical texts, as well as literary ones. The aim, here, is not to elaborate on the well-established understanding of colonial landscapes as embodying a paradoxical imaginary space of prelapsarian tropical idyll and Pandora's box of deadly diseases. Rather, it is to highlight the medical contexts of literary imagery, and to show the importance of broader cultural discourses of landscape to medical attempts to understand the very different disease environments in the sugar colonies. Emphasizing the ideological underpinnings of landscape production, Jill Casid argues that 'landscaping – whether in the form of painting, planting, poetry, or aesthetics – should be understood as united discursive and material practices that came to the fore in the eighteenth century as techniques of empire'.[7] Geoff Quilley writes that the narrative of connection and difference between Britain and the West Indies which formed a crucial conceptual vehicle of empire was 'articulated through the discourse of and on landscape'.[8] At the heart of the body of descriptive practices which articulated Atlantic landscapes is the 'colonial picturesque' – a range of aesthetic and topographical textual forms and tropes deployed in terms of narratives of aesthetic and agricultural 'improvement'. By describing the points of thematic and stylistic exchange between medical topography and landscape aesthetics, this chapter establishes the unique qualities of colonial picturesque imagery which was underpinned by medical precepts, and highlights the significant role played by medicine in the circum-Atlantic production of colonial landscapes.

The Diagnostics of Description

The medical association between space and health was by no means a new idea. The notion that geographical location had a significant effect on human health had a long history behind it: the texts of the Hippocratic Corpus trace the source of epidemic diseases to seasonal changes and meteorological conditions.[9] The period of European exploration and expansion on a massive scale between the sixteenth and nineteenth centuries, however, brought renewed awareness of the global variations of disease. The fatal consequences of colonial travel for both indigenous and alien populations had made the existence of unique disease environments an increasingly important medical preoccupation. Indeed, the problems attendant on adapting to new climates were a more persistently significant obstacle to imperial expansion than the moral problem of slavery. 'Of all the objections to colonization offered by English writers from the sixteenth century onward', as Jim Egan puts it, 'none proved more resilient than those focused on climate.'[10] The Caribbean islands as a set of geographical and medical environments were distinguished from more temperate European climes, and tropical climates were understood to be the root cause of the devastatingly high mortality rates amongst British travellers and military personnel. The growing awareness of disease agents as localized entities became the keystone of a new medical method, prompting a colonial project which engaged in mapping geographical spaces across the globe in terms of their endemic diseases. The late eighteenth century brought an age of regionalized medicine which sought to map localities according to which diseases were found to be present.[11]

Drawing on a combination of humoral-climatic and miasmatic theories, medical geography and topography constructed an opposition between healthy and unhealthy spaces, centring on a model of atmospheric infection caused by dirt, stagnation and intemperate conditions as primary disease agents. The humoral-climatic understanding of disease drew on the model of the four bodily humours and connected them to the seasons, weather and natural environment. Earlier versions of Hippocratic epidemiology and meteorology were expanded, and now focused on a hypothesis of aerial contagion. From an earlier conception of air as a simple and inactive entity, atmospheric discourse followed Robert Boyle's assertion that air was in fact a 'confus'd Aggregate of Effluviums from such differing Bodies' and developed an idea of air as a dynamic system of particles.[12] The London physician (and creator of the John Bull figure) John Arbuthnot argued in his *Essay concerning the Effects of Air on Human Bodies* (1733) that the airs of specific locations caused not only particular maladies but also different human physical and social characteristics, writing that 'the Air operates sensibly in forming the constitutions of Mankind, the Specialties of Features, Complexion, Temper, and consequently the Manners'.[13] By the 1770s, Joseph Priestley's work on airs had become integrated into a programme of reformist policy based on the possibility of meliorating the noxious qualities of particular airs.[14] Meteorological observation became a crucial part of medical practice: influential Irish physician and surgeon James Johnson noted from his experience in India that in assessing the effects on health of tropical climates 'the direction and prevalence of winds are ever to be coupled with the medical topography of a place'.[15] Medical opinion was now unified in the idea that different geographical settings held different airs and different diseases. The movement of disease occurred via noxious vapours rising from putrescent organic matter, and the West Indian environment, with its overheated, humid atmosphere and the resulting production of stagnating airs emanating either from marshlands or from densely forested areas, was considered a hotbed of disease. Within the contemporary aetiological and epidemiological understanding, malaria, yellow fever and other diseases were airborne, so colonial medical geographies focused their attention on the miasmata in the 'bad air' caused by environmental corruption and on the identification of visible signs of aerial sources of disease.

Following the work of earlier British medics such as Sydenham, whose work examined the significance of seasonal weather changes, the practice of medical geography was developed and institutionalized by German physicians such as Leonhard Ludwig Finke.[16] Medical geography, as Finke wrote, 'looked at the whole world from a medical point of view'.[17] This 'medical point of view' was grounded in the belief that all human diseases had environmental origins: 'to which diseases and evils man is exposed, because he lives here and not somewhere else, because he breathes this and no other air, he eats this and no other food, drinks this and no other water, has this and no other way of living and so on'.[18] Finke's work charted the world's diseases, establishing correlations between the places where people lived and the diseases from which they suffered. This medicalization of the atmosphere, as Richard Grove writes, created a new role for medical practitioners in relation to the management of disease and the regulation of social and environmental health.[19] Both the need to control disease and the new supervisory role of medical professionals were particularly significant in colonial plantation societies, and doctors and surgeons in large numbers took upon themselves the project of diagnosing tropical environments. The empirical study of the relationship between geography and disease aimed to create a set of practices which were concerned with either warnings against human inhabitation or proactive measures to alter an environment's salubrity. By the early nineteenth century, 'medical geography' had become a discipline encompassing elements of cartography, geography, geology, medicine, meteorology and topography. The focus on pathogenic places structured physical space in medical terms; disease was perceived as a geographical phenomenon, and the concept of 'place' was fundamentally medicalized.

On the basis of topographical accounts of natural surroundings, medical practitioners produced knowledge of which noxious environmental features – and therefore which diseases – were local to the area. German physician and European public health pioneer Johann Peter Frank instructed medical topographers in the importance of description in his *A System of Complete Medical Police* (1779–1817). For Frank, medical topographies made an 'extremely important contribution for those who have to look after the health and well-being of a country. Every publicly employed physician or district physician, should supply the medical description of his region as accurately as possible, and compare every change in weather, every phenomenon concerning the healthiness of a place'.[20] The medical description of climatic regions meant detailed written and pictorial accounts of the appearance of landscapes, catalogues of plant and animal life, descriptions of human living spaces and agricultural structures and assessing the purity of the air. Meticulous examination was crucial: 'humane physicians should be set to explore the nature, condition and constitution of the tiniest village. They should investigate its

diseases and their causes in the most precise detail'.[21] This work was not
only the domain of the physician, however: 'correct topographies supplied
by art experts' were also an essential part of medical geographical work.[22]
In the context of such professional overlap between physicians and artists,
medical topographies and imaginative representations of landscape should
be read as co-existing within a wider discourse of medical aesthetics. The
cultural prioritization of the visual – what Peter de Bolla describes as 'a
culture based on the visual, on modalities of visualization, the production and consumption of visual matter' – emerged in medical discourse as
an affirmation of medical models which presumed visible markers of the
presence of disease.[23] This visual focus was connected to the identification
of environmental pollution and meteorological and geographical markers
as signs of disease. The leading medical geographer of the West Indies,
James Lind, identifies and categorizes the 'signs of an unhealthy country',
such as swarms of insects, thick fogs, densely wooded areas, marshes,
swamps and particular types of soil and sand, and pays particular attention
to the miasmata caused by environmental corruption found in particular
geographical formations.[24]

Perhaps the best forewarning of disease, though, was the weather. The
heat, humidity and volatility of the tropical climate were considered primary disease agents, and medics began to combine meteorological observation with records of associated illnesses. William Hillary, a student
of Herman Boerhaave, who went on to practise medicine in Barbados
between 1747 and 1758, published one of the best-known and most widely
followed treatises on Caribbean diseases, *Observations on the Changes of the
Air, and the Concomitant Epidemical Diseases of Barbadoes* (1759). For six
years Hillary kept detailed daily records of the temperature and pressure
of the air and the quantities of rain that fell in each month and year. He
summarized the Barbadian weather and concurrent diseases on a monthly
basis, finding variations in the types and number of occurrences of particular maladies depending on the weather and season, concluding that
most of the diseases he encountered in Barbados were 'indigenous and
endemial in the West-India islands, or peculiar to the Torrid Zone; and
are seldom or never seen in the colder European nations'.[25] Within this
differential climatic model, weather was understood as global, patterned
change, structured within a Virgilian tradition of meteorological and agricultural prognostication based on the observation of natural signs such as
the appearance of the sky or plant life – Mary Favret's 'georgic weather'.[26]
Favret's use of 'georgic' as a framing term highlights the role of weather in
the diagnosis and 'improvement' of land.[27]

Meteorological observation was put to use in partnership with medical topography as part of the visual decoding of the physical environment, as early work by Lind, Hillary and others formed the beginning of a collective attempt to expose and interpret the visible signifiers of unhealthy tropical places. John Williamson, Fellow of the Royal College of Physicians in Edinburgh, worked in Jamaica from 1798 to 1812 and kept monthly records of weather and the relative health of plants and people. The humid climate of the West Indies, he found, was far from the picture of health. In his entry for January 1806, Williamson notes: 'a visit among woody parts, or along the banks of rivers, where immense masses of vegetable matter are passing into decomposition, and their sensible effects on the atmosphere, will convince any person how injurious to health such impregnations must be'.[28] Williamson's emphasis on the visible source of atmospheric corruption highlights the visual politics of pollution at stake in the medical geographical model. Though its atmospheric effects are unseen, the visible existence of rotting plants appears to trigger other kinds of unspecified 'sensible effects' which alert the observer to the presence of disease. While the actual point of contagion – especially miasmatic clouds – was not always directly visible, the look of the land could instruct the medic or the traveller in essential local medical knowledge.

The notion of the beautiful but torpid and pathogenic tropical climate was situated within a medicalized visual framework which shaped landscape imagery and the examination of natural surroundings. Description, already the cornerstone of Enlightenment natural knowledge, took on even greater significance in colonial contexts, where distance prevented most Europeans from closer contact with exotic people, objects, landscapes and diseases – indeed, the textual labour of description was particularly important in the West Indies.[29] By the 1790s, American physician Valentine Seaman was making use of the new practice of medical cartography to depict yellow fever epidemics in New York; in the nineteenth century, medical maps were used to illustrate cholera outbreaks in Europe.[30] However, while it is possible that medical cartography was practised in the Caribbean to some extent (although the expense of publishing images is likely to have been prohibitive), no medical maps from the region during this period appear to remain extant today. Rather, the texts produced by physicians and surgeons working in the Caribbean use topographical description to assess the relative health of particular environmental regions, descriptive textual practices became a crucial aspect of colonial medical science holding great diagnostic and prognostic significance. The idea of the natural sign as diagnostic aid is expressed in medical geography through the use of description as an interpretative tool; meteorological and topographical signs were understood as the key to demystifying tropical environments. Medical topography focused on the detailed comparison between the surface appearances of landscapes: what a landscape looked like meant as much in terms of its relative health as did a record of which diseases had been witnessed there, and the alignment of health and visibility characterizes the scientific understanding of landscape in this period.

Colonial Picturesque

Alongside the thickening descriptive practices of colonial science, literary authors also used textual practices of description to articulate the immense cultural, economic and medical significance of landscape. Heriot's *Descriptive Poem* followed the fashion for descriptive and didactic styles which shaped literary accounts of the Caribbean colonies such as Grainger's *The Sugar-Cane*, John Singleton's blank verse *General Description of the West-Indian Islands* (1767), sailor-turned-abolitionist Edward Rushton's *West-Indian Eclogues* (1787), Thomas Moore's *Epistles, Odes and Other Poems* (1806) (Moore is perhaps best known for burning Byron's memoirs but also worked for the Admiralty in Bermuda) and William Beckford's *Descriptive Account of the Island of Jamaica* (1790). Through the transition from georgic to pastoral and picturesque modes, writers used aesthetic description to prioritize landscape over labour. 'By mediating their representations of the West Indies through eclogue, and through pastoral-descriptive modes in general', Karen O'Brien argues, colonial poets suggested that, 'whatever the depredations of slavery, the real value of the colony was guaranteed by its landscape: the land was both anterior and surplus to forms of labour'.[31] The emphatically visual register of the pastoral-descriptive mode, as Geoff Quilley has written, enabled planters and travellers to 'insist on the materiality of the landscape, as a form of reaction to the destabilizing effects upon the plantocracy's economy and constitution of the events of the American Revolution and the growing metropolitan anti-slavery campaign'.[32] The political and economic significance of colonial land, and the need for the military, plantation owners and medical professionals to establish territorial, agricultural and disease control, made landscape a key conceptual and material vehicle for the production of imperial power.

The institutionalization of medical geography coincided with the fascination with scenic landscape dominating British and colonial literary and artistic imagery, and particularly with what Ann Bermingham calls 'the cult of the picturesque'.[33] As well as the agricultural boom beginning in the mid-1790s and the subsequent changing social relations between urban and rural areas, the picturesque emerged in relation to increasing travel and imperial concerns. W. J. T. Mitchell stresses the importance of recognizing the colonial contexts of domestic landscape production, arguing that 'landscape is a particular historical formation associated with European imperialism':

> Empires move outward in space as a way of moving forward in time; the 'prospect' that opens up is not just a spatial scene but a projected future of 'development' and exploitation. And this movement is not confined to the external, foreign fields toward which the empire directs itself; it is typically accompanied by a renewed interest in the re-presentation of the home land-scape, the 'nature' of the imperial centre.[34]

More specifically, Jeffrey Auerbach and Geoff Quilley draw a line between English and colonial forms of picturesque aesthetics. 'While scholars of the picturesque have generally focused on its English origins', Auerbach writes, 'it is important to note that many of its foremost practitioners drew their inspiration as much from the empire itself as from the English Lake District.'[35] In the colonies, the picturesque was the predominant mode employed to represent the plantation, and a crucial part of transforming the colonization of peoples, plants and spaces into an aesthetically pleasing and morally gratifying vision. For Auerbach, the picturesque was a homogenizing force which functioned to unite the disparate regions of Empire.[36] But the picturesque was an elastic, capacious mode that was easily adapted for diverse ideological ends in both the metropole and the colonies. While some colonial physicians and authors drew on the picturesque imagery of 'home' in order to stake their claim over the colonies, other representations of colonial landscapes were motivated by the desire to create a differential aesthetic between Europe and the Caribbean.[37] Elizabeth Bohls describes the picturesque as a 'paradoxically placeless' aesthetics of place 'grounded in mobility and comparison'.[38] This lack of geographical rootedness meant that just as the domestic picturesque was formed in the wider context of empire, images of New World landscapes were able to draw on, recontextualize and renegotiate the British picturesque.

West Indian planters and slavery apologists often engaged with the principles of medical geography to depict a genial, salubrious colonial environment. The Wiltshire-born planter, politician and historian Bryan Edwards, who lived in Jamaica for much of his adult life, draws on the aerial model of health in his construction of the island as a rural haven, envisaging himself:

> reclin'd amid the coco grove,
> Or where the interwoven plantain spreads
> Her verdant canopy, let gentle sleep
> Envelop, 'till the sultry hours are past.
> The sportive zephyrs, rustling o'er my head,
> Shall fan the undulating air, and soothe
> My slumbers—to the paradise of dreams
> My waking fancy waft.[39]

The breezy luxury of Edwards's self-congratulatory colonial scene invites the metropolitan reader into a rich, leisurely tropical environment. Jamaica's pleasing airs are held up in explicit contrast with other tropical climates: Mexico is 'fraught with poison' from its contaminating silver mines and Africa is filled with 'stagnate air' which 'o'erpow'rs / Life's functions'.[40] Indeed, Jamaica was thought of by some as one of the healthiest islands in the West Indies, because its mountainous regions were refreshed by vigorous breezes, though others preferred the flatter topography of Barbados on the assumption that it was less likely to retain noxious miasmata.

Edwards's erasure of labour and violence, and exaltation in a healthy environment, characterize ameliorationist writing at this point. But no one aestheticized the Caribbean more fervently than William Beckford. Beckford was the Jamaica-born first cousin of William Thomas Beckford of Fonthill Abbey – the English Beckford was the author of the Orientalist gothic classic *Vathek* (1786). On his father's death in 1756, the Jamaican Beckford inherited four sugar plantations, and after an education at Oxford and travels through Europe he and his wife returned to Jamaica in 1774 and remained there until 1786. Hurricanes depleted his enormous fortunes, and on his return to England Beckford was incarcerated as a debtor in the Fleet Prison and found himself with time on his hands to write the *Descriptive Account of the Island of Jamaica* (1790). During his time in the West Indies, Beckford was patron to several artists whom he invited to visit his plantation, including the landscape painter George Robertson. The *Descriptive Account* is immersed in tropical landscape through the visual lens of the picturesque; Jill Casid reads it as a 'painting of words', while Elizabeth Bohls describes Beckford's aesthetic enthrallment as 'compulsive'.[41] Seeing land in terms of its potential for being rendered artistically, Beckford's fascination with the visual realm is expressed through the use of painting analogies to present an idealized and harmonious landscape:

> The variety and brilliancy of the verdure in Jamaica are particularly striking; and the trees and shrubs that adorn the face of the country are singular for

the richness of their tints, the depths of their shadows, and the picturesque appearance they make. It is hardly possible to conceive any vegetation more beautiful, and more congenial to a painter's eye, than that which universally prevails throughout every part of that romantic Island.[42]

The use of painting imagery and the description of landscape as superficial adornment on the 'face' of Jamaica betray a desire to empty the landscape of meaning beyond the aesthetic. Beckford bears witness to tropical nature through a visual mode that signals the colonial appropriation of land, or what Anthony Pagden calls the 'autoptic imagination'.[43] But Beckford also continually replaces his own narrative subject position, synechdochically, with the singularized but generic 'eye', distancing the colonial subject from landscape – as well as from labouring slaves, whom he assimilates into these aestheticized surroundings, and whose labour is imagined as less arduous than that experienced by the British working classes. Written at a time when the abolitionist threat to the lifestyle and livelihood of the plantocracy was growing, the aestheticizing impulse is firmly rooted in a politics of reaction to abolitionism and is concerned to legitimize what Keith Sandiford calls a 'Creole cultural imperium'.[44] Beckford's transcendent eye surveys a selective view, erasing labour and violence from its picturesque scene in ways that have been discussed by John Barrell, Tim Barringer, Édouard Glissant and others, and performing what Sara Suleri calls acts of 'profound unlooking' which indicate the 'desire to transfix a dynamic cultural confrontation into a still life, converting a pictorial imperative into a gesture of self-protection that allows the colonial gaze a license to convert its ability not to see into studiously visual representations'.[45] Beckford's *Descriptive Account* operates in this kind of colonial picturesque style, evacuating social realities and conveniently bestowing innocence on colonial imagery that might otherwise present its metropolitan audiences with disturbing scenes of horrific violence.

The title of the *Descriptive Account* announces the privilege conferred upon the interpretative labour of the author as a means of communicating the colonial world to the metropolitan reader. The aesthetic ideals of the picturesque drew on the precise, technical vocabulary of topography in creating a conjoint sense of empirical veracity and judicious taste. William Gilpin had stressed the need for an 'analytical view', writing that 'to render a description of [landscape] more intelligible; and to shew more distinctly the sources of that kind of beauty, with which it abounds; it may be proper, before we examine the scenes themselves, to take a sort of analytical view of the materials, which compose them—mountains—lakes—broken—grounds—wood—rocks—cascades—vallies—and rivers'.[46] Beckford matches Gilpin's precision and empirical motivation, emphasizing his wish to 'minutely describe' the

Jamaican environment with 'eyes unprejudiced' and praising the 'fidelity' and 'accuracy' of Robertson's engravings which were 'taken on the spot'.[47] Joining the language of aesthetic feeling to the measured grammar of climatic observation, he writes: 'between one and two o'clock, the clouds begin to brew, the sky is obscured, and the heat increases in proportion to the obnebulation of the sun: the atmosphere is, for a time, peculiarly heavy; the thermometer rises from eighty to ninety degrees; the clouds are black, the day obscured, the winds asleep, and Nature still'.[48] It is the language of 'stillness' which links Beckford's picturesque with Gilpin's emphasis on 'tranquillity', 'composure' and 'repose'. The sense of repose in Gilpin's picturesque, as Alan Liu argues, performs an act of visual 'arrest' which erases motive.[49] Beckford's aestheticizing impulse betrays the desire politically (and medically) to stabilize the colonial climate and landscape, attempting to erase the material realities of colonial life by rendering landscape as artistic, rather than actual. His emphasis is on the empirical detail of description – the text begins, for example, with detailed lists of settlements, plantations and the roads through the island – suggests an investment in the idea of landscape as a stable entity, as well as in a model of vision as singular. The Jamaican climate, he writes, 'has charms to arrest the regard; and to fix the attention of every beholder'.[50]

But Beckford's colonial picturesque is by no means entirely static or immobile, and there are moments when the tranquillity of the scene collapses. With its 'alternations of stifling heat and trembling cold, of glowing haze and flitting showers', stability is the one characteristic the volatile tropical climate does not have.[51] Picturesque imagery prized the kind of variety everywhere in abundance in Beckford's Jamaica. 'The heavens are at one time all brightness', Beckford writes, 'at another they become all gloom: they sometimes seem to be in conflict, and to struggle for transcendency; and now the light, and now the showers, prevail: and these variations may be almost daily observed'.[52] It is the extreme variations of the tropical climate, however, which push the aesthetic imagination to its limits, and Beckford's descriptive labour is emphasized in his repeated exclamations that his surroundings are 'not in [his] power' to describe.[53] The impossibility of rendering Jamaica's meteorological fluctuations in descriptive form is matched by its imperviousness to attempts to capture it in visual representation: 'during my residence of nearly thirteen years in the Island', he writes, 'I did not meet with one single artist who could take an exact outline of nature.'[54] The struggle to give a full account of his colonial surroundings is not only due to the overwhelming sublimity of the Jamaican landscape, but also, crucially, to the effects of climate on the body. Beckford attributes the artistic neglect to which Jamaica has fallen victim to the problems of aesthetic appreciation in the tropics and the 'difficulty and consequent fatigue with which the least exertion in that climate is sure to be attended; a climate that very soon, and perceptibly, in many subjects, relaxes the nervous system, makes indolence succeed to industry, disease to health, and disappointment and vexation undermine the body, and care and despondency overcome and at last destroy the vigour of the mind'.[55] Even in Beckford's Creole politics of the picturesque – what Bohls calls the 'planter picturesque' – the degrading effects of the sun threaten to arrest the act of aesthetic appreciation: 'as the sun advances, and its beams are diffused, the most enchanting landscape will hardly make amends for the excess of heat and the enervating languor with which it is constantly attended'.[56] Arresting the act of observation, the 'excesses' of the Jamaican climate forestall the colonial gaze and serve as a reminder that the colonist as viewing subject is also subject to the forces of tropical nature. Despite his pro-slavery agenda and inclination to present the desirable face of Jamaica to his metropolitan readership, Beckford's account reveals a creeping tension in the relationship between aesthetics and health that compares to that suggested by Heriot and Chisholm. Much as the plantation picturesque of Beckford's protégé George Robertson's Jamaican paintings is built on what Tim Barringer describes as the 'unresolved paradox' of the celebration of large-scale capitalist production co-existing with the premodern genre of the estate portrait, neither can their verbal counterpart sustain its aesthetic vision.[57] In Beckford's text, the 'colonial immunity' that Sara Suleri has argued underpins imperial visual production is overtly medical, and is compromised by the vulnerability of landscape and its appreciation to the tropical climate, as the pressure placed upon the aesthetic by the pathogenic Caribbean environment interferes with the transcendent eye of the picturesque.[58]

Medical Topographical Aesthetics

The anxious manoeuvre between the picturesque aesthetics of landscape and the material dangers of the tropical climate is echoed in medical treatises. Chisholm reiterates Beckford's physiognomic metaphor, offering 'some account of Grenada, as far as relates to the face of the country, its productions, its diseases, and the state of the weather'.[59] While Beckford starts his *Descriptive Account* with the empirical data of Jamaica's plantations, slaves and roads, however, Chisholm's introduction makes the reverse move by beginning with scenes of natural beauty. Describing the coastline of Grenada, Chisholm adjoins topographical detail to a vision of colonial landscape as 'ornament':

> Some of these bays insinuate themselves so far into the country, as, when seen in certain points of view, to have all the ornamental effect of winding lakes: and at Calivini, Bacaye, and a few other places, they have the additional beauty of fine sloping woods, intermixed with lawns of the brightest green, and a back ground of picturesque scenes in the interior country.[60]

Chisholm's Miltonic 'woody theatre, of stateliest view' stages the Grenadian landscape for a European eye, adding picturesque enhancements to its rough beauty: the cane fields are 'diversified' by 'irregular' and 'romantic' groups of slave huts, while 'in many places the scene is enlivened by cascades'.[61] In his medical epistolary collection *Notes on the West Indies* (1806), George Pinckard, a military physician in Barbados in the 1790s, describes a similarly aestheticized view as he sails into Carlisle Bay:

> The land is seen above the houses, the trees, and the topmasts of the ships, rising to a great distance, clothed in all the richness of its tropical apparel. Verdant fields of sugar, coffee, and of cotton; fine groves, dark with luxuriant foliage; clusters of negro huts, windmills, all present themselves to diversify and enliven the picture.[62]

Pinckard views his new surroundings as if from above, and this floating eye oversees the 'picture' of a slave-run plantation, identifying the distancing and staging effects of this colonial picturesque mode: 'the whole island, encircled by the Atlantic ocean, was under the eye, displaying a scene'.[63] Physician John Williamson begins his narrative of colonial arrival in a similar tone: 'the approach to Barbados presented a kind of scenery to my view with which it had never been entertained … The lofty cocoa-nut trees, with their green covered tops, wafting with the winds, added greatly to the distant view of grandeur which the young European first contemplates of a West India island'.[64] Williamson's 'distant view' indicates the role of imperial fantasy in this scenery, as the 'young European' is met by sights he has imagined into existence long before ever setting foot in the Caribbean.[65] For Williamson's Barbados, as for Beckford's Jamaica, the island's 'extreme beauty and luxuriance' is 'beyond the powers of description'.[66]

The picturesque vistas painted by these three medical authors, however, soon give way to another view. Pinckard's senses are overwhelmed by the 'congregated disease, crowded suffering, and accumulated wretchedness' which are 'spectacles common to the eyes of medical men', as the 'spectacle' of disease and death, rather than that of picturesque landscape, becomes the new point of focus.[67] As the aesthetic eye is transformed into the medical eye, the distressing scenes to which Pinckard bears witness are attributed to the tropical environment. It is 'lamentable and surprising', he writes, that people 'prefer the convenience of commerce to the more important advantages of health, and fix their habitations, as if it were expressly, upon the most unhealthy points of the globe'.[68] Similarly, Chisholm's and Williamson's picturesque perspectives shift seamlessly into environmental diagnostics. Chisholm stresses the geographical causes of disease: 'hepatic and pulmonary inflammations are more frequent, and more violent in these rugged mountainous islands [of Grenada] than in Barbadoes, Antigua, and others of a smoother and less divided surface'.[69] In comparison to Grenada's mountainous landscape, Williamson describes the flatter landscape of Bridgetown, Barbados, as 'a low and moist situation' – a geography which he claims harbours the agents of elephantiasis.[70]

Noxious land spaces might be recuperated, however. Joseph Priestley's hope that bad airs might be cleansed of their toxic agents was particularly significant in the colonies, where European agriculture was perceived as helping unhealthy tropical environments by clearing up noxious land spaces such as marshes and woodland. The improving work of agriculture combined health concerns with aesthetic appreciation. For Williamson, the pleasing 'aspect' of particular regions of Jamaica is clearly tied to their 'state of cultivation'.[71] Chisholm's picturesque scenery sets the stage for his medical argument that contagious disease in the tropics is caused by 'the most unpardonable neglect of cleanliness, and the retention of contagious effluvia from a total want of ventilation'.[72] His fear that the most attractive landscapes might also be the most ridden with disease, though, suggests that beauty can also disguise disease. The synthesis of aspect and improvement originates in the paradoxical desire of the picturesque traveller to explore an untouched natural world, while imaginatively enhancing it. Like Beckford, though, Williamson's idealization of agricultural improvement is also a way of voicing his ameliorationist politics. Hitching social improvement to environmental improvement, Williamson writes equally keenly on the willingness with which the Jamaican authorities have taken it upon themselves to 'instruct and improve the condition of the slaves'.[73] While the domestic picturesque eye is often understood to be motivated by a desire to add the finishing touches and thereby render nature scenic, in the tropical colonies 'improvement' was underpinned by a host of other medical and political concerns. By framing their improvement narratives in terms of artistic vision, medical geographers emphasized the potential for the Caribbean to be remade not only as healthier, but also as a more habitable and socially stable space.

Pinpointing diseases in specific climatic and topographical locations, colonial authors created topographies which invited readers to position themselves both aesthetically and medically in relation to the colonial Caribbean. The textual movement from the aesthetic observation of landscape to the medical argument that certain diseases are endemic to that landscape characterizes medical geography of the period. By situating medical descriptions within an aesthetic frame, physicians and surgeons appropriated for medical use the morally and visually distanced eye of the picturesque, constructing a visual scene suggestive of the desired objectivity of medical discourse. A key implication of Enlightenment descriptive practice, as Bender and Marrinan write in *Regimes of Description*, is 'the utopian idea that knowledge is stable and generally impervious to the vicissitudes of time'.[74] The Newtonian drive to arrive at scientific universals underpinned this model of natural knowledge, which also owed much to the immense quantities of information wrought by colonial travel. The stability of knowledge, as well as the stability of landscape, lay the conceptual groundwork for the claim that a particular region was inherently diseased. Medical geography and topography combine description with an aesthetic viewpoint that surveys colonial land from above and afar, lending an impression of unity and presenting the landscape as static and immobile, with the suggestion of a stable perspective on an unstable environment. This creates distance between the physician and landscape – the 'colonial immunity' which becomes particularly significant in the writing of colonial physicians and surgeons in imagining their own objectivity and protection from the diseased surroundings which they survey and describe. Finally, the picturesque eye situates medical writing within a narrative of aesthetic and agricultural improvement intended to make tropical land spaces appear healthy and habitable. What is revealed in the aestheticized production of medical knowledge, then, is a strain of colonial picturesque vision as it was mobilized and put to use by medical geographers in representations of the West Indian islands as a set of pathogenic spaces. Medical treatises established geographical knowledge and scientific credibility as much through the visual imagery of landscape and its figurative representation as they did through medical data.

Description, in medical topography, is productive of diagnosis, and it is the details of the surface appearance of land – Chisholm's loose sand, stagnant waters and low coastline, for example – which indicate its adverse effects on health. Imagining material environments as textual conundrums to be deciphered, the medical geographer describes the characteristics of a landscape in order to develop a causal narrative of disease that pinpoints the origins of illness in geographical space. Colonial picturesque writing makes the same imaginative leap from landscape description to medical conclusion. But the proximity between medical and picturesque topographical detail also reveals precisely what literature announcing itself as 'descriptive', such as that by Heriot, Edwards and Beckford, is endeavouring to suppress. For Beckford, the relationship between aesthetic landscape and medical environment, or between description and analysis, breaks down as the inability to fully describe the colonial landscape also acknowledges the limits of description and the epistemological gaps between landscape, representation and interpretation. The purely aesthetic descriptive mode falters – and with it the distinction between the descriptive and the analytical – at the point of intersection between the aesthetics of landscape and the physiological effects of climate, as the colonial observer's surroundings encroach upon the act of description. The tropical climate is a source of great anxiety – its volatility needs to be transcribed into aesthetic form in order to be imaginatively contained. The effects of this aestheticization, however, are multiple. On the one hand, 'landscape' forges a gap between the colonial observer and the surroundings. But the endeavour to describe climate in aesthetic terms is also an attempt to transform 'climate' or 'environment' into 'landscape', rendering the invisible visible and thereby bringing the dangers of climate closer to the observing eye.[75] The mapping of a medical rhetoric of climate or environment onto the colonial aesthetics of landscape creates a tension between landscape as a static visual entity and spatial environment as a mobile and interactive set of surroundings.

'A Change of Air and Place'

This chapter began with Heriot's celebration of the 'more various, more abundant' Caribbean landscape, quickly followed by his despair at what lies beneath the luxurious, fertile tropical surroundings. Aesthetic pleasure in the 'copious, rude variety' of tropical nature is shared by other accounts of the sugar colonies, and draws on the picturesque visual model which emphasized irregularity and gradations of light and shade in the display of improved and idealized landscapes.[76] In the colonies, the potential for improvement helped Europeans imaginatively to frame the differences between Europe and the West Indies and the agricultural and environmental improvements that might be made to noxious tropical spaces. Beckford's picturesque eye, too, feasts on the 'infinite and pleasing variety' to be found in Jamaica's natural environment and presents it in terms of an imaginative invitation to 'improvement'.[77] On his departure from Jamaica, Beckford wishes that William Mason, gardener and author of the long poem *The English Garden* (1772–81), might compose a georgic on Jamaica's landscape, a subject more 'open to genius' than England's. While English landscapes might be 'pleasing', 'tranquil' and 'refined', a Jamaican georgic would accommodate the West Indian 'sublimities of inundations, the effects of thunder, and the dread of storms'. It would also present the opportunity for a sentimental aesthetics allied to Beckford's ameliorationist standpoint: to 'weep with the afflicted, and to rejoice at the punishment of tyrants'.[78] As the sublime imagery of the tropical storm suggests, variety is not only an aesthetic category for Beckford. In the comparison between Jamaica and other climates, visual variety is allied to meteorological change:

> the cascades, the torrents, the rivers, and the rills, are enchantingly pictur-esque in their different features, and exchange the sublimity or repose of their scenes, according to the variations of the seasons, or the turmoils of the elements; and these variations, I should conceive, few climates afford in competition with that I have ventured to describe.[79]

Weather phenomena become objects of visual interest, and Beckford urges the traveller to Jamaica to take 'pleasure in the beautiful varieties of vapours and fogs'.[80] In the West Indies, one person's pleasing cloud, fog or vapour might be another's life-threatening miasma, but Beckford is careful to imagine a healthy colonial sky. Much like the topographer's record of changes in meteorological conditions – and prefiguring John Constable's 'change of weather and effect' that would become a cen-tral precept of landscape aesthetics – Beckford records and aestheticizes the fluctuating tropical climate.[81] Weather, here, serves as a visual frame for colonial landscape imagery and defines the conceptual separation between the sublime volatility of Caribbean weather and the mildness of England – which 'can hardly vie with that of Jamaica for seven, eight, nine months in the year'.[82]

The 'change of weather and effect' was also an important precept of medical theory, according to which a change of air was considered beneficial to the health, and fostered the rise in medical tourism. In Barbados, George Pinckard recommends the benefits of a 'change of air and place' for patients convalescing from fevers.[83] Chisholm, too, prescribes a 'change of air and situation' to speed up the recovery from malignant pestilential fever.[84] In Williamson's Jamaica, 'much variety of climate is afforded for the benefit of sick and convalescents: and, where a temperate air is enjoyed, untainted by those sources of disease which we understand so greatly abound in Jamaica, it is a blessing which cannot be too highly estimated'.[85] Aerial changes were not always viewed in a positive light, however. Authority on colonial meteorology William Hillary had earlier written that 'the variations of the Air' in the West Indies were more likely to cause disease, and that Africans and African-Caribbeans were subject to more 'frequent and epidemical' illnesses with greater changes in the air.[86] Chisholm, following Hillary's influential meteorological model, ascribes certain climatic diseases to the particular topography of Grenada, where the 'windings of the innumerable hills … produce a change of temperature every hundred yards'. Being one moment 'bathed in the most profuse sweat' and the next 'suddenly exposed to the prevailing winds' has an immediate adverse effect: 'the body is in an instant dried up', creating an 'aguish sensation' that is followed by 'topical pains and inflammations of a most dangerous nature'.[87] Aerial variety, in this case, means that some types of inflammatory disease occur more frequently in Grenada than in the flatter islands such as Antigua or Barbados.[88] Here, Chisholm aligns aesthetic variety with ill-health, with the picturesque 'windings' of the Grenadian hills harbouring potentially deadly disease.

Variety is also a key theme for Heriot. The great vegetable abundance of the West Indies is attributed to the lack of seasonal change: because 'no frost consolidates the purling springs', Heriot writes, '*Vegetation's* ever active power / Sends forth, with rapid growth, herbs, plants, and trees, / For various virtues, various uses form'd.'[89] While Heriot celebrates the variety of plant life, which makes for vital and luxurious tropical imagery, the poem's sense of meteorological variety is more conflicted. The 'direful vicissitude' of the West Indian storm brings financial and social destruction, as tropical winds

> Tear through the fiery, howling atmosphere,
> Sweep their impetuous current o'er the earth,
> And trees and houses level with the ground,
> In woeful ruin; spreading thro' every soul
> Dismay and terror; threat'ning them with death.[90]

But while the winds leave ruin in their wake, the 'beauteous, variegated figures' of the storm clouds herald the medical benefits of sudden meteorological change in the healthful effects of fresh winds and rain that wash away the disease-spreading particles carried in stale airs, 'Wasting quick, / The noxious, fetid parts' and work to 'render the air / Again salubrious'.[91] Like Heriot, Beckford indicates a conflicted sense of the relationship between changes in the potent tropical airs and disease. Viewing the scene from a Jamaican mountain top, he writes:

> With how much more patience and delight can these different objects be observed when the north-wind brings freshness upon its wings! (for, although it be prejudicial to those in health, yet will it often revive at least, if not restore, the convalescent); when it gives variety to every scene, and makes the skies, the waters, and the land, assume new forms, that glow with various hues, or are embrowned by different shades.[92]

Here, the observer is both delighted and frustrated by his viewing experience. The parenthetical separation of the paradoxical idea that the north wind is restorative to the sick, but injurious to the healthy, annexes Beckford's health concerns from his aesthetic vision without fully detaching the two themes. The transcendent eye is endangered by the airs which bring both aesthetic pleasure and the threat of illness. While in the medical geographical accounts by Pinckard and Williamson the aesthetic functions imaginatively to map out the terrain of disease, Beckford's alignment of the 'variety' afforded by the wind with medical variations and the variation of visual perspective suggests the closer connection between aesthetics and illness that Chisholm points to in his claim that the most beautiful Grenadian landscapes are also the most deadly. For Beckford, the north wind makes Jamaica more beautiful, but also more dangerous. Similarly, for Chisholm the most 'picturesque' and 'ornamental' parts of Grenada are associated with the corruptive airs that endanger the health of visitors.[93] The role of vision as a primary human faculty gave the credence of common sense to environmental models that rendered pathogenic qualities available to sight. Beckford and Chisholm, however, appear to turn this assumption on its head and indicate the negative association between beauty and health, suggesting the conceptual problems attendant on their proximity within the panoptic vision of medico-geographical aesthetics which renders environmental phenomena that exist on the cusp of the invisible – winds, clouds, miasmata – visible. While Pinckard and Williamson make use of a picturesque vantage point to maintain a safe distance between themselves and the unhealthy landscapes they survey, Beckford's *Descriptive Account* exhibits a more problematic relationship between aesthetics, disease and landscape. For Beckford, that which renders landscape pleasing to the eye can actually be injurious to health.

Colonial Gothic

The picturesque endeavour to improve landscape imaginatively was allied to the medical geographical aspiration to improve unhealthy spaces through agriculture and other kinds of cultivation. That hope faded in the early decades of the nineteenth century. In 1764, Grainger had placed great emphasis on the possibility of Africans and Europeans becoming 'seasoned' to new environments. By 1812, colonial surgeon James Johnson voiced growing pessimism about the possibility of Europeans successfully adapting to life in tropical climates. Johnson denied that humans shared the ability of animals to adjust to new environments, and it was this idea that came to dominate nineteenth-century medical opinion: 'the plan of seasoning troops against *yellow fever*', Johnson writes, 'has completely failed'. Accusing those doctors who have '*theorised* widely on a foundation which the foregoing *facts* completely overturn' of trusting speculative knowledge rather than empirical evidence, Johnson claims that they 'probably took the doctrine from Dr. [Benjamin] Moseley, who tells us that a *seasoning* at *Bermudas* will secure us from the yellow fever of the West Indies ... Let no such plan be trusted.'[94] By the 1830s hopes of acclimatization and large-scale European settlement throughout the East and West Indies had largely evaporated.[95]

Those fading hopes are tangible not only in medical discourse but also in the changing perspectives brought by abolition. The sense of environmental disease as haunting colonial landscapes was increasingly brought to the fore with the abolition of the slave trade in 1807. The dangers of tropical climates resonate profoundly in the writing of the Scots abolitionist poet and hymn writer James Montgomery. Montgomery's father was a Moravian minister, and in 1783 his parents travelled as missionaries to Barbados, where they both later died. Montgomery was involved in radical political activism in Sheffield, and was a prolific author, writing poetry, hymns, reviews and essays. The publication of *The Wanderer of Switzerland and other Poems* (1806) put Montgomery on the national scene – Scott and Southey both praised the work and Byron wrote that *The Wanderer* was 'worth more than a thousand Lyrical Ballads'.[96] While *The Wanderer* voices concerns about the dangers posed by the French Revolution to the British populace and interests, several of Montgomery's other works focus on the anti-slavery movement, and on the efforts of missionaries in the Americas to convert slaves to Christianity. After the success of *The Wanderer*, Montgomery was commissioned by the printer Robert Bowyer to write a poem on the subject of the abolition of the slave trade in the British Empire.

On the poem's first appearance in Bowyer's volume it failed to capture the public imagination, but when published separately in 1810 it achieved considerable popularity. The poem celebrates the liberation of Africa from the terror of the slave ship – 'Thy chains are broken, Africa, be free!' – while lamenting the continuation of slavery in the West Indies.[97] Charting the history of the European colonization of the Americas, Montgomery describes Columbus's first landing, battles between the British and Spanish empires over land ownership and the death of the indigenous peoples. 'Give me to sing', writes Montgomery, 'in melancholy strains, / Of Charib martyrdoms and negro chains'.[98] The pre-colonial Caribbean, the 'Eden-islands of the West, / In floral pomp, and verdant beauty drest', has been destroyed by imperial exploitation.[99] Imagining yellow fever – the disease which 'spares the poor slave, and smites the haughty lord' – as the righteous punishment for the suffering inflicted upon enslaved Africans, the poem uses heroic couplets and images of disease and death in building a sense of ecological and moral crisis into its condemnation of colonial slavery, the agricultural abuse of the islands and the physical abuse of slaves by the planter class.[100] While for slavery apologists like James Grainger the sugarcane is celebrated as a symbol of agricultural and economic triumph, here the plant features as the source of environmental and social decay:

> An eastern plant, ingrafted on the soil,
> Was till'd for ages with consuming toil;
> No tree of knowledge with forbidden fruit,
> Death in the taste, and ruin at the root
> Yet in its growth were good and evil found,
> It bless'd the planter, but it cursed the ground;
> While with vain wealth it gorged the master's hoard,
> And spread with manna his luxurious board,
> Its culture was perdition to the slave,
> It sapp'd his life, and flourish'd on his grave.[101]

In the context of the medico-geographical impetus toward agricultural 'improvement' to clean up noxious tropical land spaces, the description of the cane's 'ingrafting' onto the land lends a sense of ecological misuse. Echoing Grainger's earlier criticisms of colonial agricultural and forestry practice, here Montgomery combines his anti-slavery message with environmentalism. His anxieties over the dangers of the mass import of foreign plants were well founded: the sugar monoculture wrought environmental havoc on the Caribbean by decreasing soil fertility and dramatically increasing the insect population which fed on the cane. The concentration of people, plants and animals in the lowland tropical areas used for sugar plantations harboured a multitude of new pathogens. Montgomery draws on medical geographical language to warn that the 'pestilent decay' of European imperialism has brought the Caribbean environment to the brink of collapse. The 'sepulchral vapours' of the socially and environmentally corrupt plantation create an air that is 'one tremendous uproar of despair', and the once-untouched landscape is now glutted with pestilent humans: 'Captives of tyrant power and dastard wiles, / Dispeopled Africa, and gorged the isles.'[102] Montgomery's rejection of European agricultural 'improvement' sacralizes pre-colonial nature, identifies slavery as a social evil so toxic that it infects the earth and expresses the problem of European imperialism medically and geopolitically.

Montgomery's identification of the capitalist imperial economy as the cause of environmental disharmony points to the Creole planter as the source of corruption. While Montgomery imagines the slave's body rotting beneath the ground, the body of the planter festers over ground: 'The bloated vampire of a living man; / His frame, – a fungus form, of dunghill birth, / That taints the air, and rots above the earth'.[103] Imagined as a parasitic demon feeding off the land and labour of others, the planter becomes the origin of disease, and his rancid body the toxic source of environmental and social decay. Tying the agricultural debasement of nature to the planter's moral depravity, Montgomery's abolitionist politics are played out here in the idea that plantation slavery and the agricultural misuse of landscape enact a kind of denaturing of the Caribbean environment. Tropical nature is bound up with death, and the idyllic abundance of the 'wild mountains and luxurious plains' is haunted by the tormented echoes of Charib martyrs, slave chains and the night-calls of vampiric creatures: 'At sun-set, when voracious monsters burst / From dreams of blood, awaked by maddening thirst.'[104] While the planter is a decaying, corruptive influence, slave bodies become contaminated too, through the ingestion of the poisoned earth. The reference to geophagy in the African's 'earth-devouring anguish of despair' is clear enough, but Montgomery also includes a footnote.[105] Describing those slaves who 'in deep and irrecoverable melancholy, waste themselves away, by secretly swallowing large quantities of earth', Montgomery calls dirt eating an 'infectious, and even a social malady: plantations have been occasionally almost depopulated, by the slaves, with one consent, betaking themselves to this strange practice, which speedily brings them to a miserable and premature end'.[106] The grim image of the slave eating contaminated earth is matched by the poem's gothic overtones in its description of plantation society:

> Slavery's island-altars built,
> And fed with human victims;—while the cries
> Of blood, demanding vengeance from the skies.[107]

The West Indies is depicted as haunted, corrupted and diseased, populated by soulless, greedy plantation owners and thousands of starving and abused slaves suffering under the 'lingering tortures' of the overseer's lash.[108] The Atlantic Ocean, meanwhile, is filled with the 'wandering ghosts' of 'myriads of slaves' who have perished aboard the overcrowded and disease-ridden slave ships or 'pestilential barks' on which they are funnelled across the Middle Passage.[109]

Beckford, Chisholm, Heriot, Pinckard and Williamson reveal the mutual significance of geographical medicine and landscape aesthetics, and Montgomery, too, draws on the association between land and colonial disease. In the colonial picturesque, medical aesthetics function to interrupt the imperial gaze and to question the form and possibility of aesthetic sensibility in a tropical setting; or, rather, the movement between the imagery of landscape and a medical discourse of infection, pestilence and miasma means that the 'natural' is always also deployed as the 'medical'. Montgomery's poem goes further: the medicalizing of nature and of landscape structures the sense of ecological rupture or crisis in the sugar colonies which questions the idea of the Caribbean landscape as 'natural' at all. Colonial plantations were built upon a foundation of African slave labour, Caribbean climate and European agriculture. This merging of spatial, social and agricultural order is constructed by Montgomery as the denaturing of the Caribbean – a terrible geopolitical hybrid in which the ideologically potent concept of a New World paradise has become polluted and debased. Montgomery's representation of the sugar islands as corrupted by disease and death rearticulates the landscape imagery of the picturesque in terms of a colonial gothic mode which drew more overtly from the contemporary medical discourse which was by now increasingly pessimistic about the possibility of human adaptation and harmony between Europeans and tropical climates.

Colonial gothic would go through other permutations and be taken up by other authors such as Matthew Lewis, whose classic gothic novel *The Monk* (1796) and the drama *Castle Spectre* (1797) would prefigure the record of his time as a planter in Jamaica in 1816 and 1817, *Journal of a West-India Proprietor* (1834).[110] Lewis, like Beckford, frames his ameliorationist position in terms of the cultivating language of the picturesque:

> I was much pleased with the scenery of Montego Bay, and with the neatness and cleanliness of the town; indeed … the first part of the road exceeds in beauty all that I have ever seen: it wound through mountain lands of my own, their summits of the boldest, and at the same time of the most beautiful shapes; their sides ornamented with bright green woods of bamboo, log-wood, prickly-yellow, broad-leaf, and trumpet trees; and so completely covered with the most lively verdure, that once, when we found a piece of barren rock, Cubina pointed it out to me as a curiosity; – 'Look, massa, rock quite naked!'[111]

Elizabeth Bohls argues that Lewis's picturesque is a 'theatrical' presentation of colonial imagery, and certainly in this passage tropical landscape becomes the 'ornamented' stage for the slave's performance of African naïveté.[112] Like Beckford's, Lewis's visual project offers glimpses of the influence of medical geographical discourse, using the aerial medical language of vapours and odours to imagine Jamaica's climate as part of an Edenic scene:

> the air, too, was delicious; the fragrance of the Sweet-wood, and of several other scented trees, but above all, of the delicious Logwood (of which most of the fences in Westmoreland are made) composed an atmosphere, such, that if Satan, after promising them 'a buxom air, embalmed with odours', had transported Sin and Death thither, the charming couple must have acknowledged their papa's promises fulfilled.[113]

As Lewis hints here, the airs that carry the sweet scent of tropical flowering trees can just as easily carry toxic gases released from rotting vegetable matter. The moment when the picturesque is interrupted by medical anxieties occurs in one of the verse entries interspersed throughout the *Journal*, and it is in the textual juxtaposition of the descriptive prose passages and poetic sections that the *Journal*'s structure highlights the impossibility of completely removing the threat of disease from picturesque plantation scenery. Fearing the 'terrible ravages' being committed by yellow fever among the white people of Jamaica, Lewis hopes for health: 'Let not thy strange diseases prey / On my life; but scare from my couch away / The yellow Plague's imps; and safe let me rest / From that dread black demon, who racks the breast'.[114] D. L. MacDonald argues that the 'dread black demon' probably refers to the Black Death – the bubonic plague which was imported to the region via shipboard rats. Given that this black fiend 'racks the breast', however (rather than leaving black spots on the skin), it may invoke the black vomit that was understood to be a symptom of the final, fatal stages of yellow fever, described by Colin Chisholm as resembling coffee grounds.[115] Lewis's anxieties about yellow fever were well

founded: he died of the disease aboard ship on his return journey from
Jamaica in 1818. The gothic sensibility annexed to Lewis's descriptive picturesque finds its full fruition in his poem 'The Isle of Devils: A Metrical
Tale' – apparently written aboard ship on his first passage to Jamaica, but
appearing in the *Journal* between entries on his second voyage to the island.
Just as the poetic sections in his earlier work *The Monk* serve to heighten
the novel's tone of gothic romance, the fantasies of imprisonment, rape
and murder in 'The Isle of Devils' haunt the picturesque fantasy of Lewis's
Journal. The poem is a nightmare of monstrosity and miscegenation run
riot: the demon ruler of a remote island rescues a shipwrecked woman
from his swarm of monstrous, vampiric dwarfs, but rapes her and eventually murders the two children – one monstrous, one human – she bears as a
result. The 'Tempest-Fiend's' black skin, 'gigantic' form and unintelligible
'wild chaunt' allude both to Caliban and to the African slaves whom Lewis
had yet to meet, fictionalizing his colonial encounter as he sails nervously
towards it.[116] The gothic denaturing of the West Indies in Montgomery's
poem is that which can only be articulated by Lewis in allegorical poetry
that displaces the threat of colonial disease from the landscape and into the
symbolic figures of demons, imps and blood-thirsty dwarves. By the time
of Lewis's journal, a gothic sensibility, thematically differentiated and for-
mally separated from the picturesque scenery described in his prose entries,
has taken over as the literary medium of diseased colonial environments.

Medical Vision

The texts discussed in this chapter reveal the powerful influence of the
aesthetic on the colonial medical imagination, the intricate relationship
between descriptive and visual language and medical ideas and the medical utility of literary modes of knowledge production. What is positioned
here as the medical aesthetics of climate and landscape describes a linguistic exchange between medical geographical science and the aesthetics
of colonial spaces as they were constructed in literary texts and travel
narratives. As well as the association of illness with colonial climates, the
comparisons between medical and other depictions of the Caribbean show
that physicians, surgeons, planters and poets drew on a shared language
of medicalized landscape aesthetics which informed, and was informed
by, discursive exchange between art, landscape gardening, literature and
the geographical and medical sciences. The cultural proximity between
geography, landscape and health was related to the centrality of sense
impressions, primarily vision, to ideas about human health and medical

diagnosis. The diagnosis of illness and the desire to contain it physically and imaginatively in the colonies was formulated in a set of medical geographical aesthetics which constituted a method of visual and descriptive control over the tropical Caribbean landscape. Within the medical discourse of climate and geography, the understanding of landscape hinged on a model of beauty, improvement and variety drawn from the literary and artistic language of the picturesque. Medical topography conceived of disease (or, rather, its geographical origins) as visible, and took up the transcendent eye of the aesthetic realm.

For medical practitioners, the continuity between British and Caribbean landscapes enabled by the use of picturesque aesthetics also imaginatively established the authority and credibility of their medical arguments. The lack of published medical cartography in the region may be another reason that medical geography turned to the picturesque aesthetics of landscape in an attempt to materialize visually the sources of aerial disease. By the early 1800s, Dahlia Porter argues, the picturesque had been excised from the new scientific topography being carried out in England, with topographical dictionaries containing very little picturesque description by this period.[117] But in the West Indies, the drive to paint an image of colonial health and beauty that could be transported to the metropole as an invitation to the sugar colonies meant that medical and scientific discourse retained its strong connections to the language of the scenic. While Lewis evacuates disease from the picturesque to gothic verse, the association between medical science, topography and landscape aesthetics was still strong in medical writing by the time of emancipation and beyond. Writing in 1854, the physician John Davy, inspector general of army hospitals and brother of Sir Humphry Davy, echoes the alteration of earlier medical authors between scenes of picturesque wonder and medical commentary, as well as the imaginative alignment of aesthetics, climate and health. St Vincent is the most beautiful of the West Indian islands, Davy claims, structured by 'mountains clad with native forests, sufficiently high to reach the region of the clouds; hills and vallies whether wooded or cultivated, ever verdant; with variety in all, whether mountain, hill, or valley, in form and colouring more than sufficient for picturesque effect'. The island's idyllic appearance is matched by its excellent climate, 'rendering it equally favourable to agricultural fertility and success, and with a few exceptions, not less so to the health and comfort of its inhabitants'.[118] In Davy's post-emancipation era the politics of climate and health and the medically purifying effects of the tropical weather are rearticulated to celebrate the end to the evils of slavery. 'Since the last great hurricane', Davy writes, 'there has been a decided improvement in the public health, and especially in that of the planters and their families ... What the hurricane did for the physical atmosphere of Barbados, emancipation effected for its moral and domestic atmosphere.'[119]

The picturesque as described by Tim Fulford and others made landscape a mode of consumption. Associated with the commercialization of rural societies, Fulford describes the picturesque as 'voyeuristic', 'distant' and 'static'.[120] But the colonies could not sustain such a view, and the colonial picturesque strains under the weight of medical anxieties it is unable to suppress. While the dangers of tropical climates and the problems of depicting slavery prompt the turn into the aesthetic as a way of stabilizing landscape, the point of meeting between landscape imagery and the climatic and topographical model afforded by medical geography poses conceptual problems. The power of tropical vegetable life described by Grainger's organic georgic takes on new associations in the texts discussed here through the agency attributed to the inanimate matter in airs, fogs and vapours which spread disease and which prevent Caribbean environments from being 'landscaped'. Further, the labour of tropical landscape description rests on an uneasy association between beauty and disease which, because of description's diagnostic impulse (and as Beckford and Chisholm suggest), can pose a threat, as much as an inspiration, to the colonial observer. Because landscape description locates the writing subject in the diseased tropical environment, the visual impulse finds itself caught in conflict with the fact that rendering landscape visible through the act of description is precisely the source of danger. In a strange displacement of disease from the human body to landscape and its aesthetic representation, the colonial landscape writer (or painter) finds the act of writing or visualization itself to be dangerous. Not only does the beauty of the Caribbean not compensate for its deadly climate, there is even a sense in which that beauty is intrinsically bound up with disease and death. This sense of natural beauty as degraded and degrading affects the tropicalization of the Caribbean in both aesthetic and medical terms. Rather than being a setting or a background, the landscape becomes a kind of toxic agent – not only harbouring the Edenic snake, but itself venomous.

Asserting a claim of mastery over the colonial landscape, writers maintained a safe distance between that landscape and the European self, and constructed a causal medical narrative whereby landscapes were the origin of health or disease. Representations of the colonial landscape are characterized by a textual movement between the description of landscape as a static aesthetic object and a medicalized disease climate as a volatile and threatening set of surroundings. The representation of colonial spaces betrays a struggle between the work of landscape description, which imposes a certain distance between the describer and the described, and a medicalized concept of climatic environment, which constructs the writing subject as bound up in a more complex causal narrative in which they can both act and be acted upon. 'Landscape' as an aesthetic unit is interrupted by the medical diagnosis of its visual signifiers and becomes invested with layers of meaning beyond the visual. Colonial landscape description frames space statically, but the attempt to fix landscape through climatic medical knowledge necessitates a causal narrative of disease, threatening both the aesthetic and the writing subject. Whereas landscape militates towards stasis and a measured distance between the 'eye' and the thing depicted, medical discussions of environment (which seek to narrate causality) collapse that distance, relocating the body within the space it describes. 'Nature' slips between the framing concepts of 'landscape' and 'climate' or 'environment', collapsing the opposition between them. As the meeting of medical language and colonial landscape imagery maps a causal narrative of environment onto the pictorial codes of landscape description, this medicalized aesthetics of landscape undermines the possibility of the desired pure aesthetic of textual and visual forms such as the picturesque.

The tropical cloud – or, fog, vapour or miasma – epitomizes this complicated relationship between landscape and climate. Clouds are the pinnacle of picturesque natural 'variety': able to take on an infinite number of shapes, they are ephemeral, itinerant, mobile. An object of keen Romantic observation, not only are clouds 'various' in their form, but their chaos and shapelessness also produce what Mary Jacobus calls an 'aesthetic of indeterminacy'.[121] 'Clouds are confusing', Jacobus writes, because they 'mysteriously combine visibility and volume without surface' and 'challenge the phenomenology of the visible with what cannot be seen.'[122] Just as clouds consist of individually 'invisible' water droplets, miasmas consist of roving disease particles – invisible but deadly. The ambiguous distinction between a cloud and a disease-spreading miasma mirrors the relationship between picturesque imagery and medical diagnosis, as well as the blurring of the boundaries between 'landscape' and 'climate' and aesthetics and health. In terms of the focus on description as a primary mode of colonial knowledge production, tropical clouds mark the struggle to describe geographical and meteorological phenomena accurately and aesthetically and bring home the medical and aesthetic problems extending from the beautiful but deadly and tempestuous 'change of weather and effect' in the West Indies.

PART II

Colonial Bodies

CHAPTER 3

Skin, Textuality and Colonial Feeling

John Gabriel Stedman's *Narrative of a Five Years Expedition against the Revolted Negroes of Surinam* (1790) is an account of colonial military life written under the spectre of disease. Mortality ran at more than 80 per cent among the troops forming the 1772 European expedition to eliminate the maroons who threatened to undermine imperial order in the Dutch colony of Suriname. The high death toll was caused not by the frequent unsuccessful military operations against fugitive slaves, but by rampant disease, and the *Narrative* does not falter in its catalogue of the illnesses suffered by Stedman and his fellow soldiers. In the midst of illness and at a point where he despairs for his life, Stedman anticipates his own epitaph:

> *Under this Stone,*
> *Lays the Skin and the Bone,*
> *While the Flesh was Long gone of poor Stedman*
>
> *Who Still took up his Pen,*
> *And Exousted his Brain,*
> *In the Hopes these Last Lines Might be red Man*[1]

This premature eulogy encompasses Stedman's two primary concerns: the integrity of the body in a colony teeming with disease, and the ambition that his *Narrative* would stand as an exhaustive portrait of life in Suriname. With sickness all around him, Stedman is acutely aware of the fragility of his own body. Improbably, however, Stedman's fantasy of his own burial envisages his skin remaining intact. Skin is the principal motif through which Stedman imagines the corruptive influence of the colonial environment on the human body. Skin was also significant as the site of physical abuse: 'whipping or flaying', as Deirdre Coleman succinctly puts it, 'was the modus operandi of plantation slavery'.[2] Stedman bears witness to frequent acts of flagellation, mutilation and branding inflicted upon slaves, relating them in macabre detail. A constant stream of diseased, dissected, flayed, peeling and whipped skins is presented to the reader, as the fear of disease inflects Stedman's work with a mortuary imagination which focuses on gruesome imagery of the living body in a process of disintegration. Stedman's pre-obitual image of his whole, buried skin encapsulates the idea of the tropical colony as a living death.

Surrounded by death, disease and extreme violence, Stedman focuses his attention on skin as the principal site of sickness and suffering. The fascination with skin as a marker of health and human difference was nowhere more evident than in the colonies, where it was the primary locus for medical and racial models of the body. Skin had only recently surpassed religion and clothing as the primary marker of human variety, and was undergoing intense medical scrutiny as part of the emerging discipline of dermatology.[3] In its images of violent dissection, flaying and whipping, the *Narrative* also reveals the skin as performing a crucial role in the production of sympathy for the suffering of others, which Stedman embeds in a sentimental mode of address that invites the reader to share in the experience of sympathetic suffering. Quoting the anonymous anti-slavery author of *Jamaica: A Poem in Three Parts* (1777) which rejected celebratory plantation poetry such as Grainger's, Stedman writes: 'Lo! tortures, Racks, whips, Famine, Gibbets, Chains / Rise on my mind, Appall my Tear Stain'd Eye'.[4] Writing in the wake of Adam Smith's and David Hume's works on sympathy and moral sentiments and at the height of the 'colonial sentimental', a literary and rhetorical style emerging in part from abolitionist poetic and rhetorical strategies, Stedman self-consciously tests the scope and limits of human sympathetic feeling through the *Narrative*'s uncomfortable amalgam of extreme violence and sentimentalized response.

Born in 1744 to a Dutch mother and Scottish father, Stedman grew up in Dendermonde, the Netherlands, and in Fife, Scotland. In 1772, having inherited his father's commission as an officer in the Scots Brigade of the Dutch Army, Stedman was recruited by the Dutch States-General as one of an initial corps of eight hundred soldiers to assist the planters in the destruction of the maroon societies that had been engaged in regular bouts of warfare with European settlers since the arrival of the English in 1651. In the 1760s the Suriname planters had been forced by their inability to overpower the maroons to sign peace treaties including the guarantee of independence in exchange for an agreement that the maroons would not give assistance to new runaway slaves. This failed, however, when the treaties only encouraged more slaves to become runaways, and soon the country's economy was threatened by a diminished workforce. The beleaguered local troops were unable to cope with the regular ambushes staged upon plantations by groups of maroon guerrillas with tactics far superior to those of the Europeans, and by the 1770s the rebels were bringing the plantation system to the point of collapse. The Saramaka and Djuka maroon communities finally abandoned Suriname for French Guiana in 1778, but any sense of victory for the Europeans was significantly undermined by the extraordinarily high death toll.[5]

What Stedman describes as his 'Little Collection of Natural Curiosity' is, in Mary Louise Pratt's words, a 'vivid discursive compendium', combining military history with anthropology, ethnography, natural history travel narrative and sentimental romance.[6] As well as an active defence of slavery and plantation owners, it comprises one of the most compelling indictments of slave-dependent societies ever published. It is notorious for its brutal scenes of slave abuse and accompanying illustrative plates, sixteen of which were engraved on commission by William Blake and accompanied the *Narrative* on its first publication in 1796. Scholarly attention has focused on several key themes and revolved around Stedman's influence on Blake's work, which Peter Linebaugh and Marcus Rediker argue was 'deeply coloured by Stedman's text, pictures, and friendship.'[7] A key point of discussion has been what Marcus Wood calls the 'sentimentalist agendas' of Stedman's shocking descriptions of ritualized violence against slaves and the pictorial versions of these scenes which accompanied them.[8] While Wood and Mario Klarer have framed the textual and visual imagery in the *Narrative* in terms of its sexualization of suffering black bodies, Anne Mellor has emphasized the 'visual evasion of textual violence' in Blake's plates and Stedman's original watercolours which formed the basis of the engravings.[9] Another substantial theme, which has been addressed by Pratt, Jenny Sharpe, Werner Sollors and Helen Thomas, is the interracial relationship between Stedman and his 'Suriname wife' Joanna, a fifteen-year-old mulatto domestic slave.[10] Accounts of the racial dynamics of romance and sentimentality are missing a sense of the overwhelming misery and terror of sickness and death circumscribing Stedman's daily existence and which is implicitly understood simply as the inevitable backdrop to life in the colonies. Speaking to this gap, Alan Bewell describes Stedman's work as 'military disease narrative', emphasizing the proximity between slavery and military service in Stedman's 'heart-of-darkness' depiction of colonial life.[11] Like Wood and Mellor, Elizabeth Bohls focuses on the visual intertexts in the *Narrative*, and has recovered the significance of Stedman's natural historical work, showing how his dual role as soldier and naturalist meant that he was 'uniquely positioned to represent natural history's complex imbrication with colonialism'.[12] My approach reads the various discourses addressed in this recent body of work on Stedman – sentimental romance,

medical account, natural history, military memoir – as fundamentally con-
joined, and looks to understand the close relationships between colonial
sentimental and medical and scientific discourses.

To his knowledge, Stedman claims, only a single sailor on the Dutch
expedition escaped illness, and of twelve hundred Dutch soldiers sent to
Suriname during the 1770s, fewer than a hundred returned home alive.[13] In
their edition of Stedman's 1790 manuscript, Richard Price and Sally Price
record different figures, but suggest a similarly dismal mortality rate: of
the sixteen hundred and fifty soldiers sent to Suriname, only a couple of
hundred survived.[14] David Geggus writes that the 'central experience of the
soldier's life in the Caribbean was without doubt death from disease. Over
half of the troops sent out to the West Indies died there.'[15] The effect of foreign pathogens on European troops was compounded by military incom-
petence, poor resources and hopelessly inadequate medical care. After one
particularly fruitless battle, Stedman was 'left to defend a whole River with
none but seek [sick] People, without even sufficient Ammunition, and
who were hourly expiring for want of proper Medicines or even so much as
a Surgeon to attend them'.[16] Stedman does not spare the squeamish reader
in his detailed accounts of the 'broken', 'deform'd' and 'rotten' bodies of
slaves and soldiers alike.[17] The *Narrative*'s bodies – human, animal and
vegetable – are decaying, dissected, dismembered, opened up and pieced
apart. The brutality of colonial violence, as well as the more mundane daily
human deterioration from illness, are figured through images of damaged
and diseased skins. Stedman uses anatomical, ethnographic, medical and
natural historical discourses to imagine what happens to the skin when
it is injured by disease or abuse in an abundance of imagery depicting
skins being bitten, bled, cut, infected and lacerated. The assault on colonial
bodies wrought by climate, disease, combat and punishment is revealed
through a dissective lens concerned with the integrity and interiority of
bodies and their parts, with the unity of the human body undermined as
the corruption, loss and removal of skins come to symbolize the decaying
effect of the colony on all bodies.

Not only does illness form an almost-constant part of the text, but
Stedman is so often feverish, bleeding and in pain himself that his state
of ill-health functions as the lens through which he views the world. The
sense of physical corrosion in Stedman's account of colonial life is mirrored
by the disunity of the *Narrative* as text. The problem of bodily integrity
leaks into that of narrative integrity, as an endless stream of dead and dying
bodies unsettles the sense of an overarching plot scheme. Disease is woven
from content into form as Stedman leapfrogs between his key themes of

illness, military account, natural history, the abuse of enslaved people and his romance with Joanna. The disconcertingly abrupt narrative shifts between the gruesome symptoms of tropical disease and other aspects of colonial life mirror the discomfiting tide of sickness suffered by Stedman and his fellow soldiers. Disease is both a perpetual presence in Stedman's life and a strange interruption into the narration of his experiences. Indeed, neither plot nor narrative existed in Stedman's original diaries, from which the *Narrative* originated, and the history of the text is marked by Stedman's repeated efforts over many years to achieve a complete account of his experiences, despite a frustrating editorial process. After settling in Devon on his return from Suriname, Stedman spent some years rewriting the several diaries he had kept. This new account became the 1790 manuscript version of the *Narrative*, for which Stedman received an offer of publication from Joseph Johnson, then increasingly involved in radical causes.[18] In 1794, Johnson employed William Thomson to edit Stedman's manuscript. As Price and Price note, Thomson's revisions reflected his own political stance, which was more pro-slavery than Stedman's ameliorative position.[19] Stedman finally had his first look at the edited version in May 1795 and was outraged at Thomson's changes, recording his displeasure in his diary in June 1795: 'my book mard intirely'.[20] Despite vociferous complaints from Stedman, who was keen to correct the 'lies & preachings' inserted by Thomson, the *Narrative* finally published in 1796 was significantly altered from its 1790 incarnation.[21] Stedman claimed to have burned two thousand copies before the public could lay eyes on the text; nevertheless, the *Narrative* was an instant success and, despite Thomson's interventions, was quickly taken up by the abolitionist cause.[22] Stedman's reformation of his diaries as a single text and the strong resentment he felt at his editor's changes to the manuscript indicate his desire to represent his experiences in terms of a comprehensive, unified story, and mark the difference between the epigrammatic 'part' represented by the brief diary entries and the attempt at a more cohesive 'whole' in the 1790 manuscript.[23]

Stedman's own prefatory comments self-consciously announce the fragmentary quality of the text, warning that the *Narrative*, 'besides its not being interesting to Great Britain has neither stile, orthography, order, or Connection', and is told with such outrageous 'bombast' that readers will dislike it from the very first page.[24] Yet he hopes that his personal tale of misery and misfortune will inspire the sympathetic reader to look beyond his 'unaccountable Stile' and feel sufficiently moved to 'throw down the Book—& with a Sigh exclaim in the Language of Eugenious— Alas poor Stedman—'.[25] David Richards argues that it is precisely the 'incongruous awkwardness of Stedman's constant shifts' in theme and tone which represents his efforts 'to make these data, these sights, these feelings fit a scheme of narration or pattern of known categories.'[26] For Richards, Stedman's chaotic surroundings compel him to seek out forms of narrative which might forge meaning out of 'the meaninglessness of colonial Suriname'.[27] As both Richards and Stedman suggest, the *Narrative* goes to some efforts to transform Stedman's fragmentary and tumultuous life in Suriname into a stable work for readerly consumption. But his narrative style is characterized by more than a sense of rapid movement between pre-existing discourses and narrative modes. As Stedman charts a sinuous course through various discursive lenses – the anatomical and the senti-mental, the ethnographic and the medical, the literary and the natural his-torical – new imaginative frameworks and rhetorical strategies emerge, as the sentimental impacts upon the medical, and the natural historical upon the literary. Sympathy – for 'poor Stedman' and for the suffering slaves, soldiers and animals which populate his text and demand a feeling response from the reader – is fundamentally connected to skin as the focal point of physical and emotional feeling in a violent and disease-ridden colony, and it is the relationship between sympathy and skin that binds this text together. As the site of human suffering, identity, difference and disease, skin becomes in Stedman's text not only the marker of human difference but also the mediator of sympathetic response and the key source of imagery for the *Narrative*'s sentimental framework. Understanding skin as the colonial frame for the social narration of the human body, this chapter foregrounds the skin as bodily text in order to unpick the construction of the *Narrative* as sentimental text, demonstrating the cultural and textual interactions between skin, sympathy and the colonial sentimental mode. The motif of skin takes on a prominent role in Stedman's pre-disciplinary engagement with multiple cultural discourses (literature, medicine, nat-ural history, racial science). This chapter outlines the narrative shape of Stedman's bizarre and fascinating account in terms of the textual, med-ical and natural historical relationship between skin and feeling. Reading Stedman's work through a medical lens reveals insights about cultural concepts of skin and complexion in the context of colonial intercultural encounter and shows the extent to which skin became a social and physical marker of character, climate, environment, race, sensibility and sympathy. In the colonies, the mutual significance of skin and sentiment and the impact of one on the other not only highlight how race and feeling were imagined in the colonies but can also expand our understanding of sym-pathy as a governing principle of eighteenth-century and Romantic social interaction and the way in which it was structured by racial and anatomical precepts.

Climate and Complexion: The Porosity of Skin

From the leaky bodies of European soldiers suffering from the bloody flux whose 'Filth for Want of Assistance was Dreeping though their Hammocks', to the 'decay'd & Corrupted Carcasses' of slaves suffering from the highly contagious skin and bone disease yaws, Stedman imagines disease in terms of corrosion.[28] 'Not a Man Was to be Seen,' he writes, 'Without Agues, Fevers, Rotten Limbs &c.'[29] European soldiers, African slaves and Creole gentry are described, respectively, as 'Scarcrows', 'skin and bone' and 'wither'd mortals'.[30] An endless stream of dead bodies and their atrophying parts appear in the text, with colonial bodies depicted as polluted and decaying. Much-dreaded and highly contagious, leprosy was widespread amongst slaves. Describing its effects on the sufferer, Stedman writes, 'the breath Stinks, the hair falls out, and the fingers and Toes becoming Putrid drop off Joynt after Joynt, till they Expire'.[31] The image of the leper is particularly fearful, writes Rod Edmond in *Leprosy and Empire*, because it undermines the integrity of the body, and, therefore, the category of the human.[32] It is this concern with bodily integrity and the limits of humanity which fuels much of the *Narrative*'s imagery of colonial bodies falling apart at the seams. The grotesque image of the leper's slowly decomposing body functions as an image of living tropical bodies in a process of disintegration that horrifies Stedman, and signifies his repeated imaginative return to the earlier poetic vision of his own corpse.[33]

Stedman's concern for the unity of his body is revealed in the meticulous record of each illness to which he succumbs. February 1776, for example, sees him poorly with 'a Bad Foot, A Sore Arm, the Prickly Heat, and all my Teeth Loose with the Scurvey'.[34] Damage to his skin is of particular concern, and he details each injury: 'my Ancle Which had been Nearly Recover'd Was Now wounded Afresh to the Bone, the Skin and Flesh being quite torn Away'.[35] Another passage documents his narrow escape from a group of rebel slaves, leaving him with 'the Loss of the Skin on one of my Shins'.[36] Each small loss represents the susceptibility of the colonial body to illness and injury, and the particular vulnerability of skin. Following the example of the slaves assisting the Europeans in their fight against the maroons, Stedman walks barefoot to prevent the rot which plagues those men walking in socks and boots through marshes and swamps: 'in this respect I had fairly the start of them [the other soldiers] all my Skin being, the swel'd foot, or *Consaka* and a few Scratches excepted, perfectly whole from my habit of walking thus, while not a sound limb was to be found amongst the rest which were running in open Sores and Corruption'.[37] From these wounds, Stedman claims, 'some lost their limbs and others even their Lives'.[38] The integrity of the skin as a protective layer and its ready exposure to disease made keeping it 'perfectly whole' absolutely crucial to survival in the tropics. Stedman's epitaph in which his skin remains long after the decomposition of his flesh is, therefore, a fantasy which replaces in death the skin which Stedman is so anxious about losing in life.

The concern for skin evokes contemporary medical narratives of the body which focused on the epidermis as a key disease site. Dermatology was becoming institutionalized as Joseph Plenck, Robert Willan and other physicians began classifying skin diseases following a Linnaean methodology.[39] In his medical and cultural history *The Book of Skin* Steven Connor writes that the eighteenth century marked a shift in anatomical thinking: 'the functions of the skin as integument and screen, covering the body and expressing the complexion of the soul, began to give way to a second phase, a more mechanical conception of the skin as a membrane'.[40] Its excretive function, for example, made skin the visible register of internal corruption. The surface of the body could be 'read' for signs of sickness: a pallid skin, in particular, suggested all manner of illnesses from food poisoning to nervous disorders. As the layer which transported toxins between the body and the outside world, skin was now imagined less as a cloak for the body and more as a pervious barrier and a mediating structure for disease. The purgative impulse of medical practice meant that treatments often aimed to evict the diseased matter to the skin's surface. Yaws, for example, is described by Willan and other experts in cutaneous diseases as an 'eruption' of corrupted matter, and Grainger's *Essay* lists treatments for yaws: 'A fortnight's use of these means, commonly throws out all the Yawey matter upon the skin.'[41] In Stedman's *Narrative*, skin reveals the terrible symptoms of colonial diseases. Along with yaws and leprosy, another widespread contagious disease with cutaneous symptoms was ringworm, from which many of Stedman's fellow soldiers suffered. In September 1773 Stedman made the following entry in his journal: 'I have got the ringworm of which I soon get the better by an excellent receipt.'[42] The 1790 *Narrative* expands on this with a detailed description of ringworm, which 'consists in large scarlet irregular Spots particularly on the under parts of the body, and which increase in Magnitude from Day to Day, unless prevented by timely application – these Spots are surrounded with a kind of hard, Scrufulous border, that makes them look in my opinion something like *land-Maps* and which are troublesome by their itching … inconceivable are the many troubles to which one is exposed in this Climate.'[43] Given Stedman's tropical location, the move from the symptomatic description of illness to cartographic imagery to climatic reference is particularly suggestive. The new science of medical geography had institutionalized a focus on pathogenic places, providing a conceptual framework for the identification of disease with the tropical colonies. Stedman and his company were plagued by a constant fear that they would find themselves 'murdered by a Combination of misery & an Unhealthy Climate'.[44] Drawing on the medical association between disease and climatic location, his 'skin map' might even be read as that of Suriname – the image of the colony emerging on the skin of the sufferer, providing tangible evidence of the effects of tropical climates as not only deleterious but also transformative. This geographic image on the surface of the skin is also a symptom of the sufferer being medically 'colonized': that is to say that the European body infected with ringworm carries the mark of the colony on its skin – a significant medical metaphor in the context of anxiety over the possibility of European physiological and social creolization. The association between disease and geosocial environment forms a narrative flourish which brings disease into the realm of the figurative and, through the imagery of the map, the textual. The image of Stedman's diseased body changes significantly in the rewritten passage in which attention is drawn to the damaged or infected part of the body as bearing the mark of the tropical climate. While the journals represent the illness in terms of a straightforward causal narrative of disease and cure, the *Narrative* develops a sense of the diseased body and its symptoms – and of skin itself – as being entangled in far broader social and scientific narratives.

From its medieval incarnation as a covering or protective layer which provided the boundary between the self and the world, eighteenth-century skin was becoming an organ in its own right. This organ was increasingly understood as mobile and subject to change according to external conditions, and its susceptibility to climatic variation was a pressing concern. Stedman references the work of the Comte de Buffon, a monogenist who wrote that black skin was caused by the excessive heat of tropical climates, and believed that skin colour could change over successive generations according to external conditions such as climate and diet.[45] This susceptibility to external forces meant that extremes of temperature could alter the balance and appearance of the skin. The American progressive Samuel Stanhope Smith, also a monogenist (but who disagreed with Buffon's model of racial categorization), wrote in *An*

Essay on the Causes of the Variety of Complexion and Figure in the Human Species (1787) that

> when heat or cold predominates in any region ... it impresses, in the same proportion, a permanent and characteristical complexion ... this cause will affect the nerves by tension or relaxation, by dilatation or contraction— It will affect the fluids by increasing or lessening the perspiration, and by altering the proportions of the secretions—It will peculiarly affect the skin by the immediate operation of the atmosphere.[46]

Elaborating on the developing idea of skin as a porous and volatile structure, Smith highlights the connection between this new functional model of skin and the increasing significance of climatic effects on complexion. Stedman sees the negative effects of climate in 'the too many Languid Looks, Sallow Complexions, deform'd Bodies, and Broken Constitutions, of our European Contriwomen'.[47] The pallid, wan looks of Europeans in the tropics contrast unfavourably with the 'Shining skin and Remarkable Cleanliness' of women such as Joanna, who have the 'Certain Advantage in a Black Complexion'.[48] Stedman sexually elevates black women, simultaneously praising their superior health. Describing a group of enslaved barge men, Stedman again emphasizes the healthy appearance of their skin: 'all as naked as when they were born ... these men look'd very well—being healthy Strong & young, theyr skin Shining & almost as black as Ebony'.[49] Dror Wahrman has argued that complexion and physiognomy came to the fore as the final decades of the eighteenth century witnessed a transformation of ideas about race, and Roxann Wheeler has provided evidence of the semiotic abundance of the term 'complexion' in eighteenth-century usage. Referring not only to skin colour but also to health and character, complexion imaginatively linked skin to a comprehensive narrative of the 'whole' person.[50] Stedman's investment in assessing skin as a marker of health and beauty articulates the convergence of medical, aesthetic and racial significance on the term 'complexion'.

While Stedman associates black skin with health and sexual attractiveness, irregularities or imperfections in the skin become morbid and grotesque. He describes albino blacks as 'Monsters', giving the example of one who 'was Exibited in England, whose Skin was not a Natural White, but Resembling Chalk, nay evern theyr hair on every part was the Same, while theyr Eyes were a Perfect Blood Colour And which they Saw verry Little in the Sun Shine, Neyther were they fit for any kind of Labour, While theyr Mental Faculties Corresponded with the incapacity of their Bodys'.[51] In the context of limited understanding of the condition, and the medical emphasis on the relationship between skin colour and health, Stedman presumes all sorts of medical and social consequences to result from achromia. Exhibitions of albinos and vitiligo sufferers such as Jamaican John Boby, the 'Wonderful Spotted Indian', captured the public imagination. James Parsons's 'Account of the White Negro Shewn Before the Royal Society' (1765) describes several black albinos being displayed as 'rarities' to the public.[52] The whiteness of the audiences who flocked to see these exhibitions, which continued to be popular throughout the nineteenth century, was resignified in relation to the white black body on display. As Charles D. Martin writes, 'the transparency of whiteness, its pretensions to naturalness, ends in the body of this white mimic.'[53] For Martin, unpigmented African skin confirms the priority of whiteness, rendering blackness the result of a secondary, accretive layer that is understood as missing from the albino body, but simultaneously suggests the possibility that it is in fact the white patches on the African albino which form the secondary layer. For Stedman, the albino black body models whiteness as the colour of corruption. Albino skin as a physical anomaly undermines the dominant categories of human variation and prompts Stedman's assumption of poor physical and mental health. Underlining the association between complexion and medical models of the racialized body, the albino also registers the dangerous elasticity of skin colour.

Stedman's supposition that albinism was suggestive of poor health registers the shift in interest from superficial physical variation to a new emphasis on the anatomical structure and function of skin. Stedman is fascinated by the skin's potential to reveal the anatomical secrets of racial difference. Moving his attention from the damage inflicted upon his own skin by disease and injury, Stedman turns to the dissection of African skins: 'the *Epidermis* or Cuticle of the Negroes I have Seen Dissected more than once, this is very Clear and Transparent, but between which and the Real Skin lies a thin Follicle which is perfectly Black, and when Removed by verry Severe Scalding or Flagellation, Exposes a Complexion not inferior to that of the European'.[54] Stedman's variegated model of skin follows the anatomical discovery by the seventeenth-century Italian microscopic anatomist Marcello Malpighi that skin comprised multiple layers. Robert Boyle and others went on to describe three layers of skin in relation to racial difference: the outer, transparent layer; the middle layer, responsible for pigmentation and the innermost layer, always white.[55] The evidence presented by anatomists and physicians showing that people of

all races had a layer of white skin at the core lent itself to a monoge-
netic theory of racial origins while implying the priority of whiteness.
Wayne Glausser and Anne Mellor have each argued that Stedman's
(and Blake's) 'Europeanization' of black bodies in the images accompanying the *Narrative* identifies the white body as primary and underpins
Stedman's ameliorative stance on slavery.[56] If the anatomical comparison
between African and European skins positions the white complexion as
the 'original skin', then the contrast between Stedman's anxiety for the
loss of his own skin and his more analytical and detached description of
the dissection of black skins is even less equitable. The act of dissection
and the passive voice in which it is described depersonalize the point
from which text and reader view the human body. The removal of pain
from the scientific scene of dissection suggests that Stedman's interest in
the anatomical body comes with a disregard for black suffering. Scientific
investigation of African bodies at a microscopic level of focus reductively
anatomizes human difference, reducing the black body to the sum of its
parts. As Stedman changes focus from the loss of his own skin to the
removal of others', he simultaneously alters his rhetoric from the personal to the anatomical. Moving seamlessly from the fear of his own skin
falling away to the scientific interest in the dissection of African skin,
Stedman projects his fear for his own bodily integrity onto other colonial bodies. By couching his discussion of colonial bodies in anatomical
terms, Stedman displaces the dread of his own physical disintegration and
constructs a scientific narrative logic through which to make sense of various key aspects of colonial life: disease, death, interracial encounter and
the subjugation of slaves.

The relationship between skin and human variety is, for Stedman,
different to that between skin and disease. While in medical terms skin
was the surface upon which disease was writ, that surface could reveal or
conceal racial origins and other layers of meaning. The epidermis could
signify one racial identity, while what lay beneath revealed another. This
is not to suggest that Stedman saw black skin as a kind of disguise or
that blackness did not constitute for him a very real material and social
difference to whiteness. Indeed, his many ethnographic passages bear
witness to the emphasis he places on skin colour. It does suggest, however, his concern for the unstable structure of skin. The anatomical distinction between the epidermis and the dermis or 'real skin', as Stedman
calls it, highlights this ambiguity: as surface covering, mediating layer
and inner 'truth', skin operates as a body part like no other.

Inside/Out: The Body without Skin

Notorious for its images of violence against slaves, critics have read the *Narrative* as a work of sentimental 'pornography'.[57] Certainly, there is an unsettling fusion of pain, sympathy and desire framing the image of the 'beautiful *Samboe* Girl of about eighteen' who is 'tied up by both arms to a tree ... as naked as she came into the World, and lacerated in such a shocking Condition by the Whips of two Negro Drivers, that she was from her neck to her Ancles literally dyed over with blood'.[58] The image presents the suffering woman as an eroticized spectacle for sympathetic consumption by a readership heavily invested in what Marcus Wood identifies as a post-Burkeian aesthetic mode in which witnessing torture is a kind of sublime experience.[59] As Wood argues, the many representations of suffering slaves should be read in light of the popular interest in the moral dimensions of sympathy and sentimental feeling.[60] Wood's argument that Stedman's incredibly visual and visceral accounts of the physical abuse of slaves – particularly naked slaves – operate 'in a world of pure fantasy', however, obscures the reality of Stedman's existence in a colony where such violence was common practice, and assimilates the beautification of abused slave bodies in Blake's accompanying plates with the more uncomfortable and disorientating articulation of the relationship between sentiment and violence in the text.[61] Sexualized images of the flayed body should also be read alongside the countless other skinned bodies presented in the text in ways that often confuse or refuse the imaginative framework of 'sentimental pornography'. The connection between skin and feeling points to the problem of reading these images as single-mindedly sexualized, as Stedman's own experience of illness and injury is transposed onto that of the tortured slave body through the focal point of skin as the site of suffering.[62] The motif of the body alive and totally divested of its skin is both a projection of Stedman's fears for the loss of his own skin and an expression of the fragility of all bodies in the violent and unstable colony.

Mesmerized by acts of extreme violence, Stedman returns again and again to the image of the excoriated body. In a particularly charged passage he recounts the story of a rebel slave named Joli Coeur who confronts his former plantation master – a brutal man who has raped Joli Coeur's mother and flogged his father. Joli Coeur takes revenge by hanging, beheading and flaying him. Before fleeing to join the maroons, he drapes the man's skin over a cannon, thereby preventing it from being fired at the rebels.[63] As a form of revenge, skinning becomes the ultimate act of violence in its dehumanization of the plantation master's body, while his dead skin takes on a new function in its afterlife that would have its owner turning in his grave. Fascinated and horrified by the sight of such violence, Stedman repeatedly imagines these scenes as enacting the complete removal of the victims' skins. A common punishment on the plantation involved the victim being 'Beat on one Breach by a Strong negro with a Handful of Knotty Tamarind Branches, till the Verry Flesh is Cut Away—he is then Turn'd over on the Other Side Where the Same Dreadful Flagelation is inflicted till not a Bit of Skin is Left, and the Spot of Execution is died over With his Blood'.[64] The 'Samboe' Girl of about eighteen' is described as being 'Skinned alive' in a vicious whipping by a bloodthirsty overseer.[65] After the countless such whippings to which slaves are repeatedly subjected, these 'miserable objects' are then 'Left to Cure themselv's or Continue to do theyr Work *Without a Skin*'.[66] Captivated by the living skinless body, Stedman repeats the image so often that it becomes an objectified symbol of the horrors of colonial existence. Stedman's Marsyan bodies, his concern for the particular vulnerability of skin, his interest in the anatomical structures of skin and its relationship to racial identities and his fear of the effects of tropical environments on European bodies are expressed through his dissevering narrative eye. This strange abundance of bodies completely divested of their skins begs the question: just what is the body without skin? And what is the skin without a body?

Dissected skins tell the story of the body in terms of its constituent parts, while imperfections in the skin indicate the deleterious effects of climate, disease or a weak constitution, and lacerated skin can invite both sentimental and sexual response. Skin stripped entirely from the body performs a different kind of cultural work. No longer considered a simple boundary between the self and the world, skin now had an intermediary function. As climate and natural surroundings were imaginatively mapped onto the skin, which was understood to display and convey the effects of external influences, skin took on a crucial role in mediating environment. As well as displacing religion and clothing as the primary visual identifiers of human difference, skin had become the sensible form of corporeal being and an important focal point for theories of sensitivity and feeling. For Stedman, as for others, skin is the site of both physical feeling (in Stedman's explorations of the capacity for pain) and psychological feeling (Joanna's romantic blushes, for example, are given in place of verbal response to his affections).[67] In sum, skin was fashioned as a crucial medium through which humans interacted with the physical and social world. Given the important role bestowed upon skin as a medical and social mediator, the image of the body without skin takes on a particularly strange significance. The removal of the skin displaces its interactive function, disturbing the physiological processes in which it functions, as well as the operations of identity and sympathetic feeling that are dependent on skin for their social production. In terms of Stedman's invitations to respond sympathetically to skin as a site of suffering and violence, the sheer number of skinless bodies that populate his *Narrative* presents a challenge to the feeling reader. As the body's public form, skin is responsible for expressive function, and without it the self has no worldly shape or recognizable appearance. If skin is the representative image of the body whole, its removal marks the confusion of that image. Without skin, the individual ceases to be recognizable as either a social or a sympathetic subject. Stedman's skinless bodies recall the image of the *écorché* made famous by such works as the anatomist William Cowper's *Myotomia reformata or, an Anatomical Treatise on the Muscles of the Human Body* (1694), in which an excoriated figure stands holding his own skin (Figure 3.1). Cowper's *écorché* looks down and away from the lifeless skin, while the hidden face marks the erasure of identity that comes with the loss of skin. This body without skin signifies the loss of the structural boundary between the self and the world, undermines the integrity of the 'human' and, in the context of Stedman's efforts to read the skin for signs of feeling, health, illness and race, renders the body illegible. The removal of the skin displaces identity from the body, erasing a coherent narrative of the body and inviting questions about the possibility of social or sympathetic identification.

The fascination with skinned bodies is also connected to the efforts by anatomists and physicians to discover what lives on after the skin or other organs have been removed. On witnessing a slave skinning a large snake (Figure 3.2), Stedman writes of the 'terrible appearance, viz, to See a Man Stark naked, black and bloody, clung with Arms and legs around the Slimy and yet living Monster'.[68] For Stedman, the flayed body of the snake is a troubling sight, and the nakedness of the black man performing the skinning serves only to enlarge the alarming rawness of the writhing, skinless creature, which he is shocked to see alive after being deprived of its intestines and skin.[69] Familiar as he was with the work of the Scottish anatomist John Hunter (who, as Stedman notes, had in 1782 used dissection to show the capacity for hearing in fish), Stedman's living, skinless snake reverberates with the eighteenth-century examination of animal bodies to explore the origins of life. It echoes, in particular, a passage in vitalism proponent Robert Whytt's *Essay on the Vital and Other Involuntary Motions of Animals* (1751).[70] Whytt was the first to demonstrate the capacity for reflex action originating in the spinal cord, and his work participated in the hotly contested debates about the location of the soul and the boundaries between life and death, human and animal that was formalized in doctrines such

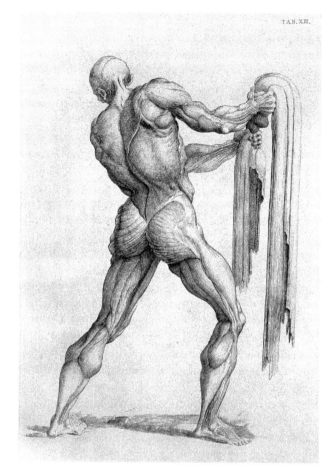

Figure 3.1 William Cowper, 'Écorché standing holding his skin, posterior view', in
Myotomia reformata: or, an Anatomical Treatise on the Muscles of the Human Body
(London: Printed for Robert Knaplock et al., 1724). Engraving. Courtesy of the
Wellcome Collection. www.creativecommons.org/licenses/by/4.0/

The skinning of the Aboma Snake, shot by Cap. Stedman.

Figure 3.2 William Blake, 'The skinning of the Aboma Snake, shot by Cap. Stedman', in John Gabriel Stedman, *Narrative of a Five Years' Expedition against the Revolted Negroes of Surinam* (London: J. Johnson, 1796). Engraving. Courtesy of The Huntington Library, San Marino, California.

as animism (the attribution of life to non-human entities) and vitalism (which explains life by reference to an immaterial principle residing in a material body – the idea of the 'vital spark' of life as self-determining and independent of the body came to the fore in the 1770s and 1780s). Whytt describes his anatomical examination of vipers, which remain 'alive' after their skin, head and entrails have been removed, in order to demonstrate his theory that 'the motions of the separated parts of animals are owing to the soul or sentient principle still continuing to act in them.'[71] As well as unsettling the boundary between life and death, the movements of the gigantic snake after it has been flayed also present a point of interest for Stedman and for his contemporaries working on skin as a site of physiological sensitivity. The new model of the skin as an organ was structured by irritability theory, the meta-framework of neural medicine during the second half of the Enlightenment. Skin was now understood as a complex structure made up of many small parts. 'All these minute parts,' wrote the physician Seguin Henry Jackson, 'when taken together, constitute a most complicated organ, endowed with a high irritability, and indubitably of great importance to the animal machine, both in sickness and in health.'[72] Skin had long had a symptomatic function as the place where disease was rendered visible, but the new understanding of skin as a permeable organ of interchange with its own structure and functions gave it a more significant role in determining and defining health. Within the physiological model of irritability (which held that motion in response to irritation by an external cause was a crucial aspect of biological life), skin was considered by some not just as having a symptomatic relationship to disease, but also as being an important site of sensibility. Skin was the subject of vigorous debate among irritability theorists, who argued over the relationship between sensibility and irritability, as well as the source of irritable function and whether organs such as the skin had the capacity for irritability. Swiss anatomist Albrecht von Haller, who introduced the term 'irritability' into the medical lexicon, became engaged in a controversy with Whytt over the nature of the relationship between body and soul expressed by the irritability of body parts. Haller held that irritability was a property of muscle fibre and that, lacking the ability to respond to stimuli by contracting, non-muscular parts of the body such as the skin could not be 'irritable'. Whytt argued that all the body's organs were sensible, and that symptoms such as inflammation in the skin proved its irritable capacity.[73] In the case of irritability being evident in body parts recently separated from the rest of the organism, Whytt hypothesized that the soul remained in the body for some time after death. This was problematic because it risked suggesting a divisible soul that might be cut into pieces on the anatomist's table – hence, the more materialist Haller concluded that irritability was independent of the soul.

Against the backdrop of anatomical interest in the muscular and neuro-logical systems and the cultural prominence of theories of irritability and sensibility, Whytt's and Stedman's snakes participate in the conversation about skin's capacity for and role in responsiveness and sensibility. The debate over skin as a sensible organ is particularly significant because it ties Stedman's anatomical interests to his fascination with skin as a sentimental object. Skin was connected to medical notions of sensibility – not only related to the sense of touch, skin had become associated with a different kind of sensitivity which revealed for the first time the body's neurophysiological processes. For Stedman, skin is also an important marker of racialized concepts such as the capacity to feel (both individually and on behalf of others) and performs a central role in the production of sympathy and of his sentimental narrative. What is the reader invited to feel on behalf of a person or an animal without a skin, given that with the loss of skin comes the loss of a principal marker of identity and feeling? In the tradition of the gentleman explorer, Stedman keeps the giant snake skin as a souvenir, along with the pelts of bats, jaguars and monkeys – tokens of colonial adventure suggesting a desire to retain something of the living whole. As the external image of the body, skin stands in figuratively for the entirety. The dead skin also serves as a reminder that the 'whole' is no longer in existence, and that bodies in Suriname are rarely intact. These bodiless skins also exist as 'things' in and of themselves: when the skin is removed it ceases to be primarily a skin and is transformed into a distinct object. Disembodied skins can even take on a strange autonomy of their own – as is the case with the skin of Joli Coeur's master, used in its afterlife as a non-violent weapon of war against those fighting on the side of the man who was once its wearer. In the case of these separated skins it is difficult to know where the skin-as-subject ends and the skin-as-object begins. Just as the skinless, living snake provokes questions about the origin of physical feeling, the objectification of skin and its separation from the body also challenge emotional response. The removal of the skin disturbs the physiological processes in which it plays a central role, as well as the social production of sympathetic feeling. As this chapter will go on to discuss, Stedman's account repeatedly invites readers to question their own sympathetic responses to the violent imagery that punctuates the text, developing a sentimental narrative style which uses a dissective viewpoint to pose problems about colonial sympathetic identification. Stedman finds himself compelled to look avidly and unflinchingly at corrupted, dissected or flayed skins with microscopic intensity, and his interest in skin and the animal or human to whom it belongs often increases with its separation

from the body: in the act of skinning he finds an amplified opportunity to
consider the problems of colonial identity and identification.

Narratives of Body and Text

Mirroring the problem of the integrity of the body is that of textual
integrity. The *Narrative* was not produced from Stedman's several diaries
by a simple act of textual merger: from the sparse, abrupt diary entries
detailing the houses at which Stedman dined, the women he bedded and
the diseases he contracted, the *Narrative* was reconstructed into a wide-
ranging reflection on life in the colonial military and on the Suriname
plantations. The focus of scholarly attention on the changes made to
Stedman's story for the 1790 text has been the alteration of his relationship with Joanna from its representation in the diaries as brief and sexually
motivated to that in the *Narrative* as a great romance.[74] Joanna's death after
Stedman's departure from Suriname, and Stedman's subsequent marriage
to a white Dutchwoman with whom he settled in Cornwall (Stedman and
Joanna's son, Johnny, followed his father to England after Joanna's death)
provides the inevitable resolution to this doomed colonial romance. While
Stedman's original diaries are notable for their total lack of feeling, sentimental modes of expression define the form and theme of the subsequent
Narrative. Jenny Sharpe notes that the romanticization of Stedman's relationship with Joanna represents both the moral connotations of romantic
love in eighteenth-century society and a set of racialized gender norms
revolving around domestic ideals of womanhood.[75] Werner Sollors argues
that Stedman's romantic re-telling self-consciously 'functions as an answer
and a specific corrective' to Richard Steele's version of the tale of Inkle and
Yarico (1711), in which the faithless Inkle sells his lover into slavery.[76] For
Sollors, Stedman's sentimentalized version establishes the moral legitimacy
of his ameliorative stance on slavery, which is 'made plausible by a focus on
its defiance of the patterns of previous fiction.'[77]

The other key subject to which feeling is retrospectively added in the
1790 *Narrative* is the violence inflicted upon enslaved people. The detailed
and explicit representation of plantation brutality centres on physical and
sympathetic feeling, as Stedman implores his reader to share in his sentimental response. The diary entry for 22 May 1773 records in extremely
perfunctory terms the execution of seven black men and the whipping of
one white man, but Stedman adds to the *Narrative* a detailed account of
violence and sympathetic suffering. Finding himself affected by the terrible sight, Stedman claims to suffer to a greater degree than the slaves.

While he is 'Surprized at the intrepidity with which the Negroes bore
theyr Punishment', Stedman announces the priority of his own pain,
exclaiming: 'how much I was hurted at the cruelty of the above execution'.[78] Stedman's sympathetic pain on witnessing the scene does not seem
to accord with his consistent claims that even the slave who is 'broke alive
upon the rack' makes no public display of suffering – a representation of
the stoic slave that echoes the implicitly pro-slavery medical theories of
black insensibility.[79] The absence of suffering on the part of the slave does
not diminish sympathetic response. For Adam Smith, sympathy is determined, in part, by what one would feel in someone else's situation: 'in every
passion of which the mind is susceptible, the emotions of the by-stander
always correspond to what, by bringing the case home to himself, he imagines should be the sentiments of the sufferer.'[80] For Stedman, as for Smith,
sympathy is an imaginative response that involves both identificatory and
judgemental impulses, as an individual assesses the attunement (or lack
thereof) of his or her own feelings and those of the other person. Stedman
enlarges his own capacity for feeling by appropriating the suffering of the
slaves he daily witnesses being brutalized and killed.

Stedman's sentimental mode of expression engages with the sublime
spectacle of pain, while the focus on his own sympathetic suffering, as
Marcus Wood points out, is part of a self-conscious attempt at creating for
himself the persona of a colonial 'Man of Feeling'.[81] Stedman foregrounds
his investment in a particular brand of masculine literary sensibility in
his overt references to his favourite writer, Laurence Sterne, and to Tobias
Smollett, and his adoption of the tone of picaresque and sentimental
romantic heroes. The emphasis on literary figures connected with the
representation of feeling reflects the major role it plays in the thematic
and stylistic processes of reconstructing the diaries as narrative, as well as
the construction of Stedman's own persona. As well as Sterne, Romantic
colonial sentimentality emerged through works by Aphra Behn, Hannah
More, William Cowper, William Wordsworth and others as a literary mode
which operated in close association with the representation of slavery and
colonial themes. Scholarly work on the relationship between sentiment
and slavery has framed the sentimental in functional terms. While Lynn
Festa has described the very particular kinds of cultural 'work' done by the
sentimental in framing the complex of social issues surrounding slavery,
Brycchan Carey has addressed the sentimental language of British abolitionist authors in terms of its role as political rhetoric.[82] On Stedman's
rewriting of his diaries as the *Narrative*, Werner Sollors outlines the 'sentimental strategies' of the 1790 text, while Marcus Wood comments on

Stedman's 'sentimentalist agendas'.[83] Sentimental labour, as Festa points out, is applied retrospectively, in a way that 'bestows coherent shape upon otherwise inchoate feelings by decanting them into contained linguistic vessels. Only retroactively does affective experience become intelligible.'[84] This sense of the sentimental as a mode which only operates with the benefit of hindsight suggests its function in producing the *Narrative* from the bare bones of the diaries. While the sentimental account of Joanna and her relationship with Stedman structures the text in terms of plot, the terrible scenes of slave suffering offer a series of supplications to Stedman's intended 'Feeling reader' to take up the position of sentimental witness to the extreme violence and to explore his or her own emotional responses to the *Narrative*'s violent imagery.[85] Feeling is productive of narrative, and with its claims on novelistic storytelling and plot function, the sentimental shifts Stedman's account into a different literary realm to that of the brief entries of the original diaries.

The frontispiece to the 1796 *Narrative* announces its sentimental agenda: Francesco Bartolozzi's engraving (Figure 3.3) of Stedman standing over a dying rebel after capturing the Maroon village of Gado Saby, blood seeping across the ground towards Stedman's naked feet, reads 'twas yours to fall, but mine to feel the wound'.[86] The sympathetic transferral of pain from the maroon's corpse to Stedman, implied by the text and by the visual movement of blood towards Stedman's feet, is incongruous with Stedman's casual posture as he leans on his gun, which is propped against the man's ribcage. The dying revolutionary is an object ripe for sentimental appropriation, and the 1796 *Narrative* uses the image to frame the story in these terms. Feelings are marked by their expression alongside scenes of horrific colonial violence and physical suffering, and the proximity of sentiment to violence complicates both the model of feeling at stake and Stedman's efforts to present his readers with a cohesive text. Stedman's portrayal of Joanna in the 1790 manuscript uses the sentimental in order, as Tassie Gwilliam puts it, to 'convert the horrors of slavery and colonial interactions into the softer pangs of love sorrow'.[87] Sentiment breaks down, however, as the 'contamination of "romance" and the domestic by colonial violence together serve to reveal the holes in sentimentality'.[88] The emotional gaps in Stedman's sentimental appropriation of slave suffering are similarly exposed by his unnerving shifts between brutally graphic descriptions of colonial violence and feeling response. So too are the *Narrative*'s textual holes revealed in its sudden changes of subject matter and tone. Reading the *Narrative* is an oddly disjointed experience. In a typically conflicted passage, Stedman tells the story of a ranger who is captured by a rebel

Figure 3.3 Francesco Bartolozzi, frontispiece from John Gabriel Stedman, *Narrative of a Five Years' Expedition against the Revolted Negroes of Surinam* (London: J. Johnson, 1796). Engraving. Courtesy of The Huntington Library, San Marino, California.

leader and suffers the punishment of having his ears, nose and lips cut off.[89] Realizing the narrative effects of such frequent accounts of extreme violence, Stedman expresses his wish to 'diversify the mind of the reader after the preceeding Scenes of Horror'.[90] The most fitting way of distracting the reader from the previous abhorrent images, for Stedman, is to offer a description of 'the beautifull Mulatto Maid Joanna', and, predictably, this description comes in the form of praise for Joanna's complexion.[91] As Stedman pauses to describe Joanna's vermillion skin and shapely lips and nose, the aestheticized image of her pleasing visage is haunted by its negative in the gruesome form of the faceless ranger. As the violence of the colonial battlefield is mapped onto the face of Stedman's enslaved beloved, beauty is revealed as yet another signifier entangled in the complicated web of disease, race and violence which makes skin the focal point of Stedman's colonial account. The slippage between Joanna's aestheticized mulatto complexion and the skinless, formless image of the ranger unsettles Stedman's romanticized construction of his lover. Stedman's romantic reshuffling of the relationship in the 1790 manuscript marks his investment in the *Narrative* as narrative, but the faceless ranger, as the negative of Joanna's exoticized beauty, stalls the production of that narrative. If skin raises issues regarding beauty, disease, identity – and, perhaps most of all, the capacity to suffer and the integrity of the colonial body – it also has a role to play in the textual unity of the *Narrative*.

An even more skittish passage sees Stedman wheel hurriedly between a natural historical account of sheep (both in their living form and skinned), a detailed description of 'dry gripes' (a stomach complaint causing pain and yellowing of the skin), a lament over the absence of a quarter of his five hundred and thirty-strong corps from sickness and death, a discussion of electric eels and, finally, a description of a slave driver mercilessly beating a young slave woman.[92] In part, Stedman's abrupt thematic turns are a consequence of the editorial process: the *Narrative* is formed as a strange hybrid of diary entries – which are reminiscent of its origins as a travel journal of the most rough and ready kind – within more novelistic chapters. But the spasmodic changes of topic also reveal the extent to which the threat of disease dominates Stedman's vision of Suriname, as well as the role of skin as a framing image for the *Narrative*. The suddenness of Stedman's shifts between natural history, illness, death and violence gesture towards the way in which skins – animal and vegetable, black and white, sick and healthy, living and dead – become the focal point of the text and draw together the *Narrative's* themes in visions of sick, damaged and dying bodies. As Stedman moves from sheep skin to diseased skin to bleeding skin, the repetition of images of disease and violence conceptually enfolds all the *Narrative*'s themes under the rubric of the corrupted body through the linking image of skin.

The tension between narrative flow and narrative interruption invites attention to the textual relationship between Stedman's natural historical accounts and the violent, sentimentalized passages intersecting them. How do we read the overlapping discourses of anatomy, medicine, natural history and sentimentality in the context of the changing boundary structures between emerging disciplines and increasing professionalization? How should we address the self-consciousness with which Stedman approaches his sentimental styling in relation to its interweaving with other discourses and textual forms? Travel narratives of Stedman's era often articulate a variety of predisciplinary colonial knowledge frameworks on the cusp of disciplinarity and are characterized by interaction between new forms of medical and natural knowledge, taxonomic systems and legal and social models produced by an expanding cultural and geographical horizon. Michel de Certeau describes the multidisciplinary shape of eighteenth-century travel writing as representing 'areas of exchange and of scientific confrontation' which are 'set in the form of narratives (in a period when collections of objects and curiosities, like the written collection of information and knowledge theorized, notably, by Francis Bacon, came into being). For this reason these narratives are of interest to a history of scientific disciplinarity and textuality: in them mobile configurations of evolving disciplines intersect, grow distinct, and become ordered'.[93] Recent work on the history of scientific disciplinarity has highlighted the loss of specificity caused by misrepresenting the soft edges of early modern disciplines, emphasizing difference over points of overlap and intersection. The call by Simon Schaffer to address the 'hybrid forms' of organized knowledge and disciplinary formation, and by Luisa Calè and Adriana Craciun to re-evaluate Romantic knowledge production in terms of its inherent structures of disorder and 'indiscipline', speak to the importance of assessing the sense of derangement at the heart of Stedman's work.[94]

In the *Narrative*, literary, medical and natural philosophical epistemological and textual modes are mutually dependent. Sentimentalized accounts of violence against slaves, framed by the motif of skin, conflict with but also conceptually underpin the production of various kinds of medical and natural knowledge, and the text is characterized as much by disorder as by the sense of structure which the sentimental belatedly imposes. For his own part, Stedman claims that the *Narrative* is structured using 'neither style, orthography, order, or Connection'. He presents the coincidence of natural history, sentiment, violence and other themes as random and his own unusual writing style as haphazard, describing the *Narrative* as being 'Patcht up with superfluous Quotations—Descriptions of Animals without so much as proper names—Trifles—Cruelties—Bombast &c.'[95] Yet Stedman's text is not so much 'patcht up' as it is contrived using a Humean associative structure, formed from contiguous discourses that circulate around skin.[96] Stedman's rapid textual movements do more than express the disjointedness and anxiety attendant on colonial military life, and more than articulate the conceptual overlap between discourses such as medicine, natural history, race, romance and the sentimental. Bohls points to the 'disturbingly incoherent' qualities of the *Narrative*, but very often these apparently fragmentary passages are in fact driven by a forceful narrative logic, much as is found in the mode of narrative deferral in the works of Stedman's literary hero, Laurence Sterne.[97] One of the most violent chapters in the text is an account of a man named Neptune being subjected to the notorious punishment of 'breaking on the rack'. The victim is tied to a flat wooden cross and beaten with an iron bar: 'Blow After Blow he Broke to Shivers every Bone in his Body till the Splinters Blood and Marrow Flew About the Field'.[98] Neptune is kept alive for some time and over the course of several pages, an episode which descends from bloodshed and sympathetic feeling into farce when the dying slave offers his dismembered hand as a meal to a white soldier. The drawn-out labour of piecing apart Neptune's body is finally completed by vultures coming to feast, leading Stedman seamlessly to a natural historical account of this particular bird – in part focusing, needless to say, on the description of its skin.

The same chapter then sees a reversal of this thematic leap from violence to natural history. Moving on to an account of indigo and the process of its production, Stedman goes through the usual motions of natural historical description. Mentioning in passing the individual he credits with bringing the first indigo to Europe, a Frenchman named Destrades, Stedman breaks off to announce that 'the Cause of his Death being verry Notorious indeed I must Relate it'. Finding himself heavily indebted, Destrades fled Suriname for Demerara, where a potentially life-threatening abscess developed on his shoulder. Mysteriously, Destrades would permit no one to examine him or uncover the shoulder, until one day gunshots are heard and he was found 'Weltering in his Blood, And Strange to tell having Stript him, the Mark of **V** for *Voleur* or Thief on the Verry Shoulder he had Strived to Conceal'. Rather than allow his tattoo to reveal this shame, Destrades shot himself, and 'thus ended the Life of this Poor Wretch who had for Years Supported the Character at Paramaribo of a polite Well Bred Gentleman'.[99] Stedman's apparently tangential sidestep from natural history and technological description is, thus, underpinned by the motif of the marked skin and the textual movement towards death. The narrative logic here is associative: Stedman gives the impression of one story leading out of another on the basis of the connection between indigo and its European 'discoverer', while underpinning this is another thematic association in the form of skin and its complex role as a marker of human social identity.

Similarly, Stedman's 'Tear Stain'd Eye', self-consciously observing the tortured Neptune's suffering throughout this long and difficult passage, functions as more than sentimental posturing. The sentimental eye frames and shapes the reader's perspective so that, as we turn from tattooed skin to the skin of the beaten slave to vulture skin, the onslaught of different registers, styles, themes and modes of knowledge creates a self-reflexive and associative text that produces knowledge about colonial bodies – natural historical, medical, social – through the lens of the sentimental. The *Narrative* demonstrates the extent to which ideas about feelings and their literary expression are interwoven with the medical and natural historical knowledge emerging from the colonies – knowledge which Stedman engages with directly in his references to such key medical and natural philosophical figures as Joseph Banks, Buffon, John Hunter, Lord Monboddo and others. In the context of the scientific interest in feeling articulated by the discourses of animism, dermatology, irritability and vitalism, Stedman creates a kind of colonial 'sentimental science'. This model goes beyond that described by Mary Louise Pratt, who treats scientific and sentimental travel writing 'in complementary fashion'.[100] Pratt draws a historical line between sentimental travel writing and older traditions of 'survival literature', showing that both forms develop sex and slavery as joint themes, but does not explore the formal relationships between sentiment and science.[101] Rather, colonial sentimental science describes a way of looking at the new knowledge associated with travel and intercultural encounter which is bound up in the tense dynamics of slavery and feeling and which structures the points of overlap and tension between the taxonomies and rhetorical modes of medicine, natural knowledge and feeling.

Sentimental Textuality

The revision of the diaries in terms of skin, race, sentiment and violence finds its bewildering, bloody apex in a passage which sees Stedman shoot a pair of black monkeys. On 21 August 1773 the diary gives the following bare statement: 'have the whole day a violent fever'.[102] The *Narrative* reformulates this, retrospectively diagnosing Stedman with a 'frenzy fever' and showing Joanna lovingly nursing Stedman back to health.[103] The passage then collapses into a torturous scene of violence, guilt, sympathy, dissection and scientific racism. In an account not recorded in the journals (and between fits of fever), Stedman describes an encounter with a monkey in terms of their mutual regard:

> Seeing me on the Side of the River in the Canoo the Creature made a Stop from Skipping after his Companions, and /being perch'd on a branch that hung over the Water/ examined me with attention and the greatest Marks of Curiosity, no doubt taking me for a Giant of his own Species, while he shewed his teeth perhaps by way of laughing–chattered prodigiously–and kept dancing and shaking of the bough on which he rested.

After these moments of natural description, Stedman shoots the monkey. Having fatally wounded but failed to kill it, Stedman is overwhelmed with guilt and desperate to end the monkey's suffering: 'I swong him round and knock'd his head against the Sides of the Canoo with such a force, that I was covered all over with blood and brains.' Still, the monkey clings to life, and Stedman is tormented by its pained looks and forced to perform a sickeningly intimate final act of killing:

> The Poor thing still continued alive, and looking at me in the most Pitiful manner that can be conceived, I knew no other Means to end this Murder than by holding him under Water till he was drown'd, while my heart felt Seek on his account. Here his dying little Eyes still Continued to follow me with seeming reproach till their light gradually forsook them and the wretched Creature expired.[104]

This agonising scene becomes part of the text's rewriting in terms of feeling, as Stedman stakes his usual claim on suffering: 'never Poor Devil felt more than I on this occasion'.[105] The monkey's pain and Stedman's sympathetic response are registered through a transaction of sentimental regard. The monkey's visual attention to Stedman is key: from looking at one another with 'curiosity', their shared looks are transformed into a sentimental exchange in which the dying monkey's eyes accuse Stedman of 'Murder'. Conceiving of the sentimental mode as a vicarious structure of visual regard underpinned by ambivalence and reflexivity, James Chandler writes that the eighteenth-century sentimental (and Sterne in particular) developed 'new structuring principles in narrative art' which negotiated the social distribution of feeling.[106] Sentiment, Chandler argues, is

'emotion that results from social circulation, passion that has been mediated by a sympathetic passage through a virtual point of view.'[107] Within
this model of sentimental sociability, looking and being looked at are the
principal ways in which feelings are developed, expressed, understood;
visual exchanges form the basis for a structure of sympathetic exchange
which distributes feeling between individuals (and readers). In the case of
the dying monkey, however, the object of sympathy is not human, or not
quite human. Stedman personifies the monkey, situating the passage in
relation to the fascination with monkeys' proximity to humans exemplified by the comparative anatomical studies of Pieter Camper and others: 'if
wisely viewed and *desected*', Stedman claims, the 'wonderfull chain of
Gradation' becomes apparent in the comparison between the African and
the orangutan.[108] The proximity of human and animal suffering speaks to
the debates concerning the 'feelings' of animals and the increasing focus
on their capacity to suffer and their function as sympathetic objects.[109] By
raising questions about what it meant to be 'human', as Laura Brown has
argued, animals 'helped Europeans imagine Africans, Native Americans
and themselves'.[110] Triangulated through animals, ideas about the distinction between the human and the non-human emerge. In Giorgio
Agamben's words: 'the inside is obtained through the inclusion of an outside, and the non-man is produced by the humanization of an animal: the
man-ape, the *enfant sauvage* or *Homo ferus*, but also and above all, the
barbarian, and the foreigner, as figures of an animal in human form.'[111]
From Gulliver's Houyhnhnms and their enslaved Yahoos to Yorick's caged
starling, anthropomorphized animals were being used in fiction to take
the measure of fellow-feeling and to explore the personal politics of slavery
– one step removed from reality.

So how does the reader interpret the sympathetic exchange of regard
between Stedman and the monkey? Why are animals so important to
Stedman's articulation of sentiment? What can they tell us about the scope
and limits of humanity and feeling in the colonies? While for much of the
Narrative Stedman describes violence against slaves committed by others,
this passage shows him re-enacting this colonial violence on the monkey,
replacing the human object of sympathy with an animal and casting a
different light on his claim to sympathetic suffering on behalf of the tortured and dying black people who populate the *Narrative*. In one sense,
Stedman uses feeling to distance himself from responsibility for colonial
acts of torture – by killing a monkey he explores his own capacity for violence but is guilty of a lesser crime than the murders of slaves to which he

bears witness.[112] One reading of the passage, then, accounts for the monkey as figurative expression of Stedman's colonial guilt. Here, the communality of sentimental feeling is significant. While Chandler emphasizes the 'virtual' production of distributed feeling which characterizes the sentimental mode, for Lynn Festa sentimental identification invites a 'perilous absorption in another's affect and interests that may threaten the autonomy of the self', leading to an agonistic 'tension between the sociable benefits and pleasures of sympathetic affect and the desire to uphold the singularity of the self.'[113] Stedman creates a complex interplay of feeling between narrator, monkey, African slave and reader, in which feelings are socially produced and expressed through an exchange of looks. This 'relay of regard' is self-consciously virtual not only in that it is mediated – Stedman's resolute claim on feeling means that he acts as a double both for the suffering slave (and the slave's simian analogue) and for the feeling reader – but also in that it is so evidently a work of imagination as Stedman constructs sentimental episodes in which African and animal objects of sympathy appear as objectified others in order to play out scenes of colonial violence to test the scope and limits of feeling and community.[114]

Yet the monkey is more than a figurative vessel for human feeling. Stedman's feelings in this passage hinge on the monkey as object of sympathy – but just what the monkey is and represents is ambiguous. As its 'dying little Eyes still Continued to follow [Stedman] with seeming reproach', the monkey's 'seeming' resemblance of human feeling highlights the fact that Stedman's sympathy is also 'seeming', because it is not directed towards a properly human object, but towards the monkey as human proxy and its 'Mock-Mimicry of the Human'.[115] Eighteenth-century monkeys were often modelled as imitative of humans, and were costumed anthropomorphically in singeries. The idea of the monkey as mimic makes it an illusory object of sympathy, and the confusion over whether it is the monkey or its African parallel that constitutes the sympathetic object disrupts Stedman's sentimental response. But Stedman also imitates the monkey: what separates humans from apes is language, but here he emphasizes his communication with the monkey through vision alone, with their silent exchange creating an affinity between Stedman and the pre-linguistic human further back along the line of the 'wonderfull chain of gradation, from man to the most diminuative of the above Species'.[116] Stedman's repeated invocation of *Tristram Shandy* also invites a reading through the many animals that figure in Sterne's sentimental narrative. In his triangulated exchange with Maria and her goat, Tristram takes her glancing from him to the goat and back again to mean that she is weighing up the resemblance between the two, concluding 'what a *Beast* man is'. Stedman agrees – the sense of mutual regard with the monkey, and their imitative exchange, blur the boundaries between animal and human. In one sense, this ambiguity permits Stedman to appropriate the monkey's pain, but the monkey is also afforded the kind of Lockean personhood described by Heather Keenleyside as emerging in Sterne's Buffonian vitalist model of human–animal relations. Taking Tristram's account of his sympathetic encounter with an ass as an example, Keenleyside shows that the ass's first-person 'speech' (as Tristram fancies it) is 'patently an effect of Tristram's projective and personifying imagina-tion'.[117] At the same time, however, the ass is an 'animate living body … with the capacity to say "I"'. Like the ass, the monkey silently responds to Stedman, and elicits his response in return, 'outside of language but in con-versation'.[118] The monkey's personhood emerges from the acts of looking and being looked at, and from the visual 'conversation' with Stedman and rejects, as Keenleyside does, the understanding of the figurative animals which populate eighteenth-century texts as entirely conventional. Rather, the monkey's claim on personhood provokes, asking Stedman troubling questions about his ability to feel for and on behalf of others, and rejecting a reading of it as merely a repository for Stedman's colonial guilt.[119] In its heavily mediated, vicarious, belated and displaced articulation of feeling, deeply invested in exploring the animal–human relation, Stedman's colo-nial sentimental constructs a model of sympathy as illusory and transient, troubling the boundaries of both feeling subject and sympathetic object.

Stedman's emotional response to the dying monkey does not prevent him from once again interpreting the experience through the grotesque imagery of the skinned body: 'I have eat them boild, roasted, and stew'd, and found their flesh white juicy and Good; the only thing which disgusted me–being their little hands, and their heads, which when dress'd by being depriv'd of the Skin look like the hands and the Skull of a young infant.'[120] The humanization of the monkey simultaneously dehumanizes the African to which it is compared, and the parallel drawn between the monkey's body and the black body conveys the latter into the realm of 'Mock-Mimicry of the Human'. The comparison between simian and African bodies, and between the skinned monkey and the body of a small child, not only make for uncomfortable reading but also raise questions about the object of sympathetic feeling to which the reader is being directed. As the passage progresses from the ordinary act of killing an animal for food to the murder of the monkey as human mimic and finally to infanticide and cannibalism, any clear sense of sympathetic affinity between Stedman and his reader is dissolved. Just as the proximity between Joanna's exoticized skin and the ranger's skinless face haunts Stedman's sentimental romance, so the blurred boundaries between monkey skin, black skin and baby skin leaves the reader wondering just what, or who, is the object of sympathy in this horrific scene. If skin is an important social prompt for sympathetic feeling, Stedman's blurry, disfigured and leaking skins complicate the feeling reader's entry into the *Narrative*.

Revealed in this elaborate, obfuscated interweaving of natural history, ethnography, racial science, anthropomorphism, medicine and sympathetic feeling is the problem of the relationship between feeling and violence which Stedman creates in rewriting his diaries in sentimental terms – and, more broadly, the problem of the colonial sentimental as a textual mode. Stedman offers his reader a range of sympathetic objects which usually take the form of humans and animals with their skin removed to varying degrees. The confusion of the sympathetic object, as well as the tension created between sympathy and violence, forestall any straightforward identification of the reader with either the object of sympathy or Stedman as sympathetic subject. Stedman's colonial sentimental mode creates a disordered reading experience in which he invites the reader to share in his feeling responses to extreme visual and visceral experiences, but his sympathetic pains also displace the suffering of African slaves. The *Narrative*'s fragmented, dissected, dismembered and violated bodies sit uneasily within the cohesive sentimental text for which Stedman voices his desire. Stedman himself abruptly cuts short his discussion of monkey dissection and the gradation of man: 'I acknowledge the theme almost to[o] delicate to bear investigation—here I shall end it for the present.'[121] The attempt to stabilize textual meaning by framing the *Narrative* in terms of feeling proves to be in vain as corrupted and violated bodies interrupt and renegotiate Stedman's story at every turn.

Skin is the objectified locus upon which Stedman hangs the themes of beauty, disease, race, sexuality and violence. As the point of mediation between the human body and the rest of the world, skin is the place where the insides of the body become exposed and expunged, and has a crucial role in the production of social and medical narratives of the human. In the colonies, skin is also particularly important as a social prompt for sympathetic feeling. As such, it has a crucial role in the production of social and medical narratives of the body. Stedman's *Narrative* documents the way in which the eighteenth-century fascination with skin plays out in a colonial context, revealing the vulnerability and ambiguity of skin to undermine a stable narrative of the colonial body, as well as a stable narrative of sympathetic social relations between people. In the context of concerns about tropical disease, social creolization and colonial violence, Stedman's skinless and decaying bodies suggest the tropics as a site of pathology not just for the body, but also for the self and, indeed, for the text. Stedman attempts to master the disconnectedness of the colonial experience through a vision of bodily and narrative wholes which cannot but reveal their diseased, decaying and dissected parts.

CHAPTER 4

'A Seasoned Creole' and 'a Citizen of the World'
White West Indians and Atlantic Medical Knowledge

While Stedman's biggest fear was the corruptive influence of the tropical environment on skin, many Europeans travelling to the Caribbean
focused their anxieties on the notoriously lethal yellow fever. In his medical epistolary collection *Notes on the West Indies* (1806) George Pinckard
gives a detailed account of his traumatic experience of this most feared
of colonial diseases. In April 1796, during the first leg of his tour of the
Caribbean as a military physician, Pinckard is dismissive of the startling
reports circulating in England of the 'yellow visaged monster' hungrily
ravaging European troops in the region: 'be not deceived', he writes, 'that
so many are about to become the victims of climate, and yellow fever; nor
suffer yourself to be persuaded that the whole of us have "sailed to our
graves"'.[1] But after a close personal encounter with the disease that very
nearly proves fatal, much of the third volume of Pinckard's letters is dedicated to the topic of yellow fever – its symptoms, methods of prevention
and treatment, the types of noxious geographical region which harboured
it, the groups most susceptible to its deathly grip and a contribution to the
vigorous transatlantic debate about whether or not it was spread by contagion. Yellow fever was a brutal disease – accounts varied among physicians,
but all registered the fierceness of its symptoms. As Pinckard describes it,
the fever came on with extreme rapidity, bringing acute hot flushes, cold
sweats and severe pains. James Clark, a Fellow of the Royal College of
Physicians of Edinburgh who practised medicine in Dominica, notes that
the early signs included headaches and nosebleeds, followed by vomiting,
with bile changing in colour from yellow to green.[2] Finally, as the disease
progressed towards what the Grenada surgeon Colin Chisholm calls the
'fatal crisis', the bile turned to black.[3] The sufferer's liver inflamed, the
skin became dry, the face flushed and the eyes swollen and the neck and
eyeballs yellowed. At the fever's apex, patients would usually become delirious; Clark notes that strong, athletic men suffered a kind of 'outrageous'
derangement, while women and those of a delicate constitution became

dejected and suffered from a more 'melancholic sort of delirium'.[4] Figures for yellow fever's mortality rate across the Caribbean are difficult to ascertain with precision, not least because of vast medical differences in diagnosis. Pinckard highlights this problem in his emphasis on the disease's misleading denomination: many patients did not present with yellowing of the skin. Those statistics that are available, however, point towards an immense death toll. J. R. McNeill writes that the mortality rate in British garrisons in Jamaica was seven times that of garrisons in Canada, largely due to yellow fever and other tropical fevers like malaria.[5] Philip Curtin writes that 71 per cent of all deaths in the West Indies were from a fever of some sort; in Britain, that figure was 12 per cent.[6] Trevor Burnard indicates that yellow fever kills around 10 to 20 per cent of the nonimmune population when it first strikes, with outbreaks spiralling out of control on sugar plantations, where an abundance of stagnant water bodies provided an ideal breeding ground for mosquitoes.[7]

Pinckard studied medicine at St Thomas's and Guy's, later moving to Edinburgh University and finally to Leiden, where he graduated in 1792. In 1795 he was appointed as a physician to the British Army, travelling with Sir Ralph Abercromby's expedition against the French possessions in the West Indies. In 1824, after his time in the Caribbean, Pinckard would go on to found the Medical, Clerical and General Life Assurance Office (later Clerical Medical), the aim of which was to extend the advantages of life assurance to individuals subject to 'deviations from the common standard of health'.[8] *Notes on the West Indies* is an account of the period between setting sail from Southampton in October 1795 and his final departure from Demerara in May 1797. The letters are in part a personal travel account of many of the Caribbean islands and Suriname, and include landscape description, observations on slavery and racist diatribe aimed particularly at black women as well as medical observations of the diseases suffered by troops and local populations. Pinckard's sixteen-page autopathographical account of the 'yellow-fanged monster' is the most emotive passage in his fourteen hundred–page work and echoes the violence of contemporary medical descriptions of yellow fever, as the 'colonial immunity' of his earlier letters of picturesque travelogue breaks down when he becomes afflicted by the disease himself. As an illness narrative Pinckard's is unusual in that the patient is also the doctor; he insists on treating himself and ignores the advice of other medical practitioners when they doubt the efficacy of his self-prescribed treatments. Describing his symptoms in the detached, objective tone of the physician, Pinckard begins his narrative by distancing himself from his own pain: 'the skin was burning, and conveyed a pungent

sensation when touched: the pulse was quickened but not very full: the
tongue was white and parched, with excessive thirst, and constant dryness
of the mouth, lips, and teeth'. His suffering soon becomes so intense, however, that Pinckard begins to slip between this detached style and a more
personal viewpoint:

> All the violence of disease now rushed in upon me, hurrying on towards
> rapid destruction. The light was intolerable and the pulsations of the head
> and eyes were most excruciating—conveying a sensation as if three or four
> hooks were fastened into the globe of each eye, and some person, standing
> behind me, was dragging them forcibly from their orbits back into the head,
> the cerebrum being, at the same time, detached from its membranes, and
> leaping about violently within the cranium.[9]

Physical feeling is so acute that it is expelled from the location of sensation,
with Pinckard now distanced from his body not by medical perspective
but by severity of suffering as he objectifies each newly foreign part that no
longer seems to belong to him – the head, the eyes, the cranium – while
using the first person to convey the physical sensations associated with
each symptom.

The most intense symptoms, though, are those that affect the mind, and
the sense of physical dismemberment in the preceding passage prefigures
the mental derangement of fever and the impact it has on the sufferer's
sense of identity. Describing the very worst moments of the illness,
Pinckard emphasizes his psychological vulnerability:

> The mind was crowded with confused and incoherent ideas, painting the
> world as new, and altogether different from that I had so lately left; indeed
> so distorted and unnatural did every thing seem around me, that I felt a
> kind of hesitation whether to accept of my return to life, or proceed onward
> to the grave, which I saw wide open before me.[10]

Pinckard's moment of hesitation at the peak of a fever-induced 'peculiar
sense of confusion, or horror', makes him pause at the crossroads between
life and death and consider his own mortality with delirious equanimity.[11]
It is this moment, when 'annihilating' sensations make him feel his
life hangs 'by a slender filament', which forms the 'crisis' of Pinckard's
fever.[12] His mind becomes 'sickened' with a 'restless, deadly horror' that
corresponds with the backdrop of the tropical elements: 'it rained and
blew; fierce lightning tore the heavens, and loud thunder, bursting from
the clouds, ruptured the elements into unison with the confusion and
disorder with which my feelings were pervaded. All nature seemed to par-
take of the unaccountable change, and to administer to the horrors which

beset me'. The meteorological disturbance at the apex of the fever reflects what Pinckard calls 'the tumult and distress of regaining an existence'. Pinckard regains his claim on life, but it is no longer the same: 'the whole order of things was inverted, and, for a time, I could not divest myself of the idea that the heavens were agitated with the convulsive throes of bringing forth a new world'. As his symptoms (and the stormy weather conditions) recede, Pinckard becomes acclimatized: 'I am become better reconciled to the world, and again recognise it as the same which I had so quietly resigned.'[13] While the world may not have changed, though, Pinckard recognizes that he has: 'having passed the fiery ordeal, I shall now deem myself quite a *seasoned* creole, and feel that I am entitled to the privileges of West India freedom'.[14]

Likening himself to 'creoles, or persons who have become creolised', Pinckard's use of the verb form differs not only from the common definition of a native West Indian but also from other types of usage in the period.[15] Most often, 'to creolize' was associated with the renowned Creole languor and the West Indian practice of reclining with the feet up on a table or sofa. Maria Nugent's diary, kept during her residence in Jamaica while her husband was the governor of the island between 1801 and 1806, records her 'usual routine' of 'writing, reading, and creolizing'.[16] The 'perfect Creole', she writes, 'says very little, and drawls out that little, and has not an idea beyond her own Penn.'[17] While Nugent appropriates various Creole social practices, she does not take up the identity as her own. Having travelled back to England, however, Nugent indicates the more lasting effects of Creole society on her own children in her description of the general amusement at 'their funny little talk, and Creole ideas and ways'.[18] Writing from Indonesia, the military surgeon John M'Leod highlights the popular reach of the term in the manner of Nugent's use of it: 'creolizing is an easy and elegant mode of lounging in a warm climate; so called, because much in fashion among the ladies of the West Indies'.[19] But some followed Pinckard's lead in defining the term along medical lines: George Birnie, assistant surgeon on the naval ship *Antelope*, wrote in 1817 from St Kitts that 'it is well known that the remittants of this country attack the same person frequently, though each succeeding attack is generally milder, in proportion as the constitution becomes *creolised*'.[20] The cartoon strip 'Johnny New-come in Jamaica' (1800, Figure 4.1) links the social and medical definitions of the term, connecting nonchalance and languor with disease. The story is a graphic narrative of the newly arrived planter as he quickly feels the ill effects of the tropical climate. After a period of poor health, Johnny mistakenly believes himself to be fully recovered and

'Seasoned', so he 'domesticates', 'creolizes' and 'puffs sickness away' with a cigar as he lounges with his feet up on a table full of empty wine glasses, before quickly succumbing to the 'Yellow Claw of Febris', which this time gives him a 'mortal nip'.[21]

While Johnny's imprudent 'creolizing' brings about his untimely end, for Pinckard the process of becoming 'creolized' heralds a new freedom which is both medical and psychological. As well as the 'privileges' of creolization through seasoning, most especially freedom from the threat of yellow fever, the fever crisis marks the moment in which Pinckard achieves a fresh perspective on his colonial surroundings. During the initial stages of his illness Pinckard becomes homesick, longing for the salubrious, picturesque England he has left behind. But the fever's physical and mental oscillations and his ultimate reconciliation with the 'new world' which greets him on his recovery – representing both the metaphorical site of his physical and emotional return to health and the geographically specific site of the New World – are part of reframing his identity as a colonial subject.[22] What is perhaps most surprising about Pinckard's account is that colonial disease could prove, for some, to be not such a terrible thing. Pinckard's 'new world', in which the yellow fever survivor, in the wake of immense physical and mental upheaval, experiences a reconciliation with the New World and is thereby afforded new medical and social freedoms, suggests that this process of medical creolization brings with it a new and different kind of colonial body and identity. Through his personal account of the aggressive symptoms of yellow fever, Pinckard constructs a narrative of the progression of disease through the body which results in something other than either death or the return to life as normal. Afforded a different perspective through the lens of disease, Pinckard claims a new identity – one that is no longer localized and British but transatlantic and displaced from the category of the national. An unequivocal polygenist, Pinckard does not believe that a process of creolization signifies underlying changes in racial identity. While he writes that climate alters the firmness or tone of the body's fibres, Pinckard also documents West Indian families who can trace their Creole 'pedigree' to eight or nine generations but show no physical mark of the tropical environment: 'in fairness of skin, and in figure, they might have been mistaken for children born in England'.[23] The Creole, here, does not signify a simple loss of Englishness – Pinckard's medical Creole does not rupture, for him, the hierarchized categories of nation and race which that loss might suggest – but it does describe a new way of being in the world.

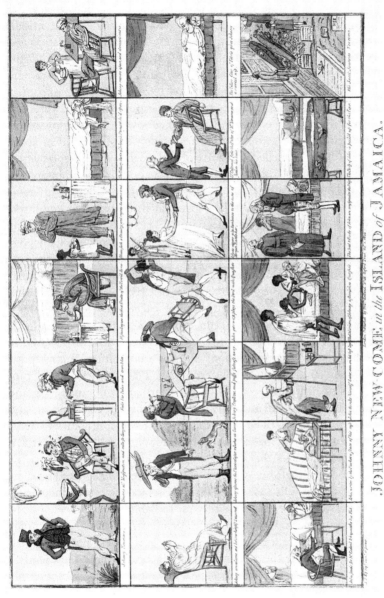

Figure 4.1 James Sayers [?], 'Johnny New-come in the Island of Jamaica' (London: William Holland, 1800). Etching with aquatint. Courtesy of the Lewis Walpole Library, Yale University.

The modern understanding of the 'Creole' relates to the non-indigenous Caribbean-born individual, as well as the idea that the colonial encounter between African enslaved peoples, Caribbean-born slaves, free black people, Indo-Caribbeans, the plantocracy and the white middle and labouring classes resulted in various forms of cultural integration and hybridization which forged a distinctive West Indian society.[24] 'Cultural intermixing', writes Kathleen Wilson, 'was, paradoxically, an instrument of national self-fashioning and definition' as 'under the pressure of contact and exchange, boundaries deemed crucial to national identity – white and black, civilised and savage, law and vengeance – were blurred, dissolved, or rendered impossible to uphold.'[25] In postcolonial studies, ideas about Creoles have been modelled in terms of the duality of existence which they represent – native and non-native, British and Caribbean, peripheral authority and imperial subject, colonizer and colonized – so that the Creole has come to occupy a liminal social space on the margins of key imperial categories of normativity, including race, class and gender. Following Homi Bhabha's model of colonial 'ambivalence', the Creole is usually positioned at the blurry boundary between European and Other, signifying both the hegemony of colonial power and the possibility of transgression.[26] Edward Kamau Brathwaite's understanding of Creole society as 'the result of a complex situation where a colonial polity reacts, as a whole, to external metropolitan pressures, and at the same time to internal adjustments made necessary by the juxtaposition of master and slave, élite and labourer, in a culturally heterogeneous relationship' has underpinned many postcolonial understandings of Creole cultures.[27] David Lambert has provided a detailed historical geography of the formation of competing and overlapping white Barbadian identities during the age of abolition, and Keith Sandiford has described the creation of an 'evolving ideal of Creole civilization' and its 'marginal relation to metropolitan cultures'.[28] Carolyn Vellenga Berman writes that Creoles undermine the unity of imperial national identity: 'Englishness itself is disconcerted or dis-composed by its Creole shadow.'[29] Discussion of literary Creoles has often attended to the notorious stereotype of the white West Indian planter – cruel, greedy, licentious, rum-soaked. As Wylie Sypher demonstrates in his early survey of the West Indian as a literary character, 'no anti-slavery novel or poem fails to inveigh against the Barbadian planter, or the sugar-grower of St Kitts, Neavis, or Jamaica.'[30] But medical discourse has been noticeably absent from, or has played a minor role in, these accounts.[31]

The 'Creole' of colonial medical discourse describes another type of individual – one who is not identified as Creole by birth or by process of cultural hybridization but rather one who has become 'creolized' by disease. This kind of medical creolization has been subsumed within a broader understanding of colonial hybridity as involving dress, food, speech, social events and other cultural practices. Pinckard's model of creolization – which he associates with specific psychological and social changes, as well as the physical changes in health that most medical practitioners believed occurred in Africans and Europeans after arrival in the New World due to processes of physical acclimatization and adaptation – suggests that the Creole could be made, as well as born. His claim that he has been 'creolized' by disease serves as an alternative metamorphic model of the Creole which structures colonial identities in medical terms. The medical understanding of Creole bodies and Pinckard's description of creolization as a physical and mental process are useful lenses through which to revisit the current understanding of the role of the Creole in Atlantic literature and culture and the prevalent stereotypes described by Sypher. By examining this specific kind of Creole body, this chapter engages in the etymological recovery of the medical underpinnings of the term 'Creole'. It uses the idea of 'creolization' as a process of alteration to the European body, psychology and national identity to re-examine postcolonial studies models of the Creole and to show how the ambiguous and contentious figure of the Creole was used to articulate and explore various key medical and social issues of the era. Rather than focusing on the notorious caricature of the white West Indian, I examine the radical author and lecturer John Thelwall's novel *The Daughter of Adoption* (1801), partly set in St Domingue, which places Creoles at the heart of its Jacobin and abolitionist agendas. Thelwall enlists white West Indian characters in order to intervene in issues central to British society at the height of empire, and in which the Creole had become a pivotal figure: gender, marriage, consanguineous and sympathetic human relationships, education, mental and physical health, colonial degeneration and the relationship between environment and inherited traits. Like Pinckard, Thelwall's Creoles express the sense of confusion and disorder at the heart of empire. But, while Pinckard writes from a mostly ameliorative perspective, Thelwall's interest in Atlantic medical and moral health emerges in a vehemently abolitionist politics. The medical dimensions of the Creole, this chapter argues, reveal new ways of seeing the important role of West Indian identities and forms of knowledge within the wider Atlantic world. From the idea of the Creole as an object of medical knowledge, this chapter uses Pinckard's model of the medical Creole to highlight the ways in which the various negative caricatures associated with the Creole were recast in relation to key social debates, revealing the Creole not just as a figure of fun, but of reform.

Creole Pathologies

Renowned for their avaricious, extravagant, idle and oversexed lifestyles, by the 1790s white Creole planters found themselves a target for abolitionist press and were vilified as cartoonish slobs and cruel tyrants.[32] The anti-slavery poem 'Tea and Sugar, or the Nabob and the Creole' (1792), published under the pseudonym 'Timothy Touchstone', illustrates both the cultural association between Creole bodies and disease and the complexity of British national feeling which underpinned anti-Creole sentiment:

> Now in his native pride the Creole view,
> Slavery's Prime Minister, of swarthy hue
> And sickly look; of various tints combin'd
> A true epitome of jaundic'd mind;
> By whom the plunder'd from old Afric's shore
> Are made to sweat, nay bleed through every pore;
> Whom every generous feeling hath defy'd
> To whom, sweet, social love, is unally'd;
> Whose flinty heart, but more obdurate mind,
> No Woe can penetrate—No Virtue find;
> Who, under British Laws,—with grief I speak,
> A greater tyrant is than Algier's Chief.[33]

These lines highlight the complex political relations between Britain and the Creole societies over which it ruled, and the medical terms in which these relations were couched. The greedy, heartless planter is physiognomically tied to the West Indies by his 'swarthy' complexion, and associated with colonial disease by his 'sickly' look and a 'jaundic'd mind' that hints at the association between Creole immorality and the creolizing disease of yellow fever. While his cruelty springs from a tropical heritage, however, it is clear that the British metropole bears the ultimate responsibility for allowing slavery within its dominions: the Creole planter is the 'Prime Minister' of slavery, but Britain wears the crown. And while physical disease is located within the body of the white Creole and tied to the Caribbean islands, the source of moral corruption is undoubtedly Britain. The poem foregrounds the Creole's tropical 'nativity', and in doing so points to the complex of issues extending from colonial birth which were articulated in relation to white West Indian cultures: miscegenation and sexual morality, gender, heredity, national identity and the transatlantic flow of wealth.

The Creole was a figure defined by ideas about health and illness; it was commonly understood by British medics that West Indians were sicklier than Europeans. Pinckard himself notes the dangers of being and becoming Creole: 'notwithstanding the severity of disease among those who are recently arrived in the West Indies', he writes, 'we remark that the creoles, or creolised, are generally much greater invalids, than those who are but lately from Europe'.[34] Those who were medically creolized enjoyed some health benefits because after an initial 'seasoning' – which in Europeans was usually thought to be initiated by a severe bout of yellow fever or another inflammatory illness – subsequent fevers were usually less violent, but many became permanently weakened by the ravages of disease.[35] The climatic model of disease emphasized the overwhelming impact of environment and suggested a causal relationship between the tropical climate and the West Indian character, as well as elevating European white people in a global geomedical hierarchy. On arriving in Jamaica in 1740, Charles Leslie found that none of the faces he saw 'resemble the gay Bloom of a *Briton.*' 'The People', he writes in the first letter of his epistolary collection, 'seem all sickly, their Complection is muddy, their Colour wan, and their Bodies meagre; they look like so many Corpses.'[36] With the growth of the abolitionist movement, white West Indians became associated with moral disorder, as well as physical ills. An aquatint depicting 'The Torrid Zone, or, Blessings of Jamaica' (Figure 4.2) by Lieutenant Abraham James of the 67th Regiment, who served in the West Indies in 1798–1801, displays the correlation between Jamaica's tropical climate, disease and the sloth for which Creoles were, by this time, notorious. In the image, West Indians doze on couches or smoke cigars, either overfed and enervated or underweight and infirm. They are framed from above by the relentless heat of the tropical sun and from below by a terrifying underworld inhabited by the gruesome, skeletal figure of personified yellow fever. The hideous angel watching over them clutches a rum bottle, warning of the illnesses that plagued those who drank in tropical climes. Medical practitioners harboured particular concerns about what Creoles ingested. By contrast to their husbands' insatiable taste for rum, white West Indian women were noted for their sobriety, with their refusal of alcohol seen as being taken to unnatural extremes. Benjamin Moseley, the Jamaican surgeon general, wrote that white Creole women's insistence on drinking only water was unhealthy and that their lack of exercise and 'crude' diet caused pallid complexions and brought on nervous complaints.[37] 'Health is retainable by Europeans in hot climates', wrote Moseley with an optimism that was not universally shared, but human weakness made 'dangerous enjoyment'

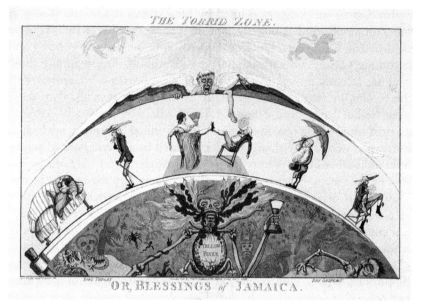

Figure 4.2 'The Torrid Zone, or, Blessings of Jamaica' (London: William Holland, 1803).
Etching with aquatint. Courtesy of the Lewis Walpole Library, Yale University.

more appealing than the 'rigid restrictions, and self-denials, which are still
necessary to keep the body and soul in unison.'[38] The luxurious West Indian
diet was also, according to Dr Robert Thomas, who practised medicine on
Nevis for nine years, 'undoubtedly highly pernicious to the constitution.'[39]
While the men were permanently intoxicated and the women dangerously
sober, Creole children were at risk from ingesting the medically and morally toxic milk of black wet nurses. Incredulous at this practice, which he
considered abhorrent and dangerous, Edward Long exclaims: 'they give
them up to a Negroe or Mulatto wet nurse, without reflecting that her
blood may be corrupted, or considering the influence which the milk may
have with respect to the disposition, as well as health, of their little ones.'[40]
    The notoriously pro-slavery Long also defends Jamaican slave owners
from abolitionist criticism: 'the planters of this island have been very
unjustly stigmatized with an accusation of treating their Negroes with
barbarity'.[41] 'There are no men, nor orders of men, in Great-Britain',
Long claims, 'possessed of more disinterested charity, philanthropy, and
clemency, than the Creole gentlemen of this island.'[42] But even Long is
quick to maintain the distinction between the British and their Creole

counterparts. The personality traits of white West Indians are associated with the tropical climate of their birth: Jamaican gentlemen are 'liable to sudden transports of anger', which come and go with all the violence of 'hurricanes'.[43] White West Indians are also physiognomically distinct from Europeans, with some climatic effects immediately recognizable in the Creole visage: 'their cheeks are remarkably high-boned, and the sockets of their eyes deeper than is commonly observed among the natives of England'.[44] The significant role of the environment in the structure of the body, however, meant that Creoles could rid their children of these physiological peculiarities: 'they, who leave it in their infancy, and pass into Britain for education, where they remain until their growth is pretty well compleated, are not so remarkably distinguished either in their features or their limbs.'[45]

British writing about Creole health was often aimed at those travelling abroad and offered instruction on which Creole habits it might be wise to imitate (staying out of the midday sun) and which to avoid (overindulgence in rich foods and other luxuries). There were also anxieties about the influx of moral and physical disease from Europeans travelling back from the Caribbean, bearing the marks of tropical climate on their bodies and carrying the threat of colonial medical and social contagion. The figure of the returning traveller tainted by colonial disease entered the metropolitan imagination: Austen's *Mansfield Park* (1814), Coleridge's 'Ancient Mariner' (1798) and William Wordsworth's 'The Brothers' (1800) participate in the construction of a medical opposition between a healthy rural England and the medical and moral dangers of the Caribbean. Charlotte Brontë's *Jane Eyre* (1847) is the work which points most explicitly to the threat of Creole disease to British health; Alan Bewell reads it as written squarely in the context of anxieties surrounding the phenomenon of tropical invalidism, arguing that Edward Rochester is forced to return from the West Indies to seek health in England – and, ultimately, in Jane as the embodiment of an Englishness that is the very opposite of the mad Creole Bertha Mason.[46] But while the representation of the infirm, languid West Indian persisted, some believed that both black and white Creoles were in fact healthier than Europeans and Africans. Black Creoles were often thought to be a better investment for slave owners than African slaves precisely because they did not need to undergo the process of 'seasoning' or acclimatization. As a consequence, they were more expensive than newly imported Africans. In 1789 the British Board of Trade published statistics which record the value of a black Creole field slave as averaging sixty pounds sterling, while a newly imported African fetched a mere thirty-six pounds.[47] Moral, as well as physical health, was at stake: the abolitionist and ship's surgeon James Ramsay's *Essay on the treatment and conversion of African Slaves in the British sugar colonies* (1784) points to the widespread understanding that black Creole slaves were 'more hardy, diligent, and trusty than Africans'.[48] Both black and white Creoles were understood to be less vulnerable to diseases of climate. For Pinckard, Europeans might benefit from disease protection after a bout of yellow fever after the disease creates an altered state of 'laxer fibre' which 'more nearly approaches that of the creoles and natives' who are less likely to suffer the dreaded yellow fever – and less likely to die from it when they do.[49] The physician Robert Thomas echoes Pinckard's description: 'the body, from long exposure to the climate, has become creolized, approaching to the confirmation of the natives, by having their original firmness of fibre reduced to the appropriate standard for continuing the healthy action under preternatural heat.'[50] Hector M'Lean, assistant inspector of hospitals at St Domingue, claims that white Creoles who have lived constantly in their native country have never been known to suffer from yellow fever.[51]

Pinckard himself participated in the negative press received by Creoles, joining Long's horrified response to various common practices such as the 'indecent' use of black wet-nurses to feed white children, and criticizing the colonial culture of 'languor and inactivity'.[52] He also viciously derides those West Indian medical practitioners who are 'only pre-eminent in ignorance' and who, 'in learning and in manners, are not far removed above the slaves.'[53] But the medical model of Creole identity deviates from the stereotypes with which it was associated, and Pinckard's personal claim to the Creole extends not only to his own body but also to a specifically Creole medical knowledge. The cause of yellow fever was unknown, and Pinckard was writing in the context of particularly high levels of public anxiety about the disease's spread across the Caribbean and North America during the 1790s. On the U.S. Eastern Seaboard, yellow fever outbreaks were having devastating effects. Martin Pernick estimates that in the first three months of the 1793 outbreak in Philadelphia between 10 and 15 per cent of the city's population died.[54] A desperate search for the cause of the disease triggered a transatlantic controversy over whether yellow fever was caused by contagion or some other means.[55] The problem originated in a broader disagreement about the category of fever itself. Febrile disorders were probably the most highly contested subject in British medicine – Michel Foucault's attention to the Enlightenment classificatory rule which 'appears as the immanent logic of morbid forms, the principle of their decipherment, and the semantic rule of their definition' is nowhere more justified than in the medical interest in the nosology of fever.[56] British medics approached yellow fever in the same way as they did domestic febrile disorders and treated it as contagious, arguing that its dominance in coastal regions indicated it was spread via maritime traffic. In the United States, many were particularly quick to lay the blame for the outbreak on the arrival of white French refugees from St Domingue. But opinion became divided between these contagionists and the non-contagionists who argued that miasmata from local swamps and effluvia from unsanitary docks were the origin of the fever.[57] With the development of vibrant transatlantic medical epistolary and print cultures, the discussion surrounding these conflicting ideas gathered momentum, and soon medical practitioners in America, Britain and the Caribbean were locked in a strenuous debate. At stake in this dispute was not only a growing American nationalism which saw foreign travellers to the new republic as a disease threat, but also the politically rooted claim over medical knowledge being asserted in varying ways amongst doctors from the three regions.[58] Mark Harrison describes the hospitals established in the British colonies as straining to mark themselves out as distinct from metropolitan medicine as they 'fostered a proudly independent medical culture that was antagonistic to the bastions of medical tradition' and 'rejected the genteel, text-based medicine of the physician elite for an avowedly empirical form of medicine supported by the twin pillars of bedside observation and post-mortem dissection'.[59]

In relation to yellow fever, there was an increasing sense of divide, played out through an Atlantic epistolary network, between British medical theory and an emerging discourse of empiricism which American and Caribbean practitioners argued was based on first-hand experience as a more accurate mode of gathering knowledge. Charles Caldwell, a Philadelphian physician, wrote that British doctors, who were 'removed a thousand leagues from the scene of action' and only had experience of the limited diseases to be found in 'a few country-towns', had no place writing about yellow fever.[60] In Britain, the contagionist model of yellow fever maintained strong endorsement among the medical elite, including members of the Royal College of Physicians. Non-contagionism, by contrast, became prominent amongst Americans and British medics who had practised overseas. Challenging the doctrine of contagionism became part of a symbolic attempt by American and colonial doctors to establish the authority of primary local experience over what they regarded as the theoretical speculation of British physicians. A powerful minority, and especially those in the medical military such as Colin Chisholm, continued to support the contagionist theory and made forceful attempts to undermine the growth of non-contagionism – but Pinckard is a notable exception within this group. Writing that 'the presence of contagion, is in no degree, necessary to the production of this fever', Pinckard explicitly grounds his description of the process of medical creolization in anti-contagionist argument:

> Indeed its invasion is governed by circumstances very opposite to all the known laws of contagion: for, in proportion as the body approaches the creole structure, so is it able to support the change of temperature, and to resist the fatal effects of the seasoning malady. If the constitution, either from natural organization, or from long residence, be assimilated to the climate, i.e. if it be reduced to the common standard of the creoles, it has nothing to apprehend from the disease:—but if it be not, the fever will, assuredly, make its attack, without waiting for any such cause as contagion.[61]

It was precisely the disease's partiality for fresh blood which marked it out as a non-contagious disease. If yellow fever were contagious, Pinckard writes, 'it must be a contagion of a very uncommon and peculiar appetite', for it was unheard-of that an 'active and wide-spreading contagion, prevailing in any particular country, should, expressly, avoid the inhabitants of that country, and only lie in wait for strangers'.[62] Arguing that medical practice should be grounded in primary observation, Pinckard stresses the difference between seeing yellow fever patients on a daily basis and the abstracted advice of those writing in theory, and from a distance:

> From experience, and examination of the diseased appearances, I may hope for more accurate elucidation, and perhaps be enabled to arrive at some general maxim, which, in vain, I have looked for in the discordant opinions of the ingenious men who have devoted their pens to this great – this interesting, and most important subject.[63]

The prioritization of experience is carried through in the case of his own encounter with yellow fever, for which he employs only those remedies which 'my own sensations had dictated'.[64] Writing back to the metropole, Pinckard participates in a colonial medical discourse that not only placed the Creole body at the centre of its claims but also belonged to a specifically colonial body of medical knowledge being developed by Caribbean and American medical practitioners which argued against the British medical status quo, grounded as it was in abstract ideas rather than local knowledge. It is this sense of the Creole's curative possibilities within an Atlantic world haunted by death and disease, of a Creole epistemology which might function in the manner of a corrective to metropolitan learning, as well as Pinckard's model of creolization as a process of medical, personal and social transition, that form useful lenses through which to examine the ways in which the Creole is imagined in contemporary literary works such as John Thelwall's transatlantic philosophical and social commentary *The Daughter of Adoption: A Tale of Modern Times.*

'Not One of the World's Family'

By the time he published *The Daughter of Adoption* pseudonymously in 1801, John Thelwall had, before his period of political exile, penned two anti-imperial dramas, *Incle and Yarico* (1787) and *The Incas* (1792), reclaiming what had become sentimental New World fables and setting them to his own anti-slavery and liberal ideas. The novel develops his abolitionist stance and unites it with a Wollstonecraftian perspective on women and marriage and a reassessment of contemporary radical politics to form a work of the kind Jon Klancher calls 'republican romance'.[65] A post-Jacobin fiction that draws on elements from gothic and sentimental genres, the story is set in England and Saint Domingue and coincides with the beginning of the Haitian Revolution in 1791.[66] Thelwall was writing in 1798–1800, just after Pinckard, who arrived in Barbados in 1796 and whose letters end the following year with the arrival of orders to proceed to Santo Domingo. The empire was booming and the abolitionist movement was struggling against the tide of anti-revolutionary feeling that had emerged in the context of French bloodshed. There remained anti-Creole sentiment, but this was fostered less vehemently by the ameliorationists who now led the slavery debate than by the abolitionists from whom they had won political ground. In his version of the slave uprising, Thelwall draws on Bryan Edwards's *An Historical Survey of the French Colony in the Island of St. Domingo* (1797), a work notorious for representing the revolution in the most grisly and unsympathetic terms. Likening the revolutionary slaves to 'so many famished tygers thirsting for human blood', Edwards describes the attack on the 'peaceful and unsuspicious planters' as brutal and ruthless: 'death, in all its horrors, or cruelties and outrages compared to which immediate death is mercy, await alike the old and the young, the matron, the virgin, and the helpless infant'.[67] Thelwall uses some of the bloodiest scenes from Edwards's account to debate the moral possibilities and social processes of revolution, reflecting on the ethics of violence in collective action through the story of the St Domingue uprising. Sitting atop the mountains of St Domingue, the young protagonist Henry Montfort exclaims: 'what a scene, and what an hour … to hatch

treason in!' 'What a scene, and what an hour, sir,' his companion Edmunds
returns, 'to make one forget that treason was ever necessary in the world.'⁶⁸
The revolutionary island presents the 'scene' in which to examine liberal
politics in practice, to criticize the weaknesses of sentimental abolitionism
and to partner anti-slavery argument with a Jacobin social agenda:

> these rocks, these pendant forests—this deep solitude, with the foaming
> eddies beneath, and all those splendid luminaries above, might only
> embolden us, by a sense of security, to question the authority of our
> oppressors, and to demonstrate that against the ravages of foreign usurpa-
> tion, at least, it is at all times lawful both to conspire and to act.⁶⁹

Thelwall's political perspective is Atlantic: he uses the context of slavery,
violence and rebellion to deliberate issues concerning social resistance,
education, gender and marriage in relation to Britain and its colonies.⁷⁰

His Jacobin view was certainly not shared by Pinckard, who makes very
clear his views on the 'maniacal fever of change' sweeping across Europe as
a consequence of the 'infectious revolution' in France.⁷¹ But, like Pinckard,
Thelwall explores Creole identities and creolized social practices and
processes in relation to the far-reaching changes happening during this
period of empire. Examining colonial society on both sides of the Atlantic,
Thelwall associates Creoles with crisis and change, and positions them in
terms of a broader Atlantic view crucial to the development of modern
society. And, like Pinckard's, Thelwall's understanding of medicine was
directly related to his ideas about empire, race and slavery. *The Daughter
of Adoption* was composed during a period when Thelwall's failing agricultural endeavours 'drove him upon expedients of literary projection';
but, significantly, this was also the period in which he was beginning to
establish his medical elocutionary practice.⁷² Having been a 'most conspicuous' member of the Physical Society at Guy's Hospital in the early 1790s,
Thelwall's most significant medical influences were the surgeon and republican Astley Cooper and the anatomist Henry Cline, to whom Thelwall
later addressed his *Letter to Henry Cline* (1810), which outlines his ideas
in relation to the 'Science of human speech'.⁷³ His medical and scientific
interests are 'inextricable from his radical politics', and inform the way
Thelwall structures Creole identities and Atlantic social politics in medical
terms.⁷⁴ Like Pinckard, Thelwall identifies Creoles with health, and not
just disease, as he uses the figure of the Creole to respond to issues relating
to adaptation, degeneration, heredity and the relationship between natural character and external environment, and explores the possibility of a
Creole cure for the English body and body politic.

The novel ostensibly focuses on Henry, son of the domineering, licentious English slave-owner Percival Montfort and his abolitionist wife Amelia Montfort, and the story follows Henry's moral and sentimental education. But it is through his Creole characters and colonial context that Thelwall's philosophical and political ideas emerge. Just as Pinckard sees the violent process of medical creolization as one which propels the sufferer into a feverish reconsideration of national identity, so Thelwall views Creole familial and domestic structures and social practices as a lens through which to scrutinize British ones. Both authors see chaotic potential in the figure of the Creole. For Pinckard, this erupts during the mental and physical crisis during the process of creolization: an 'indescribable' moment of 'distracting incoherences', 'deadly horror' and 'unaccountable change' when the natural world is deranged and disordered.[75] In Thelwall's novel, the disorder inherent in the Creole is marked by the repeated attention to the kinds of extra-institutional familial and romantic relationships widely associated with colonial societies. Central to Thelwall's political aims is the argument against institutionalized familial structures determined by consanguineous or marital laws. The novel aligns the questions raised by Creole identities and transatlantic societies concerning birthrights, consanguinity and heredity with its examination of women's subjugation within marriage and the legitimacy of children born outside it. Marcus Wood argues that Thelwall's abolitionist works present 'one of the most trenchant pleas for the ideological unification of abolition and reform theory'.[76] In *The Daughter of Adoption*, that plea is structured in terms of a domestic parallel to the Haitian Revolution. Alongside the battle between Amelia and Percival Montfort over Henry's education and Percival's masculine 'counter-revolution' against Amelia's genteel parenting practices, Thelwall's complicated webs of adoptions, extra-marital relationships and non-traditional families, developed around the separated Creole siblings Lucius and Seraphina, are used to examine issues of ancestry, class, education, kinship, nationhood, sexual morality and the movement of wealth.[77]

Thelwall did not form a good impression of the white West Indians whom he encountered at anatomy and physiology lectures in London in the early 1790s, describing the Creole character in terms of 'childish vivacity', 'unfeeling and tyrannical vehemence' and a 'sort of hoggish voluptuousness'.[78] The novel paints the generality of West Indians in terms of their 'pride, ferocity and effeminate licentiousness' as well as the usual luxurious excess, violent temper, intellectual ennui and 'sickly delicacy'.[79] Far more dangerous than these traits, though, was the Creole notoriety for sexual dissipation. Connecting West Indians to public concern about the potential for consanguineous, sexual and moral pollution that they represented, Thelwall's re-evaluation of the moral and political dimensions of marriage and other relationships is structured by a series of transatlantic deceptions, discoveries and reunions in which incest plays a central role.[80] Seraphina narrowly escapes various incestuous scenarios (first with her lost brother, Lucius Moroon, then with her lover Henry, who is mistakenly believed to be her brother). Incest is understood as a specifically colonial practice, with what the novel describes as the Caribbean moral 'confusion' seen at its extreme in the romantic relationship between Moroon and his adoptive mulatto mother, which continues after they murder her husband when she and Moroon 'live together in the most open and undisguised intercourses of criminality'.[81] Percival Montfort sums up Thelwall's vision of the social disorder created by such forms of sexual and familial derangement when, cast onto his deathbed by guilt and the ill-effects of a life of corruption, he regrets the colonial debauchery which has led to the suspected incest between Henry and Seraphina: 'I—shall see all Nature's abominations thickening round me!—a sea of chaos of unnatural lusts—All order mingle—dall connections jarred, all ties, and all affinities confounded—with uncle fathers, and sister wives.'[82] The 'sea of chaos' surrounding Thelwall's acts of incest also washes over the novel's interracial, extra-marital and non-consanguineous relationships, as human affinities are explored within and without their institutional and biological ties through the figure of the Creole as representative of alternative forms of social relations.

But while Thelwall presents colonial society as debauched and disordered, he also identifies Creoles as a catalyst for positive social change. Renowned as a space of sexual and social freedoms, the colonies function as an imaginative site of liberation. Pregnant and unmarried, Seraphina defies the limitations imposed on women by challenging the world's dim view of her relationship with Henry: she identifies as his partner in principle, whether or not they have uttered the 'gingle of mystic phrases' that is the empty symbolism of the marriage vow. Seraphina, echoing Wollstonecraft, describes marriage based on matches of wealth as 'legalised prostitution', and, like her Godwinian adoptive father Parkinson, understands a relationship (whether filial or romantic) 'originating in sympathy', rather than a 'frigid sense of obligation' to be as 'indissoluble' as 'that of nature'.[83] Sarah M. S. Pearsall emphasizes the significant differences between colonial and metropolitan sexual relations: 'that the British departed from metropolitan norms in adopting local systems of gender organization, in which non-legal unions replaced legal ones, was one of the reasons that the British Creole became such a questionable character in metropolitan eyes.'[84] Thelwall's use of a Creole figure to make the argument against the prioritization of the marriage vow is pertinent, therefore, in the focus it places on colonial domestic and social practices. Through his disorderly Creole families, Thelwall uses colonial societies and their particular racial and domestic dynamics to intervene in transatlantic issues.

Ultimately, the chaotic potential of the Creole, and the moments of crisis and rupture associated with colonial society, incline towards catharsis, resolution and cure. Seraphina's sentimental education helps Montfort Sr to acknowledge his wrongs just as they cast him onto his deathbed. And her near-misses with the incestuous relations associated with Creole society only serve to purify Seraphina of any metropolitan social and sexual ills. While Lucius represents the very worst elements of the usual Creole stereotypes, Seraphina is portrayed as 'a sort of phenomenon—a literary Creole—a female philosopher'.[85] It is through Seraphina's medical, moral and sentimental beneficence that Thelwall brings home the lessons of empire, and her liberal values which form the Creole cure to English medical and social disorder. Seraphina nurses her lover Henry back to mental and physical health after his Caribbean travels and an overdose of the 'Creolean life' trigger a rapid decline and a series of illnesses worsened by the negative influence of his father and those false friends who threaten to pull him into ruin.[86] Seraphina's curative 'physical and moral operations' and the 'medicinal power in the tears of beauty' are required when his life of dissipation leads to weakened spirits and his 'mind's health' becomes 'the prey of contagious diseases.'[87] While the physician can 'only prescribe to the symptoms of the disorder' and the surgeon 'could only dress the exterior wound', Seraphina is the 'true panacea', who 'from the precious lymbics of her eyes, distilled the healing drops that went radically to the inmost causes, and stopped the threatened gangrene of the heart'.[88] Like the 'alternate medico-educational system' of Thelwall's own elocutionary practice, Seraphina's treatment operates outside the bounds of normative medical practice.[89] With the good Dr Pengarron himself acknowledging the 'superior efficacy of her prescriptions', conventional medicine cannot help Henry, but Seraphina's treatments prove effective.[90] The 'change of scene, and change of air, and little travelling about' prescribed by Pengarron (along with most doctors of the age) cannot help Henry's father, Percival, whose innate West Indian tendencies have quickened the degeneration that is the inevitable due of slave-ownership. Nor can it cure Amelia, who suffers from a cancer gravely aggravated by her fears for Henry's safety while in St Domingue, where he is not only trapped in the midst of the violent uprising but also at risk from 'the ravages of all those diseases so frequently fatal to Europeans'.[91] The English constitution is corrupted by empire, but repaired through a practice of sympathetic medicine informed by colonial knowledge. Thelwall's model of successful medical and social cure eschews the fashionable prescriptions of the day for Seraphina's sentimental medical practice, which jointly treats body and mind, just as Thelwall's elocutionary therapy was firmly rooted in the idea that 'physical and moral phænomena run a circle, and become alternately cause and effect'.[92] Overturning Creole stereotypes, the novel instead emphasizes the importance of drawing on the lessons of colonialism to develop an Atlantic perspective on the social and political problems of the day. Seraphina, Thelwall's medicinal Creole, brings fresh insights to metropolitan questions, and some of the health and hope associated with Pinckard's model of the medically creolized.

Thelwall's use of Seraphina's white Creole femininity as a model for Atlantic health can be found in other contemporary examples, and most explicitly in Helena Wells's *Constantia Neville; or, the West Indian* (1800), a novel about a white Barbadian woman who moves to England aged thirteen with her British parents.[93] A work of conduct literature for young women (Wells and her sister ran a school in London, and Wells also published her opinions on the subject of women's education and precarious social position in non-fictional didactic works), the novel's ideas about global health and illness form the backdrop to a commentary on gender in British society.[94] Like Thelwall, Wells uses her Creole protagonist to illuminate metropolitan manners and mores within the context of changing global social networks, and, like Seraphina, Constantia explicitly refutes the stereotype of the lethargic and sickly Creole woman. Instead, colonial illness is displaced onto English bodies: in *Constantia Neville* it is not languorous Creoles but rather the narrow-minded and snobbish English gentlewomen who suffer from the nervous illnesses attendant on indolence and luxury.

Constantia and Seraphina each underline the significance of Creoles to eighteenth- and nineteenth-century discourses of gender and sexuality. In her examination of slavery's role in the emerging elaboration of national and sexual freedoms, Carolyn Vellenga Berman argues that the slavery debates had a significant role to play in efforts to change women's domestic circumstances and that the Creole was 'central to revisions of gender and family norms in nineteenth-century fiction'.[95] Constantia is the conduit through which the novel's (young, female) readers are given the benefit of Wells's social instruction, with the Creole protagonist used as a foil to British snobbery, moral fault and expectations of women's behaviour.

Constantia's struggle to find her place in English society, and the strength of her rational perspective, are couched in terms of health and illness as she is held up as a medical and moral exemplar for a new Atlantic world. Wells was herself born in South Carolina to Scottish parents, and in her vision English social hierarchies are realigned in relation to postcolonial national identities. As Constantia's sense of identity shifts during the course of the novel from British, to Barbadian, to a rootless feeling of 'no particular attachment', it becomes evident that her Creole identity and transatlantic experiences have formed her sense of herself as, in her words but echoing Oliver Goldsmith's work of the same title, a 'citizen of the world'.[96] Unlike Thelwall, Wells does not permit women to exceed the confines of a polite education, and her Atlantic world remains grounded in a strict racial hierarchy upheld by the medicalized rhetoric of physical and moral contagion. By contrast, Seraphina's identity as outsider makes her unafraid of the social exclusion which inevitably follows her relationship with Henry:

> I stand not in the predicament of others of my sex, who if they are excluded from the society of those who have the world's respect about them, fall, of necessity among the abandoned and the vile.

Seraphina's love of colonial retirement over metropolitan excess insulates her from the world's judgement as she inhabits a moral space 'where the vapours of contagion cannot reach me; and, in a region of contamination, I can still be pure'.[97] As the language of disease suggests, Thelwall's interest in casting a Wollstonecraftian eye over familial and marital institutions is articulated through ideas about deterioration and medical and social corruption – while her brother Lucius represents the dangers of incestuous 'pollution', and the 'chaos' of moral confusion and natural disorder, Seraphina is the novel's voice of frustrated medical and moral sense. With her eventual marriage to Henry, Seraphina symbolizes the possibility of healing, redemption and a new social unity that originates outside the normal bounds of relationships based on consanguinity or social institution. Her rational, objective view springs precisely from her sense of being a colonial outsider who does not live by the same domestic norms, or, as she puts it, 'I am not one of the world's family.'[98] While Constantia Neville's understanding of global health is borne of her sense of universal belonging as a 'citizen of the world', Seraphina's medical, moral and sentimental compass is clearly associated with her position as outsider and exclusion from the 'world's family'. Seraphina, 'a female historian, a philosopher, and a poet', is identified as the unbiased observer – her Creole identity and upbringing in a rural colonial enclave affording her a critical eye on English social behaviours.[99] The New World, for Thelwall, is a space of danger, disease and immorality, but also of fresh possibilities in which alternative models of romantic and filial interaction might be mapped out through Seraphina's colonial proto-feminism. Pinckard and Thelwall each claim the Creole as a figure of liberation, whether in terms of health, social position or reform. Like Constantia Neville, who finally comes to see her position as outsider in terms of universal belonging as a 'citizen of the world', Pinckard has the 'freedom' of the West Indies and Seraphina finally joins the 'world's family'. Rather than being a figure of exclusion and ignominious caricature, the Creole is, in these instances, a liberated insider within a newly connected Atlantic community.

The Creole's outsider status as non-indigenous body also has a key role to play in examinations of the relationship between nature and environment. In the wake of Kant's *On the Different Races of Man* (*Über die verschiedenen Rassen der Menschen*, 1775), which proposed that natural constitutions were expressed in different ways according to local climatic and environmental circumstances, the question of interaction between predispositions, inherited traits and environment became a central problem for the life sciences. In Pinckard's model of medical creolization, this informs his exploration of the significance of natural susceptibility to disease. The impact of disease environments on individual identity is central to the idea of the medical Creole: the extreme suffering of yellow fever brings great changes to both body and mind and, as the fevered European body 'approaches the creole structure', so too does a shift in identity towards the Creole occur.[100] But some people are more inclined to undergo the process of creolization: while yellow fever attacks Europeans 'in preference to Creoles, negroes, and those who, by a long-continued residence, have become acclimatés', the disease also discriminates between new arrivals. It is known for being 'partial', Pinckard writes, to the most 'healthy and robust, and in general, those who are the earliest subjected to great exertions, and the high degrees of temperature, are sooner seized, and more rapidly destroyed, than those of laxer fibre, or those who have the opportunity of becoming more gradually acclimatés'.[101] Women, children, and those with less hardened bodily structures were not as vulnerable to the creolizing effects of yellow fever. In *The Daughter of Adoption*, there is a similarly intricate relationship between the significance of environment and that of natural character, grounded in Thelwall's particular strand of scientific materialism evinced in his argument that life is formed in the dependent relation between the organization of matter and external stimuli.[102] As ideas about inherited characteristics began to be conceptualized as a relation between parental and filial dispositions, Thelwall tests the plasticity of human temperament and the power of environment over inherited characteristics through the separated siblings Lucius and Seraphina.[103] While the lascivious, murderous Lucius was lost in a sea storm and taken in by a family of mulattoes, the Wollstonecraftian feminine ideal and 'fair Creole' Seraphina was given up by her poverty-stricken mother and raised in seclusion by the Godwinian philosopher Parkinson on the pastoral fringes of colonial life in St Domingue.[104] The novel examines the effects of social environment on character, demonstrating the importance of education, the corruptive influence of colonial greed and the significance of environment in relation to the possibility and processes of human change. But there is another kind of 'Creole' in Thelwall's novel who points to the significance of in-born traits and, therefore, to the different formations of the arrangement between natural structure and external environment. Percival Montfort, though English by birth, is portrayed as West Indian by nature. Tempted by the 'new scenes of riot and profligacy', and hardened by 'familiarity with those tyrannic cruelties which necessarily spring out of the distinctions of master and slave', Montfort begins to feel increasingly at home in the Caribbean, 'the only country of an avaricious mind'.[105] Ultimately, Montfort becomes creolized by his participation in the slave trade to the point where 'in every point of view, he became a very West-Indian'.[106] But his colonial lifestyle during a six-year residence only confirms his natural inclinations: 'the passions and vices of the climate, or, to speak more correctly, the habits of the order, or *disorder*, of society there established, had seized with irresistible violence, on a mind already predisposed to their influence.'[107] While Seraphina represents the liberal idea that education and environment win out over the accident of birth, the elder Montfort's West Indian predisposition demonstrates the role of his 'constitutional temperament', originating in 'melancholic humours' and functioning to undermine his Englishness.

Pinckard, too, queries the nature of national identity through the ambiguity of Creole identity. Commenting on Barbadians' sense of national pride, Pinckard writes that their sense of distinction as belonging to one of the 'old' Caribbean colonies prompts an unlikely claim to 'hereditary rank and privilege from priority of, establishment'.[108] This patriotic sensibility, described by G. K. Lewis as representing the 'embryonic forms' of 'Creole nationalism', manifests in what Pinckard describes as 'the sentiment conveyed by the vulgar expression so common in the island— "neither Charib, nor Creole, but true Barbadian"'.[109] Enslaved people also participate in this sense of native superiority: 'ask one of them if he was imported, or is a Creole, and he immediately replies – "Me neder Chrab, nor Creole, Massa!—me troo Barbadian born."[110] Barbadian nationalism supersedes Creole identity, which in Pinckard's understanding becomes an amorphous category that might be claimed or disclaimed by various social groups depending on cultural affiliation, or physical predisposition to or experience of colonial disease.

Creoles are commonly described in postcolonial studies as inhabiting the marginal spaces of binary oppositions – centre and periphery, black and white, authority and subject – and this liminality is usually understood to undermine categories of national and racial identity. It is the Creole's 'disturbing capacity for shape-shifting', as Berman writes, which pulls at the threads of a cohesive sense of English nationhood abroad.[111] 'All Europeans', Pinckard is warned in Barbados, 'gradually lapse into the same indolent indulgence as the natives'.[112] While Pinckard's medical creolization triggers processes of physiological, mental and social change, Seraphina's racial identity is destabilized when she is identified as born of white British parents. In *The Daughter of Adoption*, then, the Creole is an ambiguous, transitory identity that might be passed through, rather than settled in. For neither Pinckard nor Thelwall does the Creole's mobility undermine Englishness; indeed, both articulate the priority of English national identity and cultural practices. Yet, through their different models of national identity and environmental influence, Pinckard and Thelwall both rely on but also resist the stereotype of the greedy, hot-tempered, ignorant and languid Creole who is defined by a tropical birth. Both also suggest that Creoles can be made as well as born, and examine the relationship between what in Pinckard's text is framed in terms of the differences between native Creoles and 'acclimatés' or 'creolisés' and in Thelwall's is played out in terms of natural 'propensities' and the influence of environment and social 'habitude', demonstrating the tension between nature and environment through the figure of the Creole.[113]

Creole Modernities

These explorations of inherited traits, education, gender, knowledge, marriage and nationhood show the significant role of Creoles in changing cultural relationships between colony and metropole during this period of a prospering but anxious empire. The significance of Creoles to Thelwall's political philosophy and Pinckard's postcolonial ideas of selfhood points to their role in the emergence of colonial modernity – a phrase which I use not to suggest a separation from a metropolitan version but rather to indicate the centrality of colonial peoples, politics and spaces to the history of modern societies. Indeed, *The Daughter of Adoption* and *Notes on the West Indies* not only suggest that Creoles are central to the social movements that constitute colonial modernity, but also articulate the position that modernity is inherently colonial. Emerging in part from the Creole's associations with mobility and contingency, this modernity is marked by ideas about change – both at the level of the individual, and in broader social, political and epistemological dimensions. While Seraphina embodies Thelwall's Jacobin agenda and its emergence through colonial peoples, politics and spaces, Pinckard's interest in Creoles gestures towards the long transition to modernity as underpinned by the economic, individual, medical and social changes wrought by colonialism. The extreme suffering of yellow fever brings with it feelings of tremendous 'confusion and disorder', before the terrifyingly 'inverted' natural order of disease gives way to a sense of reconciliation and a new vision of the world, one created through a traumatic process of personal and social transition that gives embodied meaning to Fernando Ortiz's account of 'transculturation' as a painful 'process of transition from one culture to another, and its manifold social repercussions'.[114] Pinckard is certainly not writing from the same political perspective as Thelwall, yet the upheaval in body, mind and nation in his disease narrative marks out his sense of a medicalized modernity, and as the feverish body is racked by the 'convulsive throes of bringing forth a new world', disease and its creolizing effects activate such 'unaccountable change' that Pinckard cannot help but see the world in a new light.

In Pinckard's West Indies, the medical and natural knowledge at stake in the disease-ridden islands is crucial to empire. His local, Creole and empirical model of knowledge echoes Grainger in its emphasis on the islands as sites of modernity in which Pinckard hopes that 'local experience' and new information and resources might prove to be of global use.[115] In his early letters, knowledge is starkly metropolitan and Pinckard reserves the strictest scorn for the West Indian medics who set about their practice 'with all the bold confidence of ignorance ... without visiting the schools of Europe'.[116] Later, however, he seeks out local knowledge and argues for the primary role of regional experience over universal, abstract logic in the treatment of yellow fever and other diseases (although when writing from Berbice, Dutch Guyana, Pinckard finds disappointment in even the 'most eminent practitioners of the colony', who in their treatment of disease appear to be as dogmatic as those in the metropole with their 'one certain faith—one given routine of practice, from which it were heresy to commit the slightest deviation').[117] A wealth of new knowledge to be uncovered in the West Indies remains untapped: despairing of colonists' commercial agendas, Pinckard complains that 'no extensive progress can be expected to be made in the different branches of the natural history of the country, so long as it shall continue to be visited only from views of pecuniary gain'.[118] Divorcing scientific from commercial endeavour, Pinckard stresses that his own work is inspired by a simple but 'ardent' desire to gain new information from the 'novel scenes' around him. He does not travel to the West Indies 'engaged in a deliberate voyage of discovery', however. Rather than the 'systematic' bodies of knowledge constructed by Enlightenment medicine and natural history, Pinckard claims that it is 'more from the daily, common round, than from the great and blazoned events' that 'just knowledge' is acquired.[119] While he claims no great and blazoned discovery, Pinckard's letters document the different ways in which the contested knowledge developed in the colonies was seen as contributing to the development of a larger body of Atlantic science and medicine, and reveal the tensions between colonial and metropolitan models of knowledge that form a key part of the history of post-Enlightenment thought.[120]

The Daughter of Adoption's subtitle is 'a tale of modern times'. Modernity, for Thelwall, is a colonial category. What Judith Thompson describes as the novel's 'complex interrelations between domestic and colonial affairs' make the point that modern problems, politics and ideas can only be fully considered in relation to the globalized perspective of empire.[121] To Henry, the West Indies is a space of radical modernity that opens up imaginative and political possibilities beyond the national borders of Britain or St Domingue: 'contemplation, that began at home, gradually extended itself to more distant objects. The physical and moral universe expanded before him—the Chronicles of Time, and the world of Fiction.'[122] Born from such universalizing philosophy is Thelwall's Creole and creolizing family – one that sets aside the ties of obligation for those of feeling, which has its roots in a Jacobin argument against consanguinity and heredity in their aristocratic institutional forms, and which sees its success in the happy ending for Henry and Seraphina. The novel ends on an idealistic note, with the celebration of the family of choice in Pengarron's decree that he will 'play a bachelor's trick' and make Henry and Seraphina's unborn child his sole heir, trumping the consanguineous debts he owes to the 'rascally legion of second and third cousins that have been gaping open-mouthed like so many carrion crows, for my death, these ten or twenty years, in hopes that each may have a mouthful of my carcase'.[123] But Henry will have 'none of the Gothic savagery by which the bonds of affinity are cracked asunder – by which the first born is rendered a lordly tyrant, and the rest dependent slaves', so Pengarron instead adopts the white West Indian baby whom Henry, Edmunds and Parkinson had saved from the arms of its dead mother in the midst of the uprising.[124]

While Thelwall celebrates these Creole connections, postcolonial expectations of Romantic abolitionism have left most critics disappointed in the constraints of Thelwall's anti-racist scope. Peter Kitson argues that the novel is unsuccessful in its attempt to grapple with 'the limits of abolitionism and the failure of the Romantic imagination to fully comprehend or represent the reality of the accumulated violence of the global system of slavery and colonialism', floundering in incomprehension when confronted with the extremity of revolutionary and racial violence.[125] Michael Scrivener points out that Thelwall 'only mildly disrupts the racist categories, because the utopian community formed around Seraphina and Henry in north Yorkshire is all-white and socially homogenous'.[126] A. A. Markley writes that Seraphina's 'purely white' racial status severely limits the reformist possibilities of the novel.[127] While Seraphina may be identified as such by the end of the novel, however, her earlier racialized identification as West Indian (the eyes 'somewhat too dark for hazel' and brown hair 'glossed with a tint of orient') and her journey through the various queries and misunderstandings over her heritage are just as significant, and bear attention as a sign of Thelwall's interest in blurring racial markers.[128] Judith Thompson argues that Seraphina, 'who looks white but whose blood is tainted, becomes the receptacle for all the culture's fears and suspicions about not only racial, but sexual and class miscegenation and instability'. But while in other texts such ambiguous racial identity is a cause of deep anxiety, for Thelwall it is 'the means by which he engages in a radical subversion and critique of a culture hypocritically obsessed with purity of blood and birth'.[129] As Thompson's reading of Seraphina's ambiguous racialization suggests, what the novel is successful in doing is aligning the questions raised by Creoles and colonial society concerning consanguinity and heredity to its radical examination of women's subjugation within marriage and the legitimacy of children born outside it, as well as other issues relating to class and education. Thelwall's Creole connections signify the Atlantic reach of his novel, and demonstrate the deep association between abolitionism and metropolitan political agitation.[130]

Significantly, Thelwall's focus on transatlantic connections does not represent the model of colonial society as a microcosmic 'little England' – a term most widely associated with describing the Barbadian upper and middle classes and first documented in Daniel McKinnen's *A Tour Through the British West Indies* (1804).[131] David Lambert has shown how important this model of the Creole was in Barbadian claims to rights and identity through a discourse of 'allegiance and indispensability to the British Empire'.[132] Describing the Godwinian Parkinson's Caribbean exile as an 'allegory' of Thelwall's own exile in Wales, Michael Scrivener, like others, reads the novel's colonial setting, more broadly, as an allegory for metropolitan politics.[133] But *The Daughter of Adoption*'s Creole families in fact represent what Elizabeth Maddock Dillon calls 'the colonial relation': a way of describing colonial society that implies 'not a one-way vector of power (in which the metropole dominates the colony) but an assemblage of connections that shapes peoples and polities around the Atlantic littoral (including the metropole) in the form of colonial modernity'.[134] In her book on Thelwall in the Wordsworth circle, Thompson emphasizes the importance of the idea of reciprocity to Thelwall's literary and philosophical vision.[135] And, just as Thelwall's medical practice was grounded in ideas about the necessarily reciprocal relationships between body and mind, doctor and patient, and the idea that 'physical and moral phænomena run a circle', so too was his model of society formed around the reciprocity of metropole and colony, and on the 'social equality and reciprocal love' of his Creole families.[136] While Thelwall uses the West Indies to mirror British social problems, he also sees the colonial example as providing a space for philosophical and political reflection that might be channelled back to the metropole in the form of radical social change, and makes colonial problems contiguous with metropolitan ones.[137] By directly connecting the debates about gender, marriage and consanguineous versus sympathetic and intellectual relationships to colonial issues relating to adaptation, tropical degeneration, Creole characteristics and inherited traits versus education, Thelwall makes the case for a circum-Atlantic Jacobinism which calls for reform across the empire by facing up to the 'reciprocal barbarities' of revolutionary violence and colonialism.[138] In its efforts to make a meaningful comparison of British and Caribbean social politics in a way that eschews sentimental abolitionism for a more intellectual debate, to examine gender inequality and the slave/marriage economies and to bring home the lessons of empire through Seraphina's creolizing cure, the novel sets an important agenda for an Atlantic Jacobin and indeed a colonial proto-feminist perspective.

Creoles and Atlantic Medical and Natural Knowledge

Pinckard's and Thelwall's texts depict colonial modernities formed around Creole identities and medical knowledge. The various models of the Creole at stake in these works are each underpinned by the importance of West Indian identities, cultural practices and nationalisms within a changing Atlantic world, and are couched in terms of global medical knowledge allied to ideas about a more universal moral and sentimental benevolence. Creoles come to stand for consanguineous pollution, moral confusion and ill-health, as well as postcolonial national identities. They bring with them chaotic potential, symbolizing the complications and moments of rupture – whether medical or mental crises or familial and social catastrophe – of Atlantic intercultural movement and processes of individual and social adaptation and change. Unusually, though, Pinckard and Thelwall, like Wells, align Creoles with health, rather than disease and, ultimately, each of their central Creole figures serves to restore a sense of social equilibrium. For the medically creolized, this means the reordering of the tropical world which occurs once the suffering of fever seasoning has effected a reconciliation with the new environment. Seraphina also reconciles herself with her new reality, accepting a compromise between colonial radical principles and metropolitan social norms – but not before she has cured Henry and Percival of their mental, moral and physical disease. It is the sense of the Creole as a figure at the centre of global health that distinguishes these texts, which reveal that the stereotypical image of the languorous, sickly white West Indian is only one aspect of the significant role played by white West Indians in Atlantic discourses of health and illness. While the Creole is identified with social chaos, blurring the boundaries of familial and national identities, it is also a figure which brings health and a sense of cosmopolitan perspective.

Pinckard's idea of medical creolization as a violent and painful process of medical, mental and social transition helps to inform readings of contemporary Creole figures by alerting postcolonial analyses of the Creole to the centrality of medical discourse to the historical understanding of Atlantic identities. Folded into historical and postcolonial accounts of the Creole should be a far more detailed understanding of the medical dimensions of colonial existence. Pinckard's emphasis on local experience, for example, and the mobilization of that knowledge as part of changing colonial identities, speak directly to Brathwaite's understanding of Creoles as having 'intimate knowledge' of and being 'committed by the experience and attachment to the West Indies', as well as to Mary Louise

Pratt's account of Creole culture as enshrining 'a glorified American nature and a glorified American antiquity' which 'existed as ideological constructs, sources of Americanist identification and pride fuelling the growing sense of separateness from Europe'.[139] *Notes on the West Indies* articulates the intimate relationship between this local natural knowledge and ideas about Creole identity, as the process of medical creolization suggests a deep and embodied local understanding that underpins colonial existence and marks the importance of medical models of the body to colonial identities.

Situated within discourses of health, illness and cure, Pinckard's and Thelwall's Creoles articulate a vision of the West Indies as a site of knowledge gathering and exchange. West Indians were crucial to the production and circulation of Atlantic forms of knowledge which often competed with metropolitan ones, and discussions about the role of the Creole in the articulation of Atlantic medical ideas are productively approached as questions of epistemology.[140] The relationship between theoretical and empirical knowledge was particularly important: claims to the value of primary observation underpinned Creole patriotisms and the struggle to sustain the plantation economy in the face of abolitionist protest. 'Against our theory', Pinckard writes from Barbados, the West Indians 'urge experience.'[141] Pinckard's model of the Creole is underpinned by an emphasis on the importance of local knowledge over metropolitan medical doctrine, and his medical 'creolisés' have the hard-won freedom of the New World and the strength of empirically grounded knowledge on their side as they bend towards their 'introduction to a new existence'.[142] The process of creolization is modelled on the idea of crisis which brings new understanding in its wake: just as Pinckard's medical Creole must undergo the throes of suffering and look death 'full in the face' in order to reap yellow fever's medical rewards, Thelwall's Henry must live out the full extent of his moral and sentimental disorder before he is able to accept Seraphina's cure.[143] These Creole 'lessons' are grounded in alternative forms of knowledge: as Pinckard documents the uneasy relationship between theory and experience, Thelwall's colonial metropolitans struggle to find a compromise between old and new, metropole and colony, Creole and English, radical and pragmatic. Embodying the synthesis of old knowledge and new world, Seraphina tests Thelwall's own determined empiricism and scientific materialism as she struggles to find her place in the 'modern times' of the novel's title.[144] Here, then, Creoles present the opportunity for sustained reflection on what constitutes knowledge and its borders, categories and politics in the context of empire.

The medical dimensions of the Creole also suggest new ways of looking at the position of West Indian identities in the Atlantic world. The model of creolization as a process, as well as the sense of the Creole as a transient identity, echo widespread ideas about West Indian plasticity. Creole women, J. B. Moreton writes in *West India customs and manners* (1793), are 'as pliable as wax, and melt like butter'.[145] Creoles were often understood as colonial mimics: white West Indian women, as Kathleen Wilson describes them, were considered 'pallid imitations' of their metropolitan counterparts.[146] For Pinckard and Thelwall, though, the mobility associated with the adaptive, hybrid nature of Creole cultures, identities and knowledge lends ideas about progress within Atlantic societies which emerge in terms of narratives of increased health. Both authors use the Creole to articulate processes of acclimatization and reconciliation in which the merging of Europe and the Caribbean heralds health and new ideas. For Pinckard, medical creolization goes some small way towards resolving the fatal flaw at the heart of the colonial endeavour, though ultimately disease will 'continue to prevail, so long as greedy lucre shall impel the inhabitants of cold climates to pay their devotions to Plutus, by a pilgrimage to tropical fields; unless these fields shall be so improved, by tillage, as to destroy the serpent, and deprive the fever of the aliment necessary for its support'.[147] Thelwall uses the Creole to figure the philosophical and political exchange between colony and metropole, defined in terms of medical and moral health and the 'adoption' of new ideas. In Seraphina's Creole cosmopolitanism, as in Pinckard's local (but outward-looking) medical and natural knowledge, Creole knowledge is understood in terms of mobility. Against the backdrop of a transatlantic drive to gather ideas, information, objects and wealth, the Creole is the arbiter of new knowledge: as outsiders, Creoles bring new perspectives which enable Thelwall to test the social status quo and Pinckard to illustrate his argument for a medical practice based on colonial experience rather than European logic. Pinckard's claims for the prioritization of experience over received wisdom and Thelwall's liberal, proto-feminist arguments make for Creoles who are aligned with a colonial-facing modernity that overhauls metropolitan tradition. These turn-of-the-century West Indians demand social reform as much as they depict processes of immense personal change.

Chapter 5 analyzes the nexus of medicine, colonial identities and revolution in relation to the African-Caribbean syncretic practices of 'obeah'. Much as Creoles were satirized and vilified, the obeah doctor became a popular plantation hate figure, with a medicalized idea of the insane and contagious obeah doctor emerging alongside pantomime caricatures of superstitious and credulous slaves, as well as more fearful images of the obeah practitioner as a sinister and revenge-driven murderer. But, like Pinckard's and Thelwall's Creoles, obeah people also represent the wealth of new medical and natural knowledge that motivated colonial expansion, and voice the ways in which the medical dimensions of colonial identities reveal the complex interplay between health and knowledge at stake in colonial intercultural encounters.

PART III

Revolution and Abolition

CHAPTER 5

The 'Intimate Union of Medicine and Magic'
Obeah, Revolution and Colonial Modernity

'Tis time the boundless prospect we now leave,
To tread, with cautious feet, the per'lous path,
That thro' the braky maze winds down the steeps,
And mould'ring passes, of the mountain's side,
Commix'd with moss, and briar, and baleful weeds,
Whose juice the obeahs 'mong the sable tribe
Extracting, turn to use medicinal.
Yet oft this crafty knave, affecting skill
In pow'rful herbs, calls magic to his aid;
And, when old age has silver'd o'er his chin,
Draws in the credulous, unthinking crowd,
To venerate his art, and fill his purse.
John Singleton, *A Description of the West Indies* (1776)[1]

John Singleton's blank verse *Description of the West Indies* (1776) attests to the dim view in which the British held the African-Atlantic syncretic complex of magical, medical and spiritual practices known as 'obeah'. Singleton's 'mock-physician' is typical of contemporary representations of obeah in his performance of 'powerful fancy' to beguile a naïve and super-stitious audience. The obeah doctor's psychological hold over enslaved communities gave planters and colonial medics cause for considerable concern. The earlier incarnation of Singleton's poem, which was origi-nally published as *A General Description of the West-Indian Islands* (1767), registers even more keenly the antagonistic relationship between obeah doctors and European-trained physicians:

A true physician, who in vain prescrib'd
For a poor slave, by fancy once possess'd
So strongly, that no learned means cou'd cure,
Was led by curiosity to see
His patient treated with superior skill
By an old hag, who long had liv'd renown'd

157

> For spells, drugs, charms, and knowledge physical.
> With sapient face she handled ev'ry part;
> Till, fixing on the seat of the disease,
> She mumbled to herself some uncouth words,
> The myst'ry of her trade, and close apply'd
> Her parched lips, by suction to extract
> The cause of the complaint.[2]

Feigning the removal of rusty nails and horse teeth from the body of a person labouring under an imagined sickness, the obeah woman performs the illusion of medical treatment with strange utterances and incongruous material props. Enslaved people seek help at her door, rather than that of the 'true physician', aggravating the competitive economy of medical knowledge at stake in the rivalry between European medicine and the obeah doctors and other black medics who 'filled their purses' through the sale of expensive charms and herbal remedies.

The obeah doctor's skill reached far beyond the realm of the medical, and it was obeah's political associations with a revolutionary agenda which the plantocracy most feared. In 1760, a group of rebel slaves led by Tacky, a Koromantyn chief, had advanced the first threat to British authority in Jamaica since the First Maroon War of the 1730s. Beginning in the Parish of St. Mary but moving quickly across the island, the rebels killed sixty white people and destroyed thousands of pounds' worth of property. Tacky was supported by a number of obeah practitioners, who were said to have made the rebels invulnerable through the administration of a powder as well as a solemn oath to bind them in secrecy.[3] Betrayed by a fellow slave, the rebels were defeated by a joint party of soldiers, planter militia and maroons. Tacky's Rebellion prompted a violent backlash and the Jamaican Assembly immediately criminalized obeah:

> Any Negro or other Slave, who shall pretend to any supernatural Power, and be detected in making any use of Blood, Feathers, Parrots Beaks, Dogs Teeth, Alligators Teeth, broken Bottles, Grave Dirt, Rum, Egg-shells, or any other Materials relative to the Practice of obeah or Witchcraft, in order to delude and impose on the Minds of others, shall upon Conviction thereof, before two Magistrates and three Freeholders, suffer Death or Transportation.[4]

The most extreme violence was suffered by those obeah practitioners supporting the rebellion, who were subjected to 'various Experiments' and 'many severe shocks' made with 'Electrical Machines and Magic Lanthorns'.[5] If obeah laid claim to a wealth of false medicine through the performance of knowledge that was in thrall to material things and the supernatural powers attached to them, these theatrical experiments reveal the response from the colonial authorities was no less 'performed'. Despite the extreme violence enacted under the spell of technological power in the form of electric shocks and lighted displays, however, in the official account of the death of one of the obeah men involved in the Tacky Rebellion the colonial agent for Jamaica Stephen Fuller notes that 'at the Place of Execution he bid defiance to the Executioner, telling him that it was not in the Power of White People to kill him'.[6] The obeah practitioner's refusal of the death sentence passed upon him by the colonial judges attempted to undermine the judicial and material powers of the colonial administration. Nearly three decades after the criminalization of obeah, planters expressed their ongoing frustration at the prevalence of obeah: 'neither the Terror of this Law, the strict Investigation which has ever since been made after the Professors of *Obi*, nor the many Examples of those who from Time to Time have hanged or transported, have hitherto produced the desired Effect'.[7] The plantocracy's efforts to eradicate obeah doctors were stymied by the 'Veil of Mystery' that was 'studiously thrown over their Incantations'. 'Every precaution is taken', Fuller notes, 'to conceal them [obeah spells] from the knowledge and discovery of the White people.'[8] The gruesome scene of torture described in the parliamentary account, and the sense of performance and counter-performance which emerges in the authorities' frustrated attempts to discover and dispel the magical power obeah held on the plantation gesture towards the theatrical dimensions of plantation culture. As this chapter will show, the response to the Tacky Rebellion was enacted in the context of colonial anxieties regarding supernatural powers, the secret speech of oaths and incantations, acts of resistance and the circulation of natural philosophical knowledge (and who could claim it and use it), and emerged through a theatrical dynamic that would come to define the representation of obeah in the Caribbean colonies and in Britain well into the nineteenth century.

The obeah doctor became one of the most pervasive tropes of the colonial Caribbean. Expressing fears about authority, revolution and affected (but nonetheless powerful) knowledge, the obeah practitioner proved a popular figure for Romantic-period authors who conjured up images of crafty and malevolent practitioners laying false claim to medical knowledge and gaining power over enslaved communities. Alongside a comic figure of ridicule there existed a medicalized idea of an insane and contagious obeah practitioner, as well as more sinister representations of revenge-driven murderers. Coleridge and Wordsworth's gothic 'The Three Graves' (1798) was inspired by colonial reports on obeah, Maria Edgeworth included a sinister obeah woman in the colonial sub-plot of her novel *Belinda* (1801) and obeah doctors took up starring roles in several melodramas and pantomimes – most famously when the black American actor Ira Aldridge played the title role in William Murray's *Obi; or, Three-Fingered Jack* (1825).

Obeah became heavily weighted in colonial culture because it brought into sharp focus the problems which emerged from the plantation encounter between different belief systems, cultural practices and bodies of medical and natural knowledge. While colonial physicians and surgeons dismissed African and African-Caribbean medical practices as artful quackery, they also envied obeah doctors the profits they made from selling their herbal knowledge, protective amulets and charms. Similarly, slave-holders scoffed at what they saw as the naïve superstition of African-Caribbean belief systems while competing aggressively with obeah people for spiritual power over the enslaved. In this sense, obeah is also a crucial part of the story of modernity's dimensions on the colonial plantation. A persistent narrative of modernity's nationalizing and scientific processes has concerned a secular European Enlightenment science forging new forms of knowledge and new ways of looking at the world. But plantation obeah implicates African-Caribbean medical and spiritual practices in syncretic cultural processes and revolutionary strategies in a way that redefines Eurocentric models of the history of science and the colonial-periphery dynamic according to which it has been structured, and suggests the under-acknowledged impact of alternative approaches to health and the natural world on the plantation and beyond. The obeah practitioner is one such model of an alternative 'colonial modernity' – a spectral figure identified with moments of intercultural encounter specific to the unique social complex of the plantation that brought exchange, instability and revolution, with influence far beyond the plantation's bounds.

As Singleton's poem and the parliamentary account of the Tacky Rebellion suggest, obeah was codified as performance. And just as the obeah practitioner was imagined as performing pretended knowledge to a credulous (and literally captive) audience, so the plantocracy attempted to dispel the theatrically produced power of oaths, spells and things by performing their own spectacular acts of magical and technological mastery. The theatricalization of obeah was part of a wider sphere of colonial performance which framed moments of intercultural encounter in various medical, political and religious contexts. Focusing on the anxieties surrounding the secret knowledge of obeah practice, the mysterious language of oaths and other rituals and the various models of performance and counter-performance which emerge in relation to obeah, this chapter examines how obeah functioned as a mode of cultural resistance. It reveals obeah as a trickster discourse associated with quacks, wizards and performers who confounded Western epistemologies and moved across knowledge categories, bodies, temporalities and geosocial boundaries and shows the ways in which, from Tacky's Rebellion in 1760 to the abolition of slavery in 1834 and beyond, obeah was positioned at the centre of a nexus of colonial anxieties revolving around ideas about belief, health, magic, medicine, performance, revolution and intercultural encounter. Drawing on the history of slave resistance and rebellion to inform readings of factual and fictional accounts of the life of the notorious Jamaican bandit Three-Fingered Jack, the anonymous gothic novel *Hamel, the Obeah Man* (1827), as well as contemporary medical and political accounts of obeah, this chapter traces the literary and cultural contours of a set of practices engaged in undermining the colonial status quo.

Obeah in the Archive

Despite the cultural prevalence of obeah, nobody seemed to know quite what it was. Griffith Hughes, rector of the Parish of St Lucy in Barbados during the late 1730s and 1740s, described the local 'obeah doctors' or 'obeah Negroes' in ambiguous terms as 'a sort of physicians and conjurers'.[9] Growing efforts to classify and understand obeah in the wake of Tacky's Rebellion brought no greater clarity. A parliamentary report in 1789 was the first publication to offer a definition of the term, but its grammatical and etymological uncertainties suggest that the authorities remained unsure about what constituted the practice of obeah, as well as what to call it: 'the term obeah, obiah, or obia (for it is variously written) we conceive to be the adjective, and the obe or obi the noun substantive'.[10] The issue of pinning down meaning in relation to both the language and practice of obeah was related to the broader difficulty met with by the plantocracy in their efforts to understand, depict, control and suppress slaves' cultural practices. British colonial representations of obeah were often characterized by anxiety as people struggled to comprehend a medico-spiritual practice very different from their own, and obeah became an 'epistemological conundrum'.[11] Obeah was shrouded in a veil of suspicion and misunderstanding and presented by the plantocracy as a malign and revenge-driven form of superstition. Remaining a shadowy and inconstant figure, the obeah doctor was framed by contradictory patterns of naming and understanding as etymological discussions substituted for whites' lack of knowledge or first-hand experience of obeah practices. This linguistic issue has not gone away: almost every recent scholarly account of the practice of obeah in the British Caribbean has stressed the etymological ambiguity of the term, while Cassidy and Le Page's *Dictionary of Jamaican English* cites thirty-five different terms for an 'obeah-man'.[12]

The violence of slave-run colonies has bequeathed one-sided archives and very few first-hand reports of obeah, an illegal oral tradition. The appearance of the obeah practitioner in literary and medical texts was dependent on three sources: the planter and colonial administrator Edward Long's *History of Jamaica* (1774), the planter and politician Bryan Edwards's *History of the West Indies* (1793) and the section on obeah in the *Report of the Lords Relating to Trade and Foreign Plantations* (1789), to which both Long and Edwards made significant contributions along with Stephen Fuller. Lacking understanding of obeah, later texts continually returned to Edwards and Long as historical authorities, and the emerging figure of the obeah practitioner became increasingly ambiguous and catachrestic.[13] In all likelihood, many or most African slaves would have had some of the medical knowledge associated with what was called 'obeah'. But any proper understanding of these medical practices is difficult to achieve, given the colonial rhetoric which derided African-Caribbean medical and religious practices as, at best, quackery and, at worst, malign and devilish irrationality 'attached to the gloomy superstitions of Africa'.[14] Neither can any effort to study obeah practice under colonial rule look to accounts written by slaves. Unsurprisingly, none of the three most famous Caribbean slave authors, Olaudah Equiano, Mary Prince and Ignatius Sancho, discuss obeah in their accounts; all three were Christians and self-consciously engaged with a British reading public. Equiano's autobiography, for example, is concerned with the articulation of a newly emerging black British identity that is fundamentally bound up with the process of religious conversion. While some planters complained that sick slaves requested black medics, Equiano's response when he is taken ill with fever and ague is to pray that God will save him.[15]

Another important reason for the absence of obeah from historical records was the secrecy with which it practised its revolutionary aims. Obeah inspired and supported rebellions throughout the British, Danish and Dutch colonies of the Caribbean, including significant revolts in Jamaica in 1733, 1738 and 1760; Antigua in 1736 and Berbice in 1763.[16] As well as giving protection from physical harm through charms and amulets, obeah practitioners joined rebels in oaths of allegiance to their cause. The Haitian Revolution, the only slave revolt to succeed in founding a new state, also had its origins in West African religion: a service held by a Vodun priest named Boukman, after which slaves set fire to nearby plantations, was the starting point of the insurgency. However, for historian Karol Weaver it was small acts of resistance, particularly by enslaved healers and their collaborators, which in aggregation across Saint Domingue led to the loss of France's most important and productive New World colony. 'In order to fully understand the origins and impact of the Haitian Revolution', Weaver argues, 'one must comprehend that the enslaved healers emerged as significant leaders of slave communities through a process of cultural retention, assimilation, and creation, profited economically and politically from their healing practices, and initiated and implemented an ideology of resistance via sabotage and the destruction of human and animal life.'[17] Similarly, in the British Caribbean the circulation of medical knowledge associated with obeah people and other African-Caribbean health practitioners functioned as a form of slave resistance that often depended upon covert forms of action.

Given this context of uprising and medical and spiritual competition, it is hardly surprising that scholarly work on obeah has emphasized negative colonial attitudes towards African-Caribbean belief systems. Diana Paton and Maarit Forde write that colonial attitudes to African religious practices were 'dominated by hostility'.[18] Romantic period representations of obeah functioned to express the colonial fears borne, as Alan Richardson writes, 'of British anxieties regarding power: the fluctuations of imperial power, the power of slaves to determine their own fate, the power of democratic movements in France, England, and in the Caribbean'.[19] But in literary studies the attention to the gothic tones in which obeah was often negatively articulated risks reiterating the exoticization of African-Caribbean cultural practices against which Paton warns.[20] Neither should the scholarly focus on unfavourable attitudes lead us to the belief that obeah was successfully exiled from the plantation, or that slave health practices and spiritual ideas made no impact on European ones. In fact, this chapter will show that there was interest from some European colonial quarters in African-Caribbean treatments, bringing a new dimension to the medical and scientific history of the colonial Caribbean and its relationship to the knowledge economy of the Western world.

Recent work in the history of science has attended to the social networks and groupings which produced and circulated knowledge. James Delbourgo, Simon Schaffer, Emma Spary and others have emphasized the significance of social networks that existed both within and beyond the institutional structures of science such as the laboratory and the university.[21] In colonial contexts, questions about how knowledge was made by a variety of individuals and mobilized across geographical and social boundaries have become particularly significant. Londa Schiebinger's work on the history of the discovery of new kinds of natural knowledge (as well as areas of ignorance and loss of knowledge) in the New World has contributed to a history of science perspective that has shifted from a metropole–periphery model to an Atlantic or transnational model, displacing Europe as the centre and addressing the ways in which knowledge was produced and circulated by and between different cultural groups, many of whom have been neglected by the historical records.[22] Colonial disease was the product of closer contact between previously separate populations, and new forms of medical knowledge also developed as a result of colonial encounters between social groups and scientific practices. An important question here regards what can be learnt from how European physicians and surgeons approached, competed with and learnt from African-Caribbean health practices and what those moments of encounter can tell us about the structures of colonial life and the circum-Atlantic production of medical and natural knowledge.

Given the necessary secrecy surrounding obeah and the paucity of the colonial archive, recovering full and accurate details of obeah practice is not possible and scholars must piece together a fragmented account, working with and through what sources are available. Attempts to recover histories of enslaved peoples and, particularly, attempts to address the question of slave subjectivity are fraught with difficulty. But, as Richard Burton writes in his account of the processes of social encounter, exchange and transformation that took place as part of what he describes as the movement from African cultures to a range of hybridized Afro-Creole practices, the moments of great cultural loss marked by the fractured and partial colonial archive must be mapped alongside those of 'cultural retention and reinterpretation, cultural imitation and borrowing, and cultural creation'.[23] For Susan Scott Parrish, looking to the natural world allows scholars to conceive of black history beyond the confines of a print culture which excluded Africans and African-Caribbeans. Slaves turned to medical and natural knowledge as a way to gain power and privilege on the plantation, and Parrish writes that 'it was the talking woods more than the "Talking Book" that was the "ur-trope" of the Anglo-African experience'.[24] Yet this history of knowledge is usefully approached from a literary perspective, both because the particular complications of obeah's archival history mean that it is only accessible through its textual depictions by colonists, and because the particular kinds of textual forms used to narrate the practice of obeah are particularly dense in imagery that is productively analyzed in ways that attend to its methods of illumination and obfuscation, and to how it elicits particular kinds of responses from a range of metropolitan and colonial readers. As Kelly Wisecup and Toni Wall Jaudon argue, because the subaltern supernatural is epistemologically irreconcilable with the rational knowledge of the European Enlightenment, 'praxis and representation can never stand fully apart', and the best way to apprehend those supernatural powers is 'within the web of influences, literary and otherwise, that shaped those who would have encountered them in the past'.[25] Srinivas Aravamudan's *Tropicopolitans* approaches the partial acts of recovery which are a necessary part of this joint literary and historiographical project through the metaphor of 'tropicalization', attempting to reconstruct elements of the colonial imagination without reifying an idealized subaltern. Aravamudan views the colonial subject as existing 'both as a fictive construct of colonial tropology and actual resident of tropical space, object of representation and agent of resistance'.[26] In this model of colonial historiography, tropicopolitans are afforded agency by their existence as 'projections as well as beings' which leave behind them 'stubborn material traces even as they are discursively deconstructed'.[27] Exploring the cultural traces of obeah practitioners as an important and heavily weighted trope of colonial slavery, whose chimerical ambiguity and secret knowledge marked their resistance to colonial representation and control, it is possible to reach towards the history of obeah and other African-Caribbean medical practices as encompassing acts of seen and unseen resistance.

Obeah and Medicine in the British Caribbean

Obeah was, and is, a syncretic range of African diasporic magical, medical and spiritual practices which, like African-Atlantic religions such as Myal, Santéria, Vodun and Winti, was practised in specific regions of the Caribbean.[28] Obeah was found primarily among slaves in the British, Danish and Dutch Caribbean islands, as well as Suriname and other parts of mainland South America.[29] Practitioners tended to a broad set of physical, social and spiritual requirements; W. E. B. Du Bois characterized the obeah doctor as 'the healer of the sick, the interpreter of the Unknown, the comforter of the sorrowing, the supernatural avenger of the wrong, and the one who rudely but picturesquely expressed the longing, disappointment, and resentment of a stolen and oppressed people'.[30] Kamau Brathwaite argues that the structure of African society enabled this trans-professional function within slave communities. In African and Caribbean folk practices, where 'religion had not been externalized and institutionalized as in Europe', the obeah practitioner combined the roles of doctor, philosopher and priest: 'healing was, in a sense, an act of faith, as it was in the early Christian church'.[31] In the north-west region of Africa from which obeah originates, disease and death were often attributed to supernatural causes, and the physical, spiritual and moral aspects of disease were unified in obeah practice. While slaves in the British Caribbean often explained minor illnesses in naturalistic terms, major illness and death were more frequently thought to be caused by specific agents such as malevolent spirits, acts of God(s), the breaking of religious rules or taboos, the displeasure of ancestral spirits and magic or sorcery.[32] This unified approach to healing and spiritual practices, which worked in opposition to the Enlightenment movement towards the separation of medicine and religion (embodied in the tortured obeah practitioner's refusal to acknowledge the authorities' power to do him harm), suggests one way in which obeah emerged as a form of conceptual resistance to the colonial slave system.

African medicine was grounded in the healing power of the vegetal realm, and practitioners were possessed of an extensive plant pharmacopoeia.[33] Herbal cures were given for a wide range of illnesses including asthma, diabetes, digestive disorders, dysentery, ophthalmia, skin diseases and worms. Herbalism constituted a major part of obeah practice, and herbal compounds were accompanied by the invocation of spirits and the use of fetishes to cure or induce physical and social ills. Along with barks, grasses, herbs and roots, the ingredients of the 'obi' might include bones, dead insects, feathers, minerals and shells. Obeah practitioners made a living from the sale of herbal treatments and protective amulets, as well as the interpretation of dreams and the spirit world and giving advice on how to scare away thieves. They gained social status, Mary Turner writes, through the sanction they afforded the oath-taking ritual, which was 'the most important single manifestation of their political role in day-to-day affairs'.[34] Oaths were an important judicial apparatus and were instrumental in uniting slaves swearing allegiance to the common purpose of resisting the chattel system so were particularly significant during periods of active rebellion. Obeah was practised with socially positive aims such as curing illness or locating missing property. But it was inevitably far more renowned for its more malevolent aims, including poisoning those who had committed theft or other crimes.

African botanical medicine proved useful in treating some of the diseases endemic to tropical regions. Enslaved herbalists, obeah practitioners and black medical attendants sanctioned by plantation owners were often more successful in their treatments than their white counterparts. Black medics, according to Richard Sheridan, 'gained power and influence because their herbal remedies occasionally contained effective drugs, and even if ineffectual, they seldom harmed the patient'.[35] This was certainly not the case with the heroic medicine practised by many European-trained plantation physicians, who bled, blistered and purged their patients on such a regular basis that they undoubtedly would have done them more harm than good. George Pinckard pours particular scorn on the medical abilities of white practitioners in Barbados, whom he considers to be so lacking in training and knowledge that many black doctors 'vie with them in medical knowledge.'[36] While European medics may have had much to learn from African and African-Caribbean botanical knowledge, there was a great deal of suspicion about obeah and other medicine practised by enslaved people. Richard Towne, a physician in Barbados during the early eighteenth century, reported that Barbadian slaves were 'great pretenders to the knowledge of specifick virtues in simples', dismissing this 'pretended' knowledge as quackery: 'I could never observe the least beneficial effect produced by them.'[37] Obeah was depicted as a fraudulent and sinister practice which allowed practitioners to prey on the superstitions of other slaves, peddling charms for their own social and economic gain. With increasing unrest across several colonies this sense of suspicion only grew, and the competition faced by European physicians from their black medical competitors is registered in their increasing resentment of the financial gains made by obeah practitioners. Thomas Dancer, an Edinburgh MD who worked as a military doctor in Jamaica and Nicaragua, dismissed obeah doctors as charlatans, but retained a certain amount of respect for their powers of persuasion: 'these obeah people are very artful in their way, and have a great ascendancy over the other negroes, whom they persuade that they are able to do many miracles by means of their art; and very often get good sums of money for their imaginary charms'.[38] James Thomson, a native of Jamaica and another Edinburgh graduate, considered many of the illnesses suffered by slaves to be the result of unreasonable 'prejudices' and the expensive 'charms' provided by obeah men or women. A 'medical man', he wrote, would find the management of slave disorders extremely difficult when obeah was involved. Struggling to break the power over slaves held by obeah's 'intimate union of medicine and magic', Thomson endeavoured to 'destroy the hold of the obeah over the patient through reasoning'.[39] Associated with witchcraft, poison, fraudulent potions and midnight rituals, obeah and other forms of slave health practice were routinely represented as the antithesis of European professionalized and empirically based medical practice. With a mixture of awe, competition

and condescension, many doctors and slave-holders scoffed at the pharmacological inefficacy of slave treatments even as they documented the powerful psychological hold they had on slaves, exoticizing obeah and other
medical practices while simultaneously deriding them.

Not everyone was so dismissive of African-Caribbean medical practices,
however. The naturalist Henry Barham, an important influence on Hans
Sloane, wrote of the 'Majoe, or Macary Bitter', a plant which had its name
from 'Majoe, an old negro woman so-called who, with a simple concoc-
tion, did wonderful cures in the most stubborn diseases, as the yaws, and
in venereal cases, when the person has been given over as incurable by
skilful physicians, because their Herculean medicines failed them; *viz.*
preparations of mercury and antimony'.[40] While his correspondent Sloane
was more dismissive of African healing practices and used only English
and Latin to describe Jamaican flora and fauna, Barham adopted African
terms, acknowledged the dangerous abilities of obeah practitioners and
described a wide range of African healing treatments. This included a
treatment that Barham received at the hands of one of his own slaves.
Upon his falling ill with a severe fever which left him with violent inflammation and swelling, Barham's slave informed him: 'Master, I can cure
you.'[41] Like Barham, William Hillary pointed out that it was local slaves,
and not European-trained physicians, who had discovered a cure for
yaws.[42] That cure, Hillary complained, was kept 'as a Secret from the white
People, but preserve[d] among themselves by Tradition'.[43] Jamaican James
Knight wrote that he was 'of the Opinion, that many Secrets in the Art of
Physick, may be obtained from the Negro Doctors, were proper Methods
taken, which I think is not below our Physicians to Enquire into, as it may
be of great Service to themselves, as well as mankind'.[44] A gentleman living
in Suriname wrote in 1761 to the Swedish botanist Carl Linnaeus to inform
him of the discovery of a tree root renowned locally for its successful
treatment of stomach complaints. A slave named Kwasímukámba, later
known as Graman (great man) Quacy, had discovered the root, and
Linnaeus named the tree *Quassia amara* in Kwasi's honour.[45] Kwasi was
freed as a result of his discovery, and his subsequent recognition within the
European scientific establishment was all the more remarkable considering
his reputation as a practitioner of obeah. John Gabriel Stedman gives an
account of these events in his *Narrative*, writing that the root was known
to have 'efficacy in strengthening the stomach and restoring the appetite'.
Kwasi, Stedman claims, was 'absolutely the first Discoverer' of the root
and, as a result, 'fill'd his Pockets with no inconsiderable Profits' – status
and wealth that are illustrated by Blake's portrait of Kwasi (Figure 5.1).[46]

Figure 5.1 William Blake, 'The Celebrated Graman Quacy', in John Gabriel Stedman, *Narrative of a Five Years' Expedition against the Revolted Negroes of Surinam* (London: J. Johnson, 1796). Engraving. Courtesy of The Huntington Library, San Marino, California.

While others saw the financial gains made by obeah practitioners as fraud-
ulently won, Stedman confers legitimacy onto Kwasi's knowledge and his
earnings. William Titford's *Hortus Botanicus Americanus* (1811) details several significant examples of learning from 'Negro doctors in Jamaica' as
well as a 'negro doctress in the Red Hills' and 'Indians in North America',
documenting 'information which may prove new, curious and valuable'.[47]
Interest in African-Caribbean botanical knowledge was less controversial
in the post-Abolition era. Richard Madden, a surgeon who was appointed
in 1833 as one of the special magistrates to oversee the Jamaican transition from slavery to freedom, wrote in his *Twelvemonth's Residence in West
Indies during the Transition from Slavery to Apprenticeship* (1835) that he had
wanted to give an account of 'those whose medical properties are known
to the negroes', but had found it 'impossible to enumerate them even in
any reasonable limits'.[48] Madden notes that he is 'so thoroughly persuaded'
of the valuable medicinal plants known to the black population of Jamaica
that 'any person who would undertake an account of the popular medicine
of the negroes, would bring to light much information serviceable to medical science'.[49] The representation of obeah and slave health practices more
generally was often negative and accused black doctors of being quacks
and fraudsters more proficient in poisoning than healing, and of holding
dangerous psychological power over slaves. The significant expressions of
interest and belief in the efficacy of African-Caribbean medical knowledge,
however, complicate the history of colonial knowledge networks and highlight the pockets of influence gained by enslaved medical practitioners.
While William Hillary may have objected to the fact that enslaved doctors
did not voluntarily share the cure for yaws with European colonial medics,
his protest – and Graman Quacy's profits – indicate the significance of the
rivalry between Afro- and Anglo-Atlantic medical practices and suggest
that this economic and scientific competition was one of the reasons obeah
and other slave health practices took on such great cultural significance on
the plantation and beyond.

The Contagious Imagination

Medics' frustration at the secrecy of African-Caribbean herbalism reflected
the broader sense of mystery and threat that surrounded obeah practice. In
times of revolution, obeah was described as a practice of whispered oaths
and secret meanings that depended upon the rhetorical performances of
the obeah man or woman as a revolutionary figurehead holding immense
power over individual minds as well as the collective imagination and

political sensibilities of whole communities. A gentleman who visited the maroon leader Cudjoe in the Blue Mountains of Jamaica shortly after the 1738 treaties that ended the First Maroon War wrote that the maroons 'Consulted on every Occasion' a 'Person whom they called Obia Man whom they greatly revered, his words carried the force of an Oracle with them'.[50] James Grainger joked in 1764 about the obeah doctor who 'mutters strange jargon', but acknowledged the dread awe in which obeah men and women were held by other slaves and advised planters that obeah doctors might have a useful place in plantation life as long as their 'mischief' was 'kept by the white people in proper subordination'.[51] Grainger described the African 'addiction' to obeah at the level of the national body, identifying it as an 'imaginary woe' which might be cured with a dose of European rationalism: 'a belief in magic is inseparable from human nature, but those nations are most addicted thereto, among whom learning, and of course, philosophy have least obtained'.[52]

In Jamaica, which had a far greater history of rebellion than Grainger's St Kitts, fears about the power of obeah over other slaves were not a laughing matter, having been intensified by several attempted rebellions involving obeah doctors. In 1775, a Jamaican planter returned from London to find that a great many of the slaves on his plantation had died, and of those that remained alive a majority were 'debilitated, bloated, and in a very deplorable condition'.[53] The mortality continued for weeks, with the planter often burying several slaves in a single day. Doctors tried every medical means available to stem the tide of death, without success. Finally, a woman confided in the planter a 'very great secret': her step-mother, an octogenarian 'woman of the Popo country', had 'put Obi upon' the slaves. The planter visited the old woman's house, where he found the walls 'stuck with the implements of her Trade, consisting of Rags, Feathers, bones of Cats … a prodigious Quantity of round Balls of Earth or Clay' and 'a thousand other articles'. Upon this discovery, the woman's house was immediately burnt to the ground, 'with the whole of its contents committed to the Flames', and the woman sold to Spaniards bound for Cuba.[54] The Popo woman became a colonial legend and her story the foundation of other obeah texts in the Caribbean press, colonial histories, medical treatises, novels, poetry and theatre.[55]

During the era of revolutions and in the wake of the slave uprising in St Domingue, the tone of several obeah representations took a decidedly gothic turn, as what Grainger had called 'strange jargon' became imbued with a renewed threat of rebellion. William Shepherd's ode 'The Negro Incantation' (1797) takes up the theme of obeah's sinister use of language. Citing Bryan

Edwards as his source, Shepherd suggests the awesome potency of the obeah conjurer's words and echoes Singleton's account of obeah theatrics in his description of a frenzied 'throng' of obeah-inspired revolutionaries:

> Now beam'd upon the sable crowd,
> Now vanish'd in the thickening cloud.
> 'Twas silence all—with frantic look,
> His spells the hoary wizard took:
> Bending o'er the quiv'ring flame,
> Convulsion shook his giant frame.
> Close and more close the shuddering captives throng,
> With breath repress'd, and straining eye, they wait—
> When midst the plantains bursts the awful song
> The words of mystic might, that seal their tyrants fate.[56]

While the Woman of the Popo Country depended upon whispered threats and a multitude of props to gain control of the plantation, Shepherd's obeah conjurer works his magic through a convulsive rhetorical and physical performance which draws in and reverberates through the 'shuddering' bodies of the crowd that hold the tangible threat of revolution.[57]

The strange power of the sinister Woman of the Popo Country and Shepherd's revolutionary conjurer over the collective mind and body reflects obeah's increasing association with afflictions of the mind, as the practitioner's powerful magical and verbal performances take hold in the credulous and weak-minded and function as a contagious disease of the imagination. The parliamentary documents on obeah expressed anxiety at 'the astonishing Influence of this Superstition upon their [Africans'] Minds' and reported that the individual for whom an obi has been 'set' suffers from 'anomalous Symptoms', either from poisoning or originating in 'Causes deeply rooted in the Mind, such as the Terrours of *Obi*', and which 'baffle the Skill of the ablest Physician'.[58] Whether the symptoms of being 'obeahed' originated from the 'Imagination and Credulity' of the afflicted slave or from 'Poison secretly administered', the effects were the same. The sufferer was so prepossessed by the horror of obeah that all hope was lost: 'His disturbed Imagination is haunted without Respite, his Features wear the settled Gloom of Despondency; Dirt, or any other unwholesome Substance, becomes his only Food, he contracts a morbid habit of body, and gradually sinks into the Grave.'[59] Indeed, 'a very considerable Portion' of the Jamaican annual death rate was attributed to 'this fascinating Mischief'.[60]

From its Humean association with Roman Catholicism, 'superstition', as the authorities classified obeah, was undergoing a process of secularization, and was appropriated in the construction of a self-conscious intellectual break with pre-Enlightenment thought. Medicine was also implicated in this move towards a secular semantics of superstition, as European doctors claimed medical explanations for the bodily symptoms of 'superstitious' beliefs. If superstition could cause illness, however, the reverse was also true. Hume identifies the cause of superstition as 'the unhappy situation of private or public affairs, from ill health, from a gloomy and melancholy disposition, or from the concurrence of all these circumstances'.[61] The 'true sources of Superstition' were 'weakness, fear, melancholy, together with ignorance', originating in a fragile state of mind in which 'infinite unknown evils are dreaded from unknown agents; and where real objects of terror are wanting, the soul, active to its own prejudice, and fostering its predominant inclination, finds imaginary ones, to whose power and malevolence it sets no limits'.[62] The result was a concentration of significance, in the mind of the sufferer, on 'ceremonies, observances, mortifications, sacrifices' in order to appease the terrified imagination. What Roy Porter et al. called the 'war of attrition' waged by professional doctors in Europe against charlatans and mountebanks formed the medical and social backdrop to the colonial association between obeah, disease and conditions of the mind.[63] European doctors were aggressively claiming jurisdiction over the bodies of the demonically possessed by asserting that their symptoms were in fact associated with particular physical diseases – perhaps caused by morbid humours, such as 'melancholy', which was brought on by an excess of black bile. It was within the context of these efforts to reframe superstition and witchcraft as disease that colonial doctors and planters viewed obeah as a contagious illness of the imagination. The account of obeah as 'superstition' succeeded in conjoining medical and religious dismissals of its value by a sleight of hand which associated false belief systems with disease.

Maria Edgeworth's novel *Belinda* (1801) and her short fiction 'The Grateful Negro' (1804) combine accounts of obeah, superstition and the imaginary dimensions of illness. *Belinda* is, in part, a portrait of Lady Delacour, a fashionable *bel esprit* who is fooled by an expensive quack doctor into believing that she is dying of breast cancer, while the colonial sub-plot which culminates in the interracial marriage between Juba and Lucy sees Belinda try to appease the superstitious Juba, who is captivated by the 'terrour' of a 'fiery obeah woman'.[64] Juba, like Delacour, recovers his health and spirits only after the trickery to which he has been subjected is revealed. Edgeworth went on to explore obeah in its plantation context in 'The Grateful Negro' (1804), her story about an attempted uprising in

Jamaica led by an obeah woman but ultimately thwarted by the 'grateful negro' of the title, who feels too indebted to his paternalistic master to allow the rebellion to come to fruition. The obeah practitioner of this plot is even more sinister – a Koromantyn woman named Esther who is determined to eliminate the white population of Jamaica and sets to work on the impressionable minds of her fellow slaves. On the point of rebellion, she had 'worked their imagination to what pitch and purpose she pleased' and 'stimulated the revengeful temper of Hector almost to phrenzy'.[65] Especially potent in the context of anxiety about slave rebellions, the model of the contagious imagination also drew on contemporary themes of political contagion. Just as Edmund Burke figured the French Revolution in terms of the threat to the English political system posed by the 'contagion of the French doctrines', discussions of slave revolutions were couched in similarly medicalized terms allied to anxieties about revolutionary crowds and the communication of political sentiments.[66]

By 1803, Thomas Winterbottom classified the belief in obeah as a 'mental disease'. Winterbottom spent four years in Africa as physician to the Sierra Leone Company and observed the practices associated with what he called African 'superstitions'. He claimed that the 'effects upon the minds of slaves' of West Indian obeah practice were significantly greater than in Africa. 'Like many of those diseases to which the body is subject', writes Winterbottom, the belief in obeah 'appears to have acquired additional vigour by being transplanted from one country to another.'[67] Not only was obeah a disease which, like fevers and fluxes, was understood to be suffered with greater intensity in particular locations, but the process of geographical movement itself appeared to amplify its symptoms. The notion of a contagious and specifically West Indian 'mental disease' – to which enslaved people were particularly vulnerable, being considered of a weaker psychological constitution – conceptually structured obeah as functioning like disease. While Grainger had earlier suggested that it offered a potential treatment resource for sickening slaves, obeah and the belief in its spiritual powers and practical efficacy was generally understood as that which needed to be cured.

Three-Fingered Jack and the Performance of Prophecy

It was within the context of this revolutionary-era model of obeah as contagious illness that the tale of the notorious outlaw Jack Mansong, otherwise known as Three-Fingered Jack, emerged. Mansong was an escaped slave reported to have used obeah to plunder and terrorize the plantations of

Jamaica in the company of sixty maroons and remains an extremely popular Jamaican folk hero. The story of the 'terror of Jamaica' went through numerous permutations in the late eighteenth and nineteenth centuries, but was first reported in 1780 in the Jamaican newspaper *The Royal Gazette,* which ran the story that the Governor of Jamaica was offering a substantial reward for the head of Three-Fingered Jack. Following the press reports, the next published account of Jack's history was by the physician Benjamin Moseley, the surgeon-general of Jamaica, who had trained in London, Paris and Leiden. His *Treatise on Sugar* (1799) is most well known for its vehement opposition to the practice of smallpox vaccination, but also describes the 'occult science of OBI' and incorporates a brief account of the life of Three-Fingered Jack. Moseley claims to have seen for himself Jack's obi, which consisted of a 'goat's horn, filled with a compound of grave dirt, ashes, the blood of a black cat, and human fat; all mixed into a kind of paste'.[68] Jack's powers were so persuasive, Moseley wrote, that there were 'many white people, who believed he was possessed of some supernatural power'.[69]

Moseley's version of the Mansong story is prefaced by an account of yaws reporting that the highly contagious yaws sufferer was usually exiled from the plantation in order either to recover in solitude or to die. Most died, but

> some of these abandoned exiles lived, in spite of the common law of nature, and survived a general mutation of their muscles, ligaments, and osteology; became also hideously white in their woolly hair and skin; with their limbs and bodies twisted and turned, by the force of the distemper, into shocking grotesque figures, resembling woody excrescences, or stumps of trees; or old Egyptian figures, that seem as if they had been made of the ends of the human, and the beginnings of the brutal form; which figures are, by some antiquaries, taken for gods, and by others, for devils.[70]

Imaginatively linked through Moseley's antiquarian ethnography to the old Africa of ancient Egypt and, in their hideous appearances, to the dark arts of devilish African magical practices, the experience of suffering from disease helped yaws sufferers develop their obeah skills. Obeah's powers emerged from secret knowledge learnt during the period of isolation: as the sufferer 'grew more misshapen', claimed Moseley, so he 'generally became more subtile'.[71] Moseley claims that African-Caribbeans understood the association between obeah and disease in a more positive light than planters: 'the most wrinkled, and most deformed Obian magicians', he writes, are also the 'most venerated'.[72] Reiterating the 1789 parliamentary report's claim that 'those whose hoary heads, and a somewhat peculiarly harsh and diabolic in their Aspect, together with some Skill in plants of the medicinal and poisonous species, have qualified them for successful imposition upon the weak and credulous', Moseley claims that those individuals who suffered extreme cases of yaws and had become the most 'deformed' were also thought to be most learned.[73] The deformity of the yaws victim-turned-obeah-practitioner gives the credence of appearance to the magical performance which, for Moseley, is at the heart of the practice:

> These magicians will interrogate the patient, as to the part of the body most afflicted. This part they will torture with pinching, drawing with gourds, or calabashes, beating, and pressing. When the patient is nearly exhausted with this rough magnetizing, Obi brings out an old rusty nail, or a piece of bone, or an ass's tooth, or the jaw-bone of a rat, or a fragment of a quart bottle, from the part; and the patient is well the next day.[74]

Here, the obeah performance centres on the gathering of secret knowledge that nonetheless depends on a process of externalization in its dramatic production of physical objects from the diseased body.

Whether or not this was an accurate representation of what enslaved African-Caribbeans believed, planters found it agreeable. After all, the understanding of obeah as 'superstition', conceptually grounded in the Humean identification of superstition as originating in physical and mental weakness, offered a convenient way of exiling the obeah practitioner and the contagious disease they carried.[75] Planters and physicians could comfortably comprehend obeah as originating *in* disease because it enabled them conceptually to structure obeah *as* disease. For Moseley, obeah is an illness beyond the comprehension of European medics: 'no humanity of the master, nor skill in medicine, can relieve a negro, labouring under the influence of Obi. He will surely die; and of a disease that answers no description in nosology'.[76] It is this idea of obeah as disease, however, which empowered the practitioner. Through the colonial terror expressed in descriptions of yaws and obeah, the exile emerges as a powerful figure. By ousting the yaws victim, the planter might also hope to be rid of a potential obeah doctor. If the patient were healed, though, the obeah practitioner might return, armed with new and dangerous knowledge. Qualified by surviving yaws and exiled living, the obeah practitioner traverses the boundary between patient and doctor and returns from exile in monstrous form to haunt the plantation – and it is the 'hoary', 'wrinkled', diseased body of the practitioner which bears the mark of obeah and forms the site of resistance both to European medical methods and to slavery.[77] Moseley identifies this resistance as beyond the secular power of the colonial authorities: 'laws have been made in the West Indies to punish this *Obian* practice with death; but they have had no effect. Laws constructed in the West Indies, can never suppress the effect of ideas, the origin of which, is in the Centre of Africa.'[78]

Three further fictionalized versions of the Mansong story appeared in 1800, all of which drew on Moseley's account and brought the story to a wider audience: William Earle's sentimental epistolary novel *Obi; or, the History of Three-Fingered Jack,* plantation overseer William Burdett's novella *Life and Exploits of Mansong*; and, following Moseley's articulation of Jack's story in terms of acting, scenery and the stage, Three-Fingered Jack's first London stage appearance in John Fawcett's 'serio-pantomime' *Obi; or, Three-Fingered Jack.*[79] Following Moseley, these works associated obeah with yaws. An obeah novice, Jack must visit the secret abode of the local obeah doctor to acquire an obi to strengthen him and protect him from his enemy. In Earle's novel he encounters the 'wrinkled and deformed' Bashra, who strikes a terrible figure: 'snails drew their slimy train upon his shrivelled feet, and lizards and vipers filled the air of his hut with foul uncleanliness'.[80] Bashra's blemished and misshapen figure marks him out as having suffered from yaws, the source of his obeah knowledge.[81] Burdett's obeah practitioner, Amalkir, is even more physically afflicted: 'old and shrivelled; a disorder had contracted all his nerves, and he could scarcely crawl.'[82] As does Moseley's version, each of these works circulates around the issues relating to identity, prophecy and religion attendant on the point of meeting between obeah and Christianity, represented by the opposed characters of Jack and the loyal slave Quashee. In the culmination of the story, and just as Jack is preparing to kill his attackers, Burdett's Quashee tells him that the obi 'had no power over him now, for that he had been christened, and his name was no longer *Quashee*. Jack knew *Reeder*; and as if he was paralysed, he let his guns fall, and drew his cutlass'.[83] The audience has already witnessed Quashee's baptism, which affords him new resistance to obeah's charms. It is now revealed that Mansong had 'prophesied that *white Obi* would get the better of him', and in this moment the symbolic power of the Christian baptismal oath 'paralyses' Mansong, functioning as a corrective to the oaths of secrecy and revolution associated with obeah, and enabling Quashee to kill Jack.[84]

Obeah's prophetic capacities presented another form of threat to plantocratic control, one that challenged Christian spiritual discourse. Burdett incorporates into the text a passage from the 1789 parliamentary report which had despaired at the supernatural authority invested in obeah practitioners: 'the Negroes in general, whether Africans or Creoles, consult, and abhor them; to these Oracles they resort, and with the most implicit Faith, upon all Occasions, whether for the Cure of Disorders, the obtaining Revenge for Injuries or Insults, the conciliating of Favour, the Discovery and Punishment of the Thief or the Adulterer, and the Prediction of Future Events'.[85] According to Moseley, it was usually women obeah doctors who made a practice of prophecy, along with their responsibility for affairs of the heart:

> It is the province of the *Obi-women* to dispose of the passions. They sell foul winds for inconstant mariners; dreams and phantasies for jealousy, vexation, and pains in the heart, for perfidious love; and for the perturbed, impatient, and wretched, at the tardy acts of time,—to turn in prophetic fury to a future page in the book of Fate,—and amaze the ravished sense of the tempest-tossed querent.[86]

Obeah women's prophecies are associated with romantic dilemmas – significantly, this might also suggest responsibility for control over reproduction.[87] Jack's prophetic imagination, meanwhile, positions him at the centre of plantocratic concerns about the encounter between Christianity and obeah. Burdett, Earle and Fawcett all follow Moseley in constructing Jack's death as a moment of revelation: Reeder's disclosure of his baptismal covenant promises Jack's destruction. His death restores peace to Jamaica, and the story closes with the marriage of a young planter's daughter and a soldier. While his power of prophecy remains a potent image of obeah's mystical powers, here Christianity is the effective antidote to Jack's revenge-driven and obeah-inspired banditry.

Fawcett's pantomime was later adapted by William Murray as the melodrama *Obi; or, Three-Fingered Jack* (1825).[88] Unlike Fawcett's dumbshow, Murray's play includes extensive dialogue. The script gestures forwards to a post-slavery moment in its announcement of the changing politics of race in this period after the abolition of the Atlantic trade in slaves but before emancipation, but it also returns to the pre-revolutionary ridicule of the healing and magical powers of obeah and the focus on the practitioner's use of language.[89] The melodramatic oscillation between the comic and the tragic alternates between laughter (shared by the overseer and the audience) at the expense of African-Caribbean superstition and pity for Jack as wronged avenger seeking redress for the loss of his wife and child in Africa.[90] Murray's overseer dismisses the naïveté of the slaves who live in fear of the local obeah woman: 'nonsense, nonsense! ye black ninny-hammers. Do you think an old woman, as great a noodle as yourselves, can stop your windpipes by cramming parrots' feathers, dogs' teeth, broken bottles, rum, and egg shells into a cow's horn, and then mumbling a few words over it, as incomprehensible as your own fears?'[91] Despite the overseer's mockery, the enslaved live in fear of the awful power of the obeah woman's words to stop their own speech: 'the very name of Obi and Three-fingered Jack struck them as dumb as—'.[92] The planter shares their alarm, demanding that the overseer refrain from mentioning Jack's name in his presence, as its very utterance will 'awaken recollections which pain, which agonize [him]'.[93] Murray's sense of obeah's dreadful linguistic power was shared by those on the plantation. For planter Matthew Lewis, obeah is so toxic that he declares it 'a crime even so much as to mention the word obeah on the estate', warning his slaves that 'if any negro from that time forward should be proved to have accused another of obeahing him, or of telling another that he had been obeahed, he should forfeit his share of the next present of salt-fish'.[94] Such was the potency of the mere word 'obeah' that Lewis attempts to extinguish it, indicating that the best cure for the problem of phony obeah doctors is a mode of linguistic resistance to their persuasive powers by the use of 'plain English'.[95]

Murray replaces the disclosure of the baptismal oath with a pronouncement of freedom. Rather than revealing his baptism to Jack, the play's climactic moment sees Quashee announce that he is now a free man. Hailed by Jack as 'Slave!' Quashee replies: 'Me *no* slave! me free! me *gentleman,* me Mr. Quashee now, and no care a button for you or Obi either.'[96] Despite the change, the performance of revelation remains central to the dramatic climax and Mansong's downfall. Indeed, the rearticulations of Jack Mansong from the 1780 press reports to Moseley's theatre-inflected medical treatise, Fawcett's pantomime and Murray's melodrama reveal the theatricalizing responses to obeah. Just as Singleton's 'credulous, unthinking crowd' and Moseley's 'rough magnetizing' highlight the sense of obeah as an act of fascination or performance to a bewitched audience, the versions of the life of Three-Fingered Jack represent responses to obeah which also mobilized the dramatic. Fawcett's and Murray's use of dramatic irony in the revelation of Quashee's conversion or his new-found freedom as the antidote to the evils of obeah shows the importance of a performance of disclosure as resolution that dispels the danger. Fawcett's revenge-driven murderer and Murray's tragic hero, who elide the political and social dimensions of slavery in favour of pantomime caricature or the story of an individual seeking revenge for personal wrongs, were both comfortable articulations of the threat posed by revolutionary slaves.[97] But both – along with the other versions of the Mansong story – also reveal the obeah practitioner as caught up in a nexus of secret knowledge, illegitimate speech, revelation and prophecy which demonstrate the colonial appropriation of the obeah practitioner's performance in a restaging of plantation society that attempts to dispel his or her threat to the social order.

Colonial Gothic and Hamel, the Obeah Man (1827)

'There is always an Obeah man in every insurrection; there always has been,' declares the planter Mr Guthrie in the anonymously published gothic fiction *Hamel, the Obeah Man* (1827).[98] *Hamel* is perhaps the most significant and distinctive fiction of slave resistance from the British Caribbean: a colonial romance dealing in magic and mystery, it is a striking representation of the consciousness of its enslaved title character and combines a pro-slavery agenda with an unflinching articulation of the motivations for rebellion. It was published four years after – but set one year before – the Demerara Revolt of 1823, which saw ten thousand slaves rise up against the planter elite and which was one of the catalysts for the eventual abolition of slavery in 1833–4, and represents a fictionalized account of events surrounding the rebellion. *Hamel* was published anonymously, but contemporary reviewers identified the author as Cynric R. Williams, about whom little is known besides his other work, *A Tour through the Island of Jamaica* (1826), which shares *Hamel*'s pro-slavery politics.[99] Written in sympathy with the plantocracy, *Hamel* is acutely sensitive to the 'horrors' inflicted upon white Creole communities during the First Maroon War of Jamaica and the Haitian Revolution.[100] The narrator reproaches the self-interested and ignorant British government for the 'oppressions' it inflicts upon the colonies and views the state of social unrest as the inevitable consequence of the 'cruel and fatal policy of the mother country'.[101]

Slowly revealed through interwoven threads and against a backdrop of haunting tropical scenery, *Hamel*'s gothic plot presents the reader with an array of corrupt and villainous colonial characters. Surprisingly, Hamel himself emerges by the end of the novel as the least sinister of these. The role of gothic anti-hero is reserved for the Methodist missionary, Roland, a lustful hypocrite who plots to marry the white heroine Joanna by force, after raping her mother and laying the blame on Joanna's fiancé. Roland's sinister intentions are finally undone by the obeah man Hamel, who, having plotted revolution, turns traitor on his fellow slaves and quashes the rebellion he had instigated. Like Edgeworth's 'The Grateful Negro', *Hamel* draws on the figure of the grateful slave which George Boulukos argues was the dominant colonial trope in eighteenth-century fiction and which embodied efforts to negate the inhumanity of slavery and assuage anxieties about rebellion by suggesting that slaves lived in a paradoxical state of 'voluntary' bondage.[102] Despite some similarities with Edgeworth's story, though, *Hamel* is unique in that the obeah practitioner himself embodies both the figure of the vengeful rebel and that of the loyal slave, and retains a strong sense of agency and authority despite ending the rebellion.[103]

The novel portrays obeah and missionary Christianity as two evils competing and conspiring in their efforts to revolutionize the slave community. Obeah practitioners are denounced as pagan necromancers who fool other slaves into believing their pretended magic with gruesome 'nocturnal orgies, festivities and broils', while missionaries are 'meddling hypocrites' sent from England by interfering abolitionists.[104] Hamel and Roland are locked in a scenario of mutual dependence and loathing, spiritually opposed but jointly intent on 'the subversion of the power and authority of the whites throughout the island'.[105] Theirs is a battle of wits, with Hamel gaining the fear and respect of his fellow slaves with mysterious spells, magical potions and whispered oaths, while Roland uses his oratory powers of persuasion and deceit. The missionary couches their struggle in terms of African disease and European cure as he argues that Christianity is the only remedy for Hamel's diabolical trickery: 'he is a dealer in magic— an obeah man, whose poisonous practices are only rendered abortive and contemptible by the antidote of mine—I may say of ours—the only true religion'.[106] The political aims of missionary work are made explicit as Roland wins the spiritual support of slaves with abolitionist rhetoric: 'the Christian religion, of which you may all become members, acknowledges no such distinction as that of master and slave: it makes all men equal; I say, it makes all men equal, all brothers'.[107] While Roland hides behind a mask of anti-slavery feeling, Hamel's aims are more explicit: 'on such a revolution his own soul was bent: his arts, his influence, his every energy, were devoted to the extermination of the Whites, or to their expulsion from the island. It is not enough to say he detested them: his hatred was charged with the recollection of the outrages he had himself endured'.[108] This moment of understanding on the part of the narrator – a conflicted but sympathetic response to the plight of slaves that emerges at various points in this otherwise pro-slavery novel – hints at the sense of moral complexity that surrounds Hamel.

Despite their spiritual opposition, the revolutionary alignment in *Hamel* between Christianity and obeah reveals the proximity between African-Caribbean and European spiritual and cultural practices and the anxiety surrounding such processes of cultural syncretism which both bolstered and undermined the chattel system. The early nineteenth century had brought increasing numbers of missionaries to the Caribbean, swept across by the liberal tide of abolitionism and philanthropy. German Moravians preceded other denominations when they arrived in Jamaica in 1754, but by the 1800s others had followed. Christian missions encouraged slaves to learn to read in order to study the Bible, while slave-holders began to see literacy as dangerously associated with resistance and the abolitionist movement. The Wesleyan Methodist mission was especially aligned with the anti-slavery cause after 1807, when it forbade missionaries either to own slaves or to marry those who did. The ban prompted the Jamaican Assembly to effect an immediate criminalization of missionary work, but the British Government disallowed the new law and made it abundantly clear that religious matters would be decided upon in the metropole. Nevertheless, by refusing to license missionaries, the Kingston magistrates effectively closed the Wesleyan chapel between 1807 and 1814.[109] After the 1823 Demerara Revolt, the missionary Reverend John Smith was tried with inciting the slaves to rebel. Smith pleaded innocence but was sentenced to death; he was later pardoned by the king but died in his prison cell before the message could reach Demerara.[110] The testimony of slaves was not recognized as legal evidence against white people, but it was heard in this case. As the prominent abolitionist James Stephen commented upon Smith's conviction:

> the evidence of slaves, Sir, is sufficient, it seems, to convict a preacher of the Gospel! … Their evidence may be safely received and relied upon against a prisoner, when a whole infuriated community is clamorous for his destruction; but is too dangerous to be heard in any case before a jury of White men, all whose prepossessions, and all whose sympathies, are adverse to the prosecutor and witness, and favourable to the party accused.[111]

While earlier uprisings such as Tacky's Rebellion had been viewed as a consequence of the malignant machinations of obeah practitioners, Christian missionaries now posed an equally significant threat to the status quo of the plantation system. The role of African Christianity in the Demerara Revolt and the later Jamaica Rebellion of 1831–2 led by Samuel Sharpe (also known as the Baptist War) made conversion a far more controversial practice than it had been when early versions of the Three-Fingered Jack story staged Christianity as the bedrock of a stable plantation and plantocratic control. Missionaries were already allied with slave communities because of their role in fostering literacy, but Smith's trial now raised the thorny issue of legal testimony and demonstrates another way in which ideas about language – its private use and public performance – became central to cultural discourses of slavery, abolition and revolution.

The politics of literacy and the power dynamics at stake in public speech acts and intercultural communication play an important role in *Hamel*. The 'hideous and discordant yell' arising from Hamel's rebellious collective as they prepare to take over the island is imagined by the narrator as a 'Babel-like confusion of tongues'.[112] The incomprehensible strangeness of the rebels' cries is answered by the mysterious song of Hamel's fellow slave and co-conspirator taken by many of the novel's characters to be a duppie, or ghost, with the narrator dismissing his 'lingo (I must not call it language)' on the grounds that it 'would be utterly unintelligible to all my uncreolized countrymen'.[113] This linguistic confusion is echoed in the series of names used to describe obeah practitioners: Hamel is variously called a 'conjurer', 'wizard', 'pretended dabbler', 'dealer in magic', 'pagan necromancer', an 'infidel' and a 'strange and unaccountable creature'.[114] Obeah practitioners were mysterious individuals, of whom most colonists knew very little. According to Edward Long, planters' inability to identify which slaves were the obeah doctors meant they could do little to tackle the problem of their powerful influence: 'it is very difficult', Long complained, 'for the White Proprietor to distinguish the *Obia Professor* from any other Negro upon his Plantation'.[115] Hamel invests in his own enigmatic image by labouring to 'weave a net of mystery, by tales of enchantment and prophetic warnings, to keep all intruders from prying into his secrets'.[116] On first meeting Hamel in his cavernous lair filled with skulls and other obeah fetishes, Roland is frustrated by Hamel's refusal to identify himself as an obeah doctor and demands to know 'In the name of God or Devil … who or what art thou?' Hamel responds enigmatically: 'Master – what you will' and, after a pause, 'what you please, – a Negro'.[117] The problem of inscrutability is at the centre of the novel's representation of obeah as shrouded in gothic mystery. Recognizing the political advantages of that sense of mystery, Hamel embraces his anonymous status as, in Long's terms, 'any other Negro'.[118]

In a confrontation with the plantation attorney Mr. Fillbeer, who has fallen from a tree after being threatened with hanging by an angry group of slaves who mistakenly believe he has shot their white master, Hamel confounds the avaricious and grotesquely fat man not with charms or illusions but with word play:

> 'It is you, you black monster, who bewitch the cows, is it? – who cause abortions among the women – who make your fellow-creatures eat dirt?'

'Dirt!' said the obeah man, emphatically – 'dirt, master Fillbeer? It is such as you and preaching Roland who make my countrymen eat dirt. Who brought us from Africa? Who made slaves of us? Who treated – and treat us still – as the dirt they buy and sell? And while they affect to be for making us free, and for saving our souls, are cramming us with dirt, and trash, and filthy foolish lies?'

'Do you call my religion dirt?' said Fillbeer ... 'dirt as you are, yourself.'

'I know,' said the latter, 'we are all dust and dirt – but master is more dirt than I am, ten times, twenty times more dirt.'

The fat man rolled upon the ground, like a tame duck, after an awkward flight, alighting upon the earth, not being able to stop its course till it has performed a somerset or two. He lay at last flat on his back, gasping for breath to repeat his curses on Hamel, who stood calmly surveying him from the rock, without offering him any assistance.

'It is a bad omen, master Fillbeer! Think of it: you have brought it on yourself. You teach the Negroes to sing psalms and preach; now learn something from a Negro in return. Learn to be master of your passion and your tongue. Are you fit to talk of righteousness, and election, and salvation from hell fire, – who are proud and vain, cruel, merciless, and passionate? Think you the Negroes will reverence or love such a heap of flesh and fat as that which lies kicking before me? Who eats the dirt now?'[119]

Dirt held great significance on the plantation for two reasons: the authorities' belief that obeah depended upon the use of grave dirt for many of its treatments and spells, and their belief that the practice of geophagy was the cause of numerous deaths amongst slaves, baffling and infuriating physicians and planters alike. William Fitzmaurice, a planter in Jamaica, reported that dirt eating was a widespread method of suicide: 'I lost in one year a dozen new Negroes by dirt eating though I fed them well – when I remonstrated with them, they constantly told me, that they preferred dying to living; and a great proportion of the new Negroes who go upon sugar plantations, die in this manner.'[120] Medics gave various explanations as to what possessed slaves to take up this strange and potentially fatal habit. In his *Practical Rules for the Management and Medical Treatment of Negro Slaves* (1803), David Collins wrote that dirt eating was both a symptom of illness or malnutrition and a method of attempted suicide.[121] Physician Robert Thomas compared dirt eating, or 'Cachexia Africana', to the illness of nostalgia (commonly suffered by British sailors and often causing them to throw themselves overboard) in its 'unaccountable desire of returning to one's own country'.[122] In the *Jamaica Planter's Guide* (1823) Thomas Roughley described the 'hateful, fatal habit of eating dirt' as caused in children by the 'excessive' breastfeeding of their mothers.[123] An anonymous 'resident' of the West Indies connected dirt eating or *Mal de stomac*' to the 'mischievous effects' of obi, asserting that it was 'a frequent disease of newly imported Africans' and was therefore by this point 'disappearing'.[124] Mary Douglas's important insight that when we look back to a time prior to the nineteenth-century discovery of the bacterial transmission of disease, pathogenicity and hygiene 'we are left with the old definition of dirt as matter out of place' underscores the significance of material things which cross social and sacred boundaries.[125] In the colonial understanding of obeah practice, dirt was indeed matter out of social and metaphorical place. Obeah was a practice grounded in a belief in the transformative powers of matter such as bones, herbs, fetishes and earth. Matter that would be categorized by the colonial authorities as waste or dirt was misappropriated and took on great cultural significance. While the Woman of the Popo Country used dirt as one of the props in her plantation performance which spread disease and killed slaves in their dozens, Hamel metaphorically transforms dirt: from an object of obeah practice, dirt becomes the image and usage of chattel slaves, the hidden agendas of colonial rhetoric and Christian preaching and the substance of the human body. Slaves could not own material things of economic value, but obeah mobilizes the value of dirt as filth, waste or nothingness. The metamorphosis of dirt, and especially its crossing of the boundary from thing (but a thing that is nothing) to human (when it is imagined as the body of a slave), points to the blurry boundaries between things and people in the dehumanizing context of the plantation, where dirt could hold more power and significance than enslaved human beings. Asserting the slave as 'master' of the tongue, Hamel transmutes matter into rhetoric, inverting the image of the dirt-eating slave and revealing the hypocrisy of the capitalist and colonialist plantation system. While the climatic and geographical understandings of disease emphasized the agency of matter – of dirt – in its theory of noxious effluvia, obeah marshalled the power of dirt in in ways that opposed European models of medicine and knowledge by calling upon ideas of transformation which elide post-Enlightenment divisions of organic and inorganic, animate and inanimate.

Passages such as this raise questions about the complicated positioning of the reader in relation to a pro-slavery novel which has a powerful enslaved black hero. Revisiting and reversing the generic codification of obeah as pantomime, Hamel jokes at the expense of the white character Fillbeer, who 'performs' a 'somerset' for Hamel – a joke which is intended to be shared by Cynric Williams's slave-owning compatriots. While the humane Fairfax and the paternalistic Mr Guthrie are held up as models of the 'good' slave owner, Fillbeer's excessive greed and Roland's hypocritical

Christianity make them the scapegoats of the novel's pro-slavery argument, affording a convenient rationalization of the attempted rebellion which is blamed on the misdeeds of non-slave-owning characters. By contrast, Hamel is presented as clever, ethical and thoughtful. His rebellious word play is also indicative of the threat posed to colonial authorities by African-Caribbean speech. While *Hamel's* narrator derides the 'barbarous sound' of obeah rites, the novel also pays notable attention to the power of the word and the politics of language at stake in a society where some forms of language – such as the duppie's song and other kinds of musical practice – were the only form of public expression and resistance possible for many slaves, while others – reading, writing and legal testimony – were unavailable and became situated at the heart of abolitionist politics.[126] Just as the debate surrounding the testimony of slaves in the case against Reverend Smith registers the colonial politics of private and public language (and the performative language of the courts), *Hamel* implicitly recognizes the potential threat – it is the very incoherence of obeah language to a planter's ear that makes it so dangerous. Ultimately choosing to crush the revolution he had sought to achieve, Hamel leaves Jamaica for Africa, to be 'never heard of more!'[127] His symbolic exile from the island leaves it safe from the sinister practice of obeah and from his revolutionary followers, but the fact that it is Hamel's own choice to prevent the rebellion and leave the island conveys the sense that it is he, not the planters, administrators or missionaries, who controls the direction of events. While *Hamel* is written in allegiance to Jamaican planters, the sympathetic and complex portrayal of Hamel himself as clever and principled (albeit vengeful and revolutionary) sits uncomfortably within this frame, and it is in this pro-slavery novel that one of the most surprising images of the obeah practitioner appears.

Like the obeah doctors portrayed by Moseley, Singleton and others, Hamel is a performer: he wins over gullible slaves with spells and illusions and his cavernous abode is reached via several theatrical 'vomitories'.[128] But *Hamel* also widens the sphere of performance and renders missionary Christianity theatrical too. Roland, having formed an alliance with Combah, a key figure in the revolutionary collective Roland hopes will help him win the hand of the planter's daughter Joanna, is alarmed to find that Combah is in league with Hamel. Roland finds himself cornered by the pair, who force him to follow through on his promise to help Combah take up the position of brutchie, or king, and lead the rebellion. While Hamel, Combah and their group are engaged in obeah practice in the vault below, Roland begins a rabble-rousing anti-slavery oration to a packed crowd: "'You will perhaps say I am a white man. So I am outwardly – my skin is white; but my heart is like yours; and if that is black as your skins, so is mine. I am an exception to the white men; I have never flogged you, nor ravished your daughters.'" Here, Roland's duplicitous speech is interrupted, as 'a loud demoniac sort of laugh was heard from the cellar below'.[129] Hamel's laughter facetiously unmasks Roland's claims to honesty and the virtue of his 'black heart' – Roland may not have ravished any of his enslaved listeners' daughters, but he has raped the mother of the white woman he wishes to marry. Crucially, though, Roland is not exposed in the eyes of the unsuspecting 'audience', who are too far removed to hear the laughter emanating from beneath.[130] This gothic-comedic theatrical pattern continues, with the unseen Hamel interrupting Roland's address to voice the missionary's wrongdoing from beneath the stage. Suddenly, a violent explosion causes Roland to fall through the floor into the obeah collective's vault, which becomes the setting for a different kind of performance. Having accidentally witnessed the obeah rites, Roland is forced to swear allegiance to the rebels' cause and drink a mixture of human blood, gunpowder and the grave dirt from a skull.[131] Meanwhile, another scene has begun above ground in which 'the dancing and festivity were carried on above with an increasing energy, as the rum inspired the minds and accelerated the motions of the performers'.[132] In one sense this passage presents the congregated slaves as an unknowing audience of potential converts witnessing Roland's hypocritical rhetoric but unaware of the equally sinister plotting of their own leaders, but in another those above ground are also presented as engaged in a revolutionary social 'performance' of their own. The various comic and dramatic elements in this passage echo the earlier theatrical incarnations of Jack Mansong, but this time the reader is presented with a series of dilemmas concerning how to interpret the relationship between missionary Christianity and obeah within the moral and social context of abolitionism. Foregrounding the elements of performance in the practice of Christianity and of obeah, *Hamel* and its gothic sensibilities construct a dichotomy between the two belief systems only to collapse it dramatically and highlight their overlapping rhetorical modes and joint revolutionary agenda.

This passage finds its parallel in Cynric R. Williams's *Tour through the Island of Jamaica* (1826), a travel narrative which also represents the encounter between Christianity and obeah in a theatrical dynamic. The *Tour* also constructs this encounter in linguistic terms: finding 'the negro patois' to be 'most ludicrously diverting', Williams records eavesdropping on the conversation between two enslaved men, Abdallah and Ebeneezer, as they discuss the Bible as a corrective to obeah. Ebeneezer blurts out 'a torrent of mutilated quotations from the Old Testament' which 'came bundled out in confusion, like rocks hurried along by an avalanche, that mingles and mars and overwhelms all into chaos'.[133] The slave, here, performs the role of verbal mimic, enacting an inaccurate and comic rendering of Christian devotion. Williams uses Abdallah and Ebeneezer's misunderstanding of biblical text to connect the problem of intercultural communication to a joint attack on obeah and the missionary project. Like the cultural adaptation of the sinister obeah doctor as pantomime fiend, Abdallah and Ebeneezer's performance of Christian belief is another example of obeah theatrics – or the ways in which the 'pretend' of the obeah performance (and African-Caribbean cultural practices more broadly) was rearticulated in various forms that expressed a range of concerns about syncretic cultural change on the plantation.

Mimesis and Modernity

The various texts relating to obeah – parliamentary records, poetry, fiction, drama, plantation journals and medical treatises – reveal that colonial responses to this misunderstood set of practices used images and ideas of performance as a means to articulate the problems of knowledge and power at troubled moments of colonial intercultural exchange in which obeah was implicated. Surgeon and colonial administrator in Cuba Richard Madden was convinced that black medics had access to a wealth of useful herbal knowledge, but viewed obeah as acting principally upon the imagination: 'it is evident to any medical man who reads these trials [of obeah practitioners] that, in the great majority of cases, the trumpery ingredients used in the practice of obeah were incapable of producing mischief, except on the imagination of the person intended to be obeahed'.[134] While the victim of obeah was afflicted by a trick of the imagination, the practitioner was also suffering from a kind of madness: 'knaves and lunatics (partially insane) are commonly the persons' who take up 'the obeah character' and 'play the part of santons and sorcerers'.[135] For Madden, obeah becomes a kind of contagious illness of the mind, transmitted through the performance or 'play' of the obeah practitioner and relying on fear to spread itself across the plantation.

The idea of the contagious and potentially fatal obeah performance highlights the anti-theatrical stance of the colonial authorities, who dismissed the obeah doctor as a purveyor of the pretend. Nevertheless, these theatrics were matched by the spectacular punishments to which practitioners were subjected, and which emerged as part of a culture of spectacular violence created to exert control over enslaved communities. Vincent Brown argues that planters used 'spiritual terror' as part of the effort to win psychological control over slave communities. Responding to the suicides which depleted their workforces, planters mutilated and displayed the corpses of slaves who had killed themselves in order to assert authority and to suggest the futility of suicide.[136] For many Africans, Brown argues, death signified the possibility of returning to ancestral lands and liberation from a life of slavery. By preventing proper burial rites and exhibiting dismembered corpses, planters hoped to convince people that the spirits' passing to the homeland had been intercepted. In a potent effort to cast a moral shadow over such acts, planters incorporated dramatic visions of heaven and hell into their rhetoric. Combined with religious teachings, the violent and theatrical punishments inflicted upon rebellious slaves involved projecting a particular concept of the afterlife. Colonial authorities, writes Brown, 'supplemented physical coercion with even more menacing "government magic", as they harnessed the affective power of the dead and people's awe of the afterlife in an attempt to transmute legal mastery into sacred authority'.[137] As well as the rivalry depicted in *Hamel* between missionaries and obeah practitioners over slaves' spiritual beliefs, obeah doctors often faced aggressive competition from planters, who responded to the authority vested in obeah people by contending for spiritual power.

Punishment was not the only plantation spectacle wrought by planters. In addition to its function in the trials of the revolutionary obeah doctors in Jamaica in 1760, the magic lantern was used on the plantation for other purposes. The planter and diarist Thomas Thistlewood records displaying his magic lantern to one of his Jamaican slaves, while slave owner and politician John Stewart figured the technological spell of the magic lantern in terms of the anti-emancipationist trope of the innocent slave who is incapable of seeing beyond the theatrical trick of the lantern and gazes in awe at the miraculous optical machine:

> The author once amused a party of negroes with the deceptions of a magic-lantern. They gazed with the utmost wonder and astonishment at the hideous figures conjured up by this optical machine, and were of the opinion that nothing short of witchcraft could have produced such an instrument.[138]

In Stewart's account the accusation of witchcraft undergoes an ironic reversal, with European technology now constructed as a supernatural phenomenon, though only in order to underline Stewart's scientific mastery.

In the 1840s the explorer, scientific investigator and missionary David Livingstone would make use of the magic lantern as 'a good means of conveying instruction' in his efforts to convert Africans to Christianity.[139] While earlier the performance of European technological power had employed spectacular display in the delivery of violent punishments against obeah doctors, these same mechanical modes of display later became important for the dissemination of new knowledge and religious ideals in ways that suggest the deep-rooted proximity of religion, scientific knowledge and violence in plantation culture, as well as the function and importance of performance and spectacle in the relationship between master and slave.

The colonial theatres of death described by Vincent Brown were intended to persuade slaves that the authorities held an all-encompassing power that extended even beyond the grave. They emerged as part of a broader spectrum of colonial performance: the plantocracy sought to deride African-Caribbean medical and spiritual practices as artful pretence which drew in John Singleton's 'credulous, unthinking crowd', while taking up the mantle of performance itself as part of an effort to claim authority over slave communities.[140] Reading these violent punishments as the public spectacle of power over life after death, they present a complex interplay between the real and the spectacular, with the performance of violence to a terrified public imagined to have ideological, material and spiritual effects. At the same time, the idea of magical slave performance which could be dispelled through counter-performance emerged from the early nineteenth-century melodramas and pantomimes which diffused the violent power of obeah through comedy or tragic sentimentality. Colonial epistemology rejected superstition and 'pretend', equating obeah with theatrically produced delusion. But paradoxically it also used spectacle to compel belief in the power of the colonial project, to deploy Christian principles strategically and to break the spell cast by the powerful performances of obeah doctors. The generic codification of obeah as theatre recategorized its practices as comedy, gothic, melodrama or pantomime, viewing obeah's fiction-making devices as a threat but also exposing obeah to a model of counter-performance which drew on supernatural spectacle and kept the British audience at a comfortable distance.

The 'Electrical Machines and Magic Lanthorns' used to torture the obeah practitioners involved in Tacky's Rebellion are described by Jill Casid as the 'mimesis of mimesis', with the spectacle of obeah punishments imitating the magical illusions of obeah itself.[141] But colonial responses to obeah present more than the imitation of magical spectacle employed by what Casid calls a 'colonial order [which] required effects of necromancy to power its machinery'.[142] As *Hamel* reveals, the cultural mimesis involved in the mutually dependent relationship between obeah and Christianity was two-way. Forcing Roland to conspire in obeah spells, Hamel stresses the parallel between African-Caribbean and European spiritual practices: "'we call you brother from your participation in *our* mysteries, as you so name those initiated in *yours*'".[143] Describing an obeah practice he calls 'the book ordeal', Richard Madden identifies a 'singular instance of an African superstition engrafted on Christianity'. 'To find out the person who has committed a theft', Madden writes, 'all parties present are called upon to open a Bible, 10th chapter of Kings.'[144] A key being placed between the leaves, each individual present would hold a thread attached to the key. After a reading of the 50th psalm, the book would be struck and fall to the ground with the key remaining in the hand of the guilty party. Writing in 1834 during the process of abolition, Madden gives an example of syncretic cultural practice suggestive of something more than mimesis and which marks the increasing overlap between Christianity and obeah that developed over the colonial period.

The violent punishments to which obeah practitioners were subjected reflect a broader attempt to dispel ontological and spiritual beliefs which did not suit the planters' interests. The obeah doctors, however, regularly undermined these efforts. While planters, colonial administrators and missionaries tried to enforce one model of life and death, obeah offered alternative ideas. At stake in this struggle was the power over cultural narratives of knowledge. *Hamel* and the fictionalized and dramatized accounts of Three-Fingered Jack present obeah as a practice which unsettled British colonial authority. They reveal that obeah emerged as a mode of social resistance through slave uprisings as well as its connection to a powerful and secret herbal pharmacopoeia and, increasingly, towards the end of the period of British slavery in the Caribbean, because of its links to Christianity. But obeah's resistant practices went beyond the pragmatic: its imaginative effects and powers of psychological resistance proved just as problematic. Obeah took hold in the colonial imagination because it highlighted the issues surrounding the intercultural encounter of Afro- and Anglo-Atlantic belief systems and cultural practices. European models of life, death, disease and futurity invoked by a plantocratic regime were faced with obeah practitioners' refusal to acknowledge or operate within their medical, spiritual or social structures and with obeah's magical performance of secret knowledge allied to a revolutionary agenda that troubled the secularity and singularity of European medical and scientific modernity. The debate about whether African-Caribbean medical practitioners held any useful knowledge, and the frustration at those medicines being kept 'as a Secret from the white People', are expressive of the competitive knowledge market at stake in the production of colonial power.[145]

Obeah reveals the cultural shape of modernity on the colonial plantation in terms of the contact between African and European spiritual and religious beliefs and medical and magical knowledge, which initiated moments of cultural conflict, confusion, exchange, hybridity and revolution. In relation to obeah, these moments were persistently framed by a theatricalizing discourse. But while many obeah people are represented in colonial texts as sinister, cave-dwelling charlatans, they also embody the complexity of identities, political allegiances and processes of cultural syncretism that shaped plantation societies and the wider colonial world. The 'Babel-like confusion of tongues' of rebellious slaves described by *Hamel's* pro-slavery narrator, for example, inhabits colonizing perceptions of race, language and literacy. Yet these multiple tongues can also be understood as verbalizing the multiple social functions performed by obeah men and women which enabled them to play a subversive role in the plantation system. It was, in a sense, the very multiplicity (as well as the duplicity) of the obeah practitioner that concerned medics and planters invested in the Enlightenment separation of medicine, religion and superstition. Hamel, the narrator writes, desired 'to create a confusion in the island'.[146] It is this confusion – of language, of social roles, of performance and reality and of medicine and religion – which gestures towards the obeah practitioner as a key figure in the articulation of colonial modernity and to the origins of obeah's role as a medically and socially resistant practice.

Afterword
Colonial Modernities and after Abolition

If Hamel's 'confusion of tongues' voices the challenge obeah presents to Eurocentric narratives of medical knowledge, linguistic forms and colonial identities, it also speaks to the contingencies of predisciplinary medical knowledge. The theatricalizing discourse within which ideas about obeah were framed was just as important in the work of the surgeon-general in Jamaica, Benjamin Moseley, as it was in the stage representations of Three-Fingered Jack. These intersecting, overlapping modes of articulating the deep-rooted medicalization of colonial lives reveal some of the epistemological and narrative models associated with 'colonial modernity' – a term that suggests a way of approaching the cultural dynamics of the modern era in relation to the particularities of colonial existence while understanding the significance of their cultural reach far beyond the Caribbean locations examined here. Colonial authors were uncomfortably aware of their position on the peripheries of metropolitan creative and natural philosophical endeavour – Grainger felt he had to justify and explain the 'importance and novelty' of his 'new and picturesque images', while Stedman apologized for his work's 'not being interesting to Great Britain'.[1] This book situates itself as part of the ongoing work to situate colonial and postcolonial ideas, texts, peoples and histories at the centre of accounts of 'modern' cultures, attempting to map the terrain of connection and difference across Atlantic societies and texts. While this study does not aim to be a history of medicine, it does endeavour to emphasize the fact that the hybridized, mobile cultures of colonial medical knowledge highlighted by obeah texts are just as important to stories of modern medicine as are the histories of European scientific institutions, historical figures and 'centres of calculation'. The Caribbean plantation, with its unique economic and social structures which reconfigured bodies, identities, persons and things according to its own capitalist and colonial logic, demands more attention in terms of its transformations of metropolitan ways of thinking and writing. Modernity, as Vincent Brown writes, 'is rarely claimed for acquisitive slaveholders and

their heterogeneous armies of labourers', despite the fact that both plantation life and the traditional understanding of modernity are underpinned
by 'capitalist accumulation, the experience of dislocation, and a self-conscious sense of the novelty of one's predicament'.[2]

As well as the relationship between African-Caribbean and European
medical knowledge, other themes from this book work towards mapping
the transatlantic reverberations of the colonial medical imagination. Ideas
about environmental health and sustainability, usable bodies and lands,
about experience, empiricism and observation, about feeling for and on
behalf of others and about shifting identities and transnational politics –
these discussions demonstrate the importance of considering colonial and
metropolitan texts and histories in reciprocal relation. Attending to the
interactions and exchanges between literary and medical texts exposes
some key textual formations of colonial modernity, and ways of reading
them. Grainger's georgic organicism produces poetic figures which express
the medicalization of African-Caribbean bodies under slavery, as well as the
muffled articulation of indigenous and slave medical and natural knowledge in European form. They, like obeah texts, need to be read against the
grain in order to trace the blurred, fractured outlines of African-Caribbean
medical knowledge and forms of resistance. This study has modelled other
reading practices which form an important part of the work to examine
the medical imagination in predisciplinary context. Reading medical
topographies through the lens of the picturesque reveals not only the
proximity of aesthetic and medical articulations of landscape but also the
unique and medicalized aesthetic sensorium in the colonies. The feeling
engagement with scientific objects and the relationship between epigrammatic parts and narrative wholes, medical knowledge and romantic fiction
in Stedman's textual practice of sentimental science demonstrate the deep
bonds between Romantic era feeling and knowing. Reading through a
medical lens sheds light on broader cultural and theoretical issues: the
chaotic potential in the process of medical creolization can be used to
inform postcolonial understandings of creolization, hybridity and change.
Obeah's transmutation through various literary and historical moments
outlines patterns of colonial thought and the politics of healing, believing
and knowing in post-Enlightenment culture.

By tracing the historical configurations of colonial literature and medicine and describing the trajectory of cultural responses to the Caribbean in
the context of far-reaching epidemiological changes, this book offers a literary history of colonial health and illness that recovers the historical perspective on disease and the rich connections between form and knowledge

in a way that illuminates the history of slave societies and colonial inter-cultural encounter. This literary genealogy of disease and medicine is grounded in an argument for a multidisciplinary Romantic studies. In the humanities, science and medicine have reached beyond their previous crit-ical limitations as providing historical context for literary interpretation. A historical view of medicine has appreciated how it has structured social categories of class, gender, nationality, race and sexuality by pathologizing certain types of bodies. But more remains to be done in charting the unstable territories of epistemological and textual forms of modernity, and particularly of their colonial dimensions and dynamics. Without reading practices that try to work across and between late modern disciplinary formations – even while acknowledging their constitution within those boundaries – we risk not only the loss of the historical specificities of par-ticular knowledge cultures but also the perpetuation of European models of epistemological forms that elide the transnational circuits of Romantic cultures. A great deal of work has been done on the orders and categories of Enlightenment knowledge and how they construct the things that we know and how we know them. But in the Caribbean context of medical chaos, social disorder and obstacles to knowledge production and circula-tion, what other ways of knowing might be considered?

This study has revealed the cultural effects of colonial disease and the ways in which bodies, identities, spaces and texts were fundamentally medicalized. The post-emancipation period brought little relief from such high rates of morbidity and mortality, though it did bring different articulations of health and illness in the Caribbean. Writing in 1854, physician John Davy (brother of Sir Humphry) indicates the continued association between climatic medicine and moral health: 'what the hurri-cane did for the physical atmosphere of Barbados, emancipation effected for its moral and domestic atmosphere'.[3] For Davy, abolition had brought a period of moral cleansing to the West Indies, which had been 'purified' now that the notorious West Indian 'licentiousness' was 'almost entirely banished from society'.[4] Set against the imaginative backdrop of climatic catharsis in the wake of the hurricane of 1831, the Caribbean's post-slavery moral redemption is allied to ideas about meteorological events and med-ical health. Yellow fever, the scourge of the European traveller to the West Indies, had an important role to play in both the construction of dis-ease as racially determined and the articulation of white Creole medical knowledge and social identities, and was deployed through different forms of rhetoric: military, sublime, gothic. While in epidemiological terms yellow fever continued to pose a severe threat to Europeans, its cultural significance changed after abolition.[5] In his travelogue *The West Indies and the Spanish Main* (1859), Anthony Trollope describes a visit to Demerara, on the Caribbean coast of what is now Guyana, where he meets a local doctor and enquires about local diseases:

> 'You don't think much of the yellow fever?' I asked him.
>   'No; very little. It comes once in six or seven years; and like influenza or cholera at home, it requires its victims. What is that to consumption, whose visits with you are constant, who daily demands its hecatombs? We don't like yellow fever, certainly; but yellow fever is not half so bad a fellow as the brandy bottle.'[6]

While Davy celebrates the moral improvement of an emancipated West Indies, Trollope's doctor stresses alcoholism as the most dangerous disease now threatening Demerara. Earlier anti-Creole discourse had conflated yellow fever and the luxuriousness of white West Indian society, but in the wake of abolition the story appears to have changed. The doctor's emphasis on British epidemic diseases does not necessarily suggest that there was no longer quite the same terror associated with specifically tropical diseases, but rather that faded hopes for European acclimatization meant that the Caribbean's era as the axis of empire had come to a close.[7] 'While so large a part of North America and Australia remain still savage', writes Trollope, 'there can be no reason why we should doom our children to swelter and grow pale in the tropics ... A certain work has been ours to do there ... But when civilization, commerce, and education shall have been spread; when sufficient of our blood shall have been infused in the veins of those children of the sun; then, I think, we may be ready, without stain to our patriotism, to take off our hats and bid farewell to the West Indies.'[8]

Changing yellow fever discourse is also evident in James Anthony Froude's historical travel narrative *The English in the West Indies* (1888). Froude had already become one of the most significant historians of his time after the publication of his *History of England* (1856). Casting a retrospective eye over the yellow fever epidemics which struck revolutionary St Domingue in the 1790s, Froude sees the rapid spread of disease as having formed a crucial turning point in the history of the republic. Giving an account of the role played by the revolutionary leader Toussaint L'Ouverture, Froude writes:

> Toussaint, who had no share in the atrocities, and whose fault was only that he had been caught by the prevailing political epidemic and believed in the evangel of freedom, surrendered and was carried to France, where he died or else was made an end of. The yellow fever avenged him, and secured for his countrymen the opportunity of trying out to the uttermost the experiment

of negro self-government. The French troops perished in tens of thousands. They were reinforced again and again, but it was like pouring water into a sieve. The climate won a victory to the black man which he could not win for himself. They abandoned their enterprise at last, and Hayti was free. We English tried to recover it afterwards, but we failed also, and for the same reason.[9]

Froude invokes the disease as the righteous punishment for the French system of slavery in St Domingue. Yellow fever was indeed significant at certain points during the revolution, but C. L. R. James notes that both the English and French accounts exaggerate the effect of yellow fever in their failure to quash the revolutionary slaves.[10] For Froude, yellow fever comes to the aid of the enslaved revolutionaries; disease is perceived as a climatic, moral and historical mechanism bound up with political change. Having identified the political fervour that inspired the revolution as metaphorically 'epidemic' (like Burke before him), Froude explains the failure of the Haitian Republic in terms of social disease. Even though 'the negro race have had [St Domingue] to themselves and have not been interfered with', the new nation has not succeeded in becoming a civilized one, because 'in the heart of them has revived the old idolatry of the Gold Coast', along with other 'superstitious' practices such as child sacrifice.[11] The 'political epidemic' which infected L'Ouverture and his countrymen and resulted in the 'massacre' of innocent French civilians has doomed the free Haitian state to failure: 'from a liberty which was inaugurated by assassination and plunder', Froude writes, 'nothing better could be expected'.[12] Froude positions himself at the end of this chain of events, looking back through time at the social consequences of colonial epidemics. Disease is tied to political momentum, functioning as a corrective to French slavery, and Froude's historicizing travel narrative figures epidemic disease as a function of social change.

Davy and Froude self-consciously write back to the abolitionist predictions which claimed climatic diseases as the inevitable retribution for participating in the system of slavery. Davy's meteorological purification retrospectively attests to the Antiguan-born William Gilbert's apocalyptic prophecy in *The Hurricane: a Theosophical and Western Eclogue* (1796) that tropical weather would bring about political liberation in the Americas. Like William Blake's *America a Prophecy* (1793), *The Hurricane* envisages meteorological events as climatic and spiritual forces emanating from Africa and functioning to inspire the American and French Revolutions: 'the Tempest turned has rouzed his rage, / And blows on Europe unrelenting fury'.[13] Similarly, Froude affirms the vision of James Montgomery

and other abolitionists who wrote that yellow fever had come as the ultimate punishment for slave traders. In these historicizing accounts, the idea
of slavery as a past institution (but one which still defined the Caribbean)
is tied to that of disease as a moral and political mechanism.

If yellow fever was now identified as a disease of the past, this was in
part because a new epidemic had replaced yellow fever and malaria as the
most terrifying of tropical diseases: Asiatic cholera. While yellow fever had
not made the journey to Britain, cholera, as Charles MacKay's poem 'The
Mowers: An Anticipation of the Cholera, 1848' puts it, 'cometh over the
sea'.[14] Cholera swept across Britain and the rest of Europe in the 1830s after
it travelled from India through Afghanistan and Russia as trade increased
with the dual effect of industrialization and British imperial expansion
leading up to the creation of the British Raj in 1858.[15] As MacKay's poem
suggests, the cholera epidemics in Britain also refocused attention towards
the homeland. In the 1830s, the only island in the Caribbean to have
suffered the disease was Cuba. Having previously escaped the epidemics
which made their way across Asia, Europe and North America, the British
Caribbean finally succumbed to the disease in 1850 after cholera island-
hopped from Cuba. Making intermittent progress throughout the 1850s,
cholera finally arrived in 1854 on Barbados, where it very quickly had fatal
results – the densely populated sugar island provided a fertile breeding
ground for the disease, and an estimated twenty thousand people died.
During the hot month of July the daily death toll in the city of Bridgetown
ran between three and four hundred.[16] Earlier cholera epidemics had been
identified as caused by pestilential airs – just as Africa and the West Indies
were the aerial hot spots for malaria and yellow fever. In 1849 physician
John Snow, who had long been a miasmatic theory sceptic, discovered that
cholera was being spread from a contaminated water pump, and medical
thinking shifted away from the climatic and geographical theories which
had earlier argued that airs and fogs were the primary causal factor of epidemic diseases.[17]

The period after abolition is that most associated with the institutionalization of the sciences of empire, as it brought the construction of the
science of 'tropical medicine' and the era of scientific racism. But, no
longer the axis upon which the British Empire turned, the Caribbean
islands had lost the sense of mystique which had made figurative
articulations of disease so culturally important. With Asiatic cholera,
the creation of the British Raj, the end of the African slave trade and,
in the 1880s, the 'scramble for Africa', the Caribbean islands no longer

dominated colonial literary and medical discourse – it was now Africa that figured most prominently in the British colonial imagination as the 'white man's grave', as the physician William Falconer's earlier claim that humanity 'was intended by nature to inhabit every part of the world' had faded from view.[18]

Notes

Communicating Disease

1 Linda Colley, *Britons: Forging the Nation, 1707–1837*, third revised edition (New Haven, CT: Yale University Press, 2009), p. 101.

2 Ibid., p. 105.

3 For accounts of the relationship between disease and empire see Jared Diamond, *Guns, Germs and Steel: The Fate of Human Societies* (London: Vintage, 1997), Mark Harrison, *Contagion: How Commerce Has Spread Disease* (New Haven, CT: Yale University Press, 2012), J. N. Hays, *The Burdens of Disease: Epidemics and Human Response in Western History* (New Brunswick, NJ: Rutgers University Press, 1998), J. R. McNeill, *Mosquito Empires: Ecology and War in the Greater Caribbean, 1620–1914* (Cambridge: Cambridge University Press, 2010).

4 See Erica Charters, *Disease, War and the Imperial State: The Welfare of the British Armed Forces during the Seven Years' War* (Chicago: Chicago University Press, 2014).

5 Vincent Brown, *The Reaper's Garden: Death and Power in the World of Atlantic Slavery* (Cambridge, MA: Harvard University Press, 2008), p. 25.

6 Marcus Rediker, *The Slave Ship: A Human History* (London: John Murray, 2008), p. 5. See also Kenneth Kiple, *The Caribbean Slave: A Biological History* (Cambridge: Cambridge University Press, 1984).

7 Rediker, *The Slave Ship*, pp. 273–6.

8 Richard Harrison Shryock, *Medicine and Society in America* (New York: New York University Press, 1960), p. 12.

9 Trevor Burnard, '"The Countrie Continues Sicklie": White Mortality in Jamaica, 1655–1780', *Social History of Medicine*, Vol. 12, No. 1 (April 1999), pp. 45–72.

10 Brown, *The Reaper's Garden*, p. 2. Prior to 1816, definitive data on Caribbean morbidity and mortality are not available. See Richard B. Sheridan, 'Mortality and the Medical Treatment of Slaves in the British West Indies' in *Race and Slavery in the Western Hemisphere: Quantitative Studies*, ed. Stanley Engerman and Eugene Genovese (Princeton, NJ: Princeton University

201

Press, 1975), pp. 285–307, p. 285. However, a wealth of statistical research by Sheridan, Philip Curtin, Barry Higman and Kenneth Kiple has illustrated the enormous death toll from disease in the colonial Atlantic. Some useful data on earlier European populations are provided by military doctors, but the quantitative and statistical turn of the nineteenth century brought improved data. See Philip Curtin, *Death by Migration: Europe's Encounter with the Tropical World in the Nineteenth Century* (Cambridge: Cambridge University Press, 1989), pp. 1–2.

11 Trevor Burnard argues that the exceedingly high rate of European mortality was the reason that the Caribbean did not become a settler society of native-born whites, in the way that the plantations of British North America did. Burnard, '"The Countrie Continues Sicklie": White Mortality in Jamaica, 1655–1780'.

12 For birth and death rates in some of the islands in the British Caribbean, see Richard B. Sheridan, *Doctors and Slaves: A Medical and Demographic History of Slavery in the British West Indies, 1680–1834*, second edition (Cambridge: Cambridge University Press, 1985), pp. 195, 237, and 241. According to Sheridan, the Bahamas and Barbados managed to sustain a positive natural increase in their slave populations during the period 1816–34.

13 See Sheridan, 'Mortality and the Medical Treatment of Slaves in the British West Indies', p. 287. Kenneth Kiple writes that 'the Indians died of European and African diseases, the whites died of African diseases, but the blacks were able to survive both, and it did not take the Europeans long to conclude that Africans were especially designed for hard work in hot places.' Kenneth Kiple, 'Disease Ecologies of the Caribbean' in *The Cambridge World History of Human Disease*, ed. Kenneth Kiple (Cambridge: Cambridge University Press, 1993), pp. 497–504, p. 499.

14 See Sheridan, *Doctors and Slaves*, pp. 131–3, 187. Sheridan also notes that some diseases which proved particularly fatal to Europeans in the tropics, such as yellow fever, were endemic along the West African coast, where Africans had often contracted a mild case that made them immune to Caribbean strains. While slave-owners blamed dirt eating on attempted suicide, Kiple writes that it may have been caused in some cases by malnutrition. See Kiple, *The Caribbean Slave*, p. 101.

15 See Mark Harrison, *Disease and the Modern World: 1500 to the Present Day* (Cambridge: Polity Press, 2004), pp. 72–3.

16 Sheridan, *Doctors and Slaves*, p. xvii.

17 On the history of aerial contagion see Hays, *The Burdens of Disease: Epidemics and Human Response in Western History* and James C. Riley, *The Eighteenth-Century Campaign to Avoid Disease* (New York: St. Martin's Press, 1987). This aerial model was very different to today's understanding of contagion. In the seventeenth century, Antoni van Leeuwenhoek was the first to use microscopes to view single-cell organisms, which he called 'animalcules', but the eighteenth century did not bring any clarification as to how these microscopic organisms spread disease, or evidence of the particular diseases with which

they were associated. Charles Winslow explains why the development of the concept of contagion was slow to be fully embraced by physicians: 'until the theory of inanimate contagion was replaced by a theory of living germs, and until to that theory were added the concepts of long-distance transmission by water and food supplies and, above all, of human and animal carriers – the hypothesis of contagion simply could not work.' Charles-Edward Amory Winslow, *The Conquest of Epidemic Disease: A Chapter in the History of Ideas* (Madison: University of Wisconsin Press, 1980), p. 182.

18 Robert Jackson, *An outline of the history and cure of fever, epidemic and contagious; more especially of jails, ships, and hospitals, the concentrated endemic, vulgarly called the yellow fever of the West Indies* (London: Printed for Mundell & Son, 1798), p. 103. In particular, the tropical fevers to which Europeans almost invariably fell victim were attributed to what the Scottish military physician Sir John Pringle called the 'exhalations' of 'noxious *Effluvia*', emitted from marshy lands of plantations and other putrefying matter, drawn out by the heat of the tropical sun. John Pringle, *Observations on the Diseases of the Army*, second edition (London: Printed for A. Millar et al., 1752), p. 6. On the aerial theory of contagion see also Riley, *The Eighteenth-Century Campaign to Avoid Disease*, p. 16.

19 George Pinckard, *Notes on the West Indies: written during the expedition under the command of the late General Sir R. Abercrombie* (London: Longman et al), Vol. I, pp. 391–2.

20 Physicians and surgeons were crucial to the success of the slave trade. As well as limiting the number of slaves who could be carried aboard ship, the Slave Trade Act 1788 recommended financial incentives to doctors for limiting slave mortality. But medical discourse also offered some of the best-informed and strongest criticism of the trade in slaves. Thomas Trotter, a naval physician who worked on the slave ship *Brookes*, became an ardent abolitionist after witnessing the violent scurvy which resulted from the ship's owner's ignoring Trotter's advice to provide slaves with a fresh and varied diet during their fourteen-month voyage.

21 John Huxham, *Observations on the air and epidemic diseases from the year 1728–1738* (London: J. Hinton, 1759), pp. xxv–xxvi. Huxham studied medicine at Leiden but never visited the West Indies. Jim Egan writes that 'whereas in earlier centuries climate had been coupled with religion to explain cultural difference, many who wrote on natural history in the eighteenth century held climate entirely responsible for this difference.' Jim Egan, 'The "Long'd-for Aera" of an "Other Race": Climate, Identity, and James Grainger's *The Sugar-Cane*', *Early American Literature*, Vol. 38, No. 2, (2003), pp. 189–212, p. 189. On the relationship between religion, climate and human difference see also Roxann Wheeler, *The Complexion of Race: Categories of Difference in Eighteenth-Century British Culture* (Philadelphia: University of Pennsylvania Press, 2000).

22 William Falconer, *Remarks on the influence of climate, situation, nature of country, population, nature of food, and way of life, on the disposition and temper,*

manners and behaviour, intellects, laws and customs, form of government, and
religion, of mankind (London: Printed for C. Dilly, 1781), p. 7.

23 David Hume, *Essays, Moral, Political, and Literary* (Indianapolis: Liberty
    Fund, 1987), pp. 202, 208.

24 See Wheeler, *The Complexion of Race.*

25 Until the scientific revolution, the ancient humoralist model of the human
    body remained the principal idea underlying the diagnosis of disease and ther-
    apeutic practices. Four bodily humours – blood, phlegm, yellow bile and black
    bile – were characterized by the four elements – air, earth, fire and water –
    and defined by their manifest qualities of heat, cold, dryness and moisture.
    The humours were also associated with seasonal and atmospheric changes.
    Health derived from the proper balance of these four fluid humours; disease
    resulted from one or more of the humours getting the upper hand. Imbalance
    in the humours was generally caused by a problem with the production, cir-
    culation or elimination of the humoral fluids. The Hippocratic tradition of
    treatment focused on restoring balance to the system of the patient rather than
    treating specific diseases. If the imbalance was excessive, the disease could be
    treated by depletion (bleeding, purging or sweating); if deficient, the patient
    could be helped by restoring the humours through diet and drugs.

26 James MacKenzie, *The History of Health, and the Art of Preserving It: Or, An*
    Account of All That Has Been Recommended By Physicians and Philosophers
    (Edinburgh: Printed by William Gordon, 1758), p. 289. A more widespread
    acceptance of anatomy and pathology had raised questions about classical
    humoralism. Renaissance anatomical studies of the body revealed that its
    structures were different to those described by Galen. In 1546 the Italian phy-
    sician Girolamo Fracastoro postulated the existence of living disease 'seeds',
    advocating quarantine and fumigation to deal with epidemics. Based on
    Cartesian philosophical propositions and the idea of the physical body as
    ruled by universal laws of matter and motion and the location of the mind
    in the brain, a new functionalist method described the body in terms of
    mechanical processes. After William Harvey's revolutionary discovery of the
    circulation of blood, the body was envisioned by many as a hydraulic net-
    work pumping blood and nervous fluids through hollow pipes. Within the
    context of this more mechanical view of the human body, there were med-
    ical efforts to determine the exact structure of its parts, and to comprehend
    their activity and arrangement in terms of mechanical effects. In the wake of
    Thomas Willis's coinage of the term 'neurology' in the seventeenth century,
    descriptions of the nervous system became increasingly important as many
    diseases came to be assigned 'nervous' causes. The cardiovascular and neuro-
    logical systems expounded by Herman Boerhaave and William Cullen also
    reshaped the eighteenth-century medical model of the human body.

27 Roy Porter, *Bodies Politic: Diseases, Death and Doctors in Britain, 1650–1900*
    (London: Reaktion Books, 2001), p. 21. For details of harmful medical practices
    and the natural philosophies they were founded upon, see also David Wootton,
    Bad Medicine: Doctors Doing Harm since Hippocrates (Oxford: Oxford

University Press, 2006). For more detail on the history of eighteenth- and nineteenth-century medicine, see William F. Bynum, *Science and the Practice of Medicine in the Nineteenth Century* (Cambridge: Cambridge University Press, 1994), and Roy Porter and Dorothy Porter, *Patient's Progress: Doctors and Doctoring in Eighteenth-Century England* (Oxford: Polity Press, 1989).

28 Richard Ligon, *A True and Exact History of the Island of Barbados* (London: Printed for Humphrey Moseley, 1657), p. 118.

29 Edmund Hickeringill, *Jamaica viewed: with all the Ports, Harbours, and their several soundings, Towns, and Settlements thereunto belonging, with the nature of its climate, fruitfulnesse of the soile, and it's suitablenesse to English complexions* (London: Printed for J. Williams, 1661), p. 1.

30 Mark Harrison writes that 'a more pessimistic view of European colonization had been evident in official circles in the West Indies since the 1780s, and ambitious plans for settling white farmers in the Caribbean had been shelved.' Mark Harrison, '"The Tender Frame of Man": Disease, Climate, and Racial Difference in India and the West Indies, 1760–1860', *Bulletin of the History of Medicine*, Vol. 70, No. 1, (1996), pp. 68–93, p. 79.

31 Cynric R. Williams, *A Tour through the Island of Jamaica, from the western to the eastern end, in the year 1823* (London: Printed for Hunt and Clarke, 1826), p. 134.

32 Tracing the history of public amenities in Barbados, Richard Carter writes that in the era of slavery plantation health care varied widely and depended very much upon the whim of the individual planter. Richard Carter, 'Public Amenities after Emancipation' in *Emancipation II: Aspects of the Post-Slavery Experience in Barbados*, ed. Woodville Marshall (Cave Hill: University of the West Indies, 1987), pp. 46–69.

33 Kiple, *The Caribbean Slave*, p. 154.

34 John Stewart, *A view of the past and present state of the Island of Jamaica; with remarks on the moral and physical condition of the slaves and on the abolition of slavery in the colonies* (Edinburgh: Oliver & Boyd, 1823), p. 192.

35 Hannah More, *Slavery: A Poem* (London: Printed for T. Cadell, 1788), ll. 267–8.

36 William Hutchinson, *The Princess of Zanfara; A Dramatic Poem* (London: Printed for Mess. Wilkie, 1789), p. 11.

37 Kathleen Wilson, *The Island Race: Englishness, Empire and Gender in the Eighteenth Century* (London: Routledge, 2003), p. 130.

38 Anna Letitia Barbauld, *Epistle to William Wilberforce, Esq. on the Rejection of the Bill for Abolishing the Slave Trade* (London: Printed for J. Johnson, 1791), p. 12.

39 Ibid., p. 15.

40 James Montgomery, *The West Indies, and other poems*, third edition (London: Longman et al, 1810), p. 44.

41 George Boulukos, Brycchan Carey, Deirdre Coleman, Markman Ellis, Lynn Festa, Peter Kitson, Debbie Lee, Sarah Salih and Marcus Wood, among others, have written informatively and sensitively on the politics of abolitionist sentiment.

42 Tim Fulford, Debbie Lee and Peter J. Kitson, *Literature, Science and Exploration in the Romantic Era: Bodies of Knowledge* (Cambridge: Cambridge University Press, 2004), p. 6.

43 Alan Bewell, *Romanticism and Colonial Disease* (Baltimore: John Hopkins University Press, 1999), p. 12.

44 Mary Louise Pratt, *Imperial Eyes: Travel Writing and Transculturation* (London: Routledge, 1992), p. 138. As Pratt writes, 'Romanticism *consists*, among other things, of shifts in relations between Europe and other parts of the world,' ibid.

45 Elizabeth Bohls, *Slavery and the Politics of Place: Representing the Colonial Caribbean, 1770–1833* (Cambridge: Cambridge University Press, 2014), p. 183.

46 Richard H. Grove, *Green Imperialism: Colonial Expansion, Tropical Eden Islands and the Origins of Environmentalism, 1600–1860* (Cambridge: Cambridge University Press, 1995), p. 8. See also Londa Schiebinger, *Plants and Empire: Colonial Bioprospecting in the Atlantic World* (Cambridge, MA: Harvard University Press, 2004), especially pp. 73–104.

47 Richard Drayton, *Nature's Government: Science, Imperial Britain, and the 'Improvement' of the World* (New Haven, CT: Yale University Press, 2000), p. 45. See also Roy MacLeod, *Nature and Empire: Science and the Colonial Enterprise* (Chicago: University of Chicago Press, 2001).

48 Alan Bewell, *Natures in Translation: Romanticism and Colonial Natural History* (Baltimore: Johns Hopkins University Press, 2017).

49 Londa Schiebinger's *Secret Cures of Slaves: People, Plants, and Medicine in the Eighteenth-Century Atlantic World* (Stanford: Stanford University Press, 2017) was published when this book was in production, and promises a wealth of new information in this area.

50 William Hillary, *Observations on the Changes of the Air, and the Concomitant Epidemical Diseases of Barbadoes*, second edition (London: Printed for L. Hawes et al, 1766), p. 341.

51 See Sheridan, *Doctors and Slaves* p. 76 and D. Maier, 'Nineteenth-Century Asante Medical Practices', *Comparative Studies in Society and History*, Vol. 21, No. 1, (January 1979), pp. 63–81.

52 Brown, *The Reaper's Garden*, p. 10.

53 Paul Youngquist and Frances Botkin, 'Introduction: Black Romanticism: Romantic Circulations', in Youngquist and Botkin (eds.), Circulations: Romanticism and the Black Atlantic, a *Romantic Circles* Praxis volume (2011) www.rc.umd.edu/praxis/circulations/HTML/praxis.2011.youngquist.html.

54 Srinivas Aravamudan, *Tropicopolitans: Colonialism and Agency, 1688–1804* (Durham, NC: Duke University Press, 1999), p. 15; Peter Hulme, *Colonial Encounters: Europe and the Native Caribbean, 1492–1797* (London: Routledge, 1986), p. 46; Edward Said, *Culture and Imperialism* (London: Vintage, 1994), p. 66.

55 Roach's model of the circum-Atlantic 'insists on the centrality of the diasporic and genocidal histories of Africa and the Americas, North and South, in the creation of the culture of modernity. In this sense, a New World was not discovered

in the Caribbean, but one was truly invented there'. Joseph Roach, *Cities of the Dead: Circum-Atlantic Performance* (New York: Columbia University Press, 1996); David Lambert, *White Creole Culture, Politics and Identity during the Age of Abolition* (Cambridge: Cambridge University Press, 2005), p. 22. On the model of 'circum-Atlantic' history see also David Armitage, 'Three Concepts of Atlantic History' in *The British Atlantic World, 1500–1800*, ed. David Armitage and Michael J. Braddick (Basingstoke: Palgrave Macmillan, 2002), pp. 11–27.

56 See Bruno Latour, *Science in Action: How to Follow Scientists and Engineers through Society* (Cambridge, MA: Harvard University Press, 1987).

57 Paul Youngquist and Frances Botkin, 'Introduction: Black Romanticism: Romantic Circulations'.

58 'Imagination' also signals the 'leap of the imagination' which Deirdre Coleman associates with acts of colonization, and the textual forms it takes. Deirdre Coleman, *Romantic Colonization and British Anti-Slavery* (Cambridge: Cambridge University Press, 2005), p. 2.

59 Work in the medical humanities has tended to follow that by Sander Gilman, George Rousseau, Elaine Scarry and Susan Sontag in recognizing the cultural and linguistic formation of both the experience of disease and medical practice.

60 George Rousseau, 'Literature and Medicine: the State of the Field', *Isis*, Vol. 72, No. 3, (1981), pp. 406–24, p. 423.

61 Sharon Ruston's *Shelley and Vitality* draws on nineteenth-century medicine in order to forge links between the poet's work and contemporary medical debates. Neil Vickers's *Coleridge and the Doctors* considers how Coleridge's medical knowledge shaped his critical thought.

62 David Shuttleton, *Smallpox and the Literary Imagination 1660–1820* (Cambridge: Cambridge University Press, 2007), p. 3.

63 Candace Ward, *Desire and Disorder: Fevers, Fictions, and Feeling in English Georgian Culture* (Lewisburg, PA: Bucknell University Press, 2007).

64 See Luisa Calè and Adriana Craciun, 'The Disorder of Things', *Eighteenth-Century Studies*, Vol. 45, No. 1, (2011), pp. 1–13, Noah Heringman, *Sciences of Antiquity: Romantic Antiquarianism, Natural History, and Knowledge Work* (Oxford: Oxford University Press, 2013), Noah Heringman (ed.), *Romantic Science: The Literary Forms of Natural History* (Albany: State University of New York Press, 2003), Jon Klancher, *Transfiguring the Arts and Sciences: Knowledge and Cultural Institutions in the Romantic Age* (Cambridge: Cambridge University Press, 2013), Simon Schaffer, 'How Disciplines Look' in *Interdisciplinarity: Reconfigurations of the Social and Natural Sciences*, ed. Andrew Barry and Georgina Born (Oxford: Routledge, 2013), pp. 57–81. This book also shares Christopher Iannini's interest in the Caribbean as a site of new forms of knowledge writing articulated by his argument that 'natural history developed as a colonial genre through its efforts to describe, disseminate, and contemplate' the complexities and hidden secrets of Caribbean natures. Christopher Iannini, *Fatal Revolutions: Natural History, West Indian Slavery, and the Routes of American Literature* (Chapel Hill: University of North Carolina Press, 2012), p. 6.

65 Elizabeth Maddock Dillon, *New World Drama: The Performative Commons in the Atlantic World, 1649–1849* (Durham, NC: Duke University Press, 2014), p. 267. Dillon writes against Foucauldian and Marxist historical accounts of modernity, writing that both 'contribute, to some extent, to derealizing the colony and the significance of the colonial relation by proposing that structures of violence embodied and enacted in the colony are not germane to modernity; that is, both relegate colonial violence to a temporally distant moment, and as a result, the colony disappears from the map of modernity', ibid., p. 35. On the cultural, economic and social relationship between colonialism and modernity see also Tim Armstrong, *The Logic of Slavery: Debt, Technology and Pain in American Literature* (Cambridge: Cambridge University Press, 2012), Anthony Bogues, *Empire of Liberty: Power, Desire, and Freedom* (Lebanon, NH: Dartmouth College Press, 2010) and David Scott, *Conscripts of Modernity: The Tragedy of Colonial Enlightenment* (Durham, NC: Duke University Press, 2004).

66 F. W. Knight (ed.), *The Slave Societies of the Caribbean* (London: UNESCO Publishing, 1997), p. 3. As Christopher Iannini writes, 'throughout the long eighteenth century, the assumption that the colonial Caribbean was the site of the most significant and valuable forms of empirical knowledge to be derived from the New World was all but axiomatic'. Iannini, *Fatal Revolutions*, p. 5.

67 On the emergence of Romantic era processes of modernization in the context of empire, see Saree Makdisi, *Romantic Imperialism: Universal Empire and the Culture of Modernity* (Cambridge: Cambridge University Press, 1998).

68 Iannini, *Fatal Revolutions*, p. 14.

69 Sander Gilman, *Disease and Representation: Images of Illness from Madness to AIDS* (Ithaca, NY: Cornell University Press, 1988), p. xiii.

1 'What New Forms of Death'

1 John Gilmore, *The Poetics of Empire: A Study of James Grainger's The Sugar-Cane* (London: The Athlone Press, 2000), p. 90.

2 James Boswell, *Life of Johnson* (Oxford: Oxford University Press, 2008), p. 698, Gilmore, *The Poetics of Empire*, Book II, l. 62.

3 On the relationship between Caribbean landscape and European poetic form in *The Sugar-Cane*, see John Chalker, *The English Georgic: A Study in the Development of a Form* (London: Routledge, 1969), p. 176, Gilmore, *The Poetics of Empire*, and Keith Sandiford, 'The Sugared Muse: or the Case of James Grainger, MD (1721–66)', *New West Indian Guide*, Vol. 61, No. 1/2 (1987), pp. 39–53. On Grainger as an early example of Caribbean literature Kamau Brathwaite emphasizes the thematic and stylistic uniqueness of Grainger's poem, arguing that Grainger's focus on the difference between British and Caribbean landscapes and the uniqueness of his poetic imagery mark 'the roots of a distinctive West Indian writing'. Edward Kamau Brathwaite, *Roots*

(Ann Arbor: University of Michigan Press, 1993), p. 138. David Dabydeen pinpoints Grainger as the origin of a Caribbean literary lineage leading up to Derek Walcott. See David Dabydeen, 'Sugar and Slavery in the West Indian Georgic', *Callaloo*, Vol. 23, No. 4 (Autumn 2000), pp. 1513–14. This argument conflicts, notably, with Dabydeen's earlier statement that Grainger 'wrote with little of a West Indian context, perspective or tradition', highlighting a broader critical movement towards acknowledging writers such as Grainger as participating in the development of 'Caribbean' or 'Creole' literature. See David Dabydeen and Nana Wilson-Tagoe, 'Selected Themes in West Indian Literature: An Annotated Bibliography', *Third World Quarterly*, Vol. 9, No. 3 (July 1987), pp. 921–60, p. 921. Keith Sandiford writes that Grainger's articulation of the 'gradual transformative effects on consciousness exercised by colonial experience' represents an emerging Creole identity and poetry. Keith Sandiford, *The Cultural Politics of Sugar: Caribbean Slavery and Narratives of Colonialism* (Cambridge: Cambridge University Press, 2000), p. 76. On Grainger and the decline of the georgic form, see Karen O'Brien, 'Imperial Georgic, 1660–1789' in *The Country and the City Revisited*, ed. Gerald MacLean, Donna Landry, and Joseph P. Ward (Cambridge: Cambridge University Press, 1999), pp. 160–79.

4 Gilmore, *The Poetics of Empire*, p. 90.
5 Ibid., p. 89.
6 Ibid., p. 89.
7 Ibid., Book I, ll. 109–10, 97.
8 Ibid., Book II, ll. 194–7.
9 Ibid., p. 89.
10 Ibid., Book I, l. 327.
11 On experimental cultures in the Caribbean, see Londa Schiebinger, who writes that 'knowledge was formed in the crucible of the Atlantic exchange of peoples and cultures'. Londa Schiebinger, 'Scientific Exchange in the Eighteenth-Century Atlantic World' in *Soundings in Atlantic History: Latent Structures and Intellectual Currents, 1500–1830*, ed. Bernard Bailyn and Patricia L. Denault (Cambridge, MA: Harvard University Press, 2009), pp. 294–328, p. 328.
12 Gilmore, *The Poetics of Empire*, Book I, l. 109.
13 See Sheridan, *Doctors and Slaves*, p. 28.
14 See Douglas J. Hamilton, *Scotland, the Caribbean and the Atlantic World 1750–1820* (Manchester: Manchester University Press, 2005), p. 112.
15 See George Clark, *A History of the Royal College of Physicians of London* (Oxford: Clarendon Press, 1964) and Hamilton, *Scotland, the Caribbean and the Atlantic World*.
16 Hamilton, *Scotland, the Caribbean and the Atlantic World*, p. 7.
17 Colley, *Britons: Forging the Nation*, p. 129.
18 Gilmore, *The Poetics of Empire*, Book IV, ll. 165–9.
19 Ibid., Book II, l. 5, Book III, l. 153, Book I, l. 518. Grainger's Scots heritage in relation to Caribbean literary history has emerged in several studies of *The Sugar-Cane*. Identifying the poem as a touchstone of West Indian

literary history, Dabydeen writes 'that Grainger, a Scotsman, is the "Father" of Caribbean Literature makes his work ever more intriguing.' Dabydeen, 'Sugar and Slavery in the West Indian Georgic', p. 1513. Gilmore argues that Grainger's 'doubly colonial' identity as a Scotsman living in the Caribbean prompts a reading of the poem as 'a far-reaching attempt to rewrite the prevailing cultural discourse which, just as it relegated Scotland and Scottish concerns to a secondary position, in effect dismissed Caribbean society as an unfit subject for literature'. Gilmore, *The Poetics of Empire*, p. 35. Brathwaite notes the influence of Scots imagery on Grainger's portrayal of enslaved communities. Brathwaite, *Roots*, p. 141.

20 Gilmore, *The Poetics of Empire*, Book IV, l. 1.

21 For demographic data on slave populations, see Kiple, *The Caribbean Slave* and Sheridan, *Doctors and Slaves*.

22 Gilmore, *The Poetics of Empire*, Book IV, 211, 431–3.

23 Ibid., Book. III, l. 175.

24 Ibid., Book III, l. 272, Book IV, l. 156.

25 Ibid., Book I, ll. 616, 618–21.

26 James Grainger, *An essay on the more common West-India diseases* (London: T. Becket and P.A. De Hondt, 1764), p. 73.

27 In the colonies, some European-trained physicians were scathing about the abilities and training of Creole doctors in particular. Dr. George Pinckard describes West Indian medical practitioners as 'pre-eminent in ignorance', writing that 'in learning and in manners' they are 'not far removed above the slaves. They are more illiterate than you can believe, and the very negro doctor of the estates too justly vie with them in medical knowledge.' Pinckard, *Notes on the West Indies*, Vol. I, p. 389. Roy Porter and Dorothy Porter have given an account of the metropolitan health care that was undertaken by those who were not physicians, surgeons or apothecaries. 'Regular doctors' such as Grainger 'reviled root and branch the activities of those professional competitors they stigmatized as "quacks", that is "pretenders" to medical knowledge.' Porter and Porter, *Patient's Progress*, p. 96. See also Roy Porter, *Health for Sale: Quackery in England, 1660–1850* (Manchester: Manchester University Press, 1989).

28 Gilmore, *The Poetics of Empire*, Book IV, ll. 244–5.

29 Ibid., Book IV, ll. 263–6.

30 The tertiary stage does not occur in all of those infected. Grainger's description of the progressive development and remissions of yaws appears to coincide with this modern understanding of the disease. However, it should be noted that he does not outline the three stages of the disease in quite the manner described here.

31 Gilmore, *The Poetics of Empire*, Book IV, ll. 281–2, 273–6. 'Live-silver' refers to mercury, then in widespread use as a treatment for many medical conditions in the Caribbean, as it was in Britain.

32 Ibid., Book I, ll. 298–9.

33 Ibid., Book II, ll. 31–3.

34 Ibid., Book II, ll. 100, 35.

35 Ibid., Book III, l. 160.
36 Ibid., p. 89.
37 Ibid., Book I, l. 266.
38 Ibid., Book III, l. 147.
39 Simon Pugh, *Reading Landscape: Country–City–Capital* (Manchester: Manchester University Press, 1990), p. 5.
40 Anthony Low, *The Georgic Revolution* (Princeton, NJ: Princeton University Press, 1985).
41 John Dyer, *The Fleece: A Poem in Four Books* (London: Printed for R. and J. Dodsley, 1757), Book I, ll. 2, 9.
42 Low, *The Georgic Revolution*, p. 314.
43 Shaun Irlam, '"Wish You Were Here": Exporting England in James Grainger's *The Sugar-Cane*', *English Literary History*, Vol. 68, No. 2 (2001), pp. 377–96, p. 379. On georgic and empire see also Richard Feingold, *Nature and Society: Later Eighteenth-Century Uses of the Pastoral and Georgic* (Hassocks: Harvester, 1978), pp. 87–115.
44 James Thomson, *The Seasons: A Poem* (London: Printed for A. Hamilton, 1793), ll. 1035 and 1040–1.
45 Ibid., ll. 1029, 1037 and 1039.
46 On the cultural history of sugar, see Keith Ellis, 'Images of Sugar in English and Spanish Caribbean Poetry', *Ariel: A Review of International English Literature*, Vol. 24, No. 1 (1993), pp. 149–59, Sandiford, *The Cultural Politics of Sugar* and Carl Plasa, *Slaves to Sweetness: British and Caribbean Literatures of Sugar* (Liverpool: Liverpool University Press, 2009).
47 Nathaniel Weekes, *Barbados: A Poem* (London: Printed by J. and J. Lewis for R. and J. Dodsley, 1754), p. 42.
48 Gilmore, *The Poetics of Empire*, Book I, ll. 497–8.
49 Ibid., Book I, ll. 1–6. While other georgics 'subordinated instruction to celebration', Shields argues that Grainger 'made instruction his highest purpose.' David S. Shields, *Oracles of Empire: Poetry, Politics, and Commerce in British America, 1690–1750* (Chicago: University of Chicago Press, 1990), p. 73.
50 Mary Favret, 'War in the Air', *Modern Language Quarterly*, Vol. 65, No. 4 (2004), pp. 531–59. Gilmore, *The Poetics of Empire*, Book I, ll. 311–16.
51 While 'ken' was certainly not an exclusively Scottish word (as Samuel Johnson's *Dictionary* shows), it was certainly in more common use by Scots. Joan Beal calls it a 'Scots lexical term of ancient pedigree'. See Joan Beal, 'Syntax and Morphology' in *The Edinburgh History of the Scots Language*, ed. Charles Jones (Edinburgh: Edinburgh University Press, 1997), pp. 335–77, p. 375.
52 Gilmore, *The Poetics of Empire*, Book I, ll. 266–70.
53 On the cultural production of colonial landscape imagery, see Jill Casid, *Sowing Empire: Landscape and Colonization* (Minneapolis: University of Minnesota Press, 2005).
54 Gilmore, *The Poetics of Empire*, Book IV, l. 396–9.
55 Beth Fowkes Tobin, *Colonizing Nature: The Tropics in British Art and Letters, 1760–1820* (Philadelphia: University of Pennsylvania Press, 2005), p. 52.

56 Anonymous, *Jamaica, a Poem, in Three Parts* (London: Printed for William Nicoll, 1777), part I, ll. 186–8.

57 On Grainger's canonical status and readership, see Gilmore, *The Poetics of Empire*, p. 48.

58 O'Brien, 'Imperial Georgic', p. 173. On the poetics of slave labour in *The Sugar-Cane*, see also Markman Ellis, '"Incessant Labour": Georgic Poetry and the Problem of Slavery' in *Discourses of Slavery and Abolition: Britain and Its Colonies, 1760–1838*, ed. Brycchan Carey, Markman Ellis, and Sarah Salih (Basingstoke: Palgrave Macmillan, 2004), pp. 45–62.

59 David Fairer, *Organising Poetry: The Coleridge Circle, 1790–1798* (Oxford: Oxford University Press, 2009), p. 276.

60 Boswell, *Life of Johnson*, p. 699.

61 Anonymous, 'Review of *The Sugar-Cane*', *The Critical Review*, Vol. 18 (October 1764), pp. 270–7, p. 171. See Gilmore, *The Poetics of Empire* on the identity of Johnson as the author of the *Critical Review*'s piece on Grainger, pp. 41–3. On the politics of colonial identities at stake in Johnson's description of Grainger as an 'American poet', Egan argues that it is precisely the Johnsonian model of British versus American identities that Grainger's poem seeks to displace. Egan, 'The "Long'd-for Aera" of an "Other Race": Climate, Identity, and James Grainger's *The Sugar-Cane*', pp. 191–2.

62 Anonymous, 'Review of *The Sugar-Cane*', p. 171.

63 Gilmore, *The Poetics of Empire*, p. 89.

64 Ibid., Book IV, l. 149, Book III, l. 274, Book I, ll. 218–26.

65 Ibid., Book IV, l. 263.

66 Ibid., Book II, l. 451.

67 Vincent Carretta, 'Review: Writings of the British Black Atlantic', *Eighteenth-Century Studies*, Vol. 34, No. 1 (2000), pp. 121–6, p. 123.

68 Gilmore, *The Poetics of Empire*, Book I, ll. 84, 85, 51.

69 Ibid., Book I, ll. 75–7.

70 O'Brien, 'Imperial Georgic', p. 174.

71 Gilmore, *The Poetics of Empire*, Book I, ll. 127–31.

72 Christopher Smart, *Poems on Several Occasions* (London: Printed for the author, 1752), Book I, l. 1., Dyer, *The Fleece: A Poem in Four Books*, Book I, l. 108.

73 Fairer, *Organising Poetry*, p. 269.

74 Gilmore, *The Poetics of Empire*, p. 91, Book II, l. 387, l. 100.

75 Ibid., Book III, ll. 213.

76 Grove, *Green Imperialism*, pp. 264–308. Fredrik Jonsson argues that the Scottish Highlands functioned as a 'laboratory for the Enlightenment' and were the point of origin of modern environmentalism. Fredrik Albritton Jonsson, *Enlightenment's Frontier: The Scottish Highlands and the Origins of Environmentalism* (New Haven, CT: Yale University Press, 2013).

77 Gilmore, *The Poetics of Empire*, Book I, ll. 557–64.

78 Ibid., Book I, l. 337, Book II, ll. 46, 228–9.

79 Ibid., Book II, ll. 238–9.

80 Ibid., Book II, ll. 391–7.

81 Johann Gottfried Herder, *Philosophical Writings*, ed. Michael N. Forster (Cambridge: Cambridge University Press, 2002), p. 325.

82 Gilmore, *The Poetics of Empire*, Book II, ll. 366–8.

83 Ibid., Book IV, ll. 463–4, 494–5.

84 On plants and historical practices of acclimatization see Drayton, *Nature's Government* and Grove, *Green Imperialism*.

85 Gilmore, *The Poetics of Empire*, p. 45 and Book IV, l. 493.

86 For a history of ideas about seasoning see Mark Harrison, *Climates and Constitutions: Health, Race, Environment and British Imperialism in India, 1600–1850* (Oxford: Oxford University Press, 1999), pp. 88–92.

87 Gilmore, *The Poetics of Empire*, Book I, l. 42. On the various diseases suffered by different groups in the Caribbean, see Sheridan, *Doctors and Slaves*, pp. 131–3, 187 and Kiple, *The Caribbean Slave*.

88 Gilmore, *The Poetics of Empire*, Book IV, ll. 103–4. While many of Grainger's claims about slave health are spurious, some of his ideas about regional susceptibility may be accurate. For example, the beef tapeworm may be responsible for those referred to as originating from Mundingo, who came from the region that is now Mali and were mainly a cattle-raising society, having a higher incidence of worms. See D. Keith McE. Kevan, 'Mid-Eighteenth-Century Entomology and Helminthology in the West Indies: Dr. James Grainger', *Journal of the Society for the Bibliography of Natural History*, Vol. 8, No. 3 (1977), pp. 193–222, p. 206.

89 Gilmore, *The Poetics of Empire*, Book IV, l. 59.

90 Ibid., Book IV, l. 46.

91 Ibid., Book IV, ll. 49, 52.

92 Janet Schaw, *Journal of a Lady of Quality* (Lincoln: Bison Books, 2005), p. 128.

93 Gilmore, *The Poetics of Empire*, Book IV, ll. 49–50, 85, 86.

94 While Africans are medically and socially constituted by climate, Jim Egan writes that Grainger 'dematerializes' the effects of climate on Europeans by 'casting the colonial environment as surface phenomena'. See Egan, 'The "Long'd-for Aera" of an "Other Race": Climate, Identity, and James Grainger's *The Sugar-Cane*', p. 197.

95 James Lind, *An essay on diseases incidental to Europeans in hot climates* (London: Printed for T. Becket and P.A de Hondt, 1768), p. 2.

96 Edward Long, *History of Jamaica. Or, general survey of the antient and modern state of that island* (London: Printed for T. Lowndes, 1774), p. 518.

97 Grainger, *Essay*, pp. 12–13.

98 Gilmore, *The Poetics of Empire*, Book IV, ll. 205–6.

99 Ibid., Book IV, ll. 206–10.

100 Ibid., Book IV, ll. 213, 202. Ramesh Mallipeddi has shown that nautical medics working aboard slave ships voiced their concerns over the dangers of nostalgic melancholy amongst slaves, caused by the loss of the homeland.Ramesh Mallipeddi, '"A Fixed Melancholy": Migration, Memory and the Middle Passage', *The Eighteenth Century*, Vol. 55, No. 2–3 (2014), pp. 235–53.

101 Gilmore, *The Poetics of Empire*, Book IV, 131–41.

102 Ibid., Book IV, ll. 144–5.

103 Ibid., Book IV, l. 15. As Markman Ellis writes, Grainger's value-laden image of 'cheerful toil' is rooted in the notion of the civilizing effects of labour. Ellis, '"Incessant Labour": Georgic Poetry and the Problem of Slavery'. Beth Tobin argues that there is a tension between Grainger's elision of slave labour and his inadvertent positioning of slaves as analogous to planters. Tobin, *Colonizing Nature: The Tropics in British Art and Letters, 1760–1820*, pp. 48–9.

104 As Londa Schiebinger writes, 'by the eighteenth century there were few unadulterated indigenous plants, humans, or knowledges to be collected in the West Indies: peoples and plants, languages and knowledges had churned, mingled, and melded for over two hundred years'. Schiebinger, *Plants and Empire*, p. 14.

105 Gilmore, *The Poetics of Empire*, Book I, ll. 458–9.

106 On eighteenth-century crossbreeding experiments and natural knowledge see Mary Terrall, *Catching Nature in the Act: Réaumur and the Practice of Natural History in the Eighteenth Century* (Chicago: University of Chicago Press, 2013). On plant hybrids in imperial contexts, see Andrea Wulf, *The Brother Gardeners: Botany, Empire and the Birth of an Obsession* (St Albans: Windmill Books, 2009). On animal crossbreeding, see Louise E. Robbins, *Elephant Slaves and Pampered Parrots: Exotic Animals in Eighteenth-Century Paris* (Baltimore: Johns Hopkins University Press, 2002) and Harriet Ritvo, 'Possessing Mother Nature: Genetic Capital in Eighteenth-Century Britain', in John Brewer and Susan Staves (eds.), *Early Modern Conceptions of Property* (1995), pp. 413–26.

107 Irlam, '"Wish You Were Here": Exporting England in James Grainger's *The Sugar-Cane*', p. 386.

108 Gilmore, *The Poetics of Empire*, Book I, ll. 129–30, 4.

109 Grainger, *Essay*, p. 21. Grainger's claim that worms were responsible for more deaths than any other plantation condition may indicate that conditions secondary to worms often proved fatal. For example, the 'dragon worm' or 'Guinea worm' (*Dracunculus medinensis*), first seen by European physicians in West Africa, is a subcutaneous parasite which enters the body through infected water and eventually creates a painful ulcer on the surface of the skin through which it must be removed – this wound can lead to a fatal secondary infection. Grainger's emphasis on fatalities from worms as a primary cause of death does not appear to agree with other colonial doctors. James Lind, for example, writes that worms are one of the 'less dangerous' diseases which 'seldom prove mortal'. Lind, *An Essay on Diseases Incidental to Europeans in Hot Climates*, pp. 53–4. Generally speaking, the lack of comprehensive public health records makes it difficult to specify the most common causes of plantation deaths. As Richard Sheridan notes, the problems of interpreting data from private plantation records mean that only rough approximations may be made. Sheridan, *Doctors and Slaves*, p. 209. Sheridan offers an analysis of morbidity and mortality on specific Caribbean plantations in Jamaica,

Grenada and what was then British Guiana. Between 1792 and 1838, Sheridan gives the most common causes of slave death (discounting old age and debility) as pulmonary diseases and dropsy (the name given to excess fluids in the serous cavities; 'dropsy' was a potentially fatal symptom that could be caused by a variety of diseases, but was categorized by eighteenth-century physicians as one disorder). Not lagging far behind are fevers (including measles and smallpox) and yaws. Worms do not make an appearance on the list of causes of fatality. See ibid., p. 208.

110 Gilmore, *The Poetics of Empire*, Book IV, ll. 290–305. While Grainger's references to worms are sometimes quite general, Kevan notes that the tropical hookworm would have caused many of the symptoms Grainger describes.

111 Grainger, *Essay*, p. 21.

112 Gilmore, *The Poetics of Empire*, Book IV, l. 292.

113 Ibid., Book IV, l. 306.

114 Ibid., Book IV, ll. 365–8.

115 Ibid., Book IV, ll. 371–6.

116 Ibid., Book IV, ll. 378–80.

117 Ibid., Book IV, ll. 378, 381–2.

118 Mallipeddi, '"A Fixed Melancholy": Migration, Memory and the Middle Passage'. Indeed, the flux, which Grainger mentions as the only disease more deadly than worms, is identified by Mallipeddi as understood by eighteenth-century nautical physicians to be caused by the psychosomatic illness of melancholy or nostalgia. On the medical underpinnings and psychosomatic conditions of colonial nostalgia see Kevis Goodman, '"Uncertain Disease": Nostalgia, Pathologies of Motion, Practices of Reading', *Studies in Romanticism*, Vol. 49, No. 2 (2010), pp. 197–227 and Jonathan Lamb, *Scurvy: The Disease of Discovery* (Princeton, NJ: Princeton University Press, 2016).

119 On the imaginative power of an entomological perspective, see Kate Tunstall's re-evaluation of the early modern materialist imagination through insect imagery, which she argues was used to 'figure and figure out psycho-physiological events or states'. Kate E. Tunstall, 'The Early Modern Embodied Mind and the Entomological Imaginary' in *Mind, Body, Motion, Matter: Eighteenth-Century British and French Literary Perspectives*, ed. Mary Helen McMurran and Alison Conway (Toronto: University of Toronto Press, 2016), pp. 202–29, p. 204.

120 Fairer, *Organising Poetry*, p. 9.

121 Monique Allewaert, 'Swamp Sublime: Ecologies of Resistance in the American Plantation Zone', *PMLA*, Vol. 123, No. 2 (2008), pp. 340–57, pp. 344, 341.

122 Allewaert, *Ariel's Ecology: Plantations, Personhood, and Colonialism in the American Tropics* (Minneapolis: University of Minnesota Press, 2013), pp. 8–9, p. 3.

123 Since this book was completed, two rich papers have been published on the fugitive species which populate Grainger's poem: Allewaert's 'Insect

Poetics: James Grainger, Personification, and Enlightenments Not Taken', *Early American Literature*, Vol. 52, No 2 (2017), pp. 299–332 and Britt Rusert, 'Plantation Ecologies: The Experimental Plantation in and against James Grainger's *The Sugar-Cane*', *Early American Studies*, Vol. 13, No. 2 (2015), pp. 341–73.

124 Rachel Crawford, 'English Georgic and British Nationhood', *English Literary History*, Vol. 65, No. 1 (1998), pp. 123–58, p. 123. See also Joyce Chaplin, who emphasizes the empirical and secular structures of modernity at stake in the agricultural developments on the plantations of the lower southern states during Grainger's era. Joyce Chaplin, *An Anxious Pursuit: Agricultural Innovation and Modernity in the Lower South, 1730–1815* (Chapel Hill: University of North Carolina Press, 1993).

125 Gilmore, *The Poetics of Empire*, Book I, ll. 278–85.

126 Ibid., Book III, ll. 342–3.

127 Ibid., Book I, ll. 246.

128 Ibid., Book I, ll. 458–9, Book III, ll. 623–5.

129 Ibid., Book III, ll. 637–40.

130 Ibid., Book II, ll. 174, 179, 210–15.

131 Ibid., Book II, ll. 185–6.

132 Kevis Goodman notes that georgic verse was identified with ideas about new 'artificial organs' such as the microscope, demonstrating that James Thomson's four-book series *The Seasons* (1726–30) 'courts a microscopic eye'. Kevis Goodman, *Georgic Modernity and British Romanticism: Poetry and the Mediation of History* (Cambridge: Cambridge University Press, 2004), pp. 9, 40.

133 Gilmore, *The Poetics of Empire*, Book I, ll. 322–8.

134 Ibid., Book III, ll. 646–54.

135 Ibid., Book I, ll. 382–3.

136 See Lucile H. Brockway, *Science and Colonial Expansion: The Role of the British Royal Botanic Gardens* (New Haven, CT: Yale University Press, 2002), Richard Drayton, *Nature's Government: Science, Imperial Britain and the 'Improvement' of the World: Science, British Imperialism and the Improvement of the World* (New Haven, CT: Yale University Press, 2000) and Schiebinger, *Plants and Empire*, especially pp. 73–104.

137 Shields, *Oracles of Empire*, p. 73, Jim Egan, 'The "Long'd-for Aera" of an "Other Race": Climate, Identity, and James Grainger's *The Sugar-Cane*', p. 191.

138 Anthony Grafton, *The Footnote: A Curious History* (Cambridge, MA: Harvard University Press, 1999). See also Frank Palmeri, 'The Satirical Footnotes of Swift and Gibbon', *The Eighteenth Century*, Vol. 31, No. 3 (Autumn 1990), pp. 245–62.

139 Egan, 'The "Long'd-for Aera" of an "Other Race": Climate, Identity, and James Grainger's *The Sugar-Cane*', p. 202. Gilmore, *The Poetics of Empire*, Book III, ll. 639, 637.

140 Gilmore, *The Poetics of Empire*, p. 90. Grainger also specifies Linnaean terms. See, for example, ibid., p. 176.

141 For recent work in the history of science on the transnational production of natural knowledge in the colonial Atlantic, see for example, James Delbourgo and Nicholas Dew (eds.), *Science and Empire in the Atlantic World* (New York: Routledge, 2008), Neil Safier, *Measuring the New World: Enlightenment Science and South America* (Chicago: University of Chicago Press, 2008), Londa Schiebinger and Claudia Swan (eds.), *Colonial Botany: Science, Commerce, and Politics in the Early Modern World* (Philadelphia: University of Pennsylvania Press, 2005).

142 Gilmore, *The Poetics of Empire*, pp. 188–9.

143 Ibid., p. 90.

144 Ibid.

145 Ibid., Book IV, l. 207.

146 Ibid., Book IV, l. 143. Hans Sloane, *A Voyage to the Islands Madera, Barbados, Nieves, S. Christophers and Jamaica* (London: Printed by B. M. for the author, 1707), Vol. I, p. xc. on ideas about the different occurrence of disease in Britain and the West Indies, as well as an account of the relationship between British and Caribbean medical knowledge and practices, see Mark Harrison, *Medicine in an Age of Commerce and Empire: Britain and Its Tropical Colonies 1660–1830* (Oxford: Oxford University Press, 2010).

147 Ibid., Book IV, ll. 286–9.

148 William Douglass, *Inoculation of the small pox as practised in Boston, consider'd in a letter to A – S – M.D. & F.R.S. in London* (Boston: Printed and Sold by J. Franklin), p. 7.

149 Edmund Massey, *A Sermon against the Dangerous and Sinful Practice of Inoculation. Preach'd at St. Andrew's Holborn, on Sunday, July the 8th, 1722* (London: William Meadows), p. 15. On the history of inoculation for smallpox see Geneviève Miller, *The Adoption of Inoculation for Smallpox in England and France* (Philadelphia: University of Pennsylvania Press, 1957). For a cultural history of inoculation practices, see Shuttleton, *Smallpox and the Literary Imagination*.

150 James Grainger, *An Essay on the More Common West-India Diseases; and the Remedies which that Country itself Produces*, in *Three tracts on West-Indian agriculture, and subjects connected therewith; viz. An essay upon plantership, by Samuel Martin, Senior, Esq. of Antigua: The sugar-cane, a didactic poem in four books: and, An essay on the management and diseases of Negroes* (Jamaica: Reprinted by A. Aikman, 1802) (1802), p. 72.

151 William Cullen, *Nosology: or, a Systematic Arrangement of Diseases* (Edinburgh: Printed by C. Stewart and Co., 1800), p. 149. William Douglass, a Scots physician in Boston, had in fact discussed yaws and inoculation before Grainger. See Kelly Wisecup, *Medical Encounters: Knowledge and Identity in Early American Literatures* (Amherst: University of Masschusetts Press, 2013), pp. 103–7.

152 Benjamin Moseley, *A Treatise on Sugar* (London: G. G. and J. Robinson, 1799), p. 168. While Moseley praises the success of inoculation for yaws, there is no vaccine for the disease today and prevention is based on the interruption of transmission by early diagnosis and antibiotic treatment.

153 On experimental cultures in the Caribbean, see Schiebinger, 'Scientific Exchange in the Eighteenth-Century Atlantic World'.

154 Hans Sloane, *A Voyage to the Islands Madera, Barbados, Nieves, S. Christophers and Jamaica* (London: Printed by B. M. for the author, 1707), Vol. I, p. clxi.

155 Ibid. By 'them' Sloane appears to be referring to both black and Amerindian doctors.

156 Ibid., Vol. II, pp. 89 and 161.

157 Ibid., Vol. I, p. xcix.

158 Kenneth Dewhurst, *Dr. Thomas Sydenham (1624–1689): His Life and Original Writings* (Berkeley: University of California Press, 1966), p. 86

159 James Knight, British Library, Additional MS, 12419, Vol. II, fo. 90: History of Jamaica (ca. 1746).

160 Hillary, *Observations on the Changes of the Air*, p. 341.

161 Gilmore, *The Poetics of Empire*, p. 180.

162 Stephen W. Thomas, 'Doctoring Ideology: James Grainger's *The Sugar Cane* and the Bodies of Empire', *Early American Studies: An Interdisciplinary Journal*, Vol. 4, No. 1 (Spring), pp. 78–111, p. 86.

163 Grainger, *Essay*, p. iii.

164 Ibid., p. 55. Richard Sheridan notes that slaves frequently employed African treatments for yaws, such as inoculation, but that they usually did so in secret. Sheridan, *Doctors and Slaves*, pp. 83–7.

165 Schiebinger, *Plants and Empire*, p. 90.

166 Grainger, *Essay*, pp. 41–2.

167 Gilmore, *The Poetics of Empire*, Book IV, ll. 257–62.

168 Ibid., p. 193.

169 Ibid., Book II, ll. 135–6.

170 Ibid., Book IV, ll. 368–70. In the poem's accompanying notes, Grainger explains that it is thought that a blow from the obeah practitioner's staff will occasion ill-health or death. See ibid., p. 194.

171 Ibid. What makes this suggestion that obeah has a valid place on the plantation particularly significant is, as Kelly Wisecup points out, that the practice was outlawed in Jamaica in 1760, four years before the publication of *The Sugar-Cane* and immediately after Tacky's Revolt saw rebel slaves kill sixty white people and destroy thousands of pounds' worth of property. Wisecup, *Medical Encounters: Knowledge and Identity in Early American Literatures*, p. 128. The Tacky uprising was supported by obeah doctors who administered a powder to make the rebels invulnerable to attack, and oversaw a solemn oath to bind them in collective secrecy. But it is important to note that no such law against obeah existed in St. Kitts, which did not have the revolutionary history of Jamaica and other islands, and so had a different relationship to the practice of obeah (In 1789 the British

Government received report that on St. Kitts there were no laws which even recognized the existence of obeah. Great Britain. Parliament. *House of Commons Sessional Papers of the Eighteenth Century,* Vol. 69. *Report of the Lords of the Committee of the Council Appointed for the Consideration of All Matters Relating to Trade and Foreign Plantations* (London, 1789), part III, A. nos. 22–6). Nevertheless, obeah was most commonly represented by the plantocracy across the British West Indies as either malevolently inspired by the devil or foolish quackery designed by crafty Africans to extort payments from their less savvy fellow slaves, and the potential value Grainger attributes to its social function sets him apart from his contemporaries.

172 'Vervain', or Verbena, is a genus of which many species are native to the Americas. Gilmore notes that the strain to which Grainger is referring is probably the West Indian vervain *Stachytarpheta jamaicensis*, which was widely regarded as a panacea.

173 Gilmore, *The Poetics of Empire*, p. 178.

174 Ibid., Book II, ll. 147–8.

175 In the case of yaws, for example, Grainger notes that 'there is generally one yaw much larger than the rest; this the Negroes call the master-yaw.' Grainger, *Essay*, p. 57.

176 Dabydeen, 'Sugar and Slavery in the West Indian Georgic', p. 1513.

177 Gilmore, *The Poetics of Empire*, Book III, l. 32.

178 Grainger, *Essay*, p. 22.

179 Ibid., p. 75.

180 My use of the term 'pharmacosm' to describe Grainger's incorporation of obeah and other magical and medical forms of knowledge into his neoclassical agricultural and medical model echoes Theophus Smith's use of the word to suggest a 'world capable of hosting myriad performances of healing and harming'. *Conjuring Culture: Biblical Formations of Black America* (Oxford: Oxford University Press, 1994), p. 44.

181 Gilmore, *The Poetics of Empire*, p. 63.

182 Ibid., Book III, l. 51, Book I, l. 266. Carl Plasa draws a useful parallel between the figures of the poet and the planter in *The Sugar-Cane*, suggestively noting that both are working in 'the breaking and cultivation of new ground, metaphorical in the one case and literal in the other'. Plasa, *Slaves to Sweetness: British and Caribbean Literatures of Sugar*, p. 12.

183 Gilmore, *The Poetics of Empire*, Book II, ll. 132–3, 463.

184 On knowledge networks in the history of science see Susan Scott Parrish, *American Curiosity: Cultures of Natural History in the Colonial British Atlantic World* (Chapel Hill: University of North Carolina Press, 2012), Pratt, *Imperial Eyes*, Simon Schaffer et al., *The Brokered World: Go-Betweens and Global Intelligence, 1770–1820* (Sagamore Beach, MA: Science History, 2009), Pamela H. Smith and Benjamin Schmidt, *Making Knowledge in Early Modern Europe: Practices, Objects, and Texts, 1400–1800* (Chicago: Chicago University Press, 2008).

185 David Hume, 'Of the Rise and Progress of the Arts and Sciences' in *Essays and Treatises on Several Subjects* (London: Printed for A. Millar, 1758), pp. 77–86, p. 86.
186 Gilmore, *The Poetics of Empire*, Book I, l. 109, p. 89.
187 Bryan Edwards, *Poems, Written Chiefly in the West-Indies* (Kingston: Printed for the author by Alexander Aikman, 1792), unnumbered page.
188 O'Brien, 'Imperial Georgic', p. 175.
189 Markman Ellis, '"The Cane-Land Isles": Commerce and Empire in Late Eighteenth-Century Georgic and Pastoral Poetry' in *Islands in History and Representation*, ed. Rod Edmond and Vanessa Smith (London: Routledge, 2003), pp. 43–62, pp. 49, 50 and 54.
190 John Singleton, *A General Description of the West-Indian Islands* (Barbados: Printed by Esmand and Walker for the author, 1767), Book II, l. 20.
191 Ibid., Book IV, ll. 415–18.

2 The Diagnostics of Description

 1 George Heriot, *A Descriptive Poem, Written in the West Indies* (London: Printed for J. Dodsley, 1781), pp. 6–8.
 2 Ibid., pp. 8–9.
 3 Heriot, *Descriptive Poem*, p. 9. 'Fever' was a highly disputed category and the classes of eighteenth-century fevers are too numerous and contested to count, but included putrid, nervous, low, hectic, pestilential, malignant, intermittent and continued.
 4 Colin Chisholm, *An essay on the malignant pestilential fever introduced into the West Indian Islands from Boullam, on the coast of Guinea, as it appeared in 1793 and 1794* (London: Printed for C. Dilly, 1795), pp. 7, 11–12. Chisholm was later inspector-general of ordnance hospitals in the West Indies, and in 1808 was elected a Fellow of the Royal Society.
 5 On ideas about the different occurrence of disease in Britain and the West Indies, as well as an account of the relationship between British and Caribbean medical knowledge and practices, see Mark Harrison, *Medicine in an Age of Commerce and Empire: Britain and Its Tropical Colonies 1660–1830* (Oxford: Oxford University Press, 2010).
 6 Ludmilla J. Jordanova, 'Earth Science and Environmental Medicine: The Synthesis of the Late Enlightenment' in *Images of the Earth: Essays in the History of the Environmental Sciences*, ed. Ludmilla J. Jordanova and Roy S. Porter (Chalfont St Giles: British Society for the History of Science, 1979), pp. 119–46, p. 119.
 7 Casid, *Sowing Empire*, p. xxii.
 8 Geoff Quilley, 'Pastoral Plantations: The Slave Trade and the Representation of British Colonial Landscape in the Late Eighteenth Century' in *An Economy of Colour: Visual Culture and the Atlantic World, 1660–1830*, ed. Geoff Quilley and Kay Dian Kriz (Manchester: Manchester University Press, 2003), pp. 106–28, p. 106.

9 On the reinvigorated Hippocratism of the eighteenth century, see Riley, *The Eighteenth-Century Campaign to Avoid Disease*, pp. x, 102, 111.

10 Egan, 'The "Long'd-for Aera" of an "Other Race": Climate, Identity, and James Grainger's *The Sugar-Cane*', p. 189.

11 On the history of medical geography as a discipline, see Nicolaas A. Rupke (ed.), *Medical Geography in Historical Perspective* (London: Wellcome Trust, 2000).

12 Robert Boyle, *Tracts: containing I. Suspicions about some hidden qualities of the air; with an appendix touching celestial magnets, and some other particulars. II. Animadversions upon Mr. Hobbes's Problemata de vacuo. III. A discourse of the cause of attraction by suction* (London, 1674), p. 2. On ideas about air as a dynamic system in relation to colonial disease in India, see Harrison, *Climates and Constitutions: Health, Race, Environment and British Imperialism in India, 1600–1850*.

13 John Arbuthnot, *An Essay Concerning the Effects of Air on Human Bodies* (London: Printed for J. Tonson, 1733), p. 146.

14 Joseph Priestley, *Experiments and Observations on Different Kinds of Air*, second edition (London: Printed for J. Johnson, 1775). On Priestley's work towards a benevolent aerial economy and the science of eudiometry, see Simon Schaffer, 'Measuring Virtue: Eudiometry, Enlightenment and Pneumatic Medicine', in *The Medical Enlightenment of the Eighteenth Century*, ed. Andrew Cunningham and Roger French (Cambridge: Cambridge University Press, 1990), pp. 281–318.

15 James Johnson, *The Influence of Tropical Climates on European Constitutions; to Which is Now Added, an Essay on Morbid Sensibility of the Stomach and Bowels, as the Proximate Cause, or Characteristic Condition of Indigestion, Nervous Irritability, Mental Despondency, Hypochondriasis, &c. &c.*, fourth edition (London: Printed for Thomas and George Underwood, 1827), p. 170.

16 In *Observationes medicae* (London, 1676), Thomas Sydenham attended to the relationship between atmospheric conditions and epidemic disease.

17 Leonhard Ludwig Finke, *Versuch einer allgemeinen medicinisch-praktischen Geographie worin der historische Theil der einheimischen Voelker- und Staaten-Arzeneykunde vorgetragen wird* (An attempt at a General Medical-Practical Geography, in which the Historical Section on Folk and Public Medicine is Presented) (Leipzig, 1792–5), quoted in translation in Richard Upjohn Light, 'The Progress of Medical Geography', *Geographical Review*, Vol. 34, No. 4, (October 1944), pp. 636–41, p. 636.

18 Ibid.

19 Grove, *Green Imperialism*, p. 304.

20 Johann Peter Frank, *A System of Complete Medical Police: Selections from Johann Peter Frank*, ed. Erna Lesky (Baltimore: John Hopkins University Press, 1976), p. 180.

21 Ibid.

22 Ibid.

23 Peter de Bolla, *The Education of the Eye: Painting, Landscape and Architecture in Eighteenth-Century Britain* (Stanford, CA: Stanford University Press, 2003),

p. 4. On the significance of the visual, see also John Brewer, *The Common People and Politics 1750–1790s* (Cambridge: Chadwyck-Healey, 1986) and Terry Eagleton, *The Ideology of the Aesthetic* (Oxford: Blackwell, 1990). Recent scholarship on the colonial literature and natural history of the British and other European empires has paid particular attention to visual cultures. See, for example, Ian Baucom, *Out of Place: Englishness, Empire, and the Locations of Identity* (Princeton, NJ: Princeton University Press, 1999); Daniela Bleichmar, *Visible Empire: Botanical Expeditions and Visual Culture in the Hispanic Enlightenment* (Chicago: University of Chicago Press, 2012); Casid, *Sowing Empire*, Parrish, *American Curiosity: Cultures of Natural History in the Colonial British Atlantic World*.

24 James Lind, *An Essay on Diseases Incidental to Europeans in Hot Climates* (London: Printed for T. Becket and P.A de Hondt, 1768), p. 127.

25 Hillary, *Observations on the Changes of the Air*, 'preface', unnumbered page.

26 Favret, 'War in the Air'.

27 Weather observations became a widely used form of colonial reportage, and one that held significance beyond the local: Jan Golinski demonstrates that both modern British attitudes to weather and the nineteenth-century institutionalization of 'tropical medicine' can trace their origins to the meticulous observations of the weather by Enlightenment medics. Jan Golinski, *British Weather and the Climate of Enlightenment* (Chicago: University of Chicago Press, 2007), pp. 3, 185.

28 John Williamson, *Medical and Miscellaneous Observations Relative to the West India Islands* (Edinburgh: Printed by Alex Smellie, 1817), Vol. I, p. 292.

29 On eighteenth-century descriptive practices, see John B. Bender and Michael Marinnan (eds.), *Regimes of Description: In the Archive of the Eighteenth Century* (Stanford, CA: Stanford University Press, 2005), Joanna Stalnaker, *The Unfinished Enlightenment: Description in the Age of the Encyclopedia* (Ithaca, NY: Cornell University Press, 2010) and Cynthia Sundberg Wall, *The Prose of Things: Transformations of Description in the Eighteenth Century* (Chicago: University of Chicago Press, 2006).

30 On the history of medical cartography, see Tom Koch, *Disease Maps: Epidemics on the Ground* (Chicago: University of Chicago Press, 2011).

31 O'Brien, 'Imperial Georgic', p. 175.

32 Quilley, 'Pastoral Plantations', pp. 110–11.

33 Ann Bermingham, *Landscape and Ideology: The English Rustic Tradition, 1740–1860* (London: Thames and Hudson, 1987), p. 57. The development of medical forms of environmental description played an important role, as Alan Bewell has revealed in *Romanticism and Colonial Disease*, in the production of Romantic landscape imagery.

34 W. J. T. Mitchell, 'Imperial Landscape' in *Landscape and Power*, ed. W. J. T. Mitchell, second edition (Chicago: University of Chicago Press, 2002), pp. 5–34, pp. 5, 17.

35 Jeffrey Auerbach, 'The Picturesque and the Homogenization of Empire', *The British Art Journal*, Vol. V, No. 1, (2004), pp. 47–54, 48. Auerbach points to

William Hodges, for example: 'instead of completing his art education with a Grand Tour to Italy as his teacher [Richard Wilson] had done, he instead became the draughtsman for Cook on his second voyage to the Pacific, and carried to India tropical ideas of light and vegetation, in addition to English ideas about picturesque composition'. Ibid. Geoff Quilley points to domestic and colonial picturesque imagery as 'reciprocal representational elements within a larger discourse of imperial landscape and the pastoral and georgic modes, and within a larger cycle of circum-Atlantic exchanges'. Quilley, 'Pastoral Plantations', p. 122.

36 Auerbach, 'The Picturesque and the Homogenization of Empire', p. 47.

37 Krista Thompson has shown how nineteenth- and twentieth-century pictur-esque photography drew on a very different set of sources to those usually cited in accounts of the picturesque mode. Rather than the influence of Italian landscape traditions, argues Thompson, the tropicalizing picturesque drew on popular travel accounts such as David Livingstone's adventures in Africa, as well as fantastical representations of tropical nature from the natural and human sciences, in order to ignite a vision of the tropics as a place of 'utter difference'. Krista A. Thompson, *An Eye for the Tropics: Tourism, Photography, and Framing the Caribbean Picturesque* (Durham, NC: Duke University Press, 2006), pp. 20–1. Also against the homogeneity of domestic and colonial pic-turesque production, Jill Casid has emphasized the material and aesthetic hybridity depicted in picturesque representations of the Atlantic processes of transplanting plants, animals and humans on display on the sugar plantation. Casid, *Sowing Empire*.

38 Bohls, *Slavery and the Politics of Place*, p. 16.

39 Bryan Edwards, 'Jamaica, a Descriptive and Didactic Poem', in Edwards, *Poems*, Book I, l. 397.

40 Ibid., Book I, ll. 95–6, Book I, ll. 184–5.

41 Casid, *Sowing Empire*, p. 12, Bohls, *Slavery and the Politics of Place*, p. 29.

42 William Beckford, *A descriptive account of the island of Jamaica: with remarks upon the cultivation of the sugar-cane throughout the different seasons of the year, and chiefly considered in a picturesque point of view* (London: Printed for T. and J. Egerton, 1790), Vol. I, p. 31. On Beckford's colonial picturesque imagery, see also Casid, *Sowing Empire*.

43 Anthony Pagden, *European Encounters with the New World: From Renaissance to Romanticism* (New Haven, CT: Yale University Press, 1993), p. 52.

44 Sandiford, *The Cultural Politics of Sugar*, p. 120.

45 Sara Suleri, *The Rhetoric of English India* (Chicago: University of Chicago Press, 1992), pp. 19, 76. John Barrell argues that the picturesque eye positions itself in a 'transcendent viewing position' which surveys the natural world with appar-ently unmediated vision but erases social issues, creating aestheticized scenes that are 'devoid of ethical, political, or sentimental meanings'. John Barrell, *The Birth of Pandora and the Division of Knowledge* (Basingstoke: Macmillan, 1992), p. 97. Describing the literature of the plantation, Édouard Glissant writes that 'conventional landscape' was 'pushed to the extremes' as part of the

'propensity to blot out the shudders of life, that is, the turbulent realities of the Plantation, beneath the conventional splendour of scenery'. Édouard Glissant, *The Poetics of Relation* (Ann Arbor: University of Michigan Press, 1997), p. 70. Writing of a specifically Jamaican strand of the picturesque in the context of the historical movement from slavery to abolition, Tim Barringer writes that the picturesque form was inherently unstable, 'always tending to reveal that which it attempted to conceal'. Tim Barringer, 'Picturesque Prospects and the Labour of the Enslaved' in *Art and Emancipation in Jamaica: Isaav Mendes Belisario and His Worlds*, ed. Tim Barringer, Gillian Forrester, and Barbaro Martinez-Ruiz (New Haven, CT: Yale Centre for British Art in association with Yale University Press, 2007), pp. 41–63, p. 61. On the suppression of political and social content by the colonial picturesque, see also Bohls, 'The Gentleman Planter', Bohls, 'The Planter Picturesque: Matthew Lewis's *Journal of a West India Proprietor*', *European Romantic Review*, Vol. 12 (2001), pp. 63–76 and Stephen Copley and Peter Garside, 'Introduction' in *The Politics of the Picturesque: Literature, Landscape and Aesthetics since 1770* (Cambridge: Cambridge University Press, 1994), pp. 1–12, 6. Sandiford describes the picturesque as an 'auxiliary to georgic', in that it is allied to the interests of the landowning elite and 'naturalises the slaves to the landscape of labour and low social privilege while also suppressing and effacing any semblance of particularity or protest'. Sandiford, *The Cultural Politics of Sugar*, p. 20.

46 William Gilpin, *Observations, relative chiefly to picturesque beauty, made in the year 1772, on several parts of England* (London: Printed for R. Blamire, 1786), Vol. I, p. 81.
47 Beckford, *Descriptive Account*, Vol. II, p. 240, Vol. I, pp. vii, x. Quilley writes that Beckford 'sees the colonies as perfect training grounds for the aspirant landscape artist'. Quilley, 'Pastoral Plantations', p. 109.
48 Beckford, *Descriptive Account*, Vol. I, p. 74.
49 Alan Liu, *Wordsworth: The Sense of History* (Stanford: Stanford University Press, 1989), pp. 62, 63.
50 Beckford, *Descriptive Account*, Vol. I, p. 21.
51 Ibid., Vol. I, p. 178.
52 Ibid., Vol. II, p. 190.
53 Ibid., Vol. II, p. 240. See also Vol. I, p. 13.
54 Ibid., Vol. I, pp. 43–4.
55 Ibid., Vol. I, pp. 12, 44.
56 Bohls, *Slavery and the Politics of Place*. Beckford, *Descriptive Account*, Vol. I, p. 15.
57 Barringer, 'Picturesque Prospects and the Labour of the Enslaved', p. 50. Robertson's paintings were not reprinted for the publication of the *Descriptive Account* – in fact Robertson's view of Beckford's estate at Roaring River, Jamaica, preceded Beckford's publication by twelve years. Beckford begins his book with an account of Robertson's paintings as 'confirmation of the fidelity of the scenes which I have attempted to delineate' and lamenting that it was

not possible to include the works alongside his text. Beckford, *Descriptive Account*, Vol. I, p. x.

58 Suleri, *The Rhetoric of English India*, p. 75.

59 Chisholm, *An Essay on the Malignant Pestilential Fever*, p. 1.

60 Ibid., p. 1. Emphasis added.

61 Ibid., pp. 10, 7.

62 George Pinckard, *Notes on the West Indies: written during the expedition under the command of the late General Sir R. Abercrombie: including observations on the Island of Barbadoes, &c,. likewise remarks relating to the Creoles and Slaves of the Western Colonies and the Indians of South America, etc.* (London: Longman et al., 1806), Vol. I, p. 197.

63 Pinckard, *Notes on the West Indies*, Vol. I, p. 306.

64 John Williamson, *Medical and Miscellaneous Observations Relative to the West India Islands* (Edinburgh: Printed by Alex Smellie, 1817), Vol. I, pp. 25–6.

65 On the picturesque as a 'fantasized encounter with the real', see de Bolla, *The Education of the Eye*, p. 120.

66 Williamson, *Medical and Miscellaneous Observations*, Vol. I, p. 396.

67 Pinckard, *Notes on the West Indies*, Vol. II, p. 365.

68 Pinckard, *Notes on the West Indies*, Vol. III, p. 441.

69 Chisholm, *An Essay on the Malignant Pestilential Fever*, p. 3.

70 Williamson, *Medical and Miscellaneous Observations*, Vol. I, p. 27.

71 Ibid., Vol. I, p. 26.

72 Chisholm, *An Essay on the Malignant Pestilential Fever*, p. 79.

73 Williamson, *Medical and Miscellaneous Observations*, Vol. II, p. 217.

74 Bender and Marinnan (eds.), *Regimes of Description: In the Archive of the Eighteenth Century*, p. 5.

75 In modern history of medicine, the term 'environment' is commonly used as suggestive of the sum of external forces or conditions that act on an organism or community of organisms. Environmental factors that might be perceived to jeopardize health consist of those of a chemical or inorganic nature, those that are biological or organic (often including the effects of 'climate'), and sociocultural factors. It is worth noting, however, that this definition was not in use during this period. Samuel Johnson defines 'environ' as 'to surround or encompass' but contains no entry for 'environment'. 'Environment' appears in Nathan Bailey's *New Universal Etymological English Dictionary* (1775) as 'an encompassing round'. While I use 'environment' to suggest the sum of an individual or community's natural surroundings, 'climate', to a far greater extent, was the term used to define the causal relationship between an individual and his or her place of habitation. Climate was determined by its position between two latitudinal parallels and constituted a descriptive framing of a particular geographical space, but climates were not politically neutral and were used to organize nations hierarchically, with Britain usually located within the more temperate regions.

76 Heriot, *Descriptive Poem*, p. 13. Heriot himself would continue to develop his work in the picturesque throughout his career as an artist and writer and up

to his final work, *A picturesque tour made in the years 1817 and 1820, through the Pyrenean Mountains* (1824). Liu writes that the picturesque represented 'law and order' and the visualization of an approach to 'managing and ultimately policing the rural landscape cognate with new methods of administration learned in the industrial centres'. Liu, *Wordsworth: the Sense of History*, p. 99.

77 Beckford, *Descriptive Account*, Vol. I, p. 10.
78 Ibid., Vol. I, pp. 401–2.
79 Ibid., Vol. I, p. 12.
80 Ibid., Vol. I, p. 73.
81 John Constable, letter to John Fisher, 17 November 1824, quoted in John E. Thornes, *John Constable's Skies: A Fusion of Art and Science* (Birmingham: Birmingham University Press, 1999), p. 175.
82 Beckford, *Descriptive Account*, Vol. I, p. 9.
83 Pinckard, *Notes on the West Indies*, p. 116.
84 Chisholm, *An Essay on the Malignant Pestilential Fever*, p. 188.
85 Williamson, *Medical and Miscellaneous Observations*, Vol. I, p. 36.
86 William Hillary, *Observations on the Changes of the Air, and the Concomitant Epidemical Diseases of Barbadoes*, second edition (London: Printed for L. Hawes et al., 1766), p. 203.
87 Chisholm, *An Essay on the Malignant Pestilential Fever*, p. 81.
88 Ibid., p. 82.
89 Heriot, *Descriptive Poem*, p. 7.
90 Ibid., pp. 13, 10.
91 Ibid., p. 10.
92 Beckford, *Descriptive Account*, Vol. I, ll, pp. 89–90.
93 Chisholm, *An Essay on the Malignant Pestilential Fever*, p. 1.
94 Johnson, *The Influence of Tropical Climates on European Constitutions*, pp. 226–7. Moseley practiced in Jamaica 1768–84, rose to the post of surgeon-general on the island and was best known for his vehement anti-inoculation stance. He later graduated M.D. at St. Andrews and was admitted to the London College of Physicians.
95 Harrison, *Disease and the Modern World: 1500 to the Present Day*, p. 87.
96 Lord George Byron, *Complete Poetical Works*, ed. J. J. McGann (Oxford: Clarendon Press, 1980), Vol. I, p. 407.
97 James Montgomery, *The West Indies* (New York: Garland, 1979), p. 3.
98 Ibid., p. 10.
99 Ibid., p. 47.
100 Ibid., p. 48.
101 Ibid., p. 18.
102 Ibid., pp. 18, 21–6.
103 Ibid., p. 44.
104 Ibid., pp. 11, 21.
105 Ibid., p. 39.
106 Ibid., p. 72.
107 Ibid., p. 28.

108 Ibid., p. 39.

109 Ibid., pp. 39, 40.

110 On imperial gothic see Patrick Brantlinger, *Rule of Darkness: British Literature and Imperialism, 1830–1914* (Ithaca, NY: Cornell University Press, 1988) and Andrew Smith and William Hughes (eds.), *Empire and the Gothic: The Politics of Genre* (Basingstoke: Palgrave Macmillan, 2003).

111 Matthew Lewis, *Journal of a West India Proprietor*, ed. Judith Terry (Oxford: Oxford University Press, 1999), p. 44. See Bohls, *Slavery and the Politics of Place* for a comparison of the 'planter picturesque' in Beckford and Lewis.

112 Bohls, *Slavery and the Politics of Place*, p. 46.

113 Lewis, *Journal of a West India Proprietor*, p. 45. The quote is from Milton's *Paradise Lost*.

114 Ibid., pp. 209, 19.

115 See Chisholm, *An Essay on the Malignant Pestilential Fever*, p. 127.

116 Lewis, *Journal of a West India Proprietor*, pp. 166, 169.

117 Dahlia Porter, 'Maps, Lists, Views: How the Picturesque Wye transformed Topography', *Romanticism*, Vol. 19, No. 2, (2013), pp. 163–78, p. 171.

118 John Davy, *The West Indies, before and since Slave Emancipation, comprising the Windward and Leeward Islands' military command; founded on notes and observations collected during a three years' residence* (London: W. and F. G. Cash, 1854), p. 172.

119 Ibid., pp. 73–4.

120 Tim Fulford, *Landscape, Liberty and Authority: Poetry, Criticism and Politics from Thomson to Wordsworth* (Cambridge: Cambridge University Press, 1996), p. 117.

121 Mary Jacobus, *Romantic Things: A Tree, a Rock, a Cloud* (Chicago: University of Chicago Press, 2012), p. 11. In his *Essay on the Modifications of Clouds* (1803), Luke Howard gave cloud formations their modern scientific taxonomies. See Richard Hamblyn, *The Invention of Clouds: How an Amateur Meteorologist Forged the Language of the Skies* (London: Picador, 2001).

122 Ibid., pp. 10, 12.

3 Skin, Textuality and Colonial Feeling

1 John Gabriel Stedman, *Narrative of a Five Years Expedition against the Revolted Negroes of Surinam in Guiana on the Wild Coast of South-America. From the year 1772 to the year 1777*, ed. Richard Price and Sally Price (Baltimore: John Hopkins University Press, 1988), p. 375.

2 Deirdre Coleman, 'Janet Schaw and the Complexions of Empire', *Eighteenth-Century Studies*, Vol. 36, No. 2 (2003), pp. 169–93, p. 172.

3 On the historical relationships between Christianity, clothing and complexion as markers of human difference, see Wheeler, *The Complexion of Race*, p. 20. On the history of dermatology see Jonathan Reinarz and Kevin Siena (eds.), *A Medical History of Skin: Scratching the Surface* (London: Routledge, 2016).

4 Stedman, *Narrative*, p. 547. Stedman is citing Anonymous, *Jamaica, a Poem*, Part I, ll. 186–8.
5 For a comprehensive account of Suriname during the period of Stedman's placement there, see Price and Price's introduction to their edition of the *Narrative*.
6 Stedman, *Narrative*, p. 347, Pratt, *Imperial Eyes*, p. 9.
7 Peter Linebaugh and Marcus Rediker (eds.), *The Many-Headed Hydra: Sailors, Slaves, Commoners, and the Hidden History of the Revolutionary Atlantic* (London: Verso, 2000), p. 346. For recent discussions of Blake and Stedman see Mario Klarer, 'Humanitarian Pornography: John Gabriel Stedman's *Narrative of a Five Years Expedition against the Revolted Negroes of Surinam* (1796)', *New Literary History*, Vol. 36, No. 4 (Autumn 2005), pp. 559–87; Debbie Lee, *Slavery and the Romantic Imagination* (Philadelphia: University of Pennsylvania Press, 2002), Marcus Rediker, 'The Red Atlantic; or, "a Terrible Blast Swept Over the Heaving Sea"' in *Sea Changes: Historizing the Ocean*, ed. Bernhard Klein and Gesa Mackenthun (New York: Routledge, 2004), pp. 111–30; Marcus Wood, *Blind Memory: Visual Representations of Slavery in England and America* (Manchester: Manchester University Press, 2000) and Marcus Wood, *Slavery, Empathy, and Pornography* (Oxford: Oxford University Press, 2002). Stedman's influence on Samuel Taylor Coleridge, who was apparently very impressed by the *Narrative*, has been noted by Mary Lynn Johnson, 'Coleridge's Prose and a Blake Plate in Stedman's *Narrative:* Unfastening the "Hooks and Eyes" of Memory', *Wordsworth Circle*, Vol. 13, No. 1 (Winter 1982), pp. 36–8.
8 Wood, *Slavery, Empathy, and Pornography*, p. 95.
9 Anne K. Mellor, 'Sex, Violence and Slavery: Blake and Wollstonecraft', *The Huntington Library Quarterly*, Vol. 58, No. 3/4 (1995), pp. 345–70, p. 360. See also Wood, *Slavery, Empathy, and Pornography* and Klarer, 'Humanitarian Pornography: John Gabriel Stedman's *Narrative of a Five Years Expedition against the Revolted Negroes of Surinam* (1796)'.
10 Pratt, *Imperial Eyes*; Jenny Sharpe, *Ghosts of Slavery: A Literary Archaeology of Black Women's Lives* (Minneapolis: University of Minnesota Press, 2003) and Helen Thomas, *Romanticism and Slave Narratives: Transatlantic Testimonies* (Cambridge: Cambridge University Press, 2000).
11 Bewell, *Romanticism and Colonial Disease*, p. 89.
12 Bohls, *Slavery and the Politics of Place*, p. 55.
13 Stedman, *Narrative*, p. 607.
14 Ibid., p. xxvi.
15 David Geggus, 'The Anglo-French Conflict in the Caribbean in the 1790s' in *Britain and Revolutionary France: Conflict, Subversion and Propaganda*, ed. Colin Jones, *Exeter Studies in History* (Exeter: University of Exeter, 1983), pp. 27–39, p. 35.
16 Stedman, *Narrative*, p. 154.
17 Ibid., pp. 369, 367.
18 This chapter works primarily from Richard Price and Sally Price's 1988 unabridged edition of this text.

19 Stedman, *Narrative*, pp. lx–lxv.
20 John Gabriel Stedman, unpublished diaries, Stedman Collection (James Ford Bell Library, University of Minnesota), 24 June 1795.
21 Ibid. For a comparison of the key differences between the 1790 and 1796 texts, see Richard Price and Sally Price's introduction to the *Narrative*. Thomson made many significant changes, making the text speak much more to the pro-slavery apologist agenda espoused by Edward Long and others. For example, Stedman's accounts of the Saramaka and Djuka free blacks as the epitome of the 'natural man' are transformed, with the 1796 text depicting them as brute savages.
22 Stedman, *Narrative*, p. L.
23 Stedman appears to have been unaware that Thomson was responsible for the alterations to his manuscript; his anger was, therefore, directed at Johnson. Ibid., p. xlix.
24 Ibid., p. 7.
25 Ibid., p. 11.
26 David Richards, *Masks of Difference: Cultural Representations in Literature, Anthropology and Art* (Cambridge: Cambridge University Press, 1994), p. 107.
27 Ibid., p. 95.
28 Stedman, *Narrative*, pp. 419, 530.
29 Ibid., p. 367.
30 Ibid., pp. 451, 528, 49.
31 Ibid., p. 530.
32 Rod Edmond, *Leprosy and Empire: A Medical and Cultural History* (Cambridge: Cambridge University Press, 2006), p. 3.
33 According to Kristen Block, 'medical treatises and academic periodicals discussing leprosy identified it as primarily an African disease, and often defined it in relation to syphilis and yaws – two other ulcerative maladies with distasteful moral connotations and physical symptoms'. These (erroneous) 'conflations of leprosy with sexually transmitted and/or 'African' diseases like yaws' may explain Stedman's imaginative connection between leprosy and his own health, given his sexual activities with various women documented in his manuscript diaries. Kristen Block, 'Slavery and Inter-Imperial Leprosy Discourse in the Atlantic World', *Atlantic Studies* (2017), p. 1.
34 Stedman, *Narrative*, p. 469.
35 Ibid., p. 370.
36 Ibid., p. 327.
37 Ibid., pp. 221–2.
38 Ibid., p. 222.
39 Joseph Jacob Plenck, *Doctrina de morbis cutaneis qua hi morbid in suas classes, genera & species rediguntur* (Vienna, 1776); Robert Willan, *On Cutaneous Diseases* (London: J. Johnson, 1808). See also John Gowland, *An Essay on Cutaneous Diseases, and Impurities of the Skin* (London: Johnson and Murray, 179?).
40 Steven Connor, *The Book of Skin* (London: Reaktion Books, 2004), p. 26.

41 Grainger, *Essay*, p. 57.
42 Stedman, unpublished diaries, 20 September 1773.
43 Stedman, *Narrative*, p. 163.
44 Ibid., p. 569.
45 See George-Louis Leclerc, Comte de Buffon, *Histoire Naturelle, générale et particulière, avec la description du Cabinet du Roi* (1749–1804). Buffon's theory that the animal, human and plant life of the Americas existed in a state of degeneration making it grow smaller and less fertile was disputed by Caribbean planters including Bryan Edwards and Edward Long.
46 Samuel Stanhope Smith, *An Essay on the Causes of the Variety of Complexion and Figure in the Human Species. To which are Added Strictures on Lord Kaim's Discourse, on the Original Diversity of Mankind* (Philadelphia and London, 1789), pp. 10–11.
47 Stedman, *Narrative*, p. 369.
48 Ibid., pp. 614, 512.
49 Ibid., pp. 39–41.
50 Dror Wahrman, *The Making of the Modern Self: Identity and Culture in Eighteenth-Century England* (New Haven, CT: Yale University Press, 2006); Wheeler, *The Complexion of Race*.
51 Stedman, *Narrative*, p. 512.
52 James Parsons, 'Account of the White Negro Shewn Before the Royal Society: In a Letter to the Right Honourable Earl of Morton, President of the Royal Society, from James Parsons, M.D.F.R.S.', *Philosophical Transactions (1683–1775)*, Vol. 55 (1765), pp. 45–53. For other examples of black people being used as exhibits see Paul Edwards and James Walvin, *Black Personalities in the Era of the Slave Trade* (London: Macmillan, 1983) and Sadiah Qureshi, *Peoples on Parade: Exhibitions, Empire, and Anthropology in Nineteenth-Century Britain* (Chicago: Chicago University Press, 2011).
53 Charles D. Martin, *The White African American Body: A Cultural and Literary Exploration* (New Brunswick, NJ: Rutgers University Press, 2002), p. 6.
54 Stedman, *Narrative*, p. 512.
55 Robert Boyle, *Experiments and Considerations Touching Colours* (New York: Johnson Reprint, 1964). On the anatomical science of race, see Andrew S. Curran, *The Anatomy of Blackness: Science and Slavery in and Age of Enlightenment* (Baltimore: Johns Hopkins University Press, 2011).
56 See Wayne Glausser, *Locke and Blake: A Conversation across the Eighteenth Century* (Gainsville: University Press of Florida, 1998), p. 79 and Mellor, 'Sex, Violence and Slavery: Blake and Wollstonecraft', p. 358.
57 See Klarer, 'Humanitarian Pornography' and Wood, *Slavery, Empathy, and Pornography*.
58 Stedman, *Narrative*, p. 264.
59 Wood, *Blind Memory*, p. 235.
60 Wood, *Slavery, Empathy, and Pornography*, pp. 101–2. As Wood points out, Stedman's contemporaries would have read his accounts of the physical abuse of slaves against the central premise of Adam Smith's theory of moral sentiments.

61 Ibid., p. 139.
62 Alan Bewell also points out that the sexualization of enslaved women has ignored their important function as medical attendants: what has 'frequently been taken as a discourse on the fulfilment of desire' was in fact 'more frequently about the necessity to regulate it'. Bewell, *Romanticism and Colonial Disease*, p. 25.
63 Stedman, *Narrative*, p. 271.
64 Ibid., p. 556.
65 Ibid., pp. 264, 266.
66 Ibid., p. 531.
67 Ibid., p. 259.
68 Ibid., p. 147.
69 For Bohls, the 'violence of slavery emerges as latent content in Stedman's snake plate' through 'its visual echoes of some of his better-known images of slave torture' Bohls, *Slavery and the Politics of Place*, p. 55.
70 While there is no particular evidence that Stedman read Whytt specifically, Stedman's explicit reference to Hunter's 'Account of the Organ of Hearing in Fish' (1782) suggest that he would have been familiar with the 'vital principle' of life which was a dominant element of eighteenth-century medical discourse, and the association between dissection and the vitalist debate exemplified by Whytt's work. Stedman, *Narrative*, p. 299.
71 Robert Whytt, *An Essay on the Vital and Other Involuntary Motions of Animals* (Edinburgh: Hamilton, Balfour and Neill, 1751), p. 384.
72 Seguin Henry Jackson, *Dermato-Pathologica; or Practical Observations, from Some New Thoughts on the Pathology and and Proximate Cause of Diseases of the True Skin and its Emanations, the Rete Mucosum and Cuticle* (London: Printed by H. Reynell, 1792), p. 32.
73 Robert Whytt, *Physiological essays* (Edinburgh: Hamilton, Balfour and Neill, 1761), p. 151.
74 See Pratt, *Imperial Eyes*, and Sharpe, *Ghosts of Slavery*.
75 Sharpe, *Ghosts of Slavery*, p. 73.
76 Werner Sollors, *Neither Black Nor White Yet Both: Thematic Explorations of Interracial Literature* (Cambridge, MA: Harvard University Press, 1999), p. 193. Richard Steele, *The Spectator* (13 March 1711). The tale of the Englishman Inkle who sells his beloved, Yarico, into slavery first appeared in Ligon, *A True and Exact History of the Island of Barbados*. Forty-five different literary versions of the tale have since been identified.
77 Sollors, *Neither Black Nor White Yet Both*, p. 199.
78 Stedman, *Narrative*, p. 103.
79 Ibid., p. 102.
80 Adam Smith, *The Theory of Moral Sentiments* (Indianapolis: Liberty Classics, 1976), p. 10.
81 Wood, *Slavery, Empathy, and Pornography*, pp. 100, 138. On spectacular violence in the colonial and revolutionary period see also Ian Haywood, *Bloody Romanticism: Spectacular Violence and the Politics of Representation, 1776–1832* (Basingstoke: Palgrave Macmillan, 2006). On the association between pain

and sensibility, Ann Jessie van Sant writes that the 'association of pain with the activation of sensibility coincides with the traditional view of sensation itself as a form of pain and of passional life as a disturbance of the soul.' Ann Jessie van Sant, *Eighteenth-Century Sensibility and the Novel: The Senses in Social Context* (Cambridge: Cambridge University Press, 1993), p. 52.

82 Lynn Festa, *Sentimental Figures of Empire in Eighteenth-Century Britain and France* (Baltimore: Johns Hopkins University Press, 2005), p. 14. Brycchan Carey, *British Abolitionism and the Rhetoric of Sensibility: Writing, Sentiment, and Slavery, 1760–1807* (Basingstoke: Palgrave Macmillan, 2005).

83 Sollors, *Neither Black Nor White Yet Both*, p. 205, Wood, *Slavery, Empathy, and Pornography*, p. 95.

84 Festa, *Sentimental Figures of Empire in Eighteenth-Century Britain and France*, p. 14.

85 Stedman, *Narrative*, p. 618.

86 Ibid., p. 2.

87 See Tassie Gwilliam, '"Scenes of Horror", Scenes of Sensibility: Sentimentality and Slavery in John Gabriel Stedman's *Narrative of a Five Years Expedition against the Revolted Negroes of Surinam*', *English Literary History*, Vol. 65, No. 3 (1998), pp. 653–73, p. 669.

88 Ibid., p. 653.

89 Stedman, *Narrative*, p. 85. 'Ranger' was a term that usually referred to a slave who had been manumitted and was assisting the European military in the fight against the revolutionaries.

90 Ibid., p. 87.

91 Ibid.

92 Ibid., pp. 113–5.

93 Michel De Certeau, 'Travel Narratives of the French to Brazil: Sixteenth to Eighteenth Centuries', *Representations*, Vol. 33 (1991), pp. 221–6, p. 222.

94 Schaffer, 'How Disciplines Look', p. 60 and Luisa Calè and Adriana Craciun, 'The Disorder of Things', special issue of *Eighteenth-Century Studies*, Vol. 45, No. 1 (2011).

95 Stedman, *Narrative*, p. 7.

96 Hume identifies 'contiguity' as one of the three principles of the association of ideas, along with 'resemblance' and 'cause and effect'. David Hume, *A Treatise of Human Nature* (London: Printed for John Noon, 1739).

97 Bohls, *Slavery and the Politics of Place*, p. 81.

98 Stedman, *Narrative*, p. 546.

99 Ibid., p. 554.

100 Pratt, *Imperial Eyes*, p. 5.

101 Ibid., p. 86.

102 Stedman, unpublished diaries, 21 August 1773.

103 Stedman, *Narrative*, p. 140. 'Frenzy' denoted a fever accompanied by some element of insanity.

104 Ibid., p. 141.

105 Ibid.

106 James Chandler, *An Archaeology of Sympathy: The Sentimental Mode in Literature and Cinema* (Chicago: Chicago University Press, 2013), p. xv.
107 Ibid., p. 12.
108 Stedman, *Narrative*, p. 144.
109 See Markman Ellis, 'Suffering Things: Lapdogs, Slaves, and Counter-Sensibility' in *The Secret Life of Things: Animals, Objects, and It-Narratives in Eighteenth-Century England*, ed. Mark Blackwell (Lewisburg: Bucknell University Press, 2007), pp. 92–113; Lynn Festa, 'Person, Animal, Thing: The 1796 Dog Tax and the Right to Superfluous Things', *Eighteenth-Century Life*, Vol. 33, No. 2 (Spring 2009), pp. 1–44; Jonathan Lamb, 'Modern Metamorphoses and Disgraceful Tales', *Critical Inquiry*, Vol. 28, No. 1, 'Things' (Autumn 2001), pp. 133–66 and David Perkins, *Romanticism and Animal Rights* (Cambridge: Cambridge University Press, 2003).
110 Laura Brown, *Fables of Modernity: Literature and Culture in the English Eighteenth Century* (Ithaca: Cornell University Press, 2001), p. 262.
111 Giorgio Agamben, *The Open: Man and Animal* (Stanford, CA: Stanford University Press, 2004), p. 37.
112 George Boulukos gives an account of the distancing effects of the colonial sentimental. George Boulukos, *The Grateful Slave: the Emergence of Race in Eighteenth-Century British and American Culture* (Cambridge: Cambridge University Press, 2008), p. 14.
113 Festa, *Sentimental Figures of Empire in Eighteenth-Century Britain and France*, pp. 5–6.
114 Chandler, *An Archaeology of Sympathy*, p. 12.
115 Stedman, *Narrative*, pp. 141, 328. On imitative monkeys in the *Narrative* and Blake's engravings of monkeys for Stedman, see Lee, *Slavery and the Romantic Imagination*.
116 Stedman's full understanding of this 'chain' is not possible to delineate. But his references to Buffon's work suggest an interest in a monogenist model of human change through reproduction and determined by climatic influence that prefigured nineteenth-century evolutionary discourse. This did not include the possibility of the common descent of humans and apes, however, which Buffon rejected (arguing against James Burnett, Lord Monboddo, who claimed apes as the 'brother of man', and whose work Stedman discusses in light of Monboddo's much-ridiculed suggestion that humans had once had tails).
117 Heather Keenleyside, *Animals and Other People: Literary Forms and Living Beings in the Long Eighteenth Century* (Philadelphia: University of Pennsylvania Press, 2016), p. 157.
118 Ibid., p. 158.
119 In her richly layered account of Blake's engravings for the *Narrative* and their relationship with Stedman's prose, Debbie Lee writes that the dying monkey 'accuses Stedman of the same kinds of crimes Stedman performs against the revolted negroes, but for which Stedman seems to feel no guilt whatsoever.' Reading Blake's engravings as working against Stedman's written account,

Lee argues that Blake, too, 'enacts a sharp indictment' of Stedman in the way he constructs and pairs particular engravings relating to violence against slaves and animals. But to read Blake's animals as strategically significant while identifying Stedman's monkeys as holding an 'otherwise trivial place as a natural history specimen' in the *Narrative* is to underestimate the complexity of the text, and to emphasize Stedman's scientific reading (on animal-human relations this included Buffon and Monboddo) over the significant literary interests which shape his work. Reading Stedman through Sterne reveals the proximity between the *Narrative*'s natural historical interests and ideas about sympathetic feeling in colonial context.

120 Stedman, *Narrative*, p. 141.

121 Ibid., p. 144.

4 'A Seasoned Creole' and 'a Citizen of the World'

1 Pinckard, *Notes on the West Indies*, Vol. III, p. 134; ibid., Vol. II, pp. 141–2.

2 James Clark, *A treatise on the yellow fever, as it appeared in the island of Dominica, in the years 1793-4-5-6: to which are added, Observations on the bilious remittent fever, on intermittents, dysentery, and some other West India diseases* (London: Printed for J. Murray and S. Highley, 1797), p. 7.

3 Chisholm, *An Essay on the Malignant Pestilential Fever*, p. 127. Although this black vomit was a notorious and dreaded symptom of yellow fever much commented upon by colonial medical treatises, Sheldon Watts notes in *Epidemics and History* that the current medical understanding of the disease is that this symptom only occurs in a relatively small percentage of sufferers, indicating that the black vomit took on an imaginative significance far broader than its actual appearance. See Sheldon Watts, *Epidemics and History: Disease, Power and Imperialism* (New Haven, CT: Yale University Press, 1997), p. 218.

4 Clark, *A treatise on the yellow fever*, p. 8.

5 John McNeill, 'Yellow Fever and Geopolitics: Environment, Epidemics, and the Struggles for Empire in the American Tropics, 1650–1900', *History Now*, Vol. 8, No. 2 (2002), pp. 10–16. See also J. R. McNeill, *Mosquito Empires: Ecology and War in the Greater Caribbean, 1620–1914* (Cambridge: Cambridge University Press, 2010), David Geggus, 'Yellow Fever in the 1790s: The British Army in Occupied Saint Domingue', *Medical History*, Vol. 23 (1979), pp. 38–58, and Watts, *Epidemics and History: Disease, Power and Imperialism*.

6 Curtin, *Death by Migration*, p. 35.

7 Trevor Burnard, *Planters, Merchants, and Slaves: Plantation Societies in British America, 1650–1820* (Chicago: University of Chicago Press, 2015), pp. 69–70, and Burnard, '"The Countrie Continues Sicklie": White Mortality in Jamaica, 1655–1780'. See also Geggus, 'Yellow Fever in the 1790s: The British Army in Occupied Saint Domingue' and Geggus, 'The Anglo-French Conflict in the Caribbean in the 1790s'.

8 *The Lancet London: A Journal of British and Foreign Medicine*, Vol. 5 (London: G. L. Hutchinson, 1824), p. 320.

9 Pinckard, *Notes on the West Indies*, Vol. III, p. 138.

10 Ibid., Vol. III, p. 147.

11 Ibid., Vol. III, p. 146.

12 Ibid., Vol. III, p. 140.

13 Ibid., Vol. III, p. 148.

14 Ibid., Vol. III, p. 135. As he recovers, Pinckard develops a narrative of psycho-logical and social change from his extreme experience, which might be read, in Joanna Bourke's terms, as a 'pain event'. Bourke argues that pain should be understood 'in relation to the way it disrupts and alarms, authenticates and cultivates, the "states of being" of real people in the world'. Joanna Bourke, *The Story of Pain, from Prayer to Painkillers* (Oxford: Oxford University Press, 2014), p. 9. On the relationship between pain and national identity, see Elaine Scarry, *The Body in Pain: The Making and Unmaking of the World* (Oxford: Oxford University Press, 1985).

15 Pinckard, *Notes on the West Indies*, Vol. III, p. 24. See also Vol. I, p. 255, and Vol. III, pp. 259, 426, 428.

16 Maria Nugent, *Lady Nugent's Journal: Jamaica One Hundred Years Ago* (Cambridge: Cambridge University Press, 2010), p. 155.

17 Ibid., pp. 123–4.

18 Ibid., p. 292.

19 John M'Leod, *Narrative of a Voyage, in His Majesty's Late Ship Alceste to the Yellow Sea, Along the Coast of Corea* (London: John Murray, 1817), p. 247.

20 George Birnie, 'Extract of a Letter from Mr George Birnie', *The London Medical and Physical Journal*, Vol. 38 (1817), p. 150. 'Remittent fevers' were understood to be particular to hot, humid climates.

21 On fever discourse in the Johnny New-come cartoons see Ward, *Desire and Disorder*.

22 Pinckard, *Notes on the West Indies*, Vol. III, p. 148.

23 Ibid., Vol. III, p. 420, Vol. II, p. 134. Other colonial medics followed Buffon and argued that the process of seasoning meant that Creoles would become increasingly blacker over several generations. See Harrison, *Climates and Constitutions: Health, Race, Environment and British Imperialism in India, 1600–1850*, pp. 88–9.

24 On the model of the Creole as cultural hybrid see Edward Kamau Brathwaite, *The Development of Creole Society in Jamaica, 1770–1820* (Oxford: Clarendon Press, 1971).

25 Wilson, *The Island Race: Englishness, Empire and Gender in the Eighteenth Century*, p. 17.

26 Homi K. Bhabha, *The Location of Culture* (Abingdon: Routledge, 1994). For an examination of white Creole culture informed by Bhabha, see Carolyn Vellenga Berman, *Creole Crossings: Domestic Fiction and the Reform of Colonial Slavery* (Ithaca, NY: Cornell University Press, 2006). On the Creole as a marker of sexual norms and Lambert, *White Creole Culture* on white Barbadian class politics.

27 Brathwaite, *The Development of Creole Society in Jamaica, 1770–1820*, p. xvi.

28 Sandiford, *The Cultural Politics of Sugar*, p. 3.

29 Berman, *Creole Crossings*, p. 28.

30 Wylie Sypher, 'The West-Indian as a "Character" in the Eighteenth Century', *Studies in Philology*, Vol. 36, No. 3 (July 1939), pp. 503–20, p. 505.

31 Lambert's model of creolization as a process of negative transformation by the colonial encounter, for example, incorporates ideas about speech, dress, behaviour, morality and racial purity, but not health. Lambert, *White Creole Culture*, p. 38.

32 On the West Indian as a cultural and literary figure see Berman, *Creole Crossings*. On the history of white Creole society, see Brathwaite, *The Development of Creole Society in Jamaica, 1770–1820*, and on the figure of the white West Indian master as a 'locus of competing pro- and antislavery discourses', see Lambert, *White Creole Culture*, p. 1.

33 Timothy Touchstone, *Tea and Sugar, or the Nabob and the Creole; a poem, in two canto's* (London, 1792), p. 3.

34 Pinckard, *Notes on the West Indies*, Vol. III, pp. 258–9.

35 On seasoning, for example, Robert Jackson wrote that Europeans could gain the same immunity to yellow fever as Africans and Creoles from a year or two's residence in the West Indies and that, conversely, Africans and Creoles could lose their immunity by travelling to Europe. Robert Jackson, *A treatise on the fevers of Jamaica* (London: Printed for J. Murray, 1791), p. 250. As Mark Harrison notes, the model of seasoning was so widely agreed upon that only a few medical practitioners opposed it and instead suggested a model of innate disposition on racial or other grounds. Mark Harrison, *Medicine in an Age of Commerce and Empire: Britain and Its Tropical Colonies 1660–1830* (Oxford: Oxford University Press, 2010), p. 108.

36 Charles Leslie, *A new history of Jamaica, from the earliest accounts, to the taking of Porto Bello by Vice-Admiral Vernon. In thirteen letters from a gentleman to his friend* (London: Printed for J. Hodges, 1740), p. 1.

37 Benjamin Moseley, *A treatise on tropical diseases; and on the climate of the West-Indies*, second edition (London, 1789), p. 81.

38 Ibid., p. 2.

39 Robert Thomas, *Medical advice to the inhabitants of warm climates, on the domestic treatment of all the diseases incidental therein: with a few useful hints to new settlers, for the preservation of health, and the prevention of sickness* (London: Printed for J. Johnson et al, 1790), p. iv.

40 Long, *History of Jamaica*, Vol. II, p. 276.

41 Ibid., Vol. II, p. 267.

42 Ibid., Vol. II, p. 169.

43 Ibid., Vol. II, p. 265.

44 Ibid., Vol. II, p. 261.

45 Ibid., Vol. II, p. 262.

46 Bewell, *Romanticism and Colonial Disease*, p. 288.

47 *Report of the Lords of the Committee of the Council Appointed for the Consideration of All Matters Relating to Trade and Foreign Plantations*, Part III, A. Nos. 28–34.

48 James Ramsay, *An essay on the treatment and conversion of African slaves in the British sugar colonies* (London: Printed by J. Philips, 1784), p. 89.

49 Pinckard, *Notes on the West Indies*, Vol. III, pp. 434, 427. Women, children and convalescents are also identified as having laxer fibres and looser bodily structures than healthy men.

50 Robert Thomas, *The modern practice of physic, exhibiting the characters, causes, symptoms, prognostics, morbid appearances, and improved method of treating the diseases of all climates*, 6th ed. (London: Printed for Longman et al, 1819), p. 75.

51 Hector M'Lean, *An enquiry into the nature, and causes of the great mortality among the troops at St. Domingo: with practical remarks on the fever of that island; and directions, for the conduct of Europeans on their first arrival in warm climates* (London: Printed for T. Cadell, 1797), p. 185.

52 Pinckard, *Notes on the West Indies*, Vol. I, pp. 260, 255.

53 Ibid., Vol. I, p. 389. On Creoles and modern manners see Simon Gikandi, *Slavery and the Culture of Taste* (Princeton, NJ: Princeton University Press, 2011), pp. 97–144.

54 Martin S. Pernick, 'Politics, Parties, and Pestilence: Epidemic Yellow Fever in Philadelphia and the Rise of the First Party System' in *A Melancholy Scene of Devastation: The Public Response to the 1793 Philadelphia Yellow Fever Epidemic*, ed. J. Worth Estes and Billy G. Smith (Canton, MA: Science History, 1997), p. 119. See also Harrison, *Contagion: How Commerce Has Spread Disease*.

55 Some physicians, such as James Anderson of Edinburgh, argued that 'yellow fever' was a misnomer and was in fact more than one disease. James Anderson, *A few facts and observations on the yellow fever of the West Indies, by which it is shewn, that there have existed two species of fever in the West-India islands for several years past, indiscriminately called yellow fever, but which have proceeded from very different causes* (Edinburgh: William Mudie, 1798). On the medical debate surrounding the nosology of yellow fever and the political dimensions of the various controversies see Harrison, *Medicine in an Age of Commerce and Empire: Britain and Its Tropical Colonies 1660–1830* and John V. Pickstone, 'Dearth, Dirt and Fever Epidemics: Rewriting the History of British "Public Health", 1780–1850' in *Epidemics and Ideas: Essays on the Historical Perception of Pestilence,* ed. Terence Ranger and Paul Slack (Cambridge: Cambridge University Press, 1991), pp. 125–48. On yellow fever and scientific racism see Watts, *Epidemics and History: Disease, Power and Imperialism*, pp. 215–16.

56 Michel Foucault, *The Birth of the Clinic: An Archaeology of Medical Perception* (London: Routledge, 1976), p. 4. The eighteenth-century fascination with fever, argues Margaret DeLacy, formed the foundations of modern nosology: 'it was the gradual adoption of this conceptualization of fevers as specific entities, each directly related to a particular pathogenic substance, that created the framework for our current methods of classifying and understanding diseases.' See Margaret DeLacy, 'Nosology, Mortality, and Disease Theory in the Eighteenth Century', *Journal of the History of Medicine*, Vol. 54 (April 1999), pp. 261–84, p. 267.

57 Pernick, 'Politics, Parties, and Pestilence: Epidemic Yellow Fever in Philadelphia and the Rise of the First Party System', p. 122.

58 Katherine Arner has traced the Atlantic dimensions of the yellow fever debates in relation to American nationalism. Katherine Arner, 'Making Yellow Fever American: The Early American Republic, the British Empire and the Geopolitics of Disease in the Atlantic world', *Atlantic Studies*, Vol. 7, No. 4 (2010), pp. 447–71.

59 Harrison, *Medicine in an Age of Commerce and Empire: Britain and Its Tropical Colonies 1660–1830*, p. 27. This sense of the distinctiveness of West Indian medical practice carried through to literary texts. In E. L. Joseph's novel *Warner Arundell, The Adventures of a Creole* (1838) the medical practitioner protagonist has no diploma or surgical license, but voices his desire to work in the West Indies in terms of the less rigid institutional structures and the fact that the 'obsolete distinction' made by British medics between physicians and surgeons does not there restrict professional possibilities. E. L. Joseph, *Warner Arundell, The Adventures of a Creole* (Kingston: University of the West Indies Press, 2001), p. 165.

60 Charles Caldwell, *A reply to Dr. Haygarth's letter to Dr. Percival, on infectious fevers: and, his address to the College of Physicians at Philadelphia, on the preventing of the American pestilence, exposing the medical, philosophical, and literary errors of that author, and vindicating the right which is the faculty of the United States have to think and decide for themselves, respecting the diseases of their own country, uninfluenced by the notions of the physicians of Europe* (Philadelphia: Printed by Thomas and William Bradford, 1802), p. 47.

61 Pinckard, *Notes on the West Indies*, Vol. III, pp. 428–9. On contagionism in the British medical military see Arner, 'Making Yellow Fever American'.

62 Pinckard, *Notes on the West Indies*, Vol. III, pp. 429–30.

63 Ibid., Vol. II, p. 324.

64 Ibid., Vol. III, p. 143.

65 Jon Klancher, 'Godwin and the Republican Romance: Genre, Politics, and Contingency in Cultural History', *Modern Language Quarterly*, Vol. 56, No. 2 (1995), pp. 145–65. On Thelwall's significant role in Romantic and nineteenth-century development of socialist and liberal thought, see Yasmin Solomonescu, 'Introduction' in *John Thelwall: Critical Reassessments*, ed. Yasmin Solomonescu, Romantic Circles Praxis Series (2011), www.rc.umd .edu/praxis/thelwall/HTML/praxis.2011.solomonescu.html.

66 As Yasmin Solomonescu points out, *The Daughter of Adoption* might more accurately be described not as a 'Jacobin novel' but as its 'radical progeny, a second-generation or post-revolutionary work that is markedly aware of its formal, philosophical and historical inheritance'. Yasmin Solomonescu, *John Thelwall and the Materialist Imagination* (Basingstoke: Palgrave Macmillan, 2014), pp. 87–8.

67 Bryan Edwards, *An Historical Survey of the French Colony in the Island of St. Domingo* (London: Printed for John Stockdale, 1797), p. 63. Marcus Wood calls Edwards's *Historical Survey* 'one of the most hard-hitting pieces of

atrocity literature to come out of the British reaction to the Haytian revolution'. Marcus Wood, *The Poetry of Slavery: An Anglo-American Anthology, 1764–1865* (Oxford: Oxford University Press, 2003), p. 68. *The Daughter of Adoption* also draws on the French military explorer Stanislaus von Wimpffen's *Voyage a Saint Domingue* (1797).

68 John Thelwall, *The Daughter of Adoption* (Peterborough: Broadview, 2013), p. 142. This part of the exchange is reported by Samuel Taylor Coleridge to have taken place between him and Thelwall. See Samuel Taylor Coleridge, *Specimens of the Table Talk of the late Samuel Taylor Coleridge* (London: John Murray, 1835), Vol. I, p. 191. From its original setting in the Quantocks, Thelwall transplants the conversation to the 'unspeakably magnificent' St Domingue landscape, which is imagined as a 'majesty of horrors'. On the development of Thelwall's work and ideas as part of a reciprocal relationship with those of Wordsworth and Coleridge see Judith Thompson, *John Thelwall in the Wordsworth Circle: The Silenced Partner* (New York: Palgrave Macmillan, 2012). Thelwall, *The Daughter of Adoption*, pp. 143, 144.

69 Thelwall, *The Daughter of Adoption*, p. 142.

70 On Thelwall's political ideas see Mary Fairclough, *The Romantic Crowd: Sympathy, Controversy and Print Culture* (Cambridge: Cambridge University Press, 2013); Michael Scrivener, *Seditious Allegories: John Thelwall and Jacobin Writing* (University Park: Pennsylvania State University Press, 2001) and Solomonescu, *John Thelwall and the Materialist Imagination*. Peter Kitson has mapped Thelwall's abolitionist social circles. Peter J. Kitson, 'John Thelwall in Saint Domingue: Race, Slavery and Revolution in *The Daughter of Adoption: A Tale of Modern Times* (1801)', *Romanticism*, Vol. 16, No. 2 (2010), pp. 120–38.

71 Pinckard, *Notes on the West Indies*, Vol. I, p. 86.

72 John Thelwall, *Poems, Written Chiefly in Retirement* (Hereford: Printed by W. H. Parker, 1801), p. xlv. On the novel's rapid composition see Michael Scrivener, *The Cosmopolitan Ideal in the Age of Revolution and Reaction, 1776–1832* (London: Pickering and Chatto, 2007), p. 126.

73 See Nicholas Roe, *John Keats and the Culture of Dissent* (Oxford: Clarendon Press, 1997), p. 176. John Thelwall, *A Letter to Henry Cline, Esq on Imperfect Developments of the Faculties, Mental and Moral, as well as Constitutional and Organic, and on the Treatment of Impediments of Speech* (London: Printed by Richard Taylor and Co., 1810), p. 3.

74 Solomonescu, *John Thelwall and the Materialist Imagination*, p. 2. As Emily Stanback argues, Thelwall's medical and therapeutic elocutionary practice 'has been understood as ideologically neutral in comparison to Thelwall's earlier involvement in radical politics and materialist science' when in fact 'the political and humanistic implications of his elocutionary project are significant, and reveal an enduring dedication to democratic ideals.' Emily Stanback, 'Disability and Dissent: Thelwall's Elocutionary Project' in *John Thelwall: Critical Reassessments*, ed. Yasmin Solomonescu, Romantic Circles Praxis Series (2011), www.rc.umd.edu/praxis/thelwall/HTML/praxis.2011.stanback.html.

75 Pinckard, *Notes on the West Indies*, Vol. III, pp. 146–8.

76 Wood, *Slavery, Empathy, and Pornography*, p. 151.

77 Using abolitionist language and foreshadowing the slave revolution, Montfort is cast as the 'imperious lord of pleasure and pain' while the abolitionist Amelia complains that her husband's 'contemptuous tyranny' forces her into the role of 'slave', echoing Wollstonecraft's comparisons between the domestic, economic and sexual subjugation of women in Britain and the enslavement of women in the colonies. Thelwall, *The Daughter of Adoption*, pp. 65, 55.

78 Thelwall, *Poems, Written Chiefly in Retirement*, p. xvi. Thelwall's 'Prefatory Memoir' to the *Poems* also reveals other connections to colonial medicine: his grandfather, Walter, was a naval surgeon 'guilty (if guilt it were) of curing the wounds of his enemies as well as of his friends'. Ibid., p. iii.

79 Thelwall, *The Daughter of Adoption*, pp. 232, 128, 139.

80 On purity and pollution as themes which define the understanding of Caribbean society, see Sandiford, *The Cultural Politics of Sugar*. Ellen Pollak writes that eighteenth-century prose fiction 'implicitly gives the narrative of incest and its prohibition centrality as a discursive matrix within which "truths" about culture, gender, and desire are produced'. Ellen Pollak, *Incest and the English Novel, 1684–1814* (Baltimore: Johns Hopkins University Press, 2003), p. 5.

81 Thelwall, *The Daughter of Adoption*, p. 209. Michael Scrivener writes that the novel's various conspiracy plots are structured through the conventions of gothic romance and sentimental fiction. Scrivener, *Seditious Allegories: John Thelwall and Jacobin Writing*, p. 241.

82 Thelwall, *The Daughter of Adoption*, p. 458.

83 Ibid., pp. 217, 141.

84 Sarah M. S. Pearsall, 'Gender' in *The British Atlantic World, 1500–1800*, ed. David Armitage and Michael J. Braddick (Basingstoke: Palgrave Macmillan, 2002), pp. 113–32, pp. 142–3.

85 Thelwall, *The Daughter of Adoption*, pp. 232, 152. As A. A. Markley writes, 'like the best of the reformist heroes and heroines of the period, Seraphina embodies the finer qualities of both genders.' A. A. Markley, *Conversion and Reform in the British Novel in the 1790s* (Basingstoke: Palgrave Macmillan, 2009), p. 110.

86 Thelwall, *The Daughter of Adoption*, p. 150.

87 Ibid., pp. 223, 197, 281, 297.

88 Ibid., pp. 389–99, 197.

89 Stanback, 'Disability and Dissent: Thelwall's Elocutionary Project'.

90 Thelwall, *The Daughter of Adoption*, p. 399.

91 Ibid., pp. 454, 121.

92 Thelwall, *A Letter to Henry Cline, Esq on Imperfect Developments of the Faculties, Mental and Moral, as well as Constitutional and Organic, and on the Treatment of Impediments of Speech*, p. 66. Thelwall's medical model was firmly rooted in the idea of a reciprocal relationship between body and mind. In treating patients, he writes, problems of 'organic action' must be addressed taking

into account the 'temper and disposition' of the patient. Ibid., p. 65. Indeed, Thelwall's emphasis on reciprocity also stressed the importance to treatment of the exchange between patient and doctor. See Stanback, 'Disability and Dissent: Thelwall's Elocutionary Project'. The novel's use of alternative medical practices is fundamentally connected to his own elocutionary work, which, as Stanback shows, worked against the grain of contemporary ideas about 'normal' bodies and traditional treatments. Ibid.

93 Wells's brother was the physician William Charles Wells, who studied at Edinburgh and Leiden and wrote an *Account of a Female of the White Race of Mankind, Part of whose Skin Resembles that of a Negro*, which was read before the Royal Society in 1813. The paper suggests that blacks and mulattoes were immune to particular diseases, and discusses ideas about evolution thought by some historians of science to anticipate Charles Darwin's: 'of the accidental varieties of man, which would occur amongst the first few and scattered inhabitants of the middle regions of Africa, some one would be better fitted than the others to bear the diseases of the country. This race would consequently multiply, while the others would decrease.' Helena Wells's works do not explicitly take up her brother's arguments, but the politics of racial difference, slavery and global health forms the backdrop to Constantia's story. See William Charles Wells, *Two Essays: one upon single vision with two eyes; the other on dew. A letter to the Right Hon. Lloyd, Lord Kenyon, and an account of a female of the white race of mankind, part of whose skin resembles that of a negro; with some observations on the causes of the differences in colour and form between the white and negro races of men.* (London: Longman et al, 1818), pp. 435–6.

94 See Helena Wells, *Letters on Subjects of Importance to the Happiness of Young Females* (London: Printed for L. Peacock, 1799), and Helena Wells, *Thoughts and Remarks on Establishing an Institution for the Support and Education of Unportioned Respectable Females* (London: Longman, 1809).

95 Berman, *Creole Crossings*, p. 91.

96 Helena Wells, *Constantia Neville; or, the West Indian* (London: Printed by C. Whittingham, 1800), Vol. III, p. 107.

97 Thelwall, *The Daughter of Adoption*, pp. 253, 264.

98 Ibid., p. 214.

99 Ibid., p. 139.

100 Pinckard, *Notes on the West Indies*, Vol. III, p. 428.

101 Ibid., Vol. III, pp. 433–4.

102 John Thelwall, *An Essay Towards a Definition of Animal Vitality; Read at the Theatre, Guy's Hospital, January 26, 1793, in which Several of the Opinions of the Celebrated John Hunter are Examined and Controverted* (London: Printed by T. Rickaby, 1793), p. 12. Yasmin Solomonescu presents a detailed delineation of Thelwall's strand of scientific materialism in historical context in Solomonescu, *John Thelwall and the Materialist Imagination*.

103 For a discussion of ideas about hereditary phenomena in medicine, plant breeding and observations of families, see Mary Terrall, 'Speculation and

Experiment in Enlightenment Life Sciences' in *Heredity Produced: At the Crossroads of Biology, Politics and Culture, 1500–1870*, ed. Staffan Müller-Wille and Hans-Joerg Rheinberger (Cambridge, MA: MIT Press, 2007), pp. 253–76, as well as other essays in this volume.

104 Thelwall, *The Daughter of Adoption*, p. 200.

105 Ibid., pp. 60, 78.

106 Ibid., p. 60.

107 Ibid., p. 72.

108 Pinckard, *Notes on the West Indies*, Vol. II, p. 76.

109 G. K. Lewis, *Main Currents in Caribbean Thought: The Historical Evolution of Caribbean Society in Its Ideological Aspects, 1492–1900* (Baltimore: Johns Hopkins University Press, 1983), p. 70. Pinckard, *Notes on the West Indies*, Vol. II, p. 76.

110 Pinckard, *Notes on the West Indies*, Vol. II, p. 76.

111 Berman, *Creole Crossings*, p. 27.

112 Pinckard, *Notes on the West Indies*, Vol. I, p. 255.

113 Thelwall, *The Daughter of Adoption*, p. 72 and Pinckard, *Notes on the West Indies*, Vol. III, p. 426.

114 Fernando Ortiz, *Cuban Counterpoint: Tobacco and Sugar* (Durham, NC: Duke University Press, 1995), p. 98.

115 Pinckard, *Notes on the West Indies*, Vol. III, pp. 148, 21.

116 Ibid., Vol. I, pp. 389–90.

117 Ibid., Vol. III, p. 21.

118 Ibid., Vol. III, p. 406.

119 Ibid., Vol. I, pp. viii–x.

120 Pinckard certainly viewed *Notes on the West Indies* as providing significant information to a transatlantic scientific audience: he sent a copy to Joseph Banks, then president of the Royal Society, with a personal inscription.

121 John Thelwall, *The Peripatetic* (Detroit: Wayne State University Press, 2001), p. 17.

122 Thelwall, *The Daughter of Adoption*, p. 142.

123 Ibid., p. 411. While the novel's ending is upbeat, Yasmin Solomonescu makes the important point that the question at the heart of the *Daughter of Adoption* is whether it is 'ultimately more conducive to reform to yield to one's circumstances or sustain a lone struggle to transform them'. By way of response, Solomonescu points out, Thelwall uses Seraphina's discovery that 'no woman is an island' to propose a more pragmatic version of Godwinian social justice which accounts for the specifics of personal circumstances and human relationships. Solomonescu, *John Thelwall and the Materialist Imagination*, p. 88.

124 Thelwall, *The Daughter of Adoption*, p. 474.

125 Kitson writes that Thelwall's aim in rewriting Bryan Edwards's version of the revolution is to 'recapture the meaning or lesson of the Saint Domingue experience from the pro-slavery lobby and return it to a battered and beleaguered but never ousted British Jacobin politics'. Kitson, 'John Thelwall in Saint

Domingue: Race, Slavery and Revolution in *The Daughter of Adoption: A Tale of Modern Times* (1801)', pp. 133, 135.

126 Scrivener, *Seditious Allegories: John Thelwall and Jacobin Writing*, p. 244.

127 Markley, *Conversion and Reform in the British Novel in the 1790s*, p. 112.

128 Thelwall, *The Daughter of Adoption*, p. 154.

129 Judith Thompson, 'Transatlantic Thelwall' at the British Association for Romantic Studies Annual Conference, University of Southampton, 2013.

130 An example of the connections Thelwall draws between colonial society and the need for changes to the class structure is the flattening of social distinction which he observes in the colonies. When they travel to the Caribbean, Henry and his loyal and vehemently abolitionist servant, Edmunds, enjoy a growing closeness and sense of equality that once again becomes a much more hierarchical relationship on their return to England, before being ultimately equalized once Seraphina has worked her sentimental cure on Henry.

131 On the particular class dynamics of Barbados see Jack P. Greene, 'Changing Identity in the British Caribbean: Barbados as a Case Study' in *Colonial Identity in the Atlantic World, 1500–1800*, ed. Nicholas Canny and Anthony Pagden (Princeton, NJ: Princeton University Press, 1987), pp. 213–66 and Lambert, *White Creole Culture*.

132 Lambert, *White Creole Culture*, p. 39.

133 Scrivener, *Seditious Allegories: John Thelwall and Jacobin Writing*, p. 242.

134 Dillon, *New World Drama: The Performative Commons in the Atlantic World, 1649–1849*, p. 31. Dillon writes that Belcour in Richard Cumberland's *The West Indian* (1771), along with other Creole literary characters, 'displays the colony in association with the metropole, making visible (often fleetingly) a set of Atlantic connections that are not peripheral to life in the metropole (as traditional accounts would have it), but that underwrite and sustain evolving forms of metropolitan economic, political, and cultural life'. ibid., p. 32.

135 Thompson, *John Thelwall in the Wordsworth Circle*.

136 Thelwall, *A Letter to Henry Cline, Esq on Imperfect Developments of the Faculties, Mental and Moral, as well as Constitutional and Organic, and on the Treatment of Impediments of Speech*, p. 66. Thelwall, *The Daughter of Adoption*, p. 474.

137 Scrivener, Solomonescu and Thompson also suggest a connection between Thelwall's exploration of creolization and the 'motley' 'style, structure and philosophy' of the novel, as well as its 'elusive' and 'dizzying' wordplay. Thelwall, *The Daughter of Adoption*, p. 15.

138 Ibid., p. 137.

139 Brathwaite, *Roots*, p. 129, Pratt, *Imperial Eyes*, p. 136.

140 On Creole work in Atlantic medical and natural knowledge see Delbourgo and Dew (eds.), *Science and Empire in the Atlantic World*. In this area, scholars of the British Atlantic also have much to learn from work on the Iberian and Spanish empires. See, for example, Jorge Cañizares-Esguerra, *How to Write the History of the New World: Historiographies, Epistemologies, and Identities in the Eighteenth-Century Atlantic World* (Stanford, CA: Stanford University

Press, 2001) and Safier, *Measuring the New World: Enlightenment Science and South America*.

141 Pinckard, *Notes on the West Indies*, Vol. I, p. 255.

142 Ibid., Vol. III, p. 147.

143 Ibid., Vol. III, p. 142.

144 Seraphina embodies Thelwall's exploration of materialism: when she successfully treats Henry with the 'healing drops' of liberal rationality and sympathetic feeling, Dr Pengarron praises her 'scientific and not empirical' methods, stressing that their success proves 'the results of her merit, not of chance'. Thelwall, *The Daughter of Adoption*, p. 399. Ultimately, though, Seraphina realizes that she has been at fault in her consideration of moral questions 'only in an abstract point of view', accepting the need to adapt to material realities. Ibid., p. 301. See also Solomonescu, *John Thelwall and the Materialist Imagination*.

145 J. B. Moreton, *West India customs and manners: containing strictures on the soil, cultivation, produce, trade, officers, and inhabitants*, second edition (London: Printed for J. Parsons, W. Richardson and J. Walter, 1793), p. 109.

146 Kathleen Wilson, 'British Women and Empire' in *Women's History: Britain 1700–1850, An Introduction*, ed. Hannah Barker and Elaine Chalus (London and New York: Routledge, 2005), pp. 260–84, p. 274.

147 Pinckard, *Notes on the West Indies*, Vol. III, pp. 445–6.

5 The 'Intimate Union of Medicine and Magic'

1 John Singleton, *A description of the West-Indies. A poem, in four books* (Printed for T. Becket, 1776), Book II, pp. 23–4. There is little biographical information available for Singleton. He describes his muse as 'British-born', but the poem was first published in Barbados, before revised editions were printed in London and Dublin.

2 Singleton, *A General Description of the West-Indian Islands*, Book II, p. 57.

3 In times of rebellion, obeah doctors were essential in administering oaths of secrecy and distributing fetishes supposed to immunize the revolutionaries from harm. See Orlando Patterson, *The Sociology of Slavery: An Analysis of the Origins, Development and Structure of Negro Slave Society in Jamaica* (Rutherford, NJ: Fairleigh Dickinson University Press, 1969), p. 192; Junius P. Rodriguez (ed.), *Encyclopedia of Slave Resistance and Rebellion* (Westport, CT: Greenwood, 2007) and Walter Rucker, 'Conjure, Magic and Power: The Influence of Afro-Atlantic Religious Practices on Slave Resistance and Rebellion', *Journal of Black Studies*, Vol. 32, No. 1 (September 2001), pp. 84–103, p. 87.

4 Jamaica. Vol. II. *Acts of Assembly, Passed in the Island of Jamaica, From the Year 1681 to the Year 1769 Inclusive* (Saint Jago de la Vega: Lowry and Sherlock, 1769–71), Vol. II, p. 55.

5 *Report of the Lords of the Committee of the Council Appointed for the Consideration of All Matters Relating to Trade and Foreign Plantations*, Part III, A. Nos. 22–6.

6 Ibid., Part III, A. Nos. 22–6.

7 Ibid., Part III, A. Nos. 22–6.

8 Ibid., Part III, A. Nos. 22–6.

9 Griffith Hughes, *The Natural History of Barbados* (London: Printed for the author, 1750), p. 15.

10 *Report of the Lords of the Committee of the Council Appointed for the Consideration of All Matters Relating to Trade and Foreign Plantations*, Part III, A. Nos. 22–6.

11 Kelly Wisecup and Toni Wall Jaudon, 'On Knowing and Not Knowing about Obeah', *Atlantic Studies: Global Currents*, Vol. 12, No. 2 (2015), pp. 129–43, p. 130.

12 Frederic Gomes Cassidy and Robert Brock LePage, *Dictionary of Jamaican English* (Barbados: University of West Indies Press, 2002), p. 326. The etymology of 'obeah' has been the subject of considerable scholarly debate. Walter Rucker has suggested that the term likely derives from the Akan word 'Obayifo', which denotes witchcraft and sorcery in the Akan spiritual world. Jerome Handler and Kenneth Bilby argue that the term is more likely to be derived from Igbo or a related language, where it would have had more positive social connotations that can be roughly translated into English as 'practitioner, herbalist', 'doctor', 'spiritual power' or 'knowledge of the sacred arts'. Significantly, it has proved impossible to point to a single place of origin, and it seems very likely, as Handler and Bilby suggest, that the term has multiple origins. While it is reasonably certain that the term comes from somewhere in West Africa, the ambiguous etymology of 'obeah' reminds modern-day scholars of the fact that its meanings and origins were equally unclear during the colonial era. See Rucker, 'Conjure, Magic and Power: The Influence of Afro-Atlantic Religious Practices on Slave Resistance and Rebellion', p. 89 and Jerome S. Handler and Kenneth M. Bilby, 'On the Early Use and Origin of the Term "Obeah" in Barbados and the Anglophone Caribbean', *Slavery and Abolition*, Vol. 22, No. 2, pp. 87–100, p. 92.

13 For an account of the relationship between Edwards's and Long's texts and other obeah narratives see Diana Paton, *The Cultural Politics of Obeah: Religion, Colonialism and Modernity in the Caribbean World* (Cambridge: Cambridge University Press, 2015), p. 75.

14 Bryan Edwards, *The proceedings of the governor and Assembly of Jamaica, in regard to the Maroon Negroes: published by order of the Assembly, to which is prefixed an introductory account, containing, observations on the disposition, character, manners, and habits of life, of the Maroons* (London: Printed for J. Stockdale, 1796), p. xxvii.

15 Olaudah Equiano, *The interesting narrative of the life of Olaudah Equiano, or Gustavus Vassa, the African. Written by himself* (London: Printed by T. Wilkins, 1789), Vol. I, p. 267.

16 Rucker, 'Conjure, Magic and Power: The Influence of Afro-Atlantic Religious Practices on Slave Resistance and Rebellion', p. 89.

17 Karol K. Weaver, *Medical Revolutionaries: The Enslaved Healers of Eighteenth-Century Saint Domingue* (Urbana and Chicago: University of Illinois Press, 2006), p. 2. Sharla Fett has shown how African-American healing practices

including herbalism, conjuring and midwifery were employed as arts of resistance in the antebellum South. Sharla M. Fett, *Working Cures: Health, Healing and Power on Southern Slave Plantations* (Chapel Hill: University of North Carolina Press, 2000).

18 Diana Paton and Maarit Forde, 'Introduction' in *Obeah and Other Powers*, ed. Diana and Maarit Forde Paton (Durham, NC: Duke University Press, 2012), pp. 1–42, p. 11.

19 Alan Richardson, 'Romantic Voodoo: Obeah and British Culture, 1797–1807', *Studies in Romanticism*, Vol. 32, No. 1 (1993), pp. 3–28, p. 5.

20 Paton, *The Cultural Politics of Obeah*, pp. 7–8.

21 See Schaffer et al (eds), *The Brokered World: Go-Betweens and Global Intelligence, 1770–1820* and Ursula Klein and E. C. Spary, *Materials and Expertise in Early Modern Europe: Between Market and Laboratory* (Chicago: University of Chicago Press, 2010).

22 See Schiebinger, *Plants and Empire*.

23 Richard D. E. Burton, *Afro-Creole: Power, Opposition and Play in the Caribbean* (Ithaca, NY: Cornell University Press, 1997), p. 5.

24 Parrish, *American Curiosity: Cultures of Natural History in the Colonial British Atlantic World*, p. 260.

25 Wisecup and Jaudon, 'On Knowing and Not Knowing about Obeah', p. 138.

26 Aravamudan, *Tropicopolitans*, p. 4.

27 Ibid., p. 6.

28 While Myal, Santéria, Vodun and Winti are usually thought of as bodies of religious belief, Margarite Fernandez-Omos and Lizbeth Paravisini-Gerbert note that obeah 'is not a religion so much as a system of beliefs rooted in Creole notions of spirituality, which acknowledges the existence and power of the supernatural world'. Margarite Fernández Olmos and Lizabeth Paravisini-Gebert, *Creole Religions of the Caribbean: An Introduction from Vodou and Santería to Obeah and Espiritismo* (New York: New York University Press, 2003), p. 131.

29 See Rucker, 'Conjure, Magic and Power: The Influence of Afro-Atlantic Religious Practices on Slave Resistance and Rebellion'.

30 W. E. B. Du Bois, *The Souls of Black Folk* (Rockville, MD: Arc Manor, 2008), p. 129.

31 Brathwaite, *The Development of Creole Society in Jamaica, 1770–1820*, p. 219.

32 See Jerome S. Handler, 'Slave Medicine and Obeah in Barbados, circa 1650 to 1834', *New West Indian Guide*, Vol. 74, No. 1/2 (2000), pp. 57–90, p. 60.

33 Among some African-Caribbean populations (such as among the Saramakas of Suriname), there was also a knowledge of bone-setting and some surgical practices. See Mary Turner, 'Religious Beliefs' in *General History of the Caribbean, Vol III: The Slave Societies of the Caribbean* (London: UNESCO Publishing and Macmillan Education, 1997), pp. 287–321 and Robert Voeks, 'Magic and Medicine in the Americas', *Geographical Review*, Vol. 83, No. 1 (January 1993), pp. 66–78.

34 Mary Turner, 'Religious Beliefs', p. 303.

35 Sheridan, *Doctors and Slaves*, p. 73.

36 Pinckard, *Notes on the West Indies*, p. 389.

37 Richard Towne, *A treatise of the diseases most frequent in the West-Indies, and herein more particularly of those which occur in Barbadoes* (London: Printed for John Clarke, 1726), p. 191.

38 Thomas Dancer, *The Medical Assistant; or Jamaica Practice of Physic* (Kingston: Printed by Alexander Aikman, 1801), p. 269.

39 James Thomson, *A Treatise on the Diseases of Negroes as they occur in the Island of Jamaica, with Observations on the Country Remedies* (Kingston: Alex Aikman, Jnr., 1820), pp. 8–10.

40 Henry Barham, *Hortus Americanus: Containing an Account of the Trees, Shrubs, and other Vegetable Productions, of South-America and the West-India Islands; and particularly of the Island of Jamaica* (Kingston: Alexander Aikman, 1794), p. 96. Barham sent his original treatise, 'Hortus Americanus', to Hans Sloane in 1711.

41 Ibid., p. 148.

42 Hillary, *Observations on the Changes of the Air*, p. 341.

43 Ibid.

44 Knight, British Library, Additional MS, 12419, Vol. II, fo. 90: History of Jamaica (ca. 1746).

45 *Quassia amara* is still in popular use in South America, being used as a natural insecticide and as a remedy for digestive disorders.

46 Stedman, *Narrative*, p. 582.

47 William Titford, *Sketches towards a Hortus botanicus Americanus; or coloured plates (with concise and familiar descriptions) of new and valuable plants of the West Indies and North and South America, etc* (London, 1811), pp. v, ix.

48 Richard Robert Madden, *A Twelvemonth's Residence in the West Indies During the Transition from Slavery to Apprenticeship: With Incidental Notices of the State of Society, Prospects, and Natural Resources of Jamaica and Other Islands* (London: J. Cochrane and Co., 1835), Vol. II, p. 66.

49 Ibid.

50 Letter from Lewis to Knight, 20 December 1743, James Knight, British Library, Additional MS, 12431: Miscellaneous Papers and original Letters relating to the affairs of Jamaica (1740–3), p. 99.

51 Gilmore, *The Poetics of Empire*, Book IV, l. 392, p. 194.

52 Ibid., Book IV, l. 367, p. 194.

53 *Report of the Lords of the Committee of the Council Appointed for the Consideration of All Matters Relating to Trade and Foreign Plantations*, Part III, A. Nos. 22–6.

54 Ibid., Part III, A. Nos. 22–6.

55 Paton writes that the story of the Popo woman functioned to solidify the cultural association between obeah practitioners and European witchcraft. Paton, *The Cultural Politics of Obeah*, p. 45.

56 William Shepherd, 'The Negro Incantation', *Monthly Magazine*, Vol. 4 (1797), p. 51.

57 Toni Wall Jaudon writes that 'as it was rendered in obeah fictions, the practice of obeah gathered together a set of bodily responses to the world unlike

the reasonable, objective forms of sense perception that were gaining traction
in the Enlightenment,. Toni Wall Jaudon, 'Obeah's Sensations: Rethinking
Religion at the Transnational Turn', *American Literature*, Vol. 84, No. 4 (2013),
pp. 715–41, p. 716.

58 *Report of the Lords of the Committee of the Council Appointed for the Consideration
of All Matters Relating to Trade and Foreign Plantations*, Part III, A. Nos. 22–6.

59 Ibid., Part III, A. Nos. 22–6.

60 Ibid.

61 Hume, 'Of Superstition and Enthusiasm', p. 48.

62 Ibid., p. 48.

63 Marijke Gikswijt-Hofstra, Brian P. Levack, and Roy Porter, *Witchcraft and
Magic in Europe: The Eighteenth and Nineteenth Centuries* (London: Athlone
Press, 1999), p. 226.

64 Maria Edgeworth, *Belinda*, ed. Kathryn J. Kirkpatrick (Oxford: Oxford
University Press, 1994), p. 222.

65 Maria Edgeworth, 'The Grateful Negro' in *The Novels and Selected Works of
Maria Edgeworth*, Vol. 12, ed. Elizabeth Eger, Clíona ÓGallchoir, and Marilyn
Butler (London: Pickering and Chatto, 2003), pp. 49–63, p. 57 'Phrenzy',
in this context, suggests the hectic state of body and mind associated with
'frenzy fever', a term for a more violent form of various contagious fevers and
explained by the chemist Richard Shannon as inflicting the sufferer with a
delirium or temporary insanity. See Richard Shannon, *Practical Observations
on the Operations and Effects of certain medicines, in the Prevention and Cure
of Diseases to Which Europeans are Subject in Hot Climates* (London, 1793),
pp. 164–5.

66 Edmund Burke, *Three Memorials on French affairs. Written in the Years 1791,
1792 and 1793* (London: Printed for F. and C. Rivington, 1797), p. 18.

67 Thomas Winterbottom, *An Account of the Native Africans in the Neighbourhood
of Sierra Leone; to which is Added, an Account of the Present State of Medicine
among Them* (Printed by C. Whittingham, 1803), Vol. I, p. 262.

68 Moseley, *A Treatise on Sugar*, pp. 170, 173.

69 Ibid., p. 174.

70 Ibid., p. 179.

71 Ibid., p. 170.

72 Ibid., p. 172.

73 *Report of the Lords of the Committee of the Council Appointed for the Consideration
of All Matters Relating to Trade and Foreign Plantations*, Part III, A. Nos. 22–6.

74 Moseley, *A Treatise on Sugar*, p. 172.

75 The term 'superstition' is used in reference to obeah by Bryan Edwards,
Griffith Hughes and Edward Long, as well as the *Report of the Lords* (1789).

76 Benjamin Moseley, *Medical Tracts* (London: Printed by John Nichols, 1800),
p. 194.

77 *Report of the Lords of the Committee of the Council Appointed for the
Consideration of All Matters Relating to Trade and Foreign Plantations*, Part III,
A. Nos. 22–6, Moseley, *A Treatise on Sugar*, p. 172. For Aravamudan, the obeah

doctor's endurance reveals 'prophylactic power'. Aravamudan in William Earle, *Obi; or, the History of Three-Fingered Jack*, ed. Srinivas Aravamudan (Peterborough: Broadview Press, 2005), p. 37.

78 Moseley, *A Treatise on Sugar*, p. 173.

79 Ibid., pp. 177–8. While Earle's anti-slavery fiction depicts Jack as a noble hero and wronged avenger, Fawcett's pantomime is less sympathetic: Jack is transformed into a violent and blindly vengeful figure whose obeah practice is dangerously disruptive of the plantation social and domestic order. The pantomime also revives Grainger's joke shared with 'the laughing world' at the expense of the obeah doctor and his superstitious followers. Gilmore, *The Poetics of Empire*, Book IV, l. 385. This time, however, the joke is made not by a planter but by a slave, Quashee. In return for the promise of freedom, Quashee kills Jack, ending the reign of the 'terror of Jamaica' and dismissing the false powers of his magic: 'me laugh at Obi charm'. John Fawcett, *Songs, Duets, & Choruses, in the pantomimical drama of Obi, or Three-Finger'd Jack: (perform'd at the Theatre Royal, Hay Market) To which are prefix'd Illlustrative Extracts, and a Prospectus of the Action* (London: Printed by T. Woodfall, 1800), p. 16. Largely in dumbshow except for the songs, the pantomime was performed by the Covent Garden theatre company, with the Shakespearean actor Charles Kemble as Jack, to great success at Haymarket. It was the most frequently played afterpiece of the season, running to thirty-nine performances that summer, with other stage productions of the story following. For performance information see William J. Burling, *Summer Theatre in London, 1661–1820, and the Rise of the Haymarket Theatre* (Rutherford, NJ: Fairleigh Dickinson University Press, 2000). For a discussion of Fawcett's pantomime see Jeffrey N. Cox, 'Theatrical Forms, Ideological Conflicts, and the Staging of *Obi*', *Obi*, ed. Charles Rzepka, Romantic Circles Praxis Series (2002), www.romantic.arhu.umd.edu/praxis/obi/cox/cox.html.

80 Earle, *Obi*, p. 104.

81 Earle notes that yaws 'contracted the limbs of the wretched sufferer, and made them much deformed'. While Earle writes that 'there was no regular method of treating' yaws, he hints that there may be treatments which lie outside the domain of European practitioners. Ibid.

82 William Burdett, *Life and Exploits of Mansong, Commonly Called Three-Finger'd Jack, the Terror of Jamaica in the years 1780 & 1781: with a Particular Account of the Obi; Being the Only True One of that Celebrated and Fascinating Mischief, so Prevalent in the West Indies* (Sommers Town: A. Neil, 1800), p. 17.

83 Ibid., p. 53. In an anti-emancipationist tract the Jamaican John Stewart would later write that 'a negro under this infatuation can only be cured of his terrors by being made a Christian: refuse him this boon, and he sinks a martyr to imagined evils'. Stewart, *A view of the past and present state of the Island of Jamaica; with remarks on the moral and physical condition of the slaves and on the abolition of slavery in the colonies*, p. 278.

84 Burdett, *Life and Exploits of Mansong*, pp. 53–4.

85 *Report of the Lords of the Committee of the Council Appointed for the Consideration of All Matters Relating to Trade and Foreign Plantations*, Part III, A. Nos. 22–6.
86 Moseley, *A Treatise on Sugar*, p. 173.
87 Obeah was associated with plantation abortions and other forms of repro-
ductive resistance. See Barbara Bush, 'Hard Labor: Women, Childbirth and
Resistance in British Caribbean Slave Societies' in *More than Chattel: Black
Women and Slavery in the Americas*, ed. David Barry Gaspar and Darlene Clark
Hine (Bloomington: Indiana University Press, 1996), pp. 193–217, p. 205 and
Michael Craton, James Walvin, and David Wright, *Slavery, Abolition and
Emancipation: Black Slaves and the British Empire, a Thematic Documentary*
(London: Longman, 1976), p. 141. Caricaturist James Sayer's graphic narrative
'Johnny New-Come in Love in the West-Indies' (1808) offers an alternative
view to the association between obeah women and love spells – here, the
newly arrived planter seeks the help of an 'Oby man' to help win the affections
of a black woman named Mimbo Wampo.
88 The production was popular; Ira Aldridge played the title role at Bristol,
Northampton, Plymouth, Sheffield and Glasgow between 1830 and 1860.
Herbert Marshall and Mildred Stock (eds.), *Ira Aldridge: the Negro Tragedian*
(London: Rockliff, 1958). See also Cox, 'Theatrical Forms, Ideological
Conflicts, and the Staging of *Obi*'.
89 When Jack holds captive the planter's daughter Rosa, who is disguised as a
boy, he instructs her: 'Come, come, no muttering. To work, to work. Trim
yonder fire. Nay, pause not; obey me! the times have changed, and the white
man must now labour for the black.' Nineteenth-century melodrama played
out social dynamics for working-class theatre-goers; here, Aldridge's Jack
presents changing views about race and slavery for a metropolitan audience.
William H. Murray, *Obi; or, Three-Fingered Jack in Dick's Standard Plays*
(London: John Dick, 1825), Act. II, Sc. III. On class dynamics as a central
function of nineteenth-century melodrama, see Elaine Hadley, *Melodramatic
Tactics: Theatricalized Dissent in the English Marketplace, 1800–1885* (Stanford,
CA: Stanford University Press, 1995) and Kristen Leaver, 'Victorian Melodrama
and the Performance of Poverty', *Victorian Literature and Culture*, Vol. 27,
No. 2 (1999), pp. 443–56. While Murray's Jack strikes a surprisingly modern
figure, Hazel Waters writes that 'serious' black characters would subsequently
be completely erased by the Victorian stage: 'by the late 1830s, popular racial
commentary on the character and abilities of the black had undergone a major
shift in tone; a shift that had long been prepared for through the medium of
comedy'. Hazel Waters, *Racism on the Victorian Stage: Representation of Slavery
and the Black Character* (Cambridge: Cambridge University Press, 2009),
p. 114.
90 On melodrama's combination of the comic and the tragic, see, for example,
Matthew S. Buckley, 'Refugee Theatre: Melodrama and Modernity's Loss',
Theatre Journal, Vol. 61 (2009), pp. 175–90.
91 Murray, *Obi; or, Three-Fingered Jack in Dick's Standard Plays*, Act I, Sc. I.
92 Ibid. Act. I, Sc. I.

93 Ibid. Act. I, Sc. I.
94 Lewis, *Journal of a West India Proprietor*, p. 92.
95 Ibid., p. 62.
96 Murray, *Obi; or, Three-Fingered Jack in Dick's Standard Plays*, Act. II, Sc. VI. Diana Paton points out that the historical documents indicate that Quashee was in fact a maroon and therefore the promise of freedom would have been irrelevant. See Diana Paton, 'The Afterlives of Three-Fingered Jack' in *Slavery and the Cultures of Abolition: Essays Marking the Bicentennial of the British Abolition Act of 1807*, ed. Brycchan Carey and Peter J. Kitson (Cambridge: Boydell and Brewer, 2007), pp. 42–63, p. 51. On the history of the Quashee figure see Patterson, *The Sociology of Slavery*.
97 On melodrama's individualization of social conflict, see, for example, Robertson Davies, *The Mirror of Nature* (Toronto: University of Toronto Press, 1983), p. 12.
98 Cynric R. Williams, *Hamel, the Obeah Man* (Peterborough: Broadview, 2010), p. 222. *Hamel* has emerged as one of the novels at the centre of new interest in nineteenth-century Caribbean literature, and has been published in two new editions.
99 The identification seems likely to be accurate, given that the *Tour* shares many of the themes and much of the style of *Hamel*, and both texts were published by Hunt and Clarke of Covent Garden. On the attribution of *Hamel* to Williams see Janina Nordius, 'Racism and Radicalism in Jamaican Gothic: Cynric R. Williams '*Hamel, the Obeah Man*', *English Literary History*, Vol. 73, No. 3 (Fall 2006), pp. 673–93, p. 675. Tim Watson argues that Cynric R. Williams was the pseudonym of Creole Blue Mountain coffee planter Charles White Williams, and that the *Tour*'s disinterested English traveller–narrator was a convenient instrument through which to advance the real Williams's pro-slavery agenda. Tim Watson, *Caribbean Culture and British Fiction in the Atlantic World, 1780–1870* (Cambridge: Cambridge University Press, 2008), p. 71.
100 Williams, *Hamel, the Obeah Man*, p. 196. The First Maroon War took place in 1731 between the British military and Cudjoe and his Leeward Maroons, a group originating in a slave revolt in 1673 in St. Ann's Parish. In 1739–40, the British signed a peace treaty with the maroons, agreeing that they would keep the areas of land they had made their own, in exchange for helping to catch new runaway slaves.
101 Ibid., pp. 202, 206.
102 Boulukos, *The Grateful Slave*, p. 2. As Michael Hurst writes, Edgeworth's tale is as much an instruction on the paternalistic roles of the British aristocracy toward the labouring classes as it is a warning to Caribbean planters to treat their slaves with benevolence. Michael Hurst, *Maria Edgeworth and the Public Scene: Intellect, Fine Feeling and Landlordism in the Age of Reform* (London: Macmillan, 1969).
103 Janelle Rodriques connects Hamel to other Caribbean trickster figures such as the folkloric spider Anancy. Janelle Rodriques, 'Obeah(man) as trickster in

Cynric Williams' *Hamel, the Obeah Man'*, *Atlantic Studies: Global Currents*, Vol. 12, No. 2 (2015), pp. 219–34. On trickster figures in West Indian literature see Lawrence Levine, *Black Culture and Black Consciousness: Afro-American Folk Thought from Slavery to Freedom* (Oxford: Oxford University Press, 1977).

104 Williams, *Hamel, the Obeah Man*, pp. 300, 162, 336.
105 Ibid., p. 326.
106 Ibid., p. 287.
107 Ibid., p. 121.
108 Ibid., p. 133.
109 See Mary Turner, *Slaves and Missionaries: The Disintegration of Jamaican Slave Society 1787–1834* (Kingston: University of the West Indies Press, 1998).
110 The Wesleyan Methodist Missionary Society published a round defence of its members against allegations of involvement in the conspiracy. *The Missionary Notices* (January 1824).
111 Society for the Mitigation and Gradual Abolition of Slavery throughout the British Dominions, *Report of the committee of the Society for the Mitigation and Gradual Abolition of Slavery throughout the British Dominions, read at the general meeting of the Society, Held on the 15th day of June, 1824, together with an account, of the proceedings which took place at that meeting* (London, 1824), pp. 59–60.
112 Williams, *Hamel, the Obeah Man*, pp. 116, 119.
113 Ibid., p. 231. The duppie or duppy was (and is) a prominent figure in the Caribbean spirit world and was commented upon by Edward Long and Matthew Lewis. Healing or poisonous compounds made by the obeah practitioner from plant and animal extracts often achieved efficacy, particularly the power to take away or revive life, through the presence of duppies or spirits of the dead.
114 Ibid., pp. 279, 82, 88, 73, 300, 88, 166.
115 *Report of the Lords of the Committee of the Council Appointed for the Consideration of All Matters Relating to Trade and Foreign Plantations*, Part III, A, Nos 22–6.
116 Williams, *Hamel, the Obeah Man*, p. 425.
117 Ibid., p. 71. Indeed, it is likely that those practising obeah arts used other terms to refer to themselves, as more recent obeah practitioners have been known to do. Diana Paton argues that obeah was the legal construct of an anxious colonial authority, rather than the self-identification of practitioners. See Diana Paton, 'Obeah Acts: Producing and Policing the Boundaries of Religion in the Caribbean', *Small Axe*, Vol. 28 (March 2009), pp. 1–18. For Dianne M. Stewart, 'obeah' was a generic category that marked the 'acculturating influence of Pan-Africanization' in slaveholding context: 'the manifold and sometimes contradictory descriptions of Obeah across the centuries are snapshots of the multiple (Obeah) practices that comprise larger and differentiated institutions of African religion'. Dianne M. Stewart, *Three Eyes for the Journey: African Dimensions of the Jamaican Religious Experience* (Oxford: Oxford University Press, 2005), p. 41.

118 'The Obeah Woman. A West Indian Narrative' (1833) contains many of the same themes as *Hamel* in its pro-slavery account of a powerful obeah woman who comes into opposition with the local missionary, who, intent on rousing the enslaved community to rebellion, falls victim to obeah poison after he insults the practice.

119 Williams, *Hamel, the Obeah Man*, p. 323.

120 Testimony of William Fitzmaurice, 9 March 1791, Sheila Lambert (ed.), *House of Commons Sessional Papers of the Eighteenth Century*, Vol. 82 (Wilmington, DE: Scholarly Resources, 1975), pp. 230–1.

121 David Collins, *Practical Rules for the Management and Medical Treatment of Negro Slaves, in the Sugar Colonies. By a Professional Planter* (London: Printed by J. Barfield, 1803), pp. 340–1. For other accounts of dirt eating see David Mason, 'On Atrophia A Ventriculo (Mal d'Estomac) or Dirt-Eating', *Edinburgh Medical and Social Journal*, Vol. 39 (1833) and Williamson, *Medical and Miscellaneous Observations*.

122 Robert Thomas, *The Modern Practice of Physic, exhibiting the characters, causes and symptoms, prognostic, morbid appearances, and improved method of treating the diseases of all climates*, fourth edition (London: Printed for Longman et al, 1813), p. 440.

123 Thomas Roughley, *The Jamaica Planter's Guide* (London: Printed for Longman et al, 1823), p. 119.

124 Anonymous, *Sketches and Recollections of the West Indies* (London: Smith, Elder and Co., 1828), p. 244.

125 Mary Douglas, *Purity and Danger: An Analysis of Concepts of Pollution and Taboo* (London: Routledge, 2003), p. 44.

126 Williams, *Hamel, the Obeah Man*, p. 119.

127 Ibid., p. 427.

128 Ibid., p. 67. A 'vomitory' was an 'opening, door, or passage in a theatre, playhouse, or the like, affording ingress or egress to the spectators' (*OED*).

129 Ibid., p. 121.

130 Ibid., p. 120.

131 Ibid., pp. 129–30. The passage echoes Edward Long's account of revolutionary oath-taking ceremonies: 'when assembled for the purposes of conspiracy', according to Long, 'the obeiah-man, after various ceremonies, draws a little blood from every one present; this is mixed in a bowl with gunpowder and grave dirt; the fetishe or oath is administered, by which they solemnly pledge themselves to inviolable secrecy, fidelity to their chiefs, and to wage perpetual war against their enemies; as a ratification of their sincerity, each person takes a sup of the mixture, and this finishes the solemn rite'. Long, *History of Jamaica*, p. 473.

132 Williams, *Hamel, the Obeah Man*, p. 131. The fear of such unsanctioned meetings and the desire to 'remedy the evils arising from irregular assemblies' had prompted the Jamaican Assembly in 1760 to outlaw unauthorized groups of slaves. See *Acts of Assembly, Passed in the Island of Jamaica, From the Year 1681 to the Year 1769 Inclusive*, Act 24, 1760.

133 Williams, *A tour through the island of Jamaica*, pp. 202, 195.
134 Madden, *A Twelvemonth's Residence in the West Indies*, Vol. II, p. 109.
135 Ibid. Vol. II, pp. 108–9.
136 As well as suicide, abortion and infanticide were other forms of covert resistance which harmed the planters' interests and which colonial authorities hoped to discourage through the introduction of Christian imagery.
137 Brown, *The Reaper's Garden*, p. 131.
138 Trevor Burnard, *Mastery, Tyranny, and Desire: Thomas Thistlewood and His Slaves in the Anglo-Jamaican World* (Chapel Hill: University of North Carolina Press, 2004); Douglas Hall, *In Miserable Slavery: Thomas Thistlewood in Jamaica, 1750–86* (London: Macmillan, 1989), p. 160, Stewart, *A view of the past and present state of the Island of Jamaica; with remarks on the moral and physical condition of the slaves and on the abolition of slavery in the colonies*, p. 258.
139 David Livingstone, *Missionary Travels and Researches in South Africa* (London: John Murray, 1857), p. 244.
140 Singleton, *A General Description of the West-Indian Islands*, p. 56.
141 Jill Casid, '"His Master's Obi": Machine Magic, Colonial Violence and Transculturation' in *The Visual Culture Reader*, ed. Nicholas Mirzoeff (London: Routledge, 2002), pp. 533–45, p. 542.
142 Ibid., p. 544.
143 Williams, *Hamel, the Obeah Man*, p. 134.
144 Madden, *A Twelvemonth's Residence in the West Indies*, Vol. II, p. 100.
145 Hillary, *Observations on the Changes of the Air*, p. 341.
146 Williams, *Hamel, the Obeah Man*, p. 327.

Afterword

1 Gilmore, *The Poetics of Empire*, p. 89; Stedman, *Narrative*, p. 7.
2 Brown, *The Reaper's Garden*, p. 259.
3 Davy, *The West Indies, before and since Slave Emancipation*, p. 74. Barbados was subjected to a particularly severe hurricane in 1831, since which time Davy claims that 'there has been a decided improvement in the public health'. Ibid., p. 73.
4 Ibid., p. 73.
5 Yellow fever outbreaks continued in the British West Indies, and it was not until the 1860s, Philip Curtin writes, that the military practice of removing troops at the first signs of a yellow fever outbreak began to be used to save lives. Curtin, *Death by Migration*, p. 70. It was not until 1881 that the cause of yellow fever was established by the Cuban doctor Carlos Finlay, who proposed that yellow fever might be transmitted by mosquitoes rather than direct human contact.
6 Anthony Trollope, *The West Indies and the Spanish Main* (London: Chapman and Hall, 1859), p. 179.
7 By the 1840s, writes Philip Curtin, there was statistical evidence which suggested that death rates in the military began to climb with longer periods of service in the tropics, disproving the claims made by earlier colonists

that Europeans could be seasoned in order to build a healthy settler society. Curtin, *Death by Migration*, p. 44.

8 Trollope, *The West Indies and the Spanish Main*, pp. 67–8.

9 J. A. Froude, *The English in the West Indies, or the Bow of Ulysses* (London: Longman et al., 1888), p. 161.

10 C. L. R. James, *The Black Jacobins: Toussaint L'Ouverture and the San Domingo Revolution* (London: Penguin, 2001), pp. 161, 323, 333.

11 Froude, *The English in the West Indies*, p. 162.

12 Froude, *The English in the West Indies*, pp. 161, 162.

13 William Gilbert, *The Hurricane: a Theosophical and Western Eclogue* (Bristol: R. Edwards, 1796), p. 34. Gilbert drew on many of the same influences as Blake. On Swedenborgian ideas about Africa in Gilbert and Blake see Deirdre Coleman, *Romantic Colonization and British Anti-Slavery* (Cambridge: Cambridge University Press, 2005). For a full account of the metaphysical theory of continents underlying *The Hurricane*, see Paul Cheshire, 'The Hermetic Geography of William Gilbert', *Romanticism*, Vol. 9, No. 1 (2003), pp. 82–93.

14 Charles Mackay, *The Poetical Works of Charles Mackay, including 'Legends of the Isles'; 'Ballads and Lyrical Poems'; 'Voices from the Mountains'; 'Voices from the Crowd', and 'Town Lyrics'* (London: G. Routledge and Co., 1857), p. 94.

15 On the history of cholera see Richard J. Evans, 'Epidemics and Revolutions: Cholera in Nineteenth-Century Europe' in *Epidemics and Ideas: Essays on the Historical Perception of Pestilence*, ed. Terence Ranger and Paul Slack (Cambridge: Cambridge University Press, 1992), pp. 149–57, Kenneth Kiple, 'Cholera and Race in the Caribbean', *Journal of Latin American Studies*, Vol. 17, No. 1 (1985), pp. 157–77.

16 See Carter, 'Public Amenities after Emancipation', pp. 67–8.

17 Just as the yellow fever epidemics of the 1790s participated in the articulation of Caribbean and American Creole medical knowledge and social identities and the construction of disease as racially determined, the cholera epidemics of the nineteenth century played an important role in the articulation of racial and national sensibilities. In the wake of European cholera epidemics, collective aggression was directed at Jews and witches in particular.

18 Falconer, *Remarks on the influence of climate*, p. 2.

Bibliography

Acts of Assembly, Passed in the Island of Jamaica, From the Year 1681 to the Year 1769 Inclusive, Jamaica, Vol. II. (Saint Jago de la Vega: Lowry and Sherlock, 1769–1771).

Agamben, Giorgio, *The Open: Man and Animal* (Stanford, CA: Stanford University Press, 2004).

Allewaert, Monique, 'Swamp Sublime: Ecologies of Resistance in the American Plantation Zone', *PMLA*, Vol. 123, No. 2 (2008), pp. 340–57.

  Ariel's Ecology: Plantations, Personhood, and Colonialism in the American Tropics (Minneapolis: University of Minnesota Press, 2013).

Anderson, James, *A few facts and observations on the yellow fever of the West Indies, by which it is shewn, that there have existed two species of fever in the West-India islands for several years past, indiscriminately called yellow fever, but which have proceeded from very different causes* (Edinburgh: William Mudie, 1798).

Anonymous, 'Review of *The Sugar-Cane*', *The Critical Review*, Vol. 18 (October 1764), pp. 270–7.

Anonymous, *Jamaica, a Poem, in Three Parts* (London: Printed for William Nicoll, 1777).

Anonymous, *Sketches and Recollections of the West Indies* (London: Smith, Elder and Co., 1828).

Aravamudan, Srinivas, *Tropicopolitans: Colonialism and Agency, 1688–1804* (Durham, NC: Duke University, 1999).

Armitage, David, 'Three Concepts of Atlantic History' in *The British Atlantic World, 1500–1800*, ed. David Armitage and Michael J. Braddick (Basingstoke: Palgrave Macmillan, 2002), pp. 11–27.

Armstrong, Tim, *The Logic of Slavery: Debt, Technology and Pain in American Literature* (Cambridge: Cambridge University Press, 2012).

Arner, Katherine, 'Making Yellow Fever American: The Early American Republic, the British Empire and the Geopolitics of Disease in the Atlantic World', *Atlantic Studies*, Vol. 7, No. 4 (2010), pp. 447–71.

Auerbach, Jeffrey, 'The Picturesque and the Homogenization of Empire', *The British Art Journal*, Vol. V, No. 1 (2004), pp. 47–54.

Barbauld, Anna Letitia, *Epistle to William Wilberforce, Esq. on the Rejection of the Bill for Abolishing the Slave Trade* (London: Printed for J. Johnson, 1791).

Barham, Henry, *Hortus Americanus: Containing an Account of the Trees, Shrubs, and other Vegetable Productions, of South-America and the West-India Islands; and particularly of the Island of Jamaica* (Kingston: Alexander Aikman, 1794).

Barrell, John, *The Birth of Pandora and the Division of Knowledge* (Basingstoke: Macmillan, 1992).

Barringer, Tim, 'Picturesque Prospects and the Labour of the Enslaved' in *Art and Emancipation in Jamaica: Isaav Mendes Belisario and His Worlds*, ed. Tim Barringer, Gillian Forrester, and Barbaro Martinez-Ruiz (New Haven, CT, and London: Yale Centre for British Art in association with Yale University Press, 2007), pp. 41–63.

Beal, Joan, 'Syntax and Morphology' in *The Edinburgh History of the Scots Language*, ed. Charles Jones (Edinburgh: Edinburgh University Press, 1997), pp. 335–77.

Beckford, William, *A descriptive account of the island of Jamaica: with remarks upon the cultivation of the sugar-cane throughout the different seasons of the year, and chiefly considered in a picturesque point of view* (London: Printed for T. and J. Egerton, 1790).

Berman, Carolyn Vellenga, *Creole Crossings: Domestic Fiction and the Reform of Colonial Slavery* (Ithaca, NY: Cornell University Press, 2006).

Bermingham, Ann, *Landscape and Ideology: The English Rustic Tradition, 1740–1860* (London: Thames and Hudson, 1987).

Bewell, Alan, *Romanticism and Colonial Disease* (Baltimore: John Hopkins University Press, 1999).

Natures in Translation: Romanticism and Colonial Natural History (Baltimore: Johns Hopkins University Press, 2017).

Bhabha, Homi K., *The Location of Culture* (Abingdon: Routledge, 1994).

Birnie, George, 'Extract of a Letter from Mr George Birnie', *The London Medical and Physical Journal*, Vol. 38 (1817).

Block, Kristen, 'Slavery and Inter-imperial Leprosy Discourse in the Atlantic World', *Atlantic Studies: Global Currents,* Vol. 14, Issue 2 (2017), pp. 243–62.

Bogues, Anthony, *Empire of Liberty: Power, Desire, and Freedom* (Lebanon, NH: Dartmouth College Press, 2010).

Bohls, Elizabeth, 'The Planter Picturesque: Matthew Lewis's *Journal of a West India Proprietor*', *European Romantic Review*, Vol. 12 (2001), pp. 63–76.

Slavery and the Politics of Place: Representing the Colonial Caribbean, 1770–1833 (Cambridge: Cambridge University Press, 2014).

Boswell, James, *Life of Johnson* (Oxford: Oxford University Press, 2008).

Boulukos, George, *The Grateful Slave: the Emergence of Race in Eighteenth-Century British and American Culture* (Cambridge: Cambridge University Press, 2008).

Bourke, Joanna, *The Story of Pain, from Prayer to Painkillers* (Oxford: Oxford University Press, 2014).

Boyle, Robert, *Experiments and Considerations Touching Colours* (New York: Johnson Reprint, 1964).

Brantlinger, Patrick, *Rule of Darkness: British Literature and Imperialism, 1830–1914* (Ithaca, NY: Cornell University Press, 1988).

Brathwaite, Edward Kamau, *The Development of Creole Society in Jamaica, 1770–1820* (Oxford: Clarendon Press, 1971).

Roots (Ann Arbor: University of Michigan Press, 1993).

Brewer, John, *The Common People and Politics 1750–1790s* (Cambridge: Chadwyck-Healey, 1986).

Brown, Laura, *Fables of Modernity: Literature and Culture in the English Eighteenth Century* (Ithaca, NY: Cornell University Press, 2001).

Brown, Vincent, *The Reaper's Garden: Death and Power in the World of Atlantic Slavery* (Cambridge, MA: Harvard University Press, 2008).

Buckley, Matthew S., 'Refugee Theatre: Melodrama and Modernity's Loss', *Theatre Journal*, Vol. 61 (2009), pp. 175–90.

Burdett, William, *Life and Exploits of Mansong, Commonly Called Three-Finger'd Jack, the Terror of Jamaica in the years 1780 & 1781: with a Particular Account of the Obi; Being the Only True One of that Celebrated and Fascinating Mischief, so Prevalent in the West Indies* (Sommers Town: A. Neil, 1800).

Burke, Edmund, *Three Memorials on French affairs. Written in the Years 1791, 1792 and 1793* (London: Printed for F. and C. Rivington, 1797).

Burling, William J., *Summer Theatre in London, 1661–1820, and the Rise of the Haymarket Theatre* (Madison: Fairleigh Dickinson Press, 2000).

Burnard, Trevor, '"The Countrie Continues Sicklie": White Mortality in Jamaica, 1655–1780', *Social History of Medicine*, Vol. 12, No. 1 (April 1999), pp. 45–72.

Mastery, Tyranny, and Desire: Thomas Thistlewood and His Slaves in the Anglo-Jamaican World (Chapel Hill: University of North Carolina Press, 2004).

Planters, Merchants, and Slaves: Plantation Societies in British America, 1650–1820 (Chicago: University of Chicago Press, 2015).

Burton, Richard D. E., *Afro-Creole: Power, Opposition and Play in the Caribbean* (Ithaca, NY: Cornell University Press, 1997).

Bush, Barbara, 'Hard Labor: Women, Childbirth and Resistance in British Caribbean Slave Societies' in *More Than Chattel: Black Women and Slavery in the Americas*, ed. David Barry Gaspar and Darlene Clark Hine (Bloomington: Indiana University Press, 1996), pp. 193–217.

Bynum, William F., *Science and the Practice of Medicine in the Nineteenth Century* (Cambridge: Cambridge University Press, 1994).

Byron, Lord George, *Complete Poetical Works*, ed. J. J. McGann (Oxford: Clarendon Press, 1980).

Caldwell, Charles, *A reply to Dr. Haygarth's letter to Dr. Percival, on infectious fevers: and, his address to the College of Physicians at Philadelphia, on the preventing of the American pestilence, exposing the medical, philosophical, and literary errors of that author, and vindicating the right which is the faculty of the United States have to think and decide for themselves, respecting the diseases of their own country, uninfluenced by the notions of the physicians of Europe* (Philadelphia: Printed by Thomas and William Bradford, 1802).

Calè, Luisa and Adriana Craciun, 'The Disorder of Things', *Eighteenth-Century Studies*, Vol. 45, No. 1 (2011), pp. 1–13.

Cañizares-Esguerra, Jorge, *How to Write the History of the New World: Historiographies, Epistemologies, and Identities in the Eighteenth-Century Atlantic World* (Stanford, CA: Stanford University Press, 2001).

Carey, Brycchan, *British Abolitionism and the Rhetoric of Sensibility: Writing, Sentiment, and Slavery, 1760–1807* (Basingstoke: Palgrave Macmillan, 2005).

Carretta, Vincent, 'Review: Writings of the British Black Atlantic', *Eighteenth-Century Studies*, Vol. 34, No. 1 (2000), pp. 121–6.

Carter, Richard, 'Public Amenities after Emancipation' in *Emancipation II: Aspects of the Post-Slavery Experience in Barbados*, ed. Woodville Marshall (Cave Hill: University of the West Indies, 1987), pp. 46–69.

Casid, Jill, '"His Master's Obi": Machine Magic, Colonial Violence and Transculturation' in *The Visual Culture Reader*, ed. Nicholas Mirzoeff (London: Routledge, 2002), pp. 533–45.

   Sowing Empire: Landscape and Colonization (Minneapolis: University of Minnesota Press, 2005).

Cassidy, Frederic Gomes and Robert Brock LePage, *Dictionary of Jamaican English* (Barbados: University of West Indies Press, 2002).

Chalker, John, *The English Georgic: A Study in the Development of a Form* (London: Routledge, 1969).

Chandler, James, *An Archaeology of Sympathy: The Sentimental Mode in Literature and Cinema* (Chicago: Chicago University Press, 2013).

Charters, Erica, *Disease, War and the Imperial State: The Welfare of the British Armed Forces during the Seven Years' War* (Chicago: Chicago University Press, 2014).

Cheshire, Paul, 'The Hermetic Geography of William Gilbert', *Romanticism*, Vol. 9, No. 1 (2003), pp. 82–93.

Chisholm, Colin, *An essay on the malignant pestilential fever introduced into the West Indian Islands from Boullam, on the coast of Guinea, as it appeared in 1793 and 1794* (London: Printed for C. Dilly, 1795).

Clark, George, *A History of the Royal College of Physicians of London* (Oxford: Clarendon Press, 1964).

Clark, James, *A treatise on the yellow fever, as it appeared in the island of Dominica, in the years 1793-4-5-6: to which are added, Observations on the bilious remittent fever, on intermittents, dysentery, and some other West India diseases* (London: Printed for J. Murray and S. Highley, 1797).

Coleman, Deirdre, 'Janet Schaw and the Complexions of Empire', *Eighteenth-Century Studies*, Vol. 36, No. 2 (2003), pp. 169–93.

   Romantic Colonization and British Anti-Slavery (Cambridge: Cambridge University Press, 2005).

Coleridge, Samuel Taylor, *Specimens of the Table Talk of the late Samuel Taylor Coleridge* (London: John Murray, 1835).

Colley, Linda, *Britons: Forging the Nation, 1707–1837*, third revised edition (New Haven, CT: Yale University Press, 2009).

Collins, David, *Practical Rules for the Management and Medical Treatment of Negro Slaves, in the Sugar Colonies. By a Professional Planter* (London: Printed by J. Barfield, 1803).

Connor, Steven, *The Book of Skin* (London: Reaktion Books, 2004).

Cox, Jeffrey N., 'Theatrical Forms, Ideological Conflicts, and the Staging of *Obi*', in *Obi: A Romantic Circles Praxis Volume*, ed. Charles Rzepka (August 2002), www.romantic.arhu.umd.edu/praxis/obi/cox/cox.html.

Craton, Michael, James Walvin, and David Wright, *Slavery, Abolition and Emancipation: Black Slaves and the British Empire, a Thematic Documentary* (London: Longman, 1976).

Crawford, Rachel, 'English Georgic and British Nationhood', *English Literary History*, Vol. 65, No. 1 (1998), pp. 123–58.

Cullen, William, *Nosology: or, a Systematic Arrangement of Diseases* (Edinburgh: Printed by C. Stewart and Co., 1800).

Curran, Andrew S., *The Anatomy of Blackness: Science and Slavery in and Age of Enlightenment* (Baltimore: Johns Hopkins University Press, 2011).

Curtin, Philip, *Death by Migration: Europe's Encounter with the Tropical World in the Nineteenth Century* (Cambridge: Cambridge University Press, 1989).

Dabydeen, David, 'Sugar and Slavery in the West Indian Georgic', *Callaloo*, Vol. 23, No. 4 (Autumn 2000), pp. 1513–14.

Dabydeen, David and Nana Wilson-Tagoe, 'Selected Themes in West Indian Literature: An Annotated Bibliography', *Third World Quarterly*, Vol. 9, No. 3 (July 1987), pp. 921–60.

Dancer, Thomas, *The Medical Assistant; or Jamaica Practice of Physic* (Kingston: Printed by Alexander Aikman, 1801).

Davies, Robertson, *The Mirror of Nature* (Toronto: University of Toronto Press, 1983).

Davy, John, *The West Indies, before and since Slave Emancipation, comprising the Windward and Leeward Islands' military command; founded on notes and observations collected during a three years' residence* (London: W. and F. G. Cash, 1854).

De Certeau, Michel, 'Travel Narratives of the French to Brazil: Sixteenth to Eighteenth Centuries', *Representations*, Vol. 33, Special Issue: The New World (1991), pp. 221–6.

DeLacy, Margaret, 'Nosology, Mortality, and Disease Theory in the Eighteenth Century', *Journal of the History of Medicine*, Vol. 54 (April 1999), pp. 261–84.

Delbourgo, James and Nicholas Dew (eds.), *Science and Empire in the Atlantic World* (New York: Routledge, 2008).

Dewhurst, Kenneth, *Dr. Thomas Sydenham (1624–1689): His Life and Original Writings* (Berkeley: University of California Press, 1966).

Diamond, Jared, *Guns, Germs and Steel: The Fate of Human Societies* (London: Vintage, 1997).

Dillon, Elizabeth Maddock, *New World Drama: The Performative Commons in the Atlantic World, 1649–1849* (Durham, NC: Duke University Press, 2014).

Douglas, Mary, *Purity and Danger: An Analysis of Concepts of Pollution and Taboo* (London: Routledge, 2003).

Douglass, William, *Inoculation of the small pox as practised in Boston, consider'd in a letter to A – S – M.D. & F.R.S. in London* (Boston: Printed and Sold by J. Franklin, 1722).

Drayton, Richard, *Nature's Government: Science, Imperial Britain, and the 'Improvement' of the World* (New Haven, CT: Yale University Press, 2000).

Du Bois, W. E. B, *The Souls of Black Folk* (Rockville, MD: Arc Manor, 2008).

Dyer, John, *The Fleece: A Poem in Four Books* (London: Printed for R. and J. Dodsley, 1757).

Eagleton, Terry, *The Ideology of the Aesthetic* (Oxford: Blackwell, 1990).

Earle, William, *Obi; or, the History of Three-Fingered Jack*, ed. Srinivas Aravamudan (Peterborough: Broadview Press, 2005).

Edgeworth, Maria, *Belinda*, ed. Kathryn J. Kirkpatrick (Oxford: Oxford University Press, 1994).
    'The Grateful Negro' in *The Novels and Selected Works of Maria Edgeworth*, Vol. 12, ed. Elizabeth Eger, Clíona ÓGallchoir, and Marilyn Butler (London: Pickering and Chatto, 2003), pp. 49–63.

Edmond, Rod, *Leprosy and Empire: A Medical and Cultural History* (Cambridge: Cambridge University Press, 2006).

Edwards, Bryan, *Poems, Written Chiefly in the West-Indies* (Kingston: Printed for the author by Alexander Aikman, 1792).
    The proceedings of the governor and Assembly of Jamaica, in regard to the Maroon Negroes: published by order of the Assembly, to which is prefixed an introductory account, containing, observations on the disposition, character, manners, and habits of life, of the Maroons (London: Printed for J. Stockdale, 1796).
    An Historical Survey of the French Colony in the Island of St. Domingo (London: Printed for John Stockdale, 1797).

Edwards, Paul and James Walvin, *Black Personalities in the Era of the Slave Trade* (London: Macmillan, 1983).

Egan, Jim, 'The "Long'd-for Aera" of an "Other Race": Climate, Identity, and James Grainger's *The Sugar-Cane*', *Early American Literature*, Vol. 38, No. 2 (2003), pp. 189–212.

Ellis, Keith, 'Images of Sugar in English and Spanish Caribbean Poetry', *Ariel: A Review of International English Literature*, Vol. 24, No. 1 (1993), pp. 149–59.

Ellis, Markman, '"The Cane-Land Isles": Commerce and Empire in Late Eighteenth-Century Georgic and Pastoral Poetry' in *Islands in History and Representation*, ed. Rod Edmond and Vanessa Smith (London: Routledge, 2003), pp. 43–62.
    '"Incessant Labour": Georgic Poetry and the Problem of Slavery' in *Discourses of Slavery and Abolition: Britain and Its Colonies, 1760–1838*, ed. Brycchan Carey, Markman Ellis, and Sarah Salih (Basingstoke: Palgrave Macmillan, 2004), pp. 45–62.
    'Suffering Things: Lapdogs, Slaves, and Counter-Sensibility' in *The Secret Life of Things: Animals, Objects, and It-Narratives in Eighteenth-Century England*, ed. Mark Blackwell (Lewisburg, PA: Bucknell University Press, 2007), pp. 92–113.

Equiano, Olaudah, *The interesting narrative of the life of Olaudah Equiano, or Gustavus Vassa, the African. Written by himself* (London: Printed by T. Wilkins, 1789).

Evans, Richard J., 'Epidemics and Revolutions: Cholera in Nineteenth-Century Europe' in *Epidemics and Ideas: Essays on the Historical Perception of Pestilence*, ed. Terence Ranger and Paul Slack (Cambridge: Cambridge University Press, 1992), pp. 149–73.

Fairclough, Mary, *The Romantic Crowd: Sympathy, Controversy and Print Culture* (Cambridge: Cambridge University Press, 2013).

Fairer, David, *Organising Poetry: The Coleridge Circle, 1790–1798* (Oxford: Oxford University Press, 2009).

Falconer, William, *Remarks on the influence of climate, situation, nature of country, population, nature of food, and way of life, on the disposition and temper, manners and behaviour, intellects, laws and customs, form of government, and religion, of mankind* (London: Printed for C. Dilly, 1781).

Favret, Mary, 'War in the Air', *Modern Language Quarterly*, Vol. 65, No. 4 (2004), pp. 531–59.

Fawcett, John, *Songs, Duets, & Choruses, in the pantomimical drama of Obi, or Three-Finger'd Jack: (perform'd at the Theatre Royal, Hay Market) To which are prefix'd Illlustrative Extracts, and a Prospectus of the Action* (London: Printed by T. Woodfall, 1800).

Festa, Lynn, *Sentimental Figures of Empire in Eighteenth-Century Britain and France* (Baltimore: Johns Hopkins University Press, 2005).

'Person, Animal, Thing: The 1796 Dog Tax and the Right to Superfluous Things', *Eighteenth-Century Life*, Vol. 33, No. 2 (Spring 2009), pp. 1–44.

Fett, Sharla M., *Working Cures: Health, Healing and Power on Southern Slave Plantations* (Chapel Hill: University of North Carolina Press, 2000).

Forde, Diana Paton and Maarit Forde Paton, 'Introduction', *Obeah and Other Powers*, ed. Diana Forde Paton and Maarit Forde Paton (Durham, NC: Duke University Press, 2012), pp. 1–42.

Foucault, Michel, *The Birth of the Clinic: An Archaeology of Medical Perception* (London: Routledge, 1976).

Frank, Johann Peter, *A System of Complete Medical Police: Selections from Johann Peter Frank*, ed. Erna Lesky (Baltimore: John Hopkins University Press, 1976).

Froude, J. A., *The English in the West Indies, or the Bow of Ulysses* (London: Longman et al, 1888).

Fulford, Tim, *Landscape, Liberty and Authority: Poetry, Criticism and Politics from Thomson to Wordsworth* (Cambridge: Cambridge University Press, 1996).

Fulford, Tim, Peter Kitson and Debbie Lee, *Literature, Science and Exploration in the Romantic Era: Bodies of Knowledge* (Cambridge: Cambridge University Press, 2004).

Geggus, David, 'Yellow Fever in the 1790s: The British Army in Occupied Saint Domingue', *Medical History*, Vol. 23 (1979), pp. 38–58.

'The Anglo-French Conflict in the Caribbean in the 1790s' in *Britain and Revolutionary France: Conflict, Subversion and Propaganda*, ed. Colin Jones, Exeter Studies in History (Exeter: University of Exeter, 1983), pp. 27–39.

Gikandi, Simon, *Slavery and the Culture of Taste* (Princeton, NJ: Princeton University Press, 2011).

Gikswijt-Hofstra, Marijke, Brian P. Levack, and Roy Porter, *Witchcraft and Magic in Europe: The Eighteenth and Nineteenth Centuries* (London: The Athlone Press, 1999).

Gilbert, William, *The Hurricane: A Theosophical and Western Eclogue* (Bristol: R. Edwards, 1796).

Gilman, Sander, *Disease and Representation: Images of Illness from Madness to AIDS* (Ithaca, NY: Cornell University Press, 1988).

Gilmore, John, *The Poetics of Empire: A Study of James Grainger's The Sugar-Cane* (London: The Athlone Press, 2000).

Glausser, Wayne, *Locke and Blake: A Conversation across the Eighteenth Century* (Gainsville: University Press of Florida, 1998).

Glissant, Édouard *The Poetics of Relation* (Ann Arbor: University of Michigan Press, 1997).

Golinski, Jan, *British Weather and the Climate of Enlightenment* (Chicago: University of Chicago Press, 2007).

Goodman, Kevis, *Georgic Modernity and British Romanticism: Poetry and the Mediation of History* (Cambridge: Cambridge University Press, 2004).

'"Uncertain Disease": Nostalgia, Pathologies of Motion, Practices of Reading', *Studies in Romanticism*, Vol. 49, No. 2 (2010), pp. 197–227.

Gowland, John, *An Essay on Cutaneous Diseases, and all impurities of the skin. Proposing a specific, and, method of cure* (London: Johnson and Murray, 1792?).

Grainger, James, *An essay on the more common West-India diseases* (London: T. Becket and P. A. De Hondt, 1764).

An Essay on the More Common West-India Diseases; and the Remedies which that Country itself Produces, in *Three tracts on West-Indian agriculture, and subjects connected therewith; viz. An essay upon plantership, by Samuel Martin, Senior, Esq. of Antigua: The sugar-cane, a didactic poem in four books: and, An essay on the management and diseases of Negroes* (Jamaica: Re-printed by A. Aikman, 1802).

Great Britain. Parliament. *House of Commons Sessional Papers of the Eighteenth Century*, Vol. 69. *Report of the Lords of the Committee of the Council Appointed for the Consideration of All Matters Relating to Trade and Foreign Plantations* (London, 1789).

Greene, Jack P., 'Changing Identity in the British Caribbean: Barbados as a Case Study' in *Colonial Identity in the Atlantic World, 1500–1800*, ed. Nicholas Canny and Anthony Pagden (Princeton, NJ: Princeton University Press, 1987), pp. 213–66.

Grove, Richard H., *Green Imperialism: Colonial Expansion, Tropical Eden Islands and the Origins of Environmentalism, 1600–1860* (Cambridge: Cambridge University Press, 1995).

Gwilliam, Tassie, '"Scenes of Horror", Scenes of Sensibility: Sentimentality and Slavery in John Gabriel Stedman's *Narrative of a Five Years Expedition against the Revolted Negroes of Surinam'*, *English Literary History*, Vol. 65, No. 3 (1998), pp. 653–73.

Hadley, Elaine, *Melodramatic Tactics: Theatricalized Dissent in the English Marketplace, 1800–1885* (Stanford, CA: Stanford University Press, 1995).

Hall, Douglas, *In Miserable Slavery: Thomas Thistlewood in Jamaica, 1750–86* (London: Macmillan, 1989).

Hamilton, Douglas J., *Scotland, the Caribbean and the Atlantic World 1750–1820* (Manchester: Manchester University Press, 2005).

Handler, Jerome S., 'Slave Medicine and Obeah in Barbados, circa 1650 to 1834', *New West Indian Guide*, Vol. 74, No. 1/2 (2000), pp. 57–90.

Handler, Jerome S. and Kenneth M. Bilby, 'On the Early Use and Origin of the Term "Obeah" in Barbados and the Anglophone Caribbean', *Slavery and Abolition*, Vol. 22, No. 2, pp. 87–100.

Harrison, Mark, '"The Tender Frame of Man": Disease, Climate, and Racial Difference in India and the West Indies, 1760–1860', *Bulletin of the History of Medicine*, Vol. 70, No. 1 (1996), pp. 68–93.

Climates and Constitutions: Health, Race, Environment and British Imperialism in India, 1600–1850 (Oxford: Oxford University Press, 1999).

Disease and the Modern World: 1500 to the Present Day (Cambridge: Polity Press, 2004).

Medicine in an Age of Commerce and Empire: Britain and Its Tropical Colonies 1660–1830 (Oxford: Oxford University Press, 2010).

Contagion: How Commerce Has Spread Disease (New Haven, CT: Yale University Press, 2012).

Hays, J. N., *The Burdens of Disease: Epidemics and Human Response in Western History* (New Brunswick, NJ: Rutgers University Press, 1998).

Heriot, George, *A Descriptive Poem, Written in the West Indies* (London: Printed for J. Dodsley, 1781).

Hickeringill, Edmund, *Jamaica Viewed: with all the Ports, Harbours, and Their Several Soundings, Towns, and Settlements Thereunto Belonging. Together, with the Nature of its Climate, Fruitfulness of the Soil, and its Suitableness to English Complexions* (London: Printed for J. Williams, 1661).

Hillary, William, *Observations on the Changes of the Air, and the Concomitant Epidemical Diseases of Barbadoes*, second edition (London: Printed for L. Hawes et al, 1766).

Hughes, Griffith, *The Natural History of Barbados* (London: Printed for the author, 1750).

Hulme, Peter, *Colonial Encounters: Europe and the Native Caribbean, 1492–1797* (London: Routledge, 1986).

Hume, David, *A Treatise of Human Nature* (London: Printed for John Noon, 1739).

'Of Superstition and Enthusiasm' in *Essays and Treatises on Several Subjects* (London: Printed for A. Millar, 1758), pp. 48–51.

'Of the Rise and Progress of the Arts and Sciences' in *Essays and Treatises on Several Subjects* (London: Printed for A. Millar, 1758), pp. 77–86.

Essays, Moral, Political, and Literary (Indianapolis: Liberty Fund, 1987).

Hurst, Michael, *Maria Edgeworth and the Public Scene: Intellect, Fine Feeling and Landlordism in the Age of Reform* (London: Macmillan, 1969).

Hutchinson, William, *The Princess of Zanfara; A Dramatic Poem* (London: Printed for Mess. Wilkie, 1789).

Huxham, John, *Observations on the air and epidemic diseases from the year 1728–1738* (London: J. Hinton, 1759).

Iannini, Christopher, *Fatal Revolutions: Natural History, West Indian Slavery, and the Routes of American Literature* (Chapel Hill: University of North Carolina Press, 2012).

Irlam, Shaun, '"Wish You Were Here": Exporting England in James Grainger's *The Sugar-Cane*', *English Literary History*, Vol. 68, No. 2 (2001), pp. 377–96.

Jackson, Robert, *A treatise on the fevers of Jamaica, with some observations on the intermitting fever of America, and an appendix containing some hints on the means of preserving the health of soldiers in hot climates* (London: Printed for J. Murray, 1791).

An outline of the history and cure of fever, epidemic and contagious; more especially of jails, ships, and hospital: the concentrated endemic, vulgarly the yellow fever of the West Indies (London: Printed for Mundell & Son, 1798).

Jackson, Seguin Henry, *Dermato-Pathologica; or Practical Observations, from Some New Thoughts on the Pathology and and Proximate Cause of Diseases of the True Skin and its Emanations, the Rete Mucosum and Cuticle* (London: Printed by H. Reynell, 1792).

Jacobus, Mary, *Romantic Things: A Tree, a Rock, a Cloud* (Chicago: University of Chicago Press, 2012).

James, C. L. R., *The Black Jacobins: Toussaint L'Ouverture and the San Domingo Revolution* (London: Penguin, 2001).

Jaudon, Toni Wall, 'Obeah's Sensations: Rethinking Religion at the Transnational Turn', *American Literature*, Vol. 84, No. 4 (2013), pp. 715–41.

Johnson, James, *The Influence of Tropical Climates on European Constitutions; to Which is Now Added, an Essay on Morbid Sensibility of the Stomach and Bowels, as the Proximate Cause, or Characteristic Condition of Indigestion, Nervous Irritability, Mental Despondency, Hypochondriasis, &c. &c.*, fourth edition (London: Printed for Thomas and George Underwood, 1827).

Johnson, Mary Lynn, 'Coleridge's Prose and a Blake Plate in Stedman's *Narrative*: Unfastening the "Hooks and Eyes" of Memory', *Wordsworth Circle*, Vol. 13, No. 1 (Winter 1982), pp. 36–8.

Joseph, E. L., *Warner Arundell, The Adventures of a Creole* (Kingston: The University of the West Indies Press, 2001).

Kevan, D. Keith McE., 'Mid-Eighteenth-Century Entomology and Helminthology in the West Indies: Dr. James Grainger', *Journal of the Society for the Bibliography of Natural History*, Vol. 8, No. 3 (1977), pp. 193–222.

Kiple, Kenneth, *The Caribbean Slave: A Biological History* (Cambridge: Cambridge University Press, 1984).

'Cholera and Race in the Caribbean', *Journal of Latin American Studies*, Vol. 17, No. 1 (1985), pp. 157–77.

'Disease Ecologies of the Caribbean' in *The Cambridge World History of Human Disease*, ed. Kenneth Kiple (Cambridge: Cambridge University Press, 1993), pp. 497–504.

Kitson, Peter J., 'John Thelwall in Saint Domingue: Race, Slavery and Revolution in *The Daughter of Adoption: A Tale of Modern Times* (1801)', *Romanticism*, Vol. 16, No. 2 (2010), pp. 120–38.

Klancher, Jon, 'Godwin and the Republican Romance: Genre, Politics, and Contingency in Cultural History', *Modern Language Quarterly*, Vol. 56, No. 2 (1995), pp. 145–65.

Klarer, Mario, 'Humanitarian Pornography: John Gabriel Stedman's *Narrative of a Five Years Expedition against the Revolted Negroes of Surinam* (1796)', *New Literary History*, Vol. 36, No. 4 (Autumn 2005), pp. 559–87.

Klein, Ursula and E. C. Spary, *Materials and Expertise in Early Modern Europe: Between Market and Laboratory* (Chicago: University of Chicago Press, 2010).

Knight, F. W. (ed.), *The Slave Societies of the Caribbean* (London: UNESCO, 1997).

Knight, James, British Library, Additional MS, 12431: Miscellaneous Papers and original Letters relating to the affairs of Jamaica (1740–43).

British Library, Additional MS, 12419, Vol. II, fo. 90: History of Jamaica (ca. 1746).

Lamb, Jonathan, 'Modern Metamorphoses and Disgraceful Tales', *Critical Inquiry*, Vol. 28, No. 1, 'Things' (Autumn 2001), pp. 133–66.

Preserving the Self in the South Seas, 1680-1840 (Chicago: University of Chicago Press, 2001).

Scurvy: The Disease of Discovery (Princeton, NJ: Princeton University Press, 2016).

Lambert, David, *White Creole Culture, Politics and Identity during the Age of Abolition* (Cambridge: Cambridge University Press, 2005).

Lambert, Sheila (ed.), *House of Commons Sessional Papers of the Eighteenth Century*, Vol. 82 (Wilmington, DE: Scholarly Resources, 1975).

The Lancet London: A Journal of British and Foreign Medicine, Vol. 5 (London: G. L. Hutchinson, 1824).

Latour, Bruno, *Science in Action: How to Follow Scientists and Engineers through Society* (Cambridge, MA: Harvard University Press, 1987).

Leaver, Kristen, 'Victorian Melodrama and the Performance of Poverty', *Victorian Literature and Culture*, Vol. 27, No. 2 (1999), pp. 443–56.

Lee, Debbie, *Slavery and the Romantic Imagination* (Philadelphia: University of Pennsylvania Press, 2002).

Leslie, Charles, *A new history of Jamaica, from the earliest accounts, to the taking of Porto Bello by Vice-Admiral Vernon. In thirteen letters from a gentleman to his friend* (London: Printed for J. Hodges, 1740).

Levine, Lawrence, *Black Culture and Black Consciousness: Afro-American Folk Thought from Slavery to Freedom* (Oxford: Oxford University Press, 1977).

Lewis, G. K., *Main Currents in Caribbean Thought: The Historical Evolution of Caribbean Society in Its Ideological Aspects, 1492–1900* (Baltimore: Johns Hopkins University Press, 1983).

Lewis, Matthew, *Journal of a West India Proprietor*, ed. Judith Terry (Oxford: Oxford University Press, 1999).

Light, Richard Upjohn, 'The Progress of Medical Geography', *Geographical Review*, Vol. 34, No. 4 (October 1944), pp. 636–41.

Ligon, Richard, *A True and Exact History of the Island of Barbados* (London: Printed for Humphrey Moseley, 1657).

Lind, James, *An essay on diseases incidental to Europeans in hot climates* (London: Printed for T. Becket and P. A de Hondt, 1768).

Linebaugh, Peter and Marcus Rediker, *The Many-Headed Hydra: Sailors, Slaves, Commoners, and the Hidden History of the Revolutionary Atlantic* (London: Verso, 2000).

Liu, Alan, *Wordsworth: The Sense of History* (Stanford, CA: Stanford University Press, 1989).

Livingstone, David, *Missionary Travels and Researches in South Africa* (London: John Murray, 1857).

Long, Edward, *History of Jamaica. Or, general survey of the antient and modern state of that island* (London: Printed for T. Lowndes, 1774).

Low, Anthony, *The Georgic Revolution* (Princeton, NJ: Princeton University Press, 1985).

Mackay, Charles, *The Poetical Works of Charles Mackay, including 'Legends of the Isles'; 'Ballads and Lyrical Poems'; 'Voices from the Mountains'; 'Voices from the Crowd', and 'Town Lyrics* (London: G. Routledge and Co., 1857).

MacKenzie, James, *The History of Health, and the Art of Preserving It: Or, An Account of All That Has Been Recommended By Physicians and Philosophers* (Edinburgh: Printed by William Gordon, 1758).

MacLeod, Roy M., *Nature and Empire: Science and the Colonial Enterprise* (Chicago: University of Chicago Press, 2001).

Madden, Richard Robert, *A Twelvemonth's Residence in the West Indies During the Transition from Slavery to Apprenticeship: With Incidental Notices of the State of Society, Prospects, and Natural Resources of Jamaica and Other Islands* (London: J. Cochrane and Co., 1835).

Maier, D., 'Nineteenth-Century Asante Medical Practices', *Comparative Studies in Society and History*, Vol. 21, No. 1 (January 1979), pp. 63–81.

Makdisi, Saree, *Romantic Imperialism: Universal Empire and the Culture of Modernity* (Cambridge: Cambridge University Press, 1998).

Mallipeddi, Ramesh, '"A Fixed Melancholy": Migration, Memory and the Middle Passage', *The Eighteenth Century*, Vol. 55, No. 2–3 (2014), pp. 235–53.

Markley, A. A., *Conversion and Reform in the British Novel in the 1790s* (Basingstoke: Palgrave Macmillan, 2009).

Marshall, Herbert and Mildred Stock, *Ira Aldridge: The Negro Tragedian* (London: Rockliff, 1958).

Martin, Charles D., *The White African American Body: A Cultural and Literary Exploration* (New Brunswick, NJ: Rutgers University Press, 2002).

Mason, David, 'On Atrophia A Ventriculo (Mal d'Estomac) or Dirt-Eating', *Edinburgh Medical and Social Journal*, Vol. 39 (1833).

Massey, Edmund, *A Sermon Against the Dangerous and Sinful Practice of Inoculation. Preach'd at St. Andrew's Holborn, on Sunday, July the 8th, 1722* (London: William Meadows, 1722).

McNeill, J. R., *Mosquito Empires: Ecology and War in the Greater Caribbean, 1620–1914* (Cambridge: Cambridge University Press, 2010).

Mellor, Anne K., 'Sex, Violence and Slavery: Blake and Wollstonecraft', *The Huntington Library Quarterly*, Vol. 58, No. 3/4 (1995), pp. 345–70.

Miller, Geneviève, *The Adoption of Inoculation for Smallpox in England and France* (Philadelphia: University of Pennsylvania Press, 1957).

Mitchell, W. J. T., 'Imperial Landscape' in *Landscape and Power*, ed. W. J. T. Mitchell, second edition (Chicago: Chicago University Press, 2002), pp. 5–34.

M'Lean, Hector, *An enquiry into the nature, and causes of the great mortality among the troops at St. Domingo: with practical remarks on the fever of that island; and directions, for the conduct of Europeans on their first arrival in warm climates* (London: Printed for T. Cadell, 1797).

M'Leod, John, *Narrative of a Voyage, in His Majesty's Late Ship Alceste to the Yellow Sea, Along the Coast of Corea* (London: John Murray, 1817).

Montgomery, James, *The West Indies, and other poems*, third edition (London: Longman et al, 1810).

The West Indies (New York: Garland, 1979).

More, Hannah, *Slavery: A Poem* (London: Printed for T. Cadell, 1788).

Moreton, J. B., *West India customs and manners: containing strictures on the soil, cultivation, produce, trade, officers, and inhabitants*, second edition (London: Printed for J. Parsons, W. Richardson and J. Walter, 1793).

Moseley, Benjamin, *A treatise on tropical diseases; and on the climate of the West-Indies*, second edition (London, 1789).

A Treatise on Sugar (London: G. G. and J. Robinson, 1799).

Medical Tracts (London: Printed by John Nichols, 1800).

Murray, William H., *Obi; or, Three-Fingered Jack in Dick's Standard Plays* (London: John Dick, 1825).

Nordius, Janina, 'Racism and Radicalism in Jamaican Gothic: Cynric R. Williams' *Hamel, the Obeah Man*', *English Literary History*, Vol. 73, No. 3 (Fall 2006), pp. 673–93.

Nugent, Maria, *Lady Nugent's Journal: Jamaica One Hundred Years Ago* (Cambridge: Cambridge University Press, 2010).

O'Brien, Karen, 'Imperial Georgic, 1660–1789' in *The Country and the City Revisited*, ed. Gerald MacLean, Donna Landry, and Joseph P. Ward (Cambridge: Cambridge University Press, 1999), pp. 160–79.

Olmos, Margarite Fernández and Lizabeth Paravisini-Gebert, *Creole Religions of the Caribbean: An Introduction from Vodou and Santería to Obeah and Espiritismo* (New York: New York University Press, 2003).

Ortiz, Fernando, *Cuban Counterpoint: Tobacco and Sugar* (Durham, NC: Duke University Press, 1995).

Pagden, Anthony, *European Encounters with the New World: From Renaissance to Romanticism* (New Haven, CT: Yale University Press, 1993).

Parrish, Susan Scott, *American Curiosity: Cultures of Natural History in the Colonial British Atlantic World* (Chapel Hill: University of North Carolina Press, 2012).

Parsons, James, 'Account of the White Negro Shewn Before the Royal Society: In a Letter to the Right Honourable Earl of Morton, President of the Royal Society, from James Parsons, M.D.F.R.S.', *Philosophical Transactions (1683–1775)*, Vol. 55 (1765), pp. 45–53.

Paton, Diana, 'The Afterlives of Three-Fingered Jack' in *Slavery and the Cultures of Abolition: Essays Marking the Bicentennial of the British Abolition Act of 1807*, ed. Brycchan Carey and Peter J. Kitson (Cambridge: Boydell and Brewer, 2007), pp. 42–63.

'Obeah Acts: Producing and Policing the Boundaries of Religion in the Caribbean', *Small Axe*, Vol. 28 (March 2009), pp. 1–18.

The Cultural Politics of Obeah: Religion, Colonialism and Modernity in the Caribbean World (Cambridge: Cambridge University Press, 2015).

Patterson, Orlando, *The Sociology of Slavery: An Analysis of the Origins, Development and Structure of Negro Slave Society in Jamaica* (Rutherford, NJ: Fairleigh Dickinson University Press, 1969).

Pearsall, Sarah M. S., 'Gender' in *The British Atlantic World, 1500–1800*, ed. David Armitage and Michael J. Braddick (Basingstoke: Palgrave Macmillan, 2002), pp. 113–32.

Perkins, David, *Romanticism and Animal Rights* (Cambridge: Cambridge University Press, 2003).

Pernick, Martin S., 'Politics, Parties, and Pestilence: Epidemic Yellow Fever in Philadelphia and the Rise of the First Party System' in *A Melancholy Scene of Devastation: The Public Response to the 1793 Philadelphia Yellow Fever Epidemic*, ed. J. Worth Estes and Billy G. Smith (Canton, MA: Published for the College of Physicians of Philadelphia and the Library Company of Philadelphia by Science History Publications, 1997).

Pickstone, John V., 'Dearth, Dirt and Fever Epidemics: Rewriting the History of British "Public Health", 1780–1850' in *Epidemics and Ideas: Essays on the Historical Perception of Pestilence* ed. Terence Ranger and Paul Slack (Cambridge: Cambridge University Press, 1991), pp. 125–48.

Pinckard, George, *Notes on the West Indies: written during the expedition under the command of the late General Sir R. Abercrombie* (London: Longman et al, 1806).

Plasa, Carl, *Slaves to Sweetness: British and Caribbean Literatures of Sugar* (Liverpool: Liverpool University Press, 2009).

Plenck, Joseph Jacob, *Doctrina de morbis cutaneis qua hi morbid in suas classes, genera & species rediguntur* (Vienna, 1776).

Pollak, Ellen, *Incest and the English Novel, 1684–1814* (Baltimore: Johns Hopkins University Press, 2003).

Porter, Dahlia, 'Maps, Lists, Views: How the Picturesque Wye transformed Topography', *Romanticism*, Vol. 19, No. 2 (2013), pp. 163–78.

Porter, Roy, *Health for Sale: Quackery in England, 1660–1850* (Manchester: Manchester University Press, 1989).

Bodies Politic: Diseases, Death and Doctors in Britain, 1650–1900 (London: Reaktion Books, 2001).

Porter, Roy and Dorothy Porter, *Patient's Progress: Doctors and Doctoring in Eighteenth-Century England* (Oxford: Polity Press, 1989).

Pratt, Mary Louise, *Imperial Eyes: Travel Writing and Transculturation* (London: Routledge, 1992).

Pringle, John, *Observations on the Diseases of the Army*, second edition (London: Printed for A. Millar et al, 1752).

Quilley, Geoff, 'Pastoral Plantations: The Slave Trade and the Representation of British Colonial Landscape in the Late Eighteenth Century' in *An Economy of Colour: Visual Culture and the Atlantic World, 1660–1830*, ed. Geoff Quilley and Kay Dian Kriz (Manchester: Manchester University Press, 2003), pp. 106–28.

Qureshi, Sadiah, *Peoples on Parade: Exhibitions, Empire, and Anthropology in Nineteenth-Century Britain* (Chicago: Chicago University Press, 2011).

Ramsay, James, *An essay on the treatment and conversion of African slaves in the British sugar colonies* (London: Printed by J. Philips, 1784).

Rediker, Marcus, 'The Red Atlantic; or, "a Terrible Blast Swept Over the Heaving Sea"' in *Sea Changes: Historizing the Ocean*, ed. Bernhard Klein and Gesa Mackenthun (New York: Routledge, 2004), pp. 111–30.

The Slave Ship: A Human History (London: John Murray, 2008).

Richards, David, *Masks of Difference: Cultural Representations in Literature, Anthropology and Art* (Cambridge: Cambridge University Press, 1994).

Richardson, Alan, 'Romantic Voodoo: Obeah and British Culture, 1797–1807', *Studies in Romanticism*, Vol. 32, No. 1 (1993), pp. 3–28.

Riley, James C., *The Eighteenth-Century Campaign to Avoid Disease* (New York: St. Martin's Press, 1987).

Roach, Joseph, *Cities of the Dead: Circum-Atlantic Performance* (New York: Columbia University Press, 1996).

Rodriguez, Junius P. (ed.), *Encyclopedia of Slave Resistance and Rebellion* (Westport, CT: Greenwood, 2007).

Rodriques, Janelle, 'Obeah(man) as trickster in Cynric Williams' *Hamel, the Obeah Man*', *Atlantic Studies: Global Currents*, Vol. 12, No. 2 (2015), pp. 219–34.

Roe, Nicholas, *John Keats and the Culture of Dissent* (Oxford: Clarendon Press, 1997).

Roughley, Thomas, *The Jamaica Planter's Guide* (London: Printed for Longman et al, 1823).

Rousseau, George, 'Literature and Medicine: the State of the Field', *Isis*, Vol. 72, No. 3 (1981), pp. 406–24.

Rucker, Walter, 'Conjure, Magic and Power: The Influence of Afro-Atlantic Religious Practices on Slave Resistance and Rebellion', *Journal of Black Studies*, Vol. 32, No. 1 (September 2001), pp. 84–103.

Rupke, Nicolaas A. (ed.), *Medical Geography in Historical Perspective* (London: Wellcome Trust, 2000).

Safier, Neil, *Measuring the New World: Enlightenment Science and South America* (Chicago: University of Chicago Press, 2008).

Said, Edward, *Culture and Imperialism* (London: Vintage, 1994).

Sandiford, Keith, 'The Sugared Muse: or the Case of James Grainger, MD (1721–66)', *New West Indian Guide*, Vol. 61, No. 1/2 (1987), pp. 39–53.

   The Cultural Politics of Sugar: Caribbean Slavery and Narratives of Colonialism (Cambridge: Cambridge University Press, 2000).

van Sant, Ann Jessie, *Eighteenth-Century Sensibility and the Novel: The Senses in Social Context* (Cambridge: Cambridge University Press, 1993).

Scarry, Elaine, *The Body in Pain: The Making and Unmaking of the World* (Oxford: Oxford University Press, 1985).

Schaffer, Simon, et al., *The Brokered World: Go-Betweens and Global Intelligence, 1770–1820* (Sagamore Beach, MA: Science History, 2009).

Schaffer, Simon, 'How Disciplines Look' in *Interdisciplinarity: Reconfigurations of the Social and Natural Sciences*, ed. Andrew Barry and Georgina Born (Oxford: Routledge, 2013), pp. 57–81.

Schiebinger, Londa, *Plants and Empire: Colonial Bioprospecting in the Atlantic World* (Cambridge, MA: Harvard University Press, 2004).

   'Scientific Exchange in the Eighteenth-Century Atlantic World' in *Soundings in Atlantic History: Latent Structures and Intellectual Currents, 1500–1830*, ed. Bernard Bailyn and Patricia L. Denault (Cambridge, MA: Harvard University Press, 2009), pp. 294–328.

Scott, David, *Conscripts of Modernity: The Tragedy of Colonial Enlightenment* (Durham, NC, and London: Duke University Press, 2004).

Scrivener, Michael, *Seditious Allegories: John Thelwall and Jacobin Writing* (University Park: Pennsylvania State University Press, 2001).

   The Cosmopolitan Ideal in the Age of Revolution and Reaction, 1776–1832 (London: Pickering and Chatto, 2007).

Shannon, Richard, *Practical Observations on the Operations and Effects of certain medicines, in the Prevention and Cure of Diseases to Which Europeans are Subject in Hot Climates* (London, 1793).

Sharpe, Jenny, *Ghosts of Slavery: A Literary Archaeology of Black Women's Lives* (Minneapolis: University of Minnesota Press, 2003).

Shepherd, William, 'The Negro Incantation', *Monthly Magazine*, Vol. 4 (1797), p. 51.

Sheridan, Richard B., 'Mortality and the Medical Treatment of Slaves in the British West Indies' in *Race and Slavery in the Western Hemisphere: Quantitative Studies*, ed. Stanley Engerman and Eugene Genovese (Princeton, NJ: Princeton University Press, 1975), pp. 285–307.

   Doctors and Slaves: A Medical and Demographic History of Slavery in the British West Indies, 1680–1834, second edition (Cambridge: Cambridge University Press, 1985).

Shields, David S., *Oracles of Empire: Poetry, Politics, and Commerce in British America, 1690–1750* (Chicago: University of Chicago Press, 1990).

Shryock, Richard Harrison, *Medicine and Society in America* (New York: New York University Press, 1960).

Shuttleton, David, *Smallpox and the Literary Imagination 1660–1820* (Cambridge: Cambridge University Press, 2007).

Singleton, John, *A General Description of the West-Indian Islands* (Barbados: Printed by Esmand and Walker for the author, 1767).

A description of the West-Indies. A poem, in four books (Printed for T. Becket, 1776).

Sloane, Hans, *A Voyage to the Islands Madera, Barbados, Nieves, S. Christophers and Jamaica* (London: Printed by B. M. for the author, 1707).

Smart, Christopher, *Poems on Several Occasions* (London: Printed for the author, 1752).

Smith, Adam, *The Theory of Moral Sentiments* (Indianapolis: Liberty Classics, 1976).

Smith, Andrew and William Hughes (eds.), *Empire and the Gothic: The Politics of Genre* (Basingstoke: Palgrave Macmillan, 2003).

Smith, Samuel Stanhope, *An Essay on the Causes of the Variety of Complexion and Figure in the Human Species. To which are Added Strictures on Lord Kaim's Discourse, on the Original Diversity of Mankind* (Philadelphia and London, 1789).

Smith, Theophus H., *Conjuring Culture: Biblical Formations of Black America* (Oxford: Oxford University Press, 1994).

Society for the Mitigation and Gradual Abolition of Slavery throughout the British Dominions, *Report of the committee of the Society for the Mitigation and Gradual Abolition of Slavery throughout the British Dominions, read at the general meeting of the Society, Held on the 15th day of June, 1824, together with an account, of the proceedings which took place at that meeting* (London, 1824).

Sollors, Werner, *Neither Black Nor White Yet Both: Thematic Explorations of Interracial Literature* (Cambridge, MA: Harvard University Press, 1999).

Solomonescu, Yasmin, 'Introduction', *John Thelwall: Critical Reassessments*, ed. Yasmin Solomonescu, Romantic Circles Praxis Series (2011), www.rc.umd .edu/praxis/thelwall/HTML/praxis.2011.solomonescu.html.

John Thelwall and the Materialist Imagination (Basingstoke: Palgrave Macmillan, 2014).

Stalnaker, Joanna, *The Unfinished Enlightenment: Description in the Age of the Encyclopedia* (Ithaca, NY: Cornell University Press, 2010).

Stanback, Emily, 'Disability and Dissent: Thelwall's Elocutionary Project' in *John Thelwall: Critical Reassessments*, ed. Yasmin Solomonescu, Romantic Circles Praxis Series (2011), www.rc.umd.edu/praxis/thelwall/HTML/praxis.2011 .stanback.html.

Stedman, John Gabriel, unpublished diaries, Stedman Collection (James Ford Bell Library, University of Minnesota).

Narrative of a Five Years Expedition against the Revolted Negroes of Surinam in Guiana on the Wild Coast of South-America. From the year 1772 to the year 1777, ed. Richard Price and Sally Price (Baltimore: John Hopkins University Press, 1988).

Steele, Richard, *The Spectator* (13 March 1711).

Stewart, Dianne M., *Three Eyes for the Journey: African Dimensions of the Jamaican Religious Experience* (Oxford: Oxford University Press, 2005).

Stewart, John, *A view of the past and present state of the Island of Jamaica; with remarks on the moral and physical condition of the slaves and on the abolition of slavery in the colonies* (Edinburgh: Oliver & Boyd, 1823).

Suleri, Sara, *The Rhetoric of English India* (Chicago: University of Chicago Press, 1992).

Sypher, Wylie, 'The West-Indian as a "Character" in the Eighteenth Century', *Studies in Philology*, Vol. 36, No. 3 (July 1939), pp. 503–20.

Terrall, Mary, 'Speculation and Experiment in Enlightenment Life Sciences' in *Heredity Produced: At the Crossroads of Biology, Politics and Culture, 1500–1870*, ed. Staffan Müller-Wille and Hans-Joerg Rheinberger (Cambridge, MA: MIT Press, 2007), pp. 253–76.

Catching Nature in the Act: Réaumur and the Practice of Natural History in the Eighteenth Century (Chicago: University of Chicago Press, 2013).

Thelwall, John, *An Essay Towards a Definition of Animal Vitality; Read at the Theatre, Guy's Hospital, January 26, 1793, in which Several of the Opinions of the Celebrated John Hunter are Examined and Controverted* (London: Printed by T. Rickaby, 1793).

Poems, Written Chiefly in Retirement (Hereford: Printed by W. H. Parker, 1801).

A Letter to Henry Cline, Esq on Imperfect Developments of the Faculties, Mental and Moral, as well as Constitutional and Organic, and on the Treatment of Impediments of Speech (London: Printed by Richard Taylor and Co., 1810).

The Peripatetic (Detroit: Wayne State University Press, 2001).

The Daughter of Adoption (Peterborough: Broadview, 2013).

Thomas, Helen, *Romanticism and Slave Narratives: Transatlantic Testimonies* (Cambridge: Cambridge University Press, 2000).

Thomas, Robert, *Medical advice to the inhabitants of warm climates, on the domestic treatment of all the diseases incidental therein: with a few useful hints to new settlers, for the preservation of health, and the prevention of sickness* (London: Printed for J. Johnson et al, 1790).

The modern practice of physic, exhibiting the characters, causes, symptoms, prognostics, morbid appearances, and improved method of treating the diseases of all climates, fourth edition (London: Printed for Longman et al, 1813).

The modern practice of physic, exhibiting the characters, causes, symptoms, prognostics, morbid appearances, and improved method of treating the diseases of all climates, sixth edition (London: Printed for Longman et al, 1819).

Thomas, Stephen W., 'Doctoring Ideology: James Grainger's *The Sugar Cane* and the Bodies of Empire', *Early American Studies: An Interdisciplinary Journal*, Vol. 4, No. 1 (Spring 2006), pp. 78–111.

Thompson, Judith, *John Thelwall in the Wordsworth Circle: The Silenced Partner* (New York: Palgrave Macmillan, 2012).

'Transatlantic Thelwall' at *British Association for Romantic Studies Annual Conference*, University of Southampton, 2013.

Thompson, Krista A., *An Eye for the Tropics: Tourism, Photography, and Framing the Caribbean Picturesque* (Durham, NC, and London: Duke University Press, 2006).

Thomson, James, *The Seasons: A Poem* (London: Printed for A. Hamilton, 1793).

Thomson, James, *A Treatise on the Diseases of Negroes as they occur in the Island of Jamaica, with Observations on the Country Remedies* (Kingston: Alex Aikman, Jnr., 1820).

Titford, William, *Sketches towards a Hortus botanicus Americanus; or coloured plates (with concise and familiar descriptions) of new and valuable plants of the West Indies and North and South America, etc* (London, 1811).

Tobin, Beth Fowkes, *Colonizing Nature: The Tropics in British Art and Letters, 1760–1820* (Philadelphia: University of Pennsylvania Press, 2005).

Touchstone, Timothy, *Tea and Sugar, or the Nabob and the Creole; a poem, in two canto's* (London, 1792).

Towne, Richard, *A treatise of the diseases most frequent in the West-Indies, and herein more particularly of those which occur in Barbadoes* (London: Printed for John Clarke, 1726).

Trollope, Anthony, *The West Indies and the Spanish Main* (London: Chapman and Hall, 1859).

Tunstall, Kate E., 'The Early Modern Embodied Mind and the Entomological Imaginary' in *Mind, Body, Motion, Matter: Eighteenth-Century British and French Literary Perspectives*, ed. Mary Helen McMurran and Alison Conway (Toronto, Buffalo, NY, and London: University of Toronto Press, 2016), pp. 202–29.

Turner, Mary, 'Religious Beliefs' in *General History of the Caribbean, Vol III: The Slave Societies of the Caribbean* (London: Unesco and Macmillan Education, 1997), pp. 287–321.

Slaves and Missionaries: The Disintegration of Jamaican Slave Society 1787–1834 (Kingston: The University of the West Indies Press, 1998).

Voeks, Robert, 'Magic and Medicine in the Americas', *Geographical Review*, Vol. 83, No. 1 (January 1993), pp. 66–78.

Wahrman, Dror, *The Making of the Modern Self: Identity and Culture in Eighteenth-Century England* (New Haven, CT: Yale University Press, 2006).

Wall, Cynthia Sundberg, *The Prose of Things: Transformations of Description in the Eighteenth Century* (Chicago: Chicago University Press, 2006).

Ward, Candace, *Desire and Disorder: Fevers, Fictions, and Feeling in English Georgian Culture* (Lewisburg, PA: Bucknell University Press, 2007).

Waters, Hazel, *Racism on the Victorian Stage: Representation of Slavery and the Black Character* (Cambridge: Cambridge University Press, 2009).

Watson, Tim, *Caribbean Culture and British Fiction in the Atlantic World, 1780–1870* (Cambridge: Cambridge University Press, 2008).

Watts, Sheldon, *Epidemics and History: Disease, Power and Imperialism* (New Haven, CT: Yale University Press, 1997).

Weaver, Karol K., *Medical Revolutionaries: The Enslaved Healers of Eighteenth-Century Saint Domingue* (Urbana and Chicago: University of Illinois Press, 2006).

Weekes, Nathaniel, *Barbados: A Poem* (London: Printed by J. and J. Lewis for R. and J. Dodsley, 1754).

Wells, Helena, *Letters on Subjects of Importance to the Happiness of Young Females* (London: Printed for L. Peacock, 1799).

Constantia Neville; or, the West Indian (London: Printed by C. Whittingham, 1800).

Thoughts and Remarks on Establishing an Institution for the Support and Education of Unportioned Respectable Females (London: Longman, 1809).

Wells, William Charles, *Two Essays: one upon single vision with two eyes; the other on dew. A letter to the Right Hon. Lloyd, Lord Kenyon, and an account of a female of the white race of mankind, part of whose skin resembles that of a negro; with some observations on the causes of the differences in colour and form between the white and negro races of men.* (London: Longman et al, 1818).

Wheeler, Roxann, *The Complexion of Race: Categories of Difference in Eighteenth-Century British Culture* (Philadelphia: University of Pennsylvania, 2000).

Whytt, Robert, *An Essay on the Vital and Other Involuntary Motions of Animals* (Edinburgh: Hamilton, Balfour and Neill, 1751).

Physiological essays (Edinburgh: Hamilton, Balfour and Neill, 1761).

Willan, Robert, *On Cutaneous Diseases* (London: J. Johnson, 1808).

Williams, Cynric R., *A Tour through the Island of Jamaica, from the western to the eastern end, in the year 1823* (London: Printed for Hunt and Clarke, 1826).

Hamel, the Obeah Man (Peterborough: Broadview, 2010).

Williamson, John, *Medical and Miscellaneous Observations Relative to the West India Islands* (Edinburgh: Printed by Alex Smellie, 1817).

Wilson, Kathleen, *The Island Race: Englishness, Empire and Gender in the Eighteenth Century* (London: Routledge, 2003).

'British Women and Empire' in *Women's History: Britain 1700–1850, an Introduction*, ed. Hannah Barker and Elaine Chalus (London and New York: Routledge, 2005), pp. 260–84.

Winslow, Charles-Edward Amory, *The Conquest of Epidemic Disease: A Chapter in the History of Ideas* (Madison: The University of Wisconsin Press, 1980).

Winterbottom, Thomas *An Account of the Native Africans in the Neighbourhood of Sierra Leone; to which is Added, an Account of the Present State of Medicine Among Them* (Printed by C. Whittingham, 1803).

Wisecup, Kelly, *Medical Encounters: Knowledge and Identity in Early American Literatures* (Amherst and Boston: University of Masschusetts Press, 2013).

Wisecup, Kelly and Toni Wall Jaudon, 'On Knowing and Not Knowing About Obeah', *Atlantic Studies: Global Currents*, Vol. 12, No. 2 (2015), pp. 129–43.

Wood, Marcus, *Blind Memory: Visual Representations of Slavery in England and America* (Manchester: Manchester University Press, 2000).

Slavery, Empathy, and Pornography (Oxford: Oxford University Press, 2002).

The Poetry of Slavery: An Anglo-American Anthology, 1764–1865 (Oxford: Oxford University Press, 2003).

Wootton, David, *Bad Medicine: Doctors Doing Harm Since Hippocrates* (Oxford: Oxford University Press, 2006).

Index

CAMBRIDGE STUDIES IN ROMANTICISM

General Editor: James Chandler, University of Chicago

For EU product safety concerns, contact us at Calle de José Abascal, 56–1°,
28003 Madrid, Spain or eugpsr@cambridge.org.

www.ingramcontent.com/pod-product-compliance
Ingram Content Group UK Ltd.
Pitfield, Milton Keynes, MK11 3LW, UK
UKHW020337140625
459647UK00018B/2198